Acknowledgments

These pages constitute a continuation of the copyright page. Grateful acknowledgment for permission to republish articles and chapters that first appeared elsewhere is hereby noted:

Chapter 1: "Context versus Principles: A Misplaced Debate in Christian Ethics" was originally published in the *Harvard Theological Review* 58, no. 2 (April 1965): 171–202. Reprinted with permission of the *Harvard Theological Review*.

Chapter 2: "Moral Discernment in the Christian Life" was originally published in *Norm and Context in Christian Ethics*, ed. Gene H. Outka and Paul Ramsey (New York: Charles Scribner's Sons, 1968), 17–36. Reprinted with permission of Gene Outka.

Chapter 3: "The Relation of the Gospels to the Moral Life" was originally published in *Jesus and Man's Hope*, vol. 2, ed. Donald G. Miller and Dikran Y. Hadidian (Pittsburgh: Pittsburgh Theological Seminary, 1971), 103–17. Reprinted with permission of Pittsburgh Theological Seminary.

Chapter 4: "Down Syndrome, Parental Desires, and the Right to Life" was originally published under the title "Mongolism, Parental Desires, and the Right to Life" in *Perspectives in Biology and Medicine* 16 (1973), 529–57. © The Johns Hopkins University Press. Reprinted with permission of The Johns Hopkins University Press. Permission to change the title and the terminology of the article also granted by The Johns Hopkins University Press.

Chapter 5: "A Theocentric Interpretation of Life." Copyright 1980 *Christian Century*. Reprinted with permission from the July 30–August 6, 1980, issue of the *Christian Century*. Subscriptions: $49/year from P.O. Box 378, Mt. Morris, IL 61054. 1-800-208-4097.

Chapter 6: "Say Something Theological!" was originally published by the University of Chicago as the 1981 Nora and Edward Ryerson Lecture. Reprinted with permission of James M. Gustafson.

Chapter 7: "Nature, Sin, and Covenant: Three Bases for Sexual Ethics" was originally published in *Perspectives in Biology and Medicine* 24 (1981): 493–97. © The Johns Hopkins University Press. Reprinted with permission of The Johns Hopkins University Press.

Chapter 8: "Nature: Its Status in Theological Ethics" was originally published in *Logos* 3 (1982): 5–23. Reprinted with permission of Santa Clara University/Philosophy Department.

Chapter 9: "Professions as 'Callings'" was originally published in the *Social Service Review* 56 (December 1982): 501–15. Reprinted with permission of the University of Chicago Press. © 1982 by the University of Chicago. All rights reserved.

Chapter 10: "Death Is Not the Enemy," coauthored with Richard L. Landau, MD, originally appeared in the *Journal of the American Medical Association* 252 (November 2, 1984): 2458. Copyright © 1984, American Medical Association. All rights reserved.

Chapter 11: "The Sectarian Temptation: Reflections on Theology, the Church, and the University" was originally published in the *Catholic Theological Society of America Proceedings* 40 (1985): 83–94. Reprinted with permission of the Catholic Theological Society of America.

Chapter 12: "Christian Ethics" was originally published in *Westminster Dictionary of Christian Ethics*, ed. James F. Childress and John Macquarrie. © 1986 The Westminster Press. Used by permission of Westminster John Knox Press.

Chapter 13: "Roman Catholic and Protestant Interaction in Ethics: An Interpretation" was originally published in *Theological Studies* 50 (1989): 44–69. Reprinted with permission of *Theological Studies*.

Chapter 14: "Moral Discourse about Medicine: A Variety of Forms" was originally published in *The Journal of Medicine and Philosophy* 15 (1990): 125–42. Reprinted with permission of Taylor and Francis. Web site: www.tandf.co .uk/journals/titles/03605310.asp (*The Journal of Medicine and Philosophy*).

Chapter 15: "The Use of Scripture in Christian Ethics" was originally published in *Studia Theologica* 51 (1997): 15–29. Reprinted with permission of Taylor and Francis. Web site: www.tandf.no/studtheol (*Studia Theologica*).

Chapter 16: "A Retrospective Interpretation of American Religious Ethics, 1948–1998" was originally published in the *Journal of Religious Ethics* 25, no. 3 (1998, 25th Anniversary Supplement): 3–22. Reprinted with permission of Blackwell Publishing.

Library of Theological Ethics

General Editors' Introduction

The field of theological ethics possesses in its literature an abundant inheritance concerning religious convictions and the moral life, critical issues, methods, and moral problems. The Library of Theological Ethics is designed to present a selection of important texts that would otherwise be unavailable for scholarly purposes and classroom use. The series will engage the question of what it means to think theologically and ethically. It is offered in the conviction that sustained dialogue with our predecessors serves the interests of responsible contemporary reflection. Our more immediate aim in offering it, however, is to enable scholars and teachers to make more extensive use of classic texts as they train new generations of theologians, ethicists, and ministers. The volumes included in the Library will comprise a variety of types. Some make available English-language texts and translations that have fallen out of print; others present new translations of texts previously unavailable in English. Still others offer anthologies or collections of significant statements about problems and themes of special importance.

We hope that each volume will encourage contemporary theological ethicists to remain in conversation with the rich and diverse heritage of their discipline.

ROBIN W. LOVIN
DOUGLAS F. OTTATI
WILLIAM SCHWEIKER

Preface

Any appreciation for this anthology should go to Paul Capetz and Theo Boer, its editors, who initiated the project and added its development to their own full teaching and research schedules for several years. Neither of them owes me any obligation of academic filial piety since they were never my students. My interaction with Paul Capetz began with a very long letter in which he analyzed aspects of my *Ethics from a Theocentric Perspective*, volume 1, with sympathetic but learned and sharp critical acumen. His interest in the Reformed tradition in theology led him to my book. That exchange has been followed by more intensive correspondence and by days of conversations in our home, all of which continue. Theo Boer made contact with me from Utrecht when he was working on a thesis for a licentiate in theology from the Faculty of Theology in Uppsala, directed by Carl-Henric Grenholm, *All Things in Relation to God: A Critical Analysis of James M. Gustafson's Theocentric Ethics*. He spent several weeks in Atlanta during which he rigorously interrogated me on all facets of my work. Subsequently he wrote a doctoral dissertation in the Faculty of Theology in Utrecht under the direction of Egbert Schroten, *Theological Ethics after Gustafson: A Critical Analysis of the Normative Structure of James M. Gustafson's Theocentric Ethics*. Our intellectual and personal engagement has continued via e-mail, telephone conversations, and intensive days in Utrecht, in Uppsala, and in our home. Both men have become deep personal friends.

From the hundreds of pages I published over fifty years, they have selected articles which they believe are most significant according to several criteria. I am pleased they included a number of items that were generated by invitations to participate in nontheological, nonreligious venues, since such was a large part of my professional life. Happily, they included the essay that means the most to me, "Say Something Theological!" my Ryerson Lecture at the University of Chicago.

Most of the articles I published were evoked by invitations to lecture, to contribute to journals, or to contribute papers to conferences. Many of them had a pedagogical purpose, to clarify controverted matters in current discussions or to frame an agenda for further development rather than to articulate and defend my own points of view. Diverse causes affect changes in the course of a professional life; different circumstances elicit different facets of life and thought, and entice one to explore a variety of theological and ethical alternatives, religious, moral, and social issues that emerge, and different modes of intellectual discourse. The first article I published in a scholarly journal was a Weberian analysis of ministerial authority. Two significant movements coincided fortuitously with research I had undertaken: Vatican II and ecumenism with my study of Roman Catholic social thought and moral theology, and the modern movement in bioethics with interests I was pursuing on implications for theology and ethics of research in human genetics, neurosciences, and clinical medicine. (The latter was literally brought home to me when my wife nursed patients undergoing experimental surgical and medical procedures in Billings Hospital of the University of Chicago.) The fact that my teaching, research, and writing did not follow a goal-oriented, rational life plan is apparent in the editors' selections for this anthology.

I am honored that Paul Capetz and Theo Boer found the articles in this volume to be worthy of attention and hope that readers will find them useful for their thinking and work.

But: *Soli Deo Gloria!*

James M. Gustafson

Rio Rancho, New Mexico
July 22, 2006

Introduction

Anyone who is at all familiar with the discipline of theological ethics recognizes James M. Gustafson as one of its leading and formative figures of the past fifty years. His various contributions have helped to define and give shape to the discipline. Indeed, many of the other important writers and teachers now working in the field of theological ethics in North America received their graduate training under Gustafson's tutelage. While his is only one voice in a field marked by diverse, even conflicting perspectives as to what constitutes theological ethics and how it is to be practiced, surely it is no exaggeration to say that one cannot become a serious student of this discipline apart from close study and careful consideration of Gustafson's arguments on formal methodological questions as well as his positions on substantive material issues. It is our hope that the essays brought together in this volume represent a sufficiently broad range of Gustafson's thought so that readers may come to a deeper understanding of both fundamental debates within the discipline of theological ethics in general and Gustafson's own positions in these debates in particular.

Since one of Gustafson's guiding convictions is that the perspectives of all persons, including academics, are highly conditioned by the social and cultural circumstances as well as the personal experiences that have shaped their lives, a few words about Gustafson's biography are in order here. Gustafson was born in 1925 in Norway, Michigan, and was raised among Swedish immigrants. His father was a pastor in the Swedish Mission Covenant Church, which had its origins in Sweden as a "free church" (i.e., not connected to the state church) nourished by Lutheran pietism. The family moved to Scranton, Kansas, in 1939 when the elder Gustafson was fired from his congregation on account of theological disagreements with fundamentalists. At that time Scranton was a farming and coal-mining community in the throes of the Depression. From 1944 to 1946 Gustafson served in the army and did tours of duty in India and Burma. Experiences from these years—of tragedy and human suffering, of the larger historical and political forces to which persons and communities are subjected, of the ambiguous circumstances in which persons are often called upon to act, and of the existence of deep cultural and religious differences among civilizations—became formative influences in Gustafson's subsequent development as a student of theology and ethics.[1]

After the war, Gustafson received his BS degree in 1948 at Northwestern University, where his studies were focused primarily on sociology and other social sciences. The deep and lasting impact of sociological modes of inquiry on his thought is evident in his later theological and ethical work. He graduated in 1951 with a BD from Chicago Theological Seminary and the Federated Theological Faculty of the University of Chicago, where his primary mentors were Daniel Day Williams, Wilhelm Pauck, and James Luther Adams. Adams introduced Gustafson to the writings of Ernst Troeltsch, that pioneer in the investigation of the implications of historicism and social and cultural relativism for Christian theology and ethics. Pauck, who had been a student of Troeltsch in Germany, suggested that Gustafson read H. Richard Niebuhr's *The Meaning of Revelation*, which impressed Gustafson as a statement of how it is possible to affirm a historic religious tradition all the while fully cognizant of its historical and cultural relativity. (Interestingly, Niebuhr himself had written his doctoral dissertation at Yale on Troeltsch's philosophy of religion.) On reading this book, Gustafson knew that it was Niebuhr who would become his main mentor. So he applied for late admission to Yale University and moved to New Haven, where he began what became a deep academic, professional, and personal relationship with Niebuhr.

Gustafson was ordained a minister in the Congregational Christian Churches (later to become the United Church of Christ) and served as the minister of the Congregational Church in Northford, Connecticut, from 1951 to 1954 while working toward his doctorate at Yale. From 1954 to 1955 he served as assistant director of the Study of Theological Education in America. (Niebuhr was its director and Williams was associate director.) Together they authored the famous study *The Advancement of Theological Education* (New York: Harper and Brothers, 1957). In 1955 Gustafson graduated from Yale with a PhD after having submitted a dissertation on the topic "Community and Time in the Christian Church: A Study of the Church from a Sociological and Philosophical Perspective." His first published book, *Treasure in Earthen Vessels: The Church as a Human Community* (New York: Harper and Row, 1961), represents the continuation of this line of inquiry.

Gustafson served on the faculty of Yale from 1955 to 1972, teaching in both the Divinity School and the Department of Religious Studies; in 1972 he accepted an appointment as University Professor of Theological Ethics at the University of Chicago, where, in addition to his teaching responsibilities in the Divinity School, he regularly taught in many other departments and fields of study in the university at large. In 1988 he moved to Emory University to become the Henry

---

1. See Gustafson's autobiographical reflections in "August Seventh, 1945," *Christian Century* 112 (August 16–23, 1995): 779–81, and "Tracing a Trajectory," *Zygon* 30 (1995): 159–75.

R. Luce Professor of Humanities and Comparative Studies, an appointment he held until 1996, at which time he became the Woodruff Professor of Comparative Studies and of Religion, also at Emory. During his years at Emory, Gustafson led seminars for faculty members from various disciplines; such an interdisciplinary emphasis has also been a major factor in Gustafson's thinking about theology and ethics.[2]

During his professional life Gustafson has authored many books and articles on various topics and issues (a complete bibliography of his works may be found at the back of this anthology). Indeed, some of his writings have attained what can only be called "canonical" status for students of theological ethics; one thinks, for example, of such classics as *Christ and the Moral Life* (New York: Harper and Row, 1968), *Can Ethics Be Christian?* (Chicago: University of Chicago Press, 1975), and *Protestant and Roman Catholic Ethics: Prospects for Rapprochement* (Chicago: University of Chicago Press, 1978). Much of this work is concerned with providing a formal analysis of the elements that go into the construction of a comprehensive systematic theological ethics. Other writings focus more concretely on specific areas of moral concern and ethical inquiry. Gustafson's major constructive statement is the two-volume magnum opus *Ethics from a Theocentric Perspective* (Chicago: University of Chicago Press, 1981, 1984). In these two volumes Gustafson implements the program for theological ethics that his earlier formal analyses had called for. The first volume, *Theology and Ethics*, shows Gustafson at work as a constructive theologian, outlining a theological framework from which to construe human life in the world in relation to God; the second volume, *Ethics and Theology*, illustrates what ethics and the moral life look like when framed by the theological perspective set forth in the first volume. Gustafson understands himself to be a theologian as well as an ethicist, and anyone who reads his works will be impressed by the scholarship in both disciplines.

The editors of this volume approach Gustafson's work from two distinct disciplinary perspectives: ethics and theology. Our collaboration on this project grew out of our shared perception that Gustafson's work is of immense importance for both of these disciplines and especially for their close interaction and mutual fructification. Like Gustafson, we are convinced that the disciplinary separation of ethics from theology, while understandable and to some extent necessary for purposes of specialization, needs to be bridged by ethicists who think about the theological presuppositions of their work in ethics and by theologians who think about the ethical implications of their work in theology. Furthermore, we are at one with Gustafson in the conviction that theological ethics has to be responsive to the needs of the church and its ministry. For this reason, those who labor in this field have an obligation to write for a wider readership than merely that of their fellow scholars. Gustafson has never forgotten that his first calling

---

2. Publications by Gustafson reflecting this interdisciplinary emphasis are *Intersections: Science, Theology, and Ethics* (Cleveland: Pilgrim Press, 1996) and *An Examined Faith: The Grace of Self-Doubt* (Minneapolis: Fortress Press, 2004).

was to be a pastor, and his work in theological ethics has always been informed by his awareness of the difficult demands placed on ordained ministers.

The essays in this collection were published in a time span of more than thirty years and constitute, we believe, a representative selection of Gustafson's academic interests and research foci. The essays in this anthology are arranged in chronological order. An ordering along thematic or methodological lines would no doubt also have its merits. However, the reader will find that no essay fits neatly into any one single category. Theological ethics, in the hands of Gustafson, is an integrative process that brings together questions and concerns of theology and ethics, engages in concrete description and careful analysis of circumstances, reflects philosophically on issues of method, attends to procedures for decision making, and gathers relevant information and knowledge from the social and natural sciences. It is precisely Gustafson's criticism of much of modern ethics that it neglects the interdependence of the parts. The reader is thus free to begin with any essay of particular interest and need not read the essays in the order in which they appear in this volume. Nonetheless, we are confident that the reader of these essays will get to know a theologian and ethicist of extraordinary skill and unusual insight whose contribution to the discipline of theological ethics can hardly be overstated.[3]

Here is a brief introduction to each of the essays chosen for inclusion in this volume:

1. "Context versus Principles: A Misplaced Debate in Christian Ethics" first appeared in *Harvard Theological Review* in 1965. Thanks to its clarifying value, the essay has had several reprints. It addresses a highly polarized discussion that originated in the 1950s with publications of Paul Lehmann, Joseph Fletcher, and Paul Ramsey, and that went on deep into the following decade. On the one end, there were ethics that were described in often vague terms as "contextual," "situational," "existential," "subjective," and "immanent." The other extreme was depicted as "deontological," "objective," and "extrinsic." In this essay, Gustafson stresses the insufficiency of these categories. They not only fail to describe adequately the complex reality of moral reasoning and decision making, but also do injustice to the arguments and motives of the positions they categorize. Yet both parts of the polarity have their merits. Contextualist accounts rightly stress the need for a careful analysis of contexts and have a point in stressing God's radical sovereignty over rules and moral codes. In contextualist accounts, we also meet an understanding of the nature of human selfhood, which stresses human moral responsibility. But contextualism doesn't necessarily exclude the use of rules or principles, as is illustrated by Karl Barth, just as, on the other end of the spectrum, a "principalist" like Reinhold Niebuhr *did* have an acute "contextual awareness." Gustafson sees his task not in a further polarization, but rather in arguing that *any* serious ethical theory must in

---

3. Three previous collections of Gustafson's essays have also been published: *The Church as Moral Decision-Maker*, ed. with an introduction by Charles M. Swezey (Philadelphia: Pilgrim Press, 1970); *Christian Ethics and the Community*, ed. with an introduction by Charles M. Swezey (New York: Pilgrim Press, 1971, 1979); and *Theology and Christian Ethics*, ed. with a new introduction by Charles M. Swezey (Philadelphia: Pilgrim Press, 1974).

the final analysis pay attention to the aspects it tended to neglect in the heat of the dispute. It is characteristic of this early essay that Gustafson is hesitant to give his own opinion. ("Is there one normative starting point, or base point, for work in Christian ethics around which other discussions ought to cohere? On this question the author has convictions, but their exposition lies outside the scope of this methodological analysis.") The author's own answer is found in "The Relation of the Gospels to the Moral Life" (see below), written six years later.

2. In "Moral Discernment in the Christian Life" (1968), the believer's quest for guidance in moral issues is described in terms of a dynamic and multifaceted process of discernment—a process of seeing and weighing, taking into consideration a range of salient factors such as the potential consequences of an action, a variety of motives, moral maxims accepted by a community, empirical data, the moral ordering of the universe as understood by reason, all seen within the context of God's beneficence. It yields no predictable outcomes as the result either of a system of deductive logic, of the accumulation of information, of the expression of emotions, or of the stubborn allegiance to principles, although it may imply some of all this. Those who discern will inevitably do this from their own perspective, history, character, and community, and against the background of beliefs and principles. Gustafson's way of describing the process of discernment sheds more light on the allegation that, in the "context versus principles" debate, he is on the side of the former—that he is a situationalist, or a decisionalist: "Discernment seems to require some sensitivity and flexibility, some pluralism of consideration that is a priori ruled out by dedicated allegiance to single principles." At the same time, the clearly realistic approach avoids subjectivism: neither are moral actors merely following their own feelings nor is the rightness or wrongness of a moral choice rooted in the agent's decision. There is "some objectivity" that we must take account of. In theological terms the moral question, "What ought or are we to do?" is to be understood as "What is God enabling and requiring us to do?"[4] With all the uncertainties that this position involves, human morality is, from a theological perspective, rooted in the way things really and ultimately are.

3. "The Relation of the Gospels to the Moral Life" was presented at Pittsburgh Theological Seminary's "Festivals of the Gospels" as part of its 175th anniversary in 1971. Gustafson depicts three ways in which the Gospels are relevant to theological ethics: in depicting God's love for humans in the example of Jesus Christ, they provide a powerful reason for being moral; principles and rules can be retrieved which guide particular actions; and the narratives of the Gospels influence "the sort of persons members of the community become." In concentrating on the third, Gustafson displays both a concern for virtues and awareness of the communal character of the Christian life. Christ as the paradigm does not provide an extrinsic goal or a timeless ideal, but *in*-forms and *in*-fluences members of a community in their distinctiveness.

---

4. In later accounts, this sentence is changed into "What is God enabling and requiring us to be and to do," cf. "Say Something Theological!" in this volume.

4. "Down Syndrome, Parental Desires, and the Right to Life"[5] (1973), prepared for the Kennedy Foundation, is a case study regarding a baby with Down syndrome. In short, the case goes as follows: At the request of the parents, health care professionals do not remove a fatal intestinal blockage, and the child is allowed to die. The first part of the chapter analyzes the reasons the actors have for their decisions. In problematizing the decision and its reasons in the subsequent section, this essay provides an example of how theology may influence the way in which a moral dilemma is analyzed and, hence, the outcome that is considered morally right. Theologically, there is reason to question the view that desires form the basis of our obligations toward others, and the view that the value of a human being is qualified by its intelligence and capacity for productivity. Rather, the value of a human being is intrinsic, constituted by its very existence in relation to others and in its dependence on them. Moreover, a theological view leads to a different assessment of the significance of suffering.

5. The short essay "A Theocentric Interpretation of Life" (1980) is one of the few autobiographical essays in Gustafson's oeuvre. It appeared in the *Christian Century's* long-standing series, "How My Mind Has Changed." The invitation for this contribution could not have come at a more appropriate moment. The article, in which Gustafson for the first time describes his own ethical proposal as "theocentric," is a prelude to the first volume of his constructive statement *Ethics from a Theocentric Perspective.* That Gustafson has come to a crossroads is reflected by the remark, "I shall not cite quotations from my previous work which are no longer accurate expressions of my present thinking." It is noteworthy that this essay refers to criteria for adequate and coherent theological ethics that are found in other publications (with occasional shifts in wording), but hardly anywhere so concisely. First, a theological ethic should contain an organizing perspective, metaphor or principle; second, it should relate coherently to four base points: (1) theology in the restricted sense of an understanding of God and God's purposes in relation to the world; (2) an interpretation of "the world" and of the significance of events in the world for human beings; (3) an interpretation of persons as moral agents; and (4) criteria and principles of moral decision making; third, it should make use of four sources: the Bible and the Christian tradition, philosophical methods and principles, solid scientific data, and human experience broadly conceived.

6. Another important statement of Gustafson's constructive position is "Say Something Theological!" (1981). It is a lecture in the prestigious annual Nora and Edward Ryerson Lectures, established in 1974 in the Faculty of Humanities at the University of Chicago. It addresses a university-wide audience and is in more than one respect a benchmark in Gustafson's oeuvre: it is an eloquent declaration, concise and comprehensive at the same time, of where Gustafson stands as a person and a theologian. Here again we find the combination of intellect and piety, reflecting his career as both a teacher and a preacher. To say something the-

5. Originally published under the title "Mongolism, Parental Desires, and the Right to Life." See editors' note on the first page of this essay.

ological means three things: it is to say something about how things really and ultimately are, it is to say something religious—"Theology has its deepest significance within the context of piety, and in the context of a historic religious tradition"; and it is to say something ethical. The ethical task, then, is to discern what God is enabling and requiring us to be and to do: "We are to relate ourselves and all things in a manner appropriate to their relations to God."

7. "Nature, Sin, and Covenant: Three Bases for Sexual Ethics" was the 1981 Jake Ginsburg Sex Psychology Lecture at Stanford University. It is a theological reflection for a secular university audience on the need for a new sexual ethic against the background of changing views on the nature and purposes of sexual relationships since the 1960s. Instead of proposing his own version of a normative sexual ethic, Gustafson depicts three "bases" that any revised sexual ethic will have to take into account: facts about biological and personal nature, the human fault to which all persons are susceptible and against which they need safeguards, and the human need for some form of covenant. As in many other essays, the point of departure is analysis and description. Even if no blueprint of a single normative sexual ethic can be given, the consequence of the "isness of things" for their "oughtness" is an ethic that affirms much of the traditional tenets of marriage: "The traditional prescriptive sexual ethics of our culture are based on comprehensive vindicating reasons that continue to be valid." Although the focus of attention is on human well-being, "these necessary conditions cannot be ignored or defied without pain and harm, though acknowledgment of them does not guarantee happiness."

8. "Nature: Its Status in Theological Ethics" (1982) is an essay written for a conference at Santa Clara University in California on the topic "Biomedical Ethics: A Christian Perspective," which was part of an ongoing series of annual conferences devoted to the larger theme of "Philosophical Issues in Christian Perspective." Its critique of Protestant thinking recurs in several of Gustafson's other publications. Gustafson criticizes Protestant theology for being unable to state the relationship between theology and nature positively and for wrongfully elevating history as the primary or sole arena of divine activity. The essay offers an informative introduction to the Roman Catholic alternative, Thomist essentialism. Traditional Roman Catholic theology rightly attends more seriously to the divine sovereignty over nature. Nevertheless, there is good reason for problematizing the traditional Thomist interpretation of nature in the light of modern scientific data. Is the order of nature static and unchanging? Is it warranted to speak of a human "essence"? Are we right in assuming a natural telos of, for example, human sexuality? And should we not adjust our anthropocentric view of the place of humans in nature and adopt a view that better accounts for the interdependence of humans and nature?

9. "Professions as 'Callings'" (1982) was written at the invitation of the School of Social Service Administration at the University of Chicago. It first analyzes the two main concepts. A *calling* provides dignity to the worker and the work done and provides a sense of fulfillment and meaning. When we speak of a *profession*, it is implied that highly developed skills are used with intelligence, reflectiveness,

and discretion; moreover, a profession is highly institutionalized and is guided by publicly transparent codes of conduct; finally, a profession is highly service oriented, that is, directed at meeting the needs of individuals and communities. Common examples are found in the clergy, in the health care sector, in law, and in social service. The overlap of a profession and a calling then lies in the motivation and in a deep vision of the human and social ends that are served. "A 'calling' without professionalization is bumbling, ineffective, and even dangerous. A profession without a calling, however, has no taps of moral and humane rootage to keep motivation alive." Despite the pitfalls that the concepts of "calling" and "profession" undeniably have, they are indispensable for our future understanding of work. In times when the merits of having a job are seen primarily in terms of self-realization and financial profit, this analysis of what the calling of a professional is may prove to be relevant for people working in any occupation.

10. "Death Is Not the Enemy" was cowritten with Richard L. Landau, MD. Originally published in the *Journal of the American Medical Association* in 1984, it contains a powerful and concise statement of an almost prophetic nature. Although secularization is not criticized per se, the authors contend that, for many persons in our culture, the loss of belief in a power that transcends nature has led to a deification of life, which, in turn, results in an unprecedented and unwarranted "priestly" role for practicing physicians in fighting and postponing death. Without arguing explicitly for a return to belief in God, the authors do plead for an acceptance of death as natural and thus not to be fought against at all costs, even if our present technological capacity allows us to prolong life indefinitely.

11. The essay "The Sectarian Temptation: Reflections on Theology, the Church, and the University" (1985), written for the Catholic Theological Society of America, is Gustafson's response to the widely popular postliberal theology of George Lindbeck and his followers. An argument in favor of "Christian participation in the ambiguities of moral and social life," this article reflects a recurrent concern throughout Gustafson's whole authorship: to prevent religion and theology from becoming irrelevant through isolation. Several kinds of sectarianism are identified: the "pious" sectarianism of some churches and groups in which Christian beliefs become subjectively meaningful, but their truth is not challenged by any serious criteria of coherence and adequacy; the "academic" sectarianism that divides the language of science and the language of religion (including theology) into incommensurable realms; and the sectarianism of purely descriptive theology which refuses to ask the question of truth. In all cases, Christian faith is rendered irrelevant for the world that surrounds it. Even Barth, Luther, and Calvin, with their solid doctrine of biblical revelation, had strong views on the relevance of the Word of God. In this essay, influences from Weber, Troeltsch, and the Niebuhrs can be found. Sectarianism is sociologically wrong in assuming that the Christian community is isolable from the wider society; it is theologically wrong because it makes Christianity into a modern and trivial form of Gnosticism; and it is philosophically wrong in assuming that religious knowledge is the result of a totally incommensurable way of knowing.

12. The concise *Westminster Dictionary of Christian Ethics* article on "Christian Ethics" (1986) exemplifies the typical "Gustafsonian" combination of description and normativity. While describing the field of Christian ethics, Gustafson includes in a nutshell his own methodological proposal. The prerequisites of consistency and adequacy ("the four base points and the four sources") mentioned in the introduction to "A Theocentric Interpretation of Life" recur here. This formal proposal, first elaborated in *Protestant and Roman Catholic Ethics*, continues to be of great methodological relevance to a new generation of scholars in Christian ethics.

13. "Roman Catholic and Protestant Interaction in Ethics: An Interpretation" was first published in 1989. Throughout his writings, Gustafson displays an interest both in Roman Catholic social thought and in exploring interactions and common grounds between Protestantism and Roman Catholicism. The study *Protestant and Roman Catholic Ethics: Prospects for Rapprochement* (1978) was not only an overview of different aspects of the interactions between the traditions, but was in itself an important proposal for how such interaction might proceed. One of the tenets of that book can be summarized as follows. Theological ethics in the last century can be described in terms of persistent tensions between "classical" polarities: nature versus grace, creation versus history, order versus dynamics, law versus gospel. The former elements have originally been stressed by Roman Catholics, the latter by Protestants. In the second half of the twentieth century, especially after Vatican II, theologians from both backgrounds came to affirm the poles their traditions had typically ignored. "Roman Catholic and Protestant Interaction in Ethics" builds on the groundwork of that study and shows with some sense of tragedy how much had happened in the eleven years since. Notwithstanding its self-confessed limitations, the essay is a tour de force of analysis of a broad range of literature, including recent Protestant writers like Stanley Hauerwas, John Howard Yoder, and Allen Verhey. It raises some sharp methodological and substantive questions about ethics, ecumenism, and theology. Although interaction between the two traditions continued toward the end of the twentieth century, there is hardly reason to speak of "rapprochement." Attention shifted from a pursuit of ecumenism per se to debates of a more methodological nature.

14. "Moral Discourse about Medicine: A Variety of Forms" (1990) may serve as an eye-opener to many scholars who have become involved in the growth industry of medical ethics. In this essay, four types of moral discourse in medicine are identified: ethical, prophetical, narrative, and policy discourse.[6] Medical ethics in its restricted, modern sense as we know it—concentrated on particular actions, against the background of particular moral conventions—is but one

---

6. See also Gustafson's *Varieties of Moral Discourse: Prophetic, Narrative, Ethical, and Policy*, the Stob Lectures of Calvin College and Seminary 1987–88 (Grand Rapids: Calvin College, 1988), as well as *The Contributions of Theology to Medical Ethics*, the 1975 Pere Marquette Theology Lecture (Milwaukee: Marquette University Press, 1975).

form of moral discourse. For a complete normative evaluation of medical practice and policy, we need a variety of types of discourse.

15. In 1970 Gustafson published a now-famous essay titled "The Place of Scripture in Christian Ethics: A Methodological Study."[7] In that essay, Gustafson approached his topic by beginning with biblical materials and themes and then asking how they might be applied to ethical questions. The more recent article reprinted here, "The Use of Scripture in Christian Ethics" (1997), addresses the theme "Scripture and ethics" in a reverse order. Gustafson takes his point of departure in questions of ethics and inquires how biblical materials might answer them. He works from five questions of ethics formulated by William Schweiker in his *Responsibility and Christian Ethics* (Cambridge: Cambridge University Press, 1995): "What is going on?" "What is the norm for how to live?" "What are we to be and to do?" "What does it mean to be an agent?" and "How do we justify moral claims?" Depending on the question that is asked, different types of answers concerning the use of Scripture are needed. Using terms developed by H. Richard Niebuhr, Gustafson contends that the authority of the Bible is not hierarchical as the ultimate justification of ethics, but can rather be described in terms of its educative and corroborative value.

16. "A Retrospective Interpretation of American Religious Ethics, 1948–1998" was published in the 25th Anniversary Supplement of the *Journal of Religious Ethics* in 1998. Gustafson identifies four major shifts in the field of religious ethics: (1) from Christian ethics to religious ethics; (2) from normative ethics to descriptive, comparative, and analytical ethics; (3) from philosophical assumptions to critical philosophical consciousness; and (4) from the social gospel's traditional agenda to more and different practical issues. The question that naturally comes up is: does the development of Gustafson's own thinking fit into this description? The question can be answered in the affirmative, with one notable exception: Gustafson made a shift from descriptive ethics to normative ethics, rather than a shift in the reverse.

THEO A. BOER
PAUL E. CAPETZ

FOR FURTHER READING

Beckley, Harlan R., and Charles M. Swezey, eds. *James M. Gustafson's Theocentric Ethics: Interpretations and Assessments*. Macon, GA: Mercer University Press, 1988.
Boer, Theo A. *Theological Ethics after Gustafson: A Critical Analysis of the Normative Structure of James M. Gustafson's Theocentric Ethics*. Kampen: Kok Publishers, 1997.

---

7. Originally published in *Interpretation* 24, no. 4 (October 1970): 430–55; reprinted in *Theology and Christian Ethics*, 121–45.

Chapter 1

Context versus Principles:
A Misplaced Debate
in Christian Ethics

The field of Christian ethics has been the location of a debate over the past decades between roughly delineated parties representing an allegiance to the use of formal prescriptive principles on the one hand, and those representing the cause of the more existential response to a particular situation on the other hand. The debate has taken place in Europe and the United States, it has taken place in Catholicism and in Protestantism. In European Protestant literature Karl Barth's *Church Dogmatics*, particularly Volume II/2, Bonhoeffer's *Ethics*, and Niels Søe's *Kristelig Etik*, have represented what has been called a "contextual" approach.[1] More traditional Lutheran theologians who stress the importance of ethics under the law have a larger place for traditional ethical principles. Werner Elert and Walter Künneth

---

1. See, Barth, *Church Dogmatics*, II/2, Eng. ed. (Edinburgh: T. and T. Clark, 1957), especially pp. 631–701; see also *Against the Stream* (London: SCM Press, 1954), especially pp. 53–124, and *How to Serve God in a Marxist Land* (New York: Association Press, 1959), pp. 45–80. Dietrich Bonhoeffer, *Ethics* (London: SCM Press, 1955), especially pp. 17–25, 55–72, and 194–222. Søe, *Kristelig Etik*, 5th ed. (Copenhagen: C. E. C. Gads Forlag, 1962), pp. 11–234, especially 108–70 (the second edition of this book was translated into German, *Christliche Ethik* [Munich: Chr. Kaiser Verlag, 1949], pp. 4–187, especially 83–132). The Christian ethics of Bultmann also belong in this general camp; for a discussion see Thomas Oden, *Radical Obedience: The Ethics of R. Bultmann* (Philadelphia: Westminster, 1964). Currently the most significant ethics text that has come from the more radical Christian

1

would be representative of this group.[2] In Catholic literature there was a movement in the early years after World War II that came to be called "situational
morality." A critic has typified it in the following terms, "The ultimate differences
between this new morality and traditional morality come down then to this: In
an objective system of ethics the moral judgment is submitted to an extrinsic
norm, an ontological norm founded on the principles of being. In situational
ethics the moral judgment is measured only by the subjective, immanent light of
the individual in question."[3] In contrast to the situational emphasis is the whole
tradition of natural law ethics and moral theology as this developed in Roman
Catholicism. It should be noted that some of the recent Catholic ethics continues to be influenced by a situational approach, though not in the extreme way of
earlier materials.[4]

In American Protestant ethics, a number of writers have been called "contextual," or "situational" ethicists. Among them are Paul Lehmann, Alexander
Miller, Joseph Sittler, H. R. Niebuhr, Albert Rasmussen, Joseph Fletcher, Gordon Kaufman, Charles C. West, and the author.[5]

Writings have been published in criticism of the contextual viewpoint by John
C. Bennett, Paul Ramsey, Alvin Pitcher, Clinton Gardiner, Robert Fitch, and
Edward L. Long.[6]

---

existentialist group is Knud Løgstrup, *Den Etiske Fordring*, 4th ed. (Copenhagen: Scandinavian University Books, 1958; German ed., *Die Ethische Forderung*, Tübingen: H. Laupp, 1959). Obviously
there are severe differences of opinion among these theologians, which points already to the mistake
of trying to include too many writers under one rubric as is required in a debate formula.

2. Elert, *The Christian Ethos* (Philadelphia: Muhlenberg Press, 1957; this is generally regarded to
be a poor translation), and Künneth, *Politik zwischen Dämon und Gott* (Berlin: Lutherisches Ver-
lagshaus, 1954).

3. Robert Gleason, S. J., "Situational Morality," *Thought*, 32 (1957), p. 555. The general movement was condemned by Pope Pius XII in 1952. For a readily available example of this point of view,
see Walter Dirks, "How Can I Know God's Will for Me?" *Cross Currents*, 5 (1955), pp. 77–92. For
other discussions, see Karl Rahner, *Nature and Grace* (London: Sheed and Ward, 1963), pp. 84–111;
Josef Fuchs, *Situation und Entscheidung* (Frankfurt: Verlag Josef Knecht, 1952); and John C. Ford
and Gerald Kelly, *Contemporary Moral Theology* I (Westminster, Md.: The Newman Press, 1958), pp.
42–140.

4. See, for example, Bernhard Häring, *The Law of Christ* I (Westminster, Md.: The Newman
Press, 1961), especially pp. 35ff., and Josef Pieper, *Prudence* (New York: Pantheon, 1959).

5. See Lehmann, "The Foundation and Pattern of Christian Behavior," in John A. Hutchison,
ed., *Christian Faith and Social Action* (New York: Scribner, 1953), pp. 93–116, and *Ethics in a Christian Context* (New York: Harper and Row, 1963). Alexander Miller, *The Renewal of Man* (New York:
Doubleday, 1955). Joseph Sittler, *The Structure of Christian Ethics* (Baton Rouge: Louisiana State University Press, 1958). H. R. Niebuhr, *The Responsible Self* (New York: Harper and Row, 1963). Albert
Rasmussen, *Christian Social Ethics* (Englewood Cliffs, N.J.: Prentice-Hall, 1956). Joseph Fletcher, "A
New Look in Christian Ethics," *Harvard Divinity School Bulletin*, 24 (1959), pp. 7–18, Gordon Kaufman, *The Context of Decision* (New York: Abingdon Press, 1961). Charles C. West, *Communism and
the Theologians* (Philadelphia: Westminster, 1958). James Gustafson, "Christian Ethics and Social Policy," in Paul Ramsey, ed., *Faith and Ethics* (New York: Harper, 1957), pp. 119–39.

6. For a discussion of an unpublished paper by Bennett, see Lehmann, *Ethics in a Christian Context*, pp. 148–54. Paul Ramsey, *War and the Christian Context* (Durham: Duke University Press,
1961), pp. 3–14, and various occasional writings. Alvin Pitcher, "A New Era in Protestant Social
Ethics?" *Chicago Theological Seminary Register*, 48 (1958), pp. 8–14. Clinton Gardiner, "The Role of
Law and Moral Principles in Christian Ethics," *Religion in Life*, 28 (1959), pp. 236–47. A running

The purpose of this study is to show that the debate is no longer a fruitful one. The umbrella named "contextualism" has become so large that it now covers persons whose views are as significantly different from each other as they are different from some of the defenders of "principles." The defenders of the ethics of principles make their cases on different grounds, and use moral principles in different ways. Finally, I will argue that there have been, and legitimately can be, four different base points for Christian moral discourse, and that no matter which point a writer selects to start from, he moves into considerations that are dominant in the other three if he seeks to develop a very complete Christian ethics.

Before engaging in a development of the major theses, however, it is important to notice that the debate has located the problem of Christian ethics at a particular point, namely the question, "how does the Christian community, or any of its conscientious members go about making a particular moral judgment or decision?" This question to a great extent determines the levels of discourse in the argument. Henry David Aiken, in an essay that ought to have great importance in theological ethics, has distinguished four levels of moral discourse, of which the answer to this question is only one. He has called them the "expressive-evocative" level, the "moral" level, the "ethical" level, and the "post-ethical" level. The first is almost ejaculatory in character; it is characterized by an unreflective moral comment that expresses feelings of indignation or of approval. At the moral level, the reflective question begins to emerge, for there men are asking, "What ought I to do in this situation?" "Is that which I admire so much really good?" Reasons are given for the choices that men make; rules are turned to in order to justify moral judgments. The discourse is essentially practical, in a sense that does not derogate "practicality" to expediency. The third, or ethical level, is the one on which questions are raised about the rules or considerations that justify a particular moral judgment. "Can the rules or the reasons by which I have justified a particular decision *really* be defended?" At this level men seek to give reasons for those other reasons that more immediately determine moral conduct. For example, if the answer to the question, "what ought I to do" is decided in terms "I ought to do what the Christian community has long expected men to do in comparable situations," the ethical question becomes, "On what grounds are the expectations of the Christian community accepted as normative?" The post-ethical level raises the question, "Why be moral?" At this point perhaps the offering of "good reasons" finds its limits, and an element of commitment made in freedom enters in.[7]

discussion of the issues can be found in the following references to *Christianity and Crisis*: Robert Fitch, "The Obsolescence of Ethics," November 16, 1959; Alexander Miller, "Unprincipled Living: The Ethics of Obligation," March 21, 1960; Paul Ramsey, "Faith Effective through in-Principled Love," May 30, 1960. See also Edward L. Long, *Conscience and Compromise* (Philadelphia: Westminster, 1954). Attention should be called to Father Edward Duff's discussion in *The Social Thought of the World Council of Churches* (New York: Association Press, 1956), pp. 93ff.

7. H. D. Aiken, "Levels of Moral Discourse," in *Reason and Conduct* (New York: Knopf, 1962), pp. 65–87. The essay was previously published in *Ethics*, 62 (1952), pp. 235–46.

Aiken's pattern has been introduced here in order to indicate that the context vs. principles debate has emerged on the second level of discourse, the moral level. It has come about in an effort to clarify an essentially practical question of morality: What ought I to do? In the polarization of the discussion, some have said, "Immerse yourself in the situation in which you live, and in which God is acting, and then do what appears to be the right thing in faith." Others have said, "Look to the objective morality of the Christian and Western tradition, for there are principles of conduct that have been derived from nature and revelation that will show you what you ought to do." Obviously the discussion moves rather quickly from this "moral" level to the "ethical" level, and the defense of each side takes place in the effort to say why the contextualist or the principled approach is the right approach. Presumably, for Christian moralists, the answer to the post-ethical question is the same, namely, "one ought to be moral because it is part of one's faith in Jesus Christ to conduct one's life in a way that is good for man." Within this general answer, however, there are very different accent marks, and these in turn affect the way that discourse goes on at other levels. The concerns of this essay begin with the moral level, and move to the ethical level, although some references are necessary to the post-ethical level as well. This is so because the debate with which we are dealing itself begins with the practical moral question.[8]

THE CONTEXTUALIST UMBRELLA

Any discussion that men force into a debate inevitably polarizes opinion, partly for the sake of clarifying the fundamental issues that divide, but partially for the sake of the convenience of lecturers in survey courses. Such has occurred in the current discussion in theological ethics in the United States. The contextualist pole has been covered by an umbrella that is so large that it begins to collapse. Men of quite different persuasions are placed under it. Men who might finally argue that assessment of the context is a matter of the first order of importance in moral decisions make that particular case for very different reasons. Writers have different contexts in view. Thus I shall show that the label itself is no longer very useful, since the differences of opinion among those so called are very great indeed.

For what reasons are men called "contextualists"? There are almost as many reasons as there are contextualists. In the area of social ethics there has been a growing concern over the past few decades for accurate analysis of what is actually taking place in the world in which Christians act so that their moral conduct can be more realistic and responsible. The realism that is sought is not at this point a critical assessment of the limitations of man's capacities to know and do the good by virtue of the limitations of his finitude and sin. It is a realism about

8. The movement from one level to another in theological ethics has been very confused. Indeed, the logic of theological ethical discourse has not been very clear precisely at this point, sometimes as a matter of conscious commitment. A great deal of work could be done in the analysis of written materials on the nest of issues opened up by Aiken's essay.

what is actually occurring, and thus about where the pliable points, the interstices in human society, are in which Christians can act, and from which can come some of the desired effects or consequences. The responsibility that is sought at this point is in relation to spheres of activity already existing. Put simply, some contextualists are saying, if you wish to act out of moral intentions in the political sphere of life, you must know the context of politics with as much accuracy and insight as is humanly possible. This means, then, that the study of politics, and of the scientific interpreters of political activity is essential for Christian moral action. If you wish to act with moral intentions in the economic sphere of life, you must have a disciplined knowledge of the economic context of moral intentions and actions. If you wish to affect the social morality of a local community, you must know that social context, its power structure, its mores, its institutional arrangements, its population movements, and so forth. Thus this particular contextual intention leads to the use of technical social analysis in the moral decision making of the Christian community. It sometimes leads to primary research by the ethically motivated Christian scholar, in order to understand what forces are actually shaping events in a society.

An example of contextual analysis of this sort, motivated by this particular reason for being a "contextualist" is Kenneth Underwood's *Protestant and Catholic*. In this widely known study, Underwood's intentions are basically ethical. He analyzed the staggering weakness of the Protestant moral community in Holyoke, Massachusetts, when it faced the question, "what ought we to do" in a particular situation. The situation was an invitation extended to Margaret Sanger to lecture on planned parenthood in a dominantly Roman Catholic city in the 1940's. Underwood put detailed sociological research to the service of a moral intention. In order to understand what the Protestants did do and did not do in those circumstances he made a detailed study of the city of Holyoke and its churches. He did a comparative analysis of the authority of Protestant and Catholic religious leadership, of the beliefs of Protestants and Catholics on religious and civil questions, of the class structure of the churches, of the relation of the churches to the labor movement, to business, and to politics, and he studied the history of Protestant involvement in politics in the city, and other matters. Underwood's conclusions are in effect these: Protestants were socially ineffective partly because they failed to understand the community situation in which they lived; they were unrealistic about the social context of which they were a part. If Protestants wish to affect comparable situations in other urban centers, they ought to take the social context—its political, religious, and economic aspects—more seriously than they normally do.[9]

A similar pattern of contextualism occurs in other areas of Christian ethics. In the ethics of medical care, for example, there is a constant reference to the

9. Kenneth Underwood, *Protestant and Catholic* (Boston: Beacon Press, 1957). A more recent study partially in this mode of contextualism is Denis Munby, *God and the Rich Society* (London: Oxford Univ. Press, 1961). Other examples could be cited as well.

particular circumstances of the patient. One might bring moral generalizations to bear on the question of abortion in general, for example, but physicians will often modify the implications of such generalizations with particular reference to the situation of the pregnant woman. This became a matter of international attention in the recent Finkbine case. The possibility of malformation of the child due to the drugs that were used during the pregnancy was the most important datum used in the decision of the parents to seek abortion. Under these particular circumstances, it was argued, abortion is morally responsible. The "context" was determinative of the decision.

The importance of knowing the actual social or personal situation is obviously not the only reason for being a "contextualist." Some writers propound the point of view in the first instance for theological reasons. This is the case for Karl Barth, as every reader of the *Church Dogmatics*, II/2, knows. Christians are to be obedient to the command of God. But the command of God is not given in formal, general ethics; it is not given in traditional rules of conduct. It is given by the living God in the concrete situation. It is a particular command addressed to a particular person in a particular sphere of activity, in a particular time and place. "The command of God as it is given to us at each moment is always and only one possibility in every conceivable particularity of its inner and outer modality."

> It is always a single decision. . . . We encounter it in such a way that absolutely nothing either outward or inward, either in the relative secret of our intention or in the unambiguously observable fulfilment of our actions, is left to chance or to ourselves, or rather in such a way that even in every visible or invisible detail He wills us precisely the one thing and nothing else, and measures and judges us precisely by whether we do or do not do with the same precision the one thing that He so precisely wills. Our responsibility is a responsibility to the command as it is given us in this way.[10]

Clearly Barth is not arguing for a "contextualism" on the grounds of a social realism that exists in the case of Underwood. Behind this particular quotation there is a whole doctrine of God who is for man in Jesus Christ, who is free, who is living and present to men in faith in the world. The fact that the ethics is expounded in terms of the particularity of God's command is more the function of Barth's doctrine of God than it is the function of a theory of human moral responsibility for a particular occasion. Theological conviction is the primary criterion by which an interpretation of the moral life is to be judged for its validity. This is clear from Barth's own extended discourse on the question "What are we to do?" The answers are given primarily in theological and religious terms. "We are to respond to the existence of Jesus Christ and His people. With our action we are to render an account to this grace."[11] "We are to accept as right, and live as those who accept as right the fact that they do not belong to themselves, that they therefore do not have their life in their own hands and at their own disposal, that

10. Barth, *Church Dogmatics*, II/2, pp. 663–64.
11. Ibid., p. 576.

they are made a divine possession in Jesus Christ."[12] "We are to accept it as right that God never meets us except compassionately, except as the One who comes to the help of our misery, except apart from and against our deserts, except in such a way as to disclose that what we have deserved is death."[13] "We are to accept it as right that God is our righteousness."[14] Further discussion of the question "What ought we to do?" adds little of moral particularity to the answer. We approach God as those who are ignorant and stand in need of divine instruction and conversion. We are to have complete openness, bracketing and holding in reserve what we know about the rightness and goodness of past decisions. We are to obey the command of God joyfully. We are to accept responsibility personally.[15]

Barth's ethics is called contextual or situational because certain basic theological affirmations permit only an ethics that is open to the present and the future, that is radically concrete in its commands. God's freedom to be for man in his grace, God's lordship over all things through his creation, redemption and reconciliation of all things, God's present activity and direct speech to man, God's calling each man to responsibility to him in the particular sphere of his life: these affirmations permit no general or formal ethics, but only an ethics of obedience in the particular time and place. Among American theologians, Joseph Sittler and Paul Lehmann also come to a contextual or relational ethic out of doctrinal affirmations, rather than from independent ethical grounds.

Joseph Sittler states that the Christian moral life is the actualization of man's justification in Christ. In man's organic relationship to God's work and presence, and to other men, the will of God is met as both known and unknown. "It is known in Christ who is the incarnate concretion of God's ultimate and relentless will-to-restoration; service of this will is presented to the believer not as a general program given in advance but as an ever-changing and fluctuant obligation to the neighbor in the midst of history's life."[16] The Christian perceives the neighbor's good and acts in continuity with his life in Christ and the ever-changing and fluctuant situation of the other person. Echoing Luther, Sittler says that the Christian moral life is "faith-doing." It is not a programmatic set of ideals, or a pattern of pre-defined obligations and duties. The authorization of this point of view is Biblical.

The language of Christian ethics is in accord with the language of revelation, and the language of revelation is in accord with the nature of God's relationships to men and the world. This language or speech is organic, and not propositional. Just as the Bible does not define the nature of God, or prove his existence, or elaborate his attributes in rational categories, so in the area of ethics the Bible does not give abstract counsels, duties, obligations, or ideals. Just as "God simply *is* what God manifestly *does*," so there is an "inner logic of the living, the organic,

12. Ibid., p. 580.
13. Ibid., p. 581.
14. Ibid., p. 582.
15. Ibid., pp. 645–661.
16. Sittler, *The Structure of Christian Ethics*, p. 73.

the destiny-bound," that is expressed in "time terms," which is appropriate to the Christian moral life, and thus to ethics.[17] Biblical speech about God, the Church, and man is all characterized by the language of organic relatedness.

Thus the Christian is organically related to his neighbors, and to the events and occasions of his historical life. He is also organically related to Christ; at least there is a continuity between the Christian and Christ that is best depicted in relational language. Thus "the Christian life is here understood as a re-enactment from below on the part of men of the shape of the revelatory drama of God's holy will in Jesus Christ. . . . Suffering, death, burial, resurrection, a new life—these are actualities which plot out the arc of God's self-giving deed in Christ's descent and death and ascension; and precisely *this same shape of grace* in its recapitulation within the life of the believer and the faithful community, is the nuclear matrix which grounds and unfolds the Christian life."[18] Out of this matrix comes faith-doing in the "ever-changing and fluctuant obligation to the neighbor in the midst of history's life."[19] Christian ethics has to be in accord with these prior theological affirmations, which in turn are consonant with the character of the relations of God to man and man to other men. Thus there is an immediacy to the commands in the Christian life that is "not communicable in the causalities of propositional speech."

Paul Lehmann is the one author who extensively uses the particular term contextual. Like Barth and Sittler, his primary intention is to delineate a position in Christian ethics that is not alien to the fundamental dogmatic statements of the Christian Church. He seeks to shape an ethics that is in accord with God's revelation in Jesus Christ, particularly with an interpretation of that revelation that stresses God's freedom in his humanizing work for man. He seeks an ethics that takes the Christian community seriously as the matrix of the Christian conscience, rather than as a prescriber of Christian moral propositions. Such an ethics then is one that delineates the Christian's participation in the world as one which coincides with what God is doing for man in a very particular set of events. The Christian is to have a theonomous conscience, a conscience "immediately sensitive to the freedom of God to do in the always changing human situation what his humanizing aims and purposes require. The theonomous conscience is governed and directed by the freedom of God alone." "Christian ethics in the tradition of the Reformation seeks to provide an analysis of the environment of decision in which the principial foundations and preceptual directives of behavior are displaced by *contextual foundations* and *parabolic directives.* In a word, the environment of decision is the context for the ethical reality of conscience."[20]

17. Ibid., Chapter I, "The Confusion in Contemporary Ethical Speech."
18. Ibid., p. 36.
19. I read Sittler's book as a contemporary statement of the basic character of Luther's ethics under the gospel. Christ is the shaper of the Christian life in the participation of the believer in faith in him. Christ is also the shaper of the Christian life that is active in love to the neighbor in his particular need. In this manner Sittler is close to the theme of the best known of Luther's writings in Christian ethics, "On the Liberty of the Christian Man." See discussion of this document below.
20. Lehmann, *Ethics in a Christian Context*, pp. 358–59, 347.

Such an ethics is grounded in the divine indicative rather than the divine imperative. "The primary question is not, 'What does God command?' The primary question is 'What does God do?'"[21] Christian ethics analyzes what God is doing as its first order of business, not what the churches have said God has ordered men to do. It is the theological discipline that reflects on the question, and its answer, "What am I, as a believer in Jesus Christ and as a member of his church, to do?"[22] The answer is that I am to do what my theonomous conscience says I should do as it is immediately sensitive to what God in his freedom is doing.

There are three contexts out of which Christian behavior comes for Lehmann. The largest and most determinative is the theological one, namely the context of what God is doing. This is known in faith in Jesus Christ. Thus he develops a Christological statement that undergirds the assertion that God is doing "political activity," or "humanizing work." "A theology of messianism [Lehmann's characterization of his Christological theology] is theology with the accent upon the politics of God, that is, upon what God has done and is doing in the world to keep human life human. For such a theology, three christological affirmations acquire particular significance. They are the doctrines of the Trinity, of the three-fold office of Christ, and of the Second Adam and the Second Advent."[23]

The second context is that of the Christian community. Jesus is really present in history among the true people of God. "It is this reality of the koinonia . . . which denotes the concrete result of God's specifically purposed activity in the world in Jesus Christ. We might, therefore, say that Christian ethics is koinonia ethics. This means that it is from, and in, the koinonia that we get the answer to the question: What am I, as a believer in Jesus Christ and as a member of his church to do?"[24]

The third context is the particular situation in the world in which God is acting, and in which the Christian acts. In his affirmation of the importance of the concrete place of Christian activity, Lehmann executes his sharp critique of those who would view Christian ethics in more rationalistic terms, stressing basic moral propositions from the Christian tradition, and seeking to deduce the ways in which these can be applied to particular situations. Lehmann, on his theological grounds (not on ethical grounds, that is not on the basis of an argument about the futility of imposing rationally derived propositions on to the dynamics of human history), bypasses this more rationally reflective procedure in favor of one that perceives, apprehends, or is sensitive to what God is doing. The stress is on other aspects of the self than the purely cognitive or intellectual aspects. He finds in the koinonia a coinciding of the response of Christians to what the community knows God has done and is doing. This leads relentlessly to highly particu-

---

21. Lehmann, "The Foundation and Pattern of Christian Behavior," p. 100.

22. Op. cit., 25. Note that the particular question of Christian ethics is on the "moral" level of discourse. Note also that Lehmann asks it in terms of "what *am* I to do," and not "what *ought* I to do." In this way he very selfconsciously reduces the imperative tone in favor of a more indicative one.

23. Ibid., p. 105.

24. Ibid., p. 47.

larized responses and actions, always sensitive to the historical present, rather than to generalizations about what ought to be.

For Lehmann, as for Barth and Sittler, Christian ethics that stress the importance of the particular situation, and the immediacy of involvement and response in that situation is legitimated on theological grounds. A quarrel with these men about the issue of contextualism must properly be a theological discussion. It necessarily involves the large and important question of the relation of ethics to dogmatics, and also the more particular questions about whether these men have properly appropriated the fundamental theological affirmations of the faith. The question of independent moral responsibility, or moral realism, in itself is not an appropriate question. There is a highly concrete sense of the place of responsibility and of the character of personal responsibility in these ethics, but it is theologically authorized. Contextual ethics are sound because they are consonant with what the Christian community knows God to be saying and doing, as this is made known in Scripture.

There is yet a third reason for contextualism in Christian ethics, namely an understanding of the nature of human selfhood, of existence. Ethics is contextual because persons live in a pattern of human relations which inevitably make moral responsibility a particular response to persons or events. A social theory of the self requires a relational or situational ethic. Social views of self, however, are not the only anthropology that bring contextualism into Christian ethics; a more individualistic existentialism does so as well. Ethics is contextual because men are free to shape their own existences in faith by their responsible and creative decisions in the world. A view of social selfhood is to be found in the writings of H. Richard Niebuhr; a more individual approach can be found in the ethics of Rudolf Bultmann and others. In either case the anthropology is also authorized by an interpretation of theology; it is not absolutely independent. But each has a degree of autonomy that is notable, and on this ground can be dealt with in a way different from Barth, Sittler, and Lehmann. For purposes of brevity only Niebuhr's discussion will be used to make the point.[25]

For H. Richard Niebuhr, the notion of moral responsibility is so closely related to the idea of man as the responder that each necessarily implies the other. "What is implicit in the idea of responsibility is the image of man-the-answerer, man engaged in dialogue, man acting in response to action upon him."[26] He distinguishes this view of man, and consequently of ethics, from those that used the image of man-the-maker and thus worked with basically teleological images, and man-the-citizen and thus worked basically with legal images and with a sense of duty or obligation. The case for the view of man-the-answerer is not derived in the first instance from particular Christian doctrines; it was built upon "common

25. For a discussion of Bultmann's ethics, see Thomas Oden, op. cit. Barth also has an anthropology that stresses the immediacy of responsibility given to the particular person, and softens any lines of continuity between the person and his community, or the person and his ethos. I shall not discuss Barth here, though it would be fruitful to do so

26. Niebuhr, *The Responsible Self*, p. 56.

experience." Thus there is a phenomenology of moral experience that is common to all men that makes the relational view of ethics appropriate, whether in Christian ethics, or some other view that has a different center of loyalty. When one observes moral action, he observes persons responding to the actions of other persons, or responding to events that have effects upon him. This is to be distinguished from those views that would affirm that men live and think morally first of all with reference to rules of conduct, or to ideas of what the future state of affairs ought to be. "All action . . . is response to action upon us."[27] "In our responsibility we attempt to answer the question: 'What shall I do?' by raising as the prior question: 'What is going on?' or 'What is being done to me?' rather than 'What is my end?' or 'What is my ultimate law?'"[28]

The effect of this understanding of selfhood is the delineation of an ethics that seeks to define and do what is fitting and appropriate in the particular relationships of the self. For Christians the interpretation of the situation involves an understanding of what God is saying and doing there. "Responsibility affirms—God is acting in all actions upon you. So respond to all actions upon you as to respond to his action."[29] The Christian community acts not only in response to the natural and historical context of its life, but in the light of a particular interpretation and understanding of that very particular context, namely what God is saying and doing there. Thus Niebuhr moves with ease between a view of the nature of man's moral existence to a view of the nature of God's being and presence as an active one. The two are coherent and congenial with each other, but Niebuhr does not seek to derive his anthropology from his doctrine of God. He is perfectly willing to find it in the common human experience as this was reconstructed in quite secular thinkers such as G. H. Mead, C. H. Cooley, Josiah Royce, and others, as well as theologians such as Buber. Finally, Niebuhr would say that a contextual ethics (though he fervently disliked the adjective) is necessary because of the nature of man.[30]

The fact that Christian moralists are contextualists in tendency for quite different reasons does not in and of itself imply that there is not enough common to all of them to make the use of the umbrella term appropriate. Obviously all have a special concern that the place of moral responsibility be understood to be highly specific and concrete, and that Christian ethics attend more to acting responsibly in a given place than it has done in those times and persons that seem satisfied with broad moral generalizations. There is a kind of personalism common to all of them, though it would be interpreted differently by various of them. But the main point to be noted for purposes of this essay is that men come to contextualism from different fundamental starting or base points, and the place

27. Ibid., p. 61.
28. Ibid., p. 63.
29. Ibid., p. 126.
30. A similar view of man is penetrating Roman Catholic philosophy and ethics. See, for example, Albert Dondeyne, *Faith and the World* (Pittsburgh: Duquesne University Press, 1963), pp. 145ff., and Bernard Häring, *The Law of Christ* I (Westminster, Md.: The Newman Press, 1963), pp. 35ff.

from which they start sets the pattern for what considerations are most important in the delineation of Christian ethics. I shall return to this in a subsequent section of this study. It needs to be noted also that within a general common ground of concern for the particularities of time and place there are differences of opinion about the place and use of moral generalizations. Lehmann, for example, eschews them with a vengeance; he keeps his elaboration of the meaning of "humanizing" to a minimum. Barth, in *Church Dogmatics*, III/4, avoids formal principles, but is willing to accept the idea that for Christians certain forms of behavior are usually appropriate. Normally Christians do not take life, for example. H. Richard Niebuhr has a large place for the principles by which human action and divine action are interpreted, though he does not stipulate a series of rules of conduct.

Finally, it needs to be noted that no serious Christian moralist who champions the place of principles avoids the issues involved in their appropriation and application within unique situations. The defenders of principles seek to move from the general to the particular in a disciplined way. These observations are the occasion for the assertion that the term contextualism has been used to cover too many theological heads, and that the debate is misplaced as it has often been specified. The defenders of principles are equally hard to lump together, and to a demonstration of this I now turn.

THE AUTHORITY AND USE OF PRINCIPLES

Three of the ablest and most influential American writers in Christian ethics have defended the significance of Christian moral principles either in a self-conscious methodological way, or simply by effective use of Christian moral norms. They are Reinhold Niebuhr, John C. Bennett, and Paul Ramsey. The inclusion of the three together immediately suggests to the reader of their works that they use principles in different ways in Christian moral discourse. Niebuhr and Bennett are concerned with the use of moral generalizations to give direction to the consequences and effects of moral action; Ramsey very deliberately stresses the use of principles for the determination of the right means of conduct. To make this differentiation is not to say that Bennett and Niebuhr are unconcerned about the proper means to be used to establish a state of affairs that approximates a Christian norm, nor that Ramsey is unacquainted with the idea that right means of conduct have to be appropriate to the right ends of conduct. But the difference of concern is notable enough to indicate that the purposes for which principles are used are different, and thus these writers can not easily be lumped together.

Reinhold Niebuhr's love-justice dialectic is widely known, and thus does not require detailed exposition. In *An Interpretation of Christian Ethics*, he derives the distinctive significance of Christian ethics largely from the teachings of Jesus, in intellectual continuity with the theology of the social gospel. The problem of the Christian practical reason is then set by the discrepancy that exists between a moral ideal that is impossible of historical realization, a law of love that cannot be easily applied on the one hand, and the condition of man the sinner and the complexity of moral dilemmas on the other hand. His polemic had a particular historical reference, namely "all those forms of naturalism, liberalism, and radicalism which generate utopian illusions and regard the love commandment as ultimately realizable because history knows no limits of its progressive approximations."[31] Niebuhr's argument was not against an ethics of impossible ideals or unrealizable laws of love, but against those who too simply believed that history could be shaped by them. Thus he developed a procedure of reflection in which some approximation of the ideals could occur through the idea of justice and its ramifications for balances of power, and greater equality in the distribution of the means of power in human social affairs. Love remained the moral ideal and the moral law; indeed "the law of love is involved in all approximations of justice, not only as the source of the norms of justice, but as an ultimate perspective by which their limitations are discovered."[32] The action which seeks to achieve moral ends in the human community is always to be guided and judged by the "impossible ethical ideal" that is given in the gospel.

This basic pattern of moral reflection continued in Niebuhr's writings, though the statement of the authority of the norm and some of the concepts and their uses were slightly altered. In *The Nature and Destiny of Man* the self-sacrifice of Jesus on the cross becomes the central point for understanding the meaning of heedless *agape,* rather than the teachings of Jesus; and the dialectic is refined and complicated by the introduction of the idea of mutuality.[33] The fact that Niebuhr had an acute "contextual awareness" needs to be noted, for in the dialectic of Christian ethical thought and life it is necessary to have an understanding of what actually is going on in the realms of politics and economics, of international relations and war. Indeed, this is one pole of the dialectic. But Christian faith in effect provides a revelation of moral norms which always judges and guides the more pragmatic responses and actions to the fluctuations of human history. The norms derived from revelation are authorized by God's deed and by Scripture, but they were also supported by their basically ethical significance as well. For example, Niebuhr argues for their significance in terms of the potential perversions and distortions of justice, if justice is not judged and tempered by a higher norm of self-sacrificial love.

John C. Bennett, like Niebuhr and many persons called contextualists, seeks to avoid utopianism and the lack of realism in Christian moral reflection and action. His concern also is to be significantly related to what is actually going on in human history and society. He also shares Niebuhr's view that there are norms given in the Christian revelation that can give guidance to the involvement of Christians in social change. His procedures are also well known to students of

31. *An Interpretation of Christian Ethics* (New York: Harper, 1935), p. 117.
32. Ibid., p. 140.
33. *The Nature and Destiny of Man* II (New York: Scribners, 1943), especially chapters 9 and 10.

Christian ethics, particularly in the version of them he gave in *Christian Ethics and Social Policy*, where he shares J. H. Oldham's conception of "middle axioms" that stand between the transcendence of the Christian ethic on the one hand, and the situation of human sin and "technical autonomy" on the other hand. These middle axioms are goal oriented, and not means oriented. "The Christian ethic guides us in determining the goals which represent the purpose of God for our time."[34] Thus the church is to provide guidelines, or provisional definitions of goals that will help Christians relate the transcendent Christian ethics to given times and places. In writings subsequent to the book of 1946, Bennett has continued to indicate the necessity for more fixed principles as anchors and compasses (the words are mine, not his) for Christian ethics. Like Niebuhr, his concern is twofold; he does not wish to compromise the absoluteness of the demand of Christian ethics for indiscriminate love by some theological argument that mitigates their starkness, and yet he accepts a Christian sense of responsibility for the moral character of what is going on in human society. It is through the statement of fundamental principles and more particular derivative directives that Bennett keeps both poles in proper tension.

Paul Ramsey's polemic is against both what he deems to be the "wastelands of relativism" that are the effect of contextualism, and against those who use moral principles more for the purpose of prediction and governing of consequences than for the determination of the proper means of conduct. *"How* we do *what* we do is as important as our goals."* Ramsey, like Niebuhr and Bennett, takes love to be the central point of reference for Christian ethics, although he also suggests in various writings that he wishes to resuscitate a modified version of natural law in Protestant ethics as well. "Love posits or takes form in principles of right conduct which express the difference it discerns between permitted and prohibited action, and these are not wholly derived from reflection upon consequences."[35] Ramsey's accent on the ethics of right conduct does not mean that he ignores prudential consideration of consequences, but that he wishes to make a corrective stance against Christian ethics that seem to be exclusively governed by such calculation. He works this methodological position out with reference to the situation of the Christian community in the nuclear weapons age, largely by a contemporary formulation of the just war theory. These principles of the right conduct of war are authorized by the Christian theological and ethical tradition, as it has sought to find the "inprincipled" forms of love that enable conduct to be guided during conflict, and by the Biblical revelation of love made known in the faith that Christ died for all men. They are worked out in relation to the possible use of nuclear weapons, as the writers on military strategy have considered the potential function of these weapons in an open international conflict. Ramsey's procedures, as he does this, are much more akin to the rational procedures

34. *Christian Ethics and Social Policy* (New York: Scribners, 1946), p. 76. Oldham's suggestions are found in Visser 't Hooft and Oldham, *The Church and Its Function in Society* (London: G. Allen and Unwin, 1937), pp. 209ff.
35. *War and the Christian Conscience*, pp. 6, 4.

of the moral theology tradition of the Roman Catholic Church than they are to most of the work of his fellow Protestant theologians. This makes him the most audible and visible defender of "principled ethics," as Lehmann's use of the notion of contextualism makes him the most audible and visible critic of such ethics.

In this brief analysis of these writers, it becomes clear that principles are used in different ways by different writers, and have different degrees of authority. In the case of Reinhold Niebuhr, love and justice are norms that are given a minimum of definition, and certainly are not spelled out into a series of moral propositions given for the guidance of conduct. The weight of his work is so heavily upon the assessment of what is going on in society, and the pragmatic judgments made (to be sure under the judgment and guidance of the ideas of love and justice), that he could easily be located on the contextual side of the debate. John C. Bennett's statements of middle axioms are deliberately relativized as being the creatures of ethical reflection under very specific circumstances, and thus open to revision as circumstances change. Paul Ramsey's delineation of principles of right conduct are weighted with more authority, for he has a confidence in the tradition that makes him take its distillations of the bases of judgment very seriously in their own right, apart from the contemporary occasions in which they are to be applied. If our discussion was extended to include Roman Catholic ethics, an even greater certitude about certain traditional moral propositions would be disclosed. Niebuhr and Bennett tend to use principles for the determination of a better state of affairs, or for the delineation of proper goals; Ramsey stresses right conduct and means as well as calculation of ends, and in this sense shares the ethos of Catholic moral theology. Apart from such a refinement of what is involved in the ethic of moral principles, the lumping of these writers together is a serious oversimplification.

In an earlier essay, I suggested a distinction between the prescriptive use of principles and the illuminative use of principles.[36] The distinction is introduced here to indicate some of the difficulties inherent in the polarization of the current debate. For Paul Ramsey, traditional Christian moral principles have such authority that they in effect prescribe the right conduct of Christians. Another moralist can read Ramsey's arguments, take them with great seriousness as an illustration of how a very thoughtful Christian ethicist reflects upon a current moral situation, and find the principles to illuminate his own judgment without being determined by the authority of the principles or the argument. He can find other statements of principles and other arguments equally illuminating, and equally important for his own decision. If the moralist stresses the openness of the present situation, the responsibility of the person in it to make his own decision, and the power of affections, dispositions, and perceptiveness also to give guidance to behavior, he need not necessarily ignore traditional moral principles. Rather, they are a significant part, though only a part, of what goes into his own moral reflection. Principles enable him to *interpret* what is morally wrong and

36. "Christian Ethics and Social Policy" (1958), pp. 126–29.

morally right about a particular occasion; to interpret what direction subsequent events ought to take in order to maintain the existence of the good and preserve it from disaster; and to interpret what patterns and means of action are more appropriate morally as he participates in events. But they are not prescriptive in the sense that the principles and arguments made concerning their application are the most important or sole authority for the governing of action. Thus casuistic arguments can be read with a great deal of serious interest without being determinative of conduct. In the illuminative use of principles the center of gravity is on the newness, the openness, the freedom that is present, in which the conscientious man seeks to achieve the good and do the right. In the prescriptive use of principles the center of gravity is on the reliability of traditional moral propositions and their reasonable application in a relatively open contemporary situation.

On the basis of this distinction, it is possible for persons who appear to be contextualists actually to be very serious students of moral principles and of the science of casuistry. The function that this study has, however, is different from what it appears to have for Paul Ramsey and for traditional Catholic moral theologians. But its function can be important enough to raise a serious question about the easy identification of theological moralists into two camps. Karl Barth, for example, in *Church Dogmatics*, III/4, discusses particular instances of moral decision with some care and precision as a way for the reader to become sensitive to what God might be commanding him to be and to do in an analogous situation. Even Paul Lehmann introduces the notion that God's activity is "political" and "humanizing," terms that are susceptible to more extensive exposition than he gives them, but nevertheless function as points of illumination for the actual conduct of the Christian man.

The debate between context and principles, then, forces an unfair polarization upon a diversity of opinion that makes it both academically unjust, and increasingly morally fruitless. Persons assigned to either pole are there for very different reasons, and work under the respective umbrellas in very different ways. It also becomes clear that contextualists find some moral principles or generalizations that give guidance to existential decisions, and that the defenders of principles find some ways to proceed from generalizations to particular situations. This assertion points to the theme of the remainder of the paper, namely, that Christian ethics can and does begin from at least four base points, and no matter which one is primary for a particular theologian, he moves toward the other three as he extends his moral discourse within a Christian frame of reference.

FOUR BASE POINTS FOR CHRISTIAN MORAL DISCOURSE

The four base points have already been introduced, though one not as directly as the others. There are moralists who begin with as accurate and perceptive social analysis, or situational analysis as possible. Others begin with fundamental theological affirmations. Still others locate moral principles as the central point for discussion. In addition to these three a fourth can be discerned, namely the nature of the Christian's life in Christ and its proper expressions in moral conduct. To be related to Jesus Christ in faith is to have a certain manner or quality of life which in turn has its appropriate moral expressions in intentions and actions. I shall indicate by use of examples the way in which moral reflection beginning from each of these points moves to a consideration of the other points as it engages in moral discourse.

It is appropriate to begin with the two base points that have already received most attention, namely with moral principles and with theological affirmations. Ramsey seeks to think about the use of modern weapons within the tradition of just war principles, and particularly the principle of noncombatant immunity. Non-combatants are not to be directly and intentionally killed in warfare. This is a moral proposition that is to be applied to the conduct of war in every time and place; it is as valid for the twentieth century as it was for the fifth century. Obviously Ramsey cannot, and does not wish to remain at the level of reiteration of an honored principle. He necessarily moves toward the particular context of warfare in the twentieth century, because the conduct of warfare, and even of the testing of weapons for warfare is different by virtue of the state of technology than it was when the principle was first formulated. When a large part of the economy of a nation is marshalled for the productive effort needed to conduct modern warfare, are the producers in factories combatants or noncombatants? When the scale of destruction by weapons is so great that a precise demolition of military installations is made difficult, is it meaningful to counsel noncombatant immunity? Ramsey takes the technological situation into view when he proceeds to ask these questions that any critical person would. He indicates in a number of his writings that he has read such authors as Oskar Morgenstern, and Herman Kahn as carefully and seriously as any Christian moralist has done, writers who discuss the problems involved in the use of weapons and the potential effects of their use in terms of the contemporary international situation. The point is a simple one: Ramsey moves from a basic moral principle to the problems that exist in and for its application under very particular conditions of the technology of warfare. He is cautious to keep his argument on the moral level; what makes the conduct of war right according to the just war principles is not derived from analysis of weapons, nor merely from the potential consequences of the use of weapons now being made, but from the fact that inprincipled love requires guards against indiscriminate killing. But he cannot avoid dealing with what now potentially exists in the state of contemporary technology.

Ramsey also moves from a particular principle to some theological justification for the principle. He believes that the just war principles are authorized in at least a twofold manner. When reasonable men think reasonably about the conduct of war, they will make the means used in war proportionate to the ends to be sought, and the ends to be sought will also be reasonable. In this sense there is an appeal made to human reason, or to the natural law as a ground for the principles. When Christians in the history of the Church's involvement in Western history have sought to understand what their central theological and moral point of reference—love—implies for the restraint of evil within social responsibility, they have worked this out in terms of just war principles. Thus there is also an appeal to the particular touchstone of Christian ethics. St. Augustine, St. Thomas, and other theologians have put the principles into love so that they can give direction to human activity. There is congruity between the particularized principles such as noncombatant immunity, and the affirmation that Christ, in love, died for all men. Thus in moving from the moral level of discourse to the authorization of moral rules Ramsey turns to philosophical and theological affirmations.

In yet another way Ramsey moves toward theological affirmations. He opens the way for a revision of ethical principles when certain theological realities take over. The principles are to be used as a service, and not as a reliance; "these rules are opened for review and radical revision in the instant that *agape* controls." In indicating where he differentiates his work from certain Catholic moralists, he suggests that "in the view here proposed, charity enters into a fresh determination of what is right in the given concrete context, and it is not wholly in bondage to natural-law determination of permitted or prohibited means."[37] Love is not only the basis for moral principles, it is an active reality that makes the moral person open to revision of the principles derived from it, and enables him freshly to determine what is right in a particular context. God's love, then, is free to alter the rules that men normally live by, though normally they ought to live by the rules derived from knowledge of God's love. A contrast with Karl Barth's procedure is instructive. Barth seems to say, God in his freedom commands man in his situation ever anew. Since he is not capricious, he is likely to command similar things, indeed the same thing over and over again. But one is not to make a moral principle out of the consistencies of God's speech. Ramsey seems to say that Christian love usually acts within the law and lays down rules or principles. Thus we normally act according to these rules. But, since Jesus Christ is Lord, there can always be a "fresh determination of what should be done in situations not rightly covered by the law, by natural justice, or even by its [Christian love's] own former articulation in principle."[38] Thus in moving from principles to Christian love, presumably to God's active love, one finds the source not only of principles, but of the fresh determinations of what should be done. What is Barth's first declaration comes in as a qualification of Ramsey's ethical style, though as a theological moralist he necessarily takes account of it.

Ramsey says little about the freedom of the Christian in faith and love to apprehend freshly what he ought to do and to be, though perhaps such a view is implicit in his understanding of the moment that *agape* controls. If he were to be more completely systematic than he has been, it would be necessary for him to develop an understanding of the Christian man in faith, who is open to the love of God both in its form of rules and its freer form. He would answer questions

37. Ramsey, op. cit., p. 179.
38. Ibid., p. 190.

pertaining to the nature and authority of the Christian conscience to determine what is morally right. Thus he would move not only from principles toward the historical situation, and the theological affirmations, as he does, but also to a view of human moral life in faith.

The theological moralist whose apparent base point is certain theological affirmations about the nature and activity of God necessarily moves toward the other base points as his reflection becomes systematic. I have indicated how Paul Lehmann, like Barth, develops a view of Christian ethics that is coherent with his understanding of God's work made known in and through Jesus Christ. It is also clear from our previous exposition that Lehmann's conception of God's activity in the events in which men participate requires an acute sensitivity to what is really going on in the particular personal and social context of behavior.[39]

Although Lehmann's view of conscience has been alluded to, it is worth further elaboration here, for the possibility of the kind of contextual ethics he expounds depends in large part on the viability of his view of the nature of the Christian moral self. Certain accents are distinctive and important. Lehmann pays more attention to the role of sensitivity, imagination, and perceptiveness than do many writers in the field of ethics. In his description of the theonomous conscience we have already seen this: it is "immediately sensitive to the freedom of God to do . . . what his humanizing aims and purposes require." Immediate sensitivity to what God is doing in his freedom apparently is not something that comes from a more rationalistic ethical discourse. It assumes a transformation of the self in faith. The church is the matrix of this transformation. "The reality of the church is an ethical reality because what God is doing in the world becomes concrete in the transformation of human motivation and the structures of human relatedness which are the stuff of human fulfillment."[40] An ethics that is as free of rational calculation as Lehmann's is logically has to have a view of the self that accomplishes what precise rational discourse does for a writer such as Paul Ramsey. The activity of God, Lehmann asserts, "is brought directly to bear upon the life of the believer by means of a functional Christological content and connection . . . It is also a way of giving to the believer a clear understanding of the environment and direction of what he is to do and thus a firm foundation for behavior. The difference [between believers and unbelievers] is defined by imaginative and behavioral sensitivity to what God is doing in the world to make and keep human life human, to achieve the maturity of men, that is, the new humanity."[41] Lehmann's emphasis on transformation of motivation, on a clear understanding that is relatively unaided by moral or sociological principles, on imaginative and behavioral sensitivity locates the personal nexus between God's activity and human action. Whether it stands up under various forms of criticism is not the concern of this essay. Lehmann does move to the outlines of a view of

39. See, for example, his discussion of sexuality, op. cit., pp. 133–40.
40. Ibid., p. 72.
41. Ibid., pp. 116, 117.

Christian moral life in faith that is consistent with the other bases of his ethics. Indeed, Christian ethics aims at a quality of life of which morality is the by-product. *"Christian ethics aims, not at morality, but at maturity.* The *mature* life is the fruit of Christian faith. Morality is a by-product of maturity."[42]

Lehmann eschews moral principles, and seems to assert that any use of them falls into a false abstraction, separating morality from life.[43] Consistent with this is his emphasis on the freedom of God, about which he says much more than he does about the love of God, or the ordering work of God. Yet there is a consistency to God's activity, so that Lehmann reiterates that it is a "humanizing," or "maturing" activity. He desists from extensive exposition of what these terms mean. Maturity, he says, *"is* the integrity in and through interrelatedness which makes it possible for each individual member of an organic whole to be himself in togetherness, and in togetherness each to be himself." "For Christianity, what is fundamentally human in human nature is the gift to man of the power to be and to fulfill himself in and through a relationship of dependence and self-giving toward God and toward his fellow man. Thus, maturity is *self-acceptance through self-giving.* . . . In the fully developed Christian sense, 'maturity' and 'the new humanity' are identical."[44] In spite of the severe economy of exposition, Lehmann does have a particular content in view when he uses these key terms. The effect is that these notions become principles of illumination for sensitive Christians in discerning what God is doing. They are not to be used as the first principles in the resolution of a problem in the manner of the science of casuistry. But they provide meaningful points of reference for moral judgment. Where humanizing work is going on, God is active, and where Christians perceive this they are to act so that their behavior coincides with what God is doing.

Thus Lehmann moves from his prime base of theological affirmation to a consideration of the other three bases for Christian moral discourse. His reluctance to denote in greater details what function as principles of illumination and judgment is consistent with his starting point and the way in which he defines it, but clearly Christians are not to be immature, nor are they to engage in anything that is inhuman, or dehumanizing in its effects.

If the ethicist begins with disciplined social analysis, he has to move to other points in order to clarify the moral judgments that he makes about what he finds to be the case. Often there is a division of labor between the social analyst and the

---

42. Ibid., p. 54.
43. Ibid., pp. 148ff., and particularly p. 152. "For a *koinonia* ethic the clarification of ethical principles and their application to concrete situations is ethically unreal because such clarification is a logical enterprise and there is no way in logic of closing the gap between the abstract and the concrete." I regard this assertion to be the slaying of a straw man, for no serious moralist has believed that logic alone closed that gap. Roman Catholic moral theology, which is most susceptible to the criticism, never assumes that logic alone is the path from principle to concrete action, and always has a place for the person, with his natural and theological virtues, who acts responsibly. See, for example, Josef Pieper's *Prudence*, which admittedly makes the most of the person who is the juncture between principles and actions.
44. Ibid., pp. 55, 16–17.

moralist, though it is quite typical for the moralist to make a judgment on the information he perceives to be important or adequate pertaining to a particular instance, whether this information is derived in a disciplined way or by impressions. It is also the case that social analysis is often freighted with moral judgments. If Kenneth Underwood's study is taken as a case of social analysis done for ethical intention, the need for movement between principles or bases of moral judgment and empirical analysis can be seen. If the weakness in thought and deed of the Protestant churches in Holyoke is bad, as Underwood clearly indicates he believes, it is judged bad on the basis of moral and theological convictions, not sociological evidence. One can extrapolate from the analysis he makes to indicate what some of the bases of judgment are. Presumably the churches were not acting out a theologically defined conception of their mission; they were not being responsible to the God they confessed in worship. Presumably also they lacked the ethical clarity to order the various activities in which they ought to be engaged, and thus were institutionally subject to social pressures. Underwood does not draw out these things, for he is particularly seeking to show how moral communities must understand their social contexts through a process of social analysis. He does not claim that the book has Christian ethics as its primary subject matter. But a more extensive ethical treatise would require the movement in the directions of the other bases. There is something theologically awry with the actual situation, there is something morally weak about it, and the religious leaders and laity lack some qualities of Christian existence which prohibited them from becoming more active in accord with professed convictions.

The fourth base, that of a conception of Christian existence, has not been clearly represented in our previous analysis. In the case of H. R. Niebuhr, an interpretation of moral existence is clearly a major starting point for ethical and moral reflection, but in *The Responsible Self* he is not concerned to suggest the particular qualities that the religious life in faith brings into being. Further exploration of Bultmann's ethics would be one way of making the point. Man in faith has a radical freedom to be himself, to be obedient to the command of God. The moral life is to some extent then a situational expression of that faith, that freedom, and that obedience.

The interrelation between base points, with a particular prime focus on the state of the life of faith can best be illustrated by Luther's essay, "On the Liberty of the Christian Man." In this particular work, Luther describes the Christian life in the famous aphorisms, "A Christian man is a perfectly free Lord of all, subject to none. A Christian man is a perfectly dutiful servant of all, subject to all."[45] He goes on to describe the nature of this Christian liberty and righteousness, which cannot be produced by work or by any external influence, but only by the Word of God received in faith. Thus, in the very description of the righteousness of the Christian, Luther immediately turns to the theological source and foundation of it, that is God's gift of his Son which is the act of God's justification of man. The

---

45. Citations here are to the edition, *Three Treatises* (Philadelphia: Muhlenberg Press, 1943), p. 251.

concern for which Luther is most widely known even outside the Christian community enters in here, namely that law and works are unnecessary for any man's righteousness (in the sense of the gift of God's righteousness) and salvation. God counts men righteous, and in the faith of man gives the gift of liberty and righteousness. He unites the believer with Christ as the bride is united with the bridegroom. "Therefore, faith alone is the righteousness of a Christian man and the fulfilling of all the commandments."[46] Thus Luther describes the "inward man" with immediate reference to God's work for man in Jesus Christ.

This inward man, while never perfectly spiritual and holy in this life, nevertheless gives to the "outward man" certain characteristics. The works of the outward man never justify him before God, but they do express the desire born in faith to reduce the body to subjection and to purify its evil lusts. They are directed toward the neighbor in love. The attention given to the self in faith and the idea that the external actions are expressions of that faith can be seen when Luther writes, "These two sayings, therefore, are true: 'Good works do not make a good man, but a good man does good works; evil works do not make a wicked man, but a wicked man does evil works'; so that it is always necessary that the 'substance' or person itself be good before there can be any good works, and that good works follow and proceed from the good person, as Christ also says, 'A corrupt tree does not bring forth good fruit, a good tree does not bring forth evil fruit.'"[47] Faith, then, brings with it the gifts of righteousness and liberty, which are effectual through love. Faith "issues in works of the freest service cheerfully and lovingly done, with which a man willingly serves another without hope or reward."[48]

Luther does not digress from his primary attention to give illustrations of what the neighbor's needs are; he does not describe the kinds of personal and social contexts in which the works of love are to be effectual. But obviously he assumes that they are particular and concrete. Nor does he spell out some principles of Christian love that enter into the guidance of the action directed by love to the neighbor. He does have, however, the figure of the work of Jesus Christ in view, as that which gives something of the shape of the Christian's intentions and actions toward others. The full work of Christ presents a pattern for the relation to others. "Just as our neighbor is in need and lacks that in which we abound, so we also have been in need before God and have lacked His mercy. Hence, as our heavenly Father has in Christ freely come to our help, we also ought freely to help our neighbor through our body and its works, and each should become as it were a Christ to the other, that we may be Christs to one another and Christ may be the same in all; that is, that we may be truly Christians."[49] The work of Christ, received by Christians in faith, both empowers and shapes the arc of their rela-

46. Ibid., p. 262.
47. Ibid., p. 271.
48. Ibid., p. 276.
49. Ibid., p. 279.

tion to the neighbor, and in this sense functions as a broad, but delineated pattern for the Christian moral life.

Thus Luther touches upon the four bases that have been indicated to be necessary for a systematic Christian ethic. His primary concern in the essay on liberty is to describe the Christian life, but he cannot do this without attending to the theological sources of that existence, and to both those persons toward whom it is expressed in love, and the shape of the life that properly expresses it.

The intention of this section has now been executed, namely to show that authors of important works in and for Christian ethics tend to focus on one base point in their exposition, and even to declare that a certain base point is the proper point for beginning Christian moral reflection, and that they necessarily move toward some consideration of the other base points. This is sometimes done with great self-consciousness so that the way in which they deal with them is consistent with their starting point, or it is only indicated in a cursory fashion that cries out for further exploration. The debate over context and principles is over-simplified if it does not take into account these base points, and the way in which they are related to the discussions of context and the use and authority of principles.

FOR CLARIFICATION OF DISCUSSION

The way in which the debate has attended to the moral level of discourse, without sufficiently moving to other levels is in part responsible for its being misplaced. It has tended to assume that the matter of how moral decisions are made could be separated from other considerations. I hope it is now clear that if one chooses to argue against "contextualism" one has to direct his arguments to the theological and ethical reasons given for the stress on context. Thus against Barth, Lehmann, and Sittler, one's argument ought primarily to be a theological argument. It is because these men have a certain view of God and his activity that they find contextualism congenial as an approach to ethics. None of them is fixed upon the question, "How do men decide what to do?" as if this ethical question were capable of abstraction from fundamental *theo*logical convictions in the strict sense. If one chooses to argue against H. R. Niebuhr, he would have to argue not only on theological grounds (not explicated in this essay), but on the grounds of a moral anthropology. Is man to be understood as responder and answerer, or is he better understood as maker and citizen? If one chooses to argue against the demand for refined social analysis of the context of action, the character of one's concerns might be directed to whether that context is properly understood through the means of social research, and whether such a proposal does not carry with it unexplicated ethical and theological assumptions.

Similarly, if one argues against principles, one has to be particular about certain questions. From what sources are the principles derived? From nature, or from Biblical revelation, or from the ethos of the Christian community? How are principles used? For giving direction to goals, or for the determination of right conduct? As prescriptive principles, or as analytical and illuminating principles?

If one persists in choosing sides in a misplaced debate, there are still questions that have to be dealt with. How does one move between moral principles and theological affirmations? Do certain defenses of principles assume certain views about God that are not necessarily consistent with such ethics? What is assumed about the nature of the moral self in various uses of principles? About the amenability of the social and personal world to subjection to principles, and actions governed quite exclusively by principles? How does one move between theological affirmations, moral principles and moral judgments? Through a view of sensitivity and imagination? Through rational calculation?

Further elaboration of these questions raised by this paper is not necessary. One larger one still looms, namely, is there one normative starting point, or base point, for work in Christian ethics around which other discussions ought to cohere? On this question the author has convictions, but their exposition lies outside the scope of this methodological analysis.

Chapter 2

Moral Discernment
in the Christian Life

I. THE NOTION OF DISCERNMENT

The practical moral question is asked in various ways. Sometimes it is, "What ought we to do?" Or, if one chooses to relax the imperative and accentuate the indicative, it is, "What are we to do?" When such ways of asking the question are scrutinized, it becomes clear that the words "ought" and "are" carry a heavy load of freight. There is not only the relative moral weight or authority implied by each, the degree of obligation that each suggests, but also an unexplored process of moral judgment-making. Indeed, the polemics out of which this book emerges have attended primarily to those processes. Most of the polemics in Christian ethics have been about *how Christians ought to make judgments*. They ought to use rules in a highly rational way, or they ought to exercise their graced imaginations, or they ought to obey the tradition of the Church, or they ought to respond to the situation of which they are a part. Not enough work has yet been done by either philosophers or theologians on just how people actually do make moral judgments, though the variously propagated "oughts" claim some validation on the basis that each is correlated with what people actually do.

25

In this chapter, I wish to suggest that the practical moral question of what we ought or are *to do* be held in abeyance in its strongest existential moral sense; and that it would be fruitful to look more carefully at how we *discern* what we ought to do, or are to do. Moral agents exercise some discrimination in making judgments, and it is this exercise of discrimination that I wish to explore. Such exploration is not done on the basis of a sampling of opinion; I have not approached a cross-section of men, not even a cross-section of Christians, with a schedule of questions to find out how they actually discern what to do. Nor does this exploration lead to a full-blown theory of the relations of motives, affections, rationality, and other aspects of moral selfhood as these have engaged the attention of moral philosophers in the past. I am not proposing that what seems to me to be involved in moral discernment is something that can be packaged, delivered, and taught to people who wish to become more moral. Nor am I suggesting the absence of wide variations in the ways in which people discern what they are to do; obviously some men are more emotive in their responses, some more intuitive, some more rational.

The intention of this chapter is more limited. It is based on the following rudimentary observations. Persons of moral seriousness do exercise discrimination in making judgments. They discern what they are or ought to do. Discrimination, or discernment, takes place not only in moral experiences but in other areas of human experience as well, such as esthetic experience. Common speech uses the adjective "discerning" with reference to persons who seem to be more perceptive, wiser, more discriminating than others are in judging, whether the object judged is a performance of a symphony, a person and his behavior, a political situation, or a novel. Thus by exploring the uses of the word "discern," we might be able to see what goes into moral judgments, and particularly into moral judgments that seem to have a quality of excellence.

In one usage, to discern something is simply to see that it is there; indeed, this kind of visual use of the word is the least qualitative, or value-laden. When I am driving in a fog, I might say to my companion, "I dimly discern the white line that divides the lanes." I do not see it with unusual accuracy; I am not making a qualitative judgment about what I see; I am using the word simply to indicate that I can see the line. Perhaps more commonly we use the verb "discern" to indicate a particular accuracy in perception or observation. Often we use it when we can locate a detail that misses the perception of others. Often we use it when some subtle shading or coloring registers on us. In accord with such use, we might call a person "discerning" who has an unusual capacity to isolate significant detail, to perceive subtleties, to be penetrating and accurate in his observations. While in one sense, to discern something is simply to notice it, to see it, in another sense we reserve the word for a quality of perception, of discrimination, of observation and judgment.

It is this quality of perception, discrimination, observation, and judgment that is involved when we speak of a "discerning person" or of "discerning comments" in various realms of discourse. As one who has to read hundreds of letters of recommendations for admission to graduate school, and who has to live with admissions based upon such letters, I have come to regard certain persons who write letters regularly as being "discerning." I do not mean that they give the most detailed descriptions of the candidates, nor that they simply notice the most obvious things about them. I mean that they seem to be able to get at salient characteristics of the students that have great importance in assisting me to make my judgment about them. There is an accuracy to their descriptions and their judgments that is borne out over time; they have an eye for pertinent characteristics (pertinent to what it takes, for example, to be a good graduate student). They enable me to have some understanding of the student; I can begin to draw my own "portrait" of him. This is more than a picture of a man of twenty-four who achieved a high academic record at Princeton University, and is interested in further study of ethics. By the letter writer's discernment of the qualities of mind, spirit, and character of the man, I can grasp some of his significant features, what his strengths and weaknesses are. I rely on the discerning letters of discerning men to help me make my judgment of what I ought to do with reference to the admission of a student to graduate school.

The same sort of process occurs in other areas of experience. Good literary critics are the most "discerning" ones. The difference between the good schoolboy type of writer on literature, who does all his homework (research) and writes up accurate summaries of what he has read, and the writer who moves the discussion to another stage is one of a quality of discernment. The discerning critic helps the reader to "see" things in the literature that he might not see on his own; he helps the reader to perceive some of the subtlety of the writer's words, characters, or plots; he helps him to understand what the writer's intention is in the way in which he concretely organizes his details. The same would be involved in distinctions between types of people who go to art museums. There are time clods who pace through the rooms with nothing registering upon their consciousnesses other than the fact that at the museum they saw works by Rembrandt and Picasso, about whom everyone who reads the newspapers knows something. At the other extreme are the discerning students, who not only are open to the impressions that a painting makes upon them, but sense the significance of detail, of the arrangement of color patterns, of lines, and all other aspects of the work. The discerning observer can not only say, "I don't like that one," but he can give some reasons for his judgment that express more than his feelings, that have some objectivity to him.

By reading the works of discerning critics of art and literature my own capacities for making judgments are deepened and broadened. I begin to "see" what is involved in accurate observation so that my own perceptions of the text or the painting are altered. I learn to be more discriminating in my own judgments. Presumably my judgments will be "better," at least to the extent of being more informed. I will be less likely to miss salient points I had missed before; I will become more "sensitive" to nuances, to details and their suggestive meanings, to the structure and wholeness of the piece at hand.

What seems to be involved in the quality of discernment toward which the foregoing paragraphs point? This question might best be answered by indicating what seems not to be involved, indeed, what is excluded. First, a person who has a scheme for analysis that he woodenly and mechanically imposes on whatever he observes would probably not be called a "discerning" person. The tourist who visits art museums with one checklist of things that he ought to look at, and another of the things he ought to look for in what he looks at, would hardly at that stage of his life receive the appellation "discerning." Checklists and wooden schemes of analysis cannot attend to the subtle nuances that are involved in refined discriminations; they seem to stress the more universal elements found in all objects of a given class, rather than the particularities to be appreciated in a single representative of what might be a class. Although they may help the novice to avoid gross errors, such schemes seem to be "external," that is, imposed from the outside on both the observer and that which he observes. They do not in themselves have or require the qualities of empathy, appreciation, imagination, and sensitivity that seem to be involved in discerning perception and judgment.

Thus, also, in moral experience, someone might suggest that in making a judgment the agent ought to keep in mind a scheme that includes the following six things: the potential consequences, the variety of his motives, the moral maxims accepted by his community, the empirical data about the situation as he defines it, the love of God, and the moral order of the universe as understood by reason. A person who has to make a moral judgment might run his dilemma through such a scheme with several possible results. He might be more confused after than before. He might try to "add up" all these considerations and find that their sum is far from a judgment. Or he might find that the scheme usefully points him in a direction, and then simply follow the direction. But the critic would probably say that each of these ways of making a judgment is wooden, mechanical, external, and certainly not discerning.

Second, the person who has formulated a set of first principles, has refined his understanding of deductive logic so that he can move from the universal to the particular, and has consequently determined on a rational basis what conduct is right and good, might not be viewed as a man of moral discernment. He might be called a man of intellectual discernment on the grounds of his virtuosity in formulating the universal principles and by the authority of his deductive logic. But since moral judgments involve more than the arrangement of ideas to each other in a logical and orderly way, in actual practice such a person might not demonstrate the perceptiveness that helps one to be aware of the complexity of the details of a particular instance. Indeed, if he assumes that his intellectual virtuosity is sufficient for making a moral judgment, he has to classify the case at hand, that is, attend less to its unique elements and accentuate those it has in common with others, in order to proceed. Intellectual clarity and the use of critical reflection are involved in moral discernment, just as they are involved in discerning criticisms or discerning descriptions in response to works of art, but in themselves they are not sufficient to exhaust what we normally include in the notion of discernment.

Third, the person who is skilled in accumulating the relevant information pertaining to a subject is not necessarily a discerning judge. All teachers know

instances of students who are admirably exhaustive in their bibliographical preparation, are assiduous in reading with comprehension the important treatises on
the subject, and are even orderly in arranging this material and reasonably clear
in writing it up, but who are not really discerning students of the subject. "Discernment" seems to be appropriate for pointing to the ability to distinguish the
important from the unimportant information and the insightful interpretations
from the uninsightful. It refers to the ability to perceive relationships between
aspects of the information that enable one to see how it all fits together, or how
it cannot fit together. It refers to the ability to suggest inferences that can be drawn
from the information, and thus to an imaginative capacity. One can find sociological studies, for example, that seem to be exhaustive in the accumulation of
the data pertinent to the topic under research but are of limited value because the
researcher lacked discriminating judgment and imagination. So it is in the sphere
of moral judgments. Accurate accumulation of relevant information about a matter that is the object of moral judgment is indispensable, but such accumulation
in itself does not constitute a discerning moral decision. The raw data for making judgments might be gathered, but the act of judgment itself involves more
capacities than are required simply to pull relevant information together. Or, one
can find biographies that are encyclopedic accumulations of objective data about
the man involved, but do not enable the reader to penetrate in any way into the
"character" of the subject, that do not give a coherent "picture" of the man so that
he can be understood and not just known about.

Fourth, one might find persons who are articulate in giving their emotive and
expressive reactions to a subject. By feeling deeply about something they are able
to give an immediate reaction to its presence. But the reaction may be much more
the expression of their indignation or their inordinate admiration than a discerning account of what was worthy of approval or disapproval, what was good or bad
in the subject. The first hearing of music from India, for example, might evoke a
judgment that it is unbearable, or that it is fascinating. Neither would be considered a discerning judgment, for neither would give reasons for the reaction.
Whether it is the rhythm that either fascinates or repels, or the tonal qualities of
the sitar, or the absence of Western style of harmony, would be matters that would
be developed in a discerning judgment. Similarly in moral matters, the expressive
ejaculation of approval or disapproval in itself is not a discerning moral judgment.
Nor would response in action that was based only on the depth of one's sense of
indignation or love necessarily be a discerning response. Some disinterestedness,
some accuracy of knowledge, some reflective awareness of what the situation
entailed beyond what is immediately present would be ingredients of a more discerning response. Some thoughtful discrimination between the values that compete for actualization, between the possible consequences of possible courses of
action, would be likely to occur if the judgment were to be called "discerning."

Fifth, stubborn allegiance to a given basis for making a judgment hardly makes
for discerning judgment. Moralistic critics of literature provide interesting examples here. All literature that uses profanity, that talks about sexual relations in

four-letter words, or that details the accounts of homosexual or heterosexual relations has often been condemned as "bad." And the use of the word "bad" has seemed indiscriminately to include both moral and nonmoral (e.g., literary) values. The critic who makes such judgments may have a palpable consistency that gives him the appearance of integrity, of being a man who is clear about his principles of judgment. But such stubborn allegiance to such principles hardly enables him to have an appreciation for the varieties of values that might be present in a book, for the significance of the concrete and the detailed, for the cumulative effect of the character portrayals or the plot development. Discernment seems to require some sensitivity and flexibility, some pluralism of consideration that is a priori ruled out by dedicated allegiance to single principles of interpretation or criticism. Similarly, in moral experience, the person who has a highly visible integrity based upon stubborn dedication to one or two principles, values, or rules, is not likely to be discriminating in a complicated situation. His responses may be predictable, but they are not thereby discerning.

These remarks about what seems not to be part of "discerning" judgments all pertain to a quality of excellence in discrimination. By indicating what the discerning person (in a qualitative sense) may not be and do, perhaps we can get at the elements of a discernment both in a more descriptive sense of Everyman as a moral discerner, and in a more normative sense of what excellence in discernment is. Some of the same elements are involved in the discernment of the morally flat-footed clod and the moral virtuoso. When these can be enumerated, perhaps one can see what combinations and accents among them make for excellence.

Discernment of what one ought to do, even among the clods, no doubt involves a perception of what is morally fitting in the place and time of action. What is fitting is decided differently by different people: some attack a problem in a disinterested manner, with great objectivity involved in their collection of appropriate information, their use of generalized prescriptive principles or articulated values, and their careful assessments of possible consequences of alternative courses of action. Others are more passionate; they feel deeply about what the actual situation is, they trust their built-in compasses to guide them, and they express their courage and initiative in taking the risks involved in action. What is fitting is discerned with reference to some of the same things and some different things, and different valences are existentially placed on different things by different people. Some are more determined by emotions, and value their moral sensitivities highly; others distrust emotions, and value their moral reflection highly. But perhaps some of the same things are present in both flat-footed and virtuoso performances in each style.

What are the common elements in all moral discernment? Perhaps several. There is a "reading" of what actually is the case at hand. Sometimes this reading is simply a visual image of an event that evokes decision and action. Sometimes it is a highly researched reading. Sometimes it is checked against other readings; sometimes it is idiosyncratic. Sometimes there is a depth of interpretation: some will want to know how the case got to be what it is, what are the relations of various elements to each other, who among the participants is most important or has more at stake, what the pliable factors are, what patterns and structures are there, and how it differs from similar cases. Sometimes there is no desire to interpret in a sophisticated way; sometimes there is no time to do so. The reading is from a perspective; this is important. Because the perspectives of moral participants differ, some see certain aspects to which others are blind; different persons accent the importance of different aspects; and in some persons there is simply suppression of factual matters that are abrasive to the moral predispositions. We have seen the importance of perspectives in "factual" judgments in the arguments about what really is the case in Vietnam. Sometimes the case is read more complexly because the moral discerner understands the situation and its participants to be part of an extensive pattern of relationships to other situations and other persons; sometimes it is read more simply because the time and space box in which it is seen is limited. Even different "situationists" differ on what the situation is. But for clod and virtuoso alike moral discernment involves such a reading of the case, an assessment of pertinent facts.

It is persons who discern; and persons have histories that affect their discernment. Some have never been seriously challenged to examine the bases of their judgments; others are highly self-critical and introspective. Some have developed characters on the basis of critical evaluations of past experiences and of the exercise of their initiative in becoming what they are throughout their personal moral histories. Others have more or less bounced morally through life, accumulating the effects of one occasion or episode after the other without a sense of self-direction. Some have acute senses of justice and injustice by virtue of having been the victims of oppression, or by virtue of being members of groups that have histories of being oppressed. Others are blithely confident about the goodness of men and the world because the world and men have been blithely supportive to them. Some are committed to getting all that they can out of life for themselves, and will discern what they ought to do in the light of that commitment; others are committed to loving the neighbor and meeting his needs because they have a religious loyalty that makes them believe this is how life ought to be lived. Several things have thus been suggested about the persons who discern: they are persons of persistent moral dispositions, or the absence thereof, and some have different persistent dispositions from others. They are persons of certain moral sensitivities or sensibilities, or the absence thereof, and some have different "feelings" from others. They are persons of certain commitments or the absence thereof, and some have different commitments from others. Moral discernment in a particular occasion is determined in part by these aspects of the self. These other-than-rational aspects of selfhood partially determine perspective, partially determine what is seen and accented, partially determine what is judged to be right and wrong, and thus what one will do.

Most persons who make moral judgments live by some beliefs, rules, and moral principles that enter into their discernment. They are members of communities that have rules of conduct and some power of sanction in enforcing them. Thus, most people decide not to steal something from a store when they go shopping, for there are rules against this, and potential disruptive consequences if they should be caught stealing. Most people discern that they ought to assist someone who is suffering not merely because the observation of the suffering of others makes them feel bad, but because the "golden rule" or the principle of meeting the neighbor's need readily applies. There are not only principles, rules, and values to which men are committed that partially determine their moral discernment; there is also usually some rational reflection about how these function at least in the instances where the normal habituated responses seem not to apply readily. Both the moral clod and the virtuoso are likely to be able to give some principles that will justify their judgments, and are likely to be willing to show that they arrived at the judgment on the basis of some rational discrimination. Some men will give intellectually sophisticated justifications, indicating their reasons for selecting some principles and not others as applicable to the case at hand, and defending the principles that are applicable. Others might simply appeal to the generalized expectations of a given society of which they are a part, or appeal to the authority of an institution, such as the Church, which has taught them the principles by which they live, and supports them in their use of those principles.

Many other elements could be adumbrated either as extensions of those described, or in addition to them. At the minimum, however, discernment involves a reading of the case at hand, an expression of what constitutes the character and perspective of the person, and some appeals to reason and principles both to help one discern and to defend what one discerns. Excellence in moral discernment perhaps involves various combinations of these. There is a discriminating and accurate reading of the situation, and an understanding of the relations of elements of the situation to each other, and of its relations to other situations. There is a stipulation of the more and less important factors, and empathy for its "inner" character as well as a description of its external character. There is a refined moral sensitivity that registers subtle nuances not only of fact but of value, that is not just emotion or sentiment, but appears to contribute to the perception of what one ought to do. Moral sensitivity seems to contribute in the "discerning" moral man an intuitive element that leads to accuracy in moral aim, judiciousness in evaluation, and compelling authenticity in deed. Just as discerning critics of art know much about art, so the discerning moral man often knows much about morality. He can think clearly about potential consequences and applicable principles; he knows something of the range of values that might compete with or support each other, and he can discriminate between alternative courses of action. He is likely to have a clear head, to be able to argue with himself and others before a judgment is made, and give good reasons for it afterward.

The discerning act of moral discernment is impossible to program, and difficult to describe. It involves perceptivity, discrimination, subtlety, sensitivity, clarity, rationality, and accuracy. And while some men seem to have it as a "gift of the gods," others achieve it by experience and training, by learning and acting. It is probably more akin to the combination of elements that go into good literary criticism and good literary creativity than it is to the combination of elements that make a good mathematician or logician; it is both rational and affective. How we discern what we ought to do, whether we be morally flat-footed clods or moral virtuosos, is a complex process indeed.

II. MORAL DISCERNMENT IN THE CHRISTIAN LIFE

The human processes of discernment are no different among Christians than they are among other men. There are the moral clods and the moral virtuosos among Christians; nothing can guarantee that because a man has faith in God whom he believes to have been disclosed in Jesus Christ he will be a man of excellence in moral discernment. Nor does the morally discerning Christian have different faculties or capacities that other men are deprived of because they happen not to be Christians. No special affective capacities, logic, or rational clarity can be claimed by Christians as possessions they have by virtue of their faith. Whatever the gifts of grace are, they function in and through the human capacities of discernment that are probably fairly evenly distributed throughout all mankind. Whatever "newness" there is in the Christian life is not a replacement of insufficient moral sensitivity with more sufficient, insufficient rational clarity with more sufficient. All this, however, is not to say that moral discernment in the Christian life ought not to be different, cannot be different, and sometimes is not different. Just what some of these differences ought to be, can be, and are is the subject matter of the remainder of this chapter.

There is a text from St. Paul's Letter to the Romans that makes a good starting point for discussion of this subject.

> I implore you by God's mercy to offer your very selves to him: a living sacrifice, dedicated and fit for his acceptance, the worship offered by mind and heart. Adapt yourselves no longer to the pattern of this present world, but let your minds be remade and your whole nature thus transformed. Then you will be able to discern the will of God, and to know what is good, acceptable, and perfect. Romans 12:1-2 (New English Bible)

Although this passage will not be exegeted in detail, it is suggestive not only of substantive themes of morality in the Christian life, but also of what changes might be registered in moral discernment. I shall use it at least as a starting point for further discussion.

We might characterize the Christian's obligation to answer the practical moral question, "What ought or are we to do?" in the following way. *Man is to discern what God enables and requires him to do.* Full explication of this sentence would require a book-length exposition of Christian ethics; here I merely suggest various lines that such exposition would take.

What is said about discerning what God enables and requires man to do is not presumed to be a description of how any one Christian does this, or how some "mean" or average Christian constructed out of a sample of all Christians does it. It is clearly said in a mode that suggests that something like it is appropriate normatively, and possible actually.

Christians have a particular stance, or perspective. They stand in a particular relationship which in turn affects their self-understandings, their perceptions and interpretations of the world, and they have certain norms by which they discriminate what is right and good. In St. Paul's language, they are a people who have offered themselves up to God; they are living sacrifices dedicated and fit for His acceptance; mind and heart are offered to God in devotion and in praise. This language suggests that something more is involved than the claim that Christians are people who hold certain ideas or propositions to be meaningful or true. It suggests that Christians are not people who are distinguished from others simply by their belief in a set of propositions about God, and by inferences they draw from those propositions about what man is and what his relationship to God and other men also is. Mind and heart are offered to God; their "very selves" are given to him. A particular relationship of man's personal existence to God is implored by the apostle. It is not only belief that certain things are worthy of acceptance intellectually, but conviction and trust that it is appropriate to rely upon God and to give oneself in this reliance and its consequent service. Christians are, by virtue of this faith, in a particular position; they have by virtue of this faith a particular perspective. Just as my sons are different from my neighbor's sons partly because of their filial relations to me that are different from the filial relations other sons have to their own fathers, so Christians are different because of the relationship in which they exist to God in whom they believe and trust. Just as the understandings which my sons have of themselves are partially determined by the relationship in which they exist to me, so Christians' understandings of themselves are partially determined by the relationship in which they exist to God. Just as the perspectives my sons have on the world of which they are a part is partially determined by their relationship to me, so also are the Christians' by their relationship to God. Just as my sons "see" and interpret life around them partially under this perspective determined by their relation to me, so Christians interpret the world around them from the perspective of their faith in God.

Thus one impact of Christian faith as it affects moral discernment involves the self-understanding that it evokes and directs. If I dedicate myself to be fit for the acceptance of God in whom I believe, I will consciously intend to live in such a way that my words and deeds are worthy of Him. If I frequently offer my mind and heart to Him worshipfully, I will be renewed in this self-understanding as one who depends upon Him, who is grateful to Him, who seeks to be consistent with what He gives and requires of me. The situation is parallel in structure to the self-understandings of others who have offered themselves, so to speak, to other objects of commitment. The devotee of the *Playboy* way of life has a self-understanding that is determined in part by his devotion to the symbols of that way of life, to the values that are pointed to by these symbols. He will see himself to be "sophisticated" and "cool"; he will value highly the gratification of his desires for a maximum of pleasure; he will intend to live in a way that is consistent with his self-understanding, which in turn is evoked and directed by *Playboy*. To put it simply, Christians will answer the question, "Who am I?" differently by virtue of their faith.

Just as one's interpretation of oneself is altered by Christian faith, so one's interpretation of the world around him is altered. Interpretations are informed by perspectives; indeed what one discerns to be important in his perception of the world around him is informed by his perspective. As I have indicated elsewhere,[1] the notion of perspective in matters of moral assessment is analogous to its use in matters of visual experience. Some things are seen clearly and some are shadowed by the perspective of the observer. Some are accented and others are diminished in the impressions that they register. Perspective and self-understanding both make one more sensitive to some things and less sensitive to others. The national leader whose obligation is clearly and primarily to the self-interest of his nation is likely to "read the situation" of Vietnam, or some other one, differently from the person who views his obligation to be primarily to a universal God of love who wills the well-being of all men. The former understands himself to be one who exercises power for the sake of the interests of the nation; the latter understands himself to be one who is the servant of Jesus Christ. (I shall not deal here with the nest of issues that are involved in such a case as one who in a position of political judgment seeks to exercise his power as both a member of a nation and a Christian. The two "selves" are not necessarily either in irresolvable conflict or in perfect harmony.) Certain "facts" have greater importance from one perspective than from the other. Both might observe the same human suffering, but interpret its significance differently because one is viewing things from the perspective of national interest and the other from the perspective of redeeming love. The significance of what is going on is determined by the perspectives of those who see it and participate in it.

Surely H. Richard Niebuhr was getting at this when he suggested that "interpretation" is part of "responsibility." Interpretation is "in the light of" some things that are particular and thus partially constitute the perspective of the interpreter. Thus Christians interpret what is going on in the light of their beliefs about God, and what men and the world are and are to be before Him. Differences of opinion among Christians in their moral discernment are not only affected by differences in the data that they might have available, but also by differences in their understanding of what the "light" of the gospel is, and what it illuminates about the world and the self. (It is not our task in this chapter to enter into that technical theological realm where these differences of the latter sort are to be adjudicated.) In spite of differences, there are certain common elements. Christian affirmations about the goodness of God and the goodness of the world He created, the reign of God in the preservation of that which He created, the willful unfaith and disobedience of men, the redemptive purpose of God to reconcile the

---

1. In the last chapter of *Christ and the Moral Life* (New York: Harper and Row, 1968).

world to Himself, the hope of a consummation of all things in the coming Kingdom of God, the judgment of God on human disorder, and other affirmations,
are part of the "light" that Christians bring to bear upon their interpretation of
the world. At another level there are things believed about man: men are created
to live together in order and in love, they are to seek each other's good, their lives
are to be sustained and not oppressed or destroyed, they are to live in gratitude
to God and to others for life and loving care, they are to respect each other, etc.
Such assertions are related both to the gospel and to normal human experience;
they become "lights" that help Christians understand both what is to be affirmed
in the world and what is to be sought for the world.

The perspective of the Christian affects what he values; it gives direction to
the moral ends that he seeks, to the longings and desires that he has, to the preferences that he articulates in word and deed. Valuations and preferences are by
no means always the result of a conscious reflective process in which certain "values" are defined, judged, and determined to be worthy of acceptance, then in turn
applied in rational discrimination to the interpretation of the world in which
men live. Christians do not always first engage in a process of defining "love,"
which by tradition and experience they value highly, and then use this definition
to engage in a rational process of interpretation of events in the world in the light
of love. (It is clearly the task of the person whose vocation is theological and ethical thinking in the Christian community to engage in such deliberate, careful
thinking, more than it is the task of every Christian.) Rather, Christians may have
perspectives that are formed in their faith and belief in a God of love, who has
demonstrated His love for man in creation, and in His forgiveness and renewal
of life, who enables men to love one another as they have been loved, and who
wills that men should love each other. This "loving" perspective is likely to color
the things that Christians value and approve of in their perception, interpretation, and choices in the world. That which restores and brings life and joy is to
be preferred to that which destroys and brings death and suffering and pain, for
example. Not only in his rational discriminations, but in his moral sensitivities,
the Christian is likely to be sensitive to oppression and injustice, to physical and
mental suffering. Christians are likely to interpret not only what is the case, but
what ought to be the case in the light of valuations that are determined by the
perspective or posture of their faith.

The process of interpretation that is part of discernment is, as I have suggested,
an expression of fundamental dispositions that are shaped in part by the faith and
trust Christians have as they offer themselves up to God. Their sensibilities are
colored by their faith and its perspective. But it is also, as has been suggested, a
matter of using articulated and expressed beliefs. Both are part of the moral discernment of Christians. If Christians are to discern what God enables and
requires them to do, they are involved in rational discrimination as well as sensi-
ble response. Just as I am more likely to do what is acceptable to my sons if I *know*
what their needs and desires are, so I am more likely to do what is acceptable to
God if I have some knowledge about what God seems to require and enable. Part

of my response to my sons' needs is a matter of understanding based upon the human relationship that has been formed between us, with all the nuances of feeling and affection, of intuitive insight and perception. Part of it is a matter of thinking clearly and rationally about what they need in the light of who they are, the resources available to meet their needs, the ways in which they may not understand their needs any more clearly than I do, and the kind of order of life it takes for us to live together with some harmony and joy.

It is under this latter aspect of stipulated convictions and rational reflection that moral discernment in the Christian life uses dogma, moral principles formed in Scripture and the tradition, moral rules of the Christian community, and refined moral argumentation. If I am to discern what God enables and requires, I must be able to say some things about God. Thus the understanding and formed convictions that Christians have about God are important for the way in which they discern things morally, and what they actually discern to be morally appropriate. Variations are many, and changes both within the tradition and in the beliefs of an individual man occur through time. Some aspects of Christian belief are stressed on one occasion, others on another, and elements of belief are combined and recombined in particular times and places so that different themes are accented and muted. Sometimes we recall more cogently God as the awesome judge of human evil, sometimes God the redeemer of the world, sometimes God the restrainer of men who wills that order persist, sometimes God the just and merciful who wills a disruption of an unjust order.

Moral discernment, then, has reference to belief. It is the moral agent who discerns with reference to belief what he judges God to be enabling and requiring. This statement is important, for it precludes saying that Christians are "immediately sensitive" to what God is doing in the world (Lehmann), or that they hear in a clear and direct way what the command of God is to them (Barth). Discernment is a human act made with reference to human statements about God as these statements are forged from Scripture and from the theological tradition. Theologically, it might be said that God is enabling men to discern what God is enabling men to do; but the locus for the discernment is in the self as it relates beliefs about the God in whom it trusts to the situations in which it acts.

Moral rules and principles also play a part in the rational reflection that is part of discerning what one ought to do. Not all of them are rooted particularly in the Christian tradition, but certainly there are some that have historical origins in the Christian faith, and particular authority for Christians. Rules can be understood as having a social function and generally a social sanction in morality. They are determinations of what is definitely required and what is definitely prohibited in the community. As such they are ready and authoritative references for the man who is to discern what he ought to do in normal instances. He discerns clearly and quickly that the situation in which he is to act is one in which his behavior ought to be conformed to those rules that regulate the life of the community. Others before him have faced situations comparable to his own, and have interpreted them in such a way that it is clear that Christians ought to do very specific things on such occasions. There need be no ambiguity in discernment. Just as one need not engage in a unique process of discernment to judge that he ought to obey the traffic signals, so one need not engage in a unique process to judge that as a Christian he has the duty to respect another person as a human being. Elaborate reasons can be given for traffic rules and for the obligations that drivers and pedestrians have to obey them, but members of the civil community do not require that such reasons be given on each occasion. Elaborate theological and ethical reasons can be given for the rule that Christians must treat other persons with respect as human beings, but both because such a rule can be readily internalized and because its authority is clear and unambiguous, they can discern readily prohibited limits and required actions that are enabled and demanded of them. This is not to say that there are not situations in which reflection and interpretation is not required pertaining to how the rules apply. But it is to say that often rules have immediate applicability, and even when they do not seem to apply readily, the agent can begin with the rule (and not a series of arguments for its validity) in his discerning. For example, in the realm of sexual behavior, there has been a commonly accepted rule, "Thou shalt not commit adultery." Reasons can be given for the authority of that rule, but the rule has relative autonomy by virtue of its long usage within the Christian community so that its members do not have to face every human relationship with a man or woman who is not their marriage partner as one that offers the moral possibility of adultery. Indeed, if for various reasons a relationship suggests that adultery might be committed, Christians begin with the rule. The weight of evidence and reflection clearly has to be such as to invalidate the application of the rule in that particular instance. Exceptions to such rules are not made lightly, and the existence of exceptions is hardly evidence for the invalidity of the rule.

Moral principles function in a similar way, though perhaps they can be distinguished in some instance from rules by the absence of social sanction. Nor are they so determined by what sociologists and anthropologists have called one's status and roles in the community. In different human situations moral principles function differently. Certainly such a principle as the commandment to love the neighbor as the self would be part of the "light" that Christians would bring to bear upon their interpretation of the general situation and also be part of their intention in acting within it. It would function to set the direction of their activity: what they do ought to be in accord with what love requires. To discern what the principle seems to enable and require places an obligation on Christians to interpret what love seems to mean, and how this meaning is applicable in the particular occasion. Moral reflection on such a general principle requires a great degree of sophistication on some occasions; on others its requirements seem to be self-evident. When sophistication is required, the Christian is involved in the process in which the situation must be defined (its proper time and space limits determined, its complex of relationships delineated, its data formulated and organized); in which other principles bearing on the case that might not be easily harmonized with the love commandment have to be stipulated and recalled, other theological reference-points than love remembered, other values than love designated, and the use of "love" itself carefully delineated so that it has some particularity and does not cover everything. He is involved in a process in which analogies from Scripture or from the moral experience of the community are rehearsed and brought to bear; in which moral sensibilities are recognized, judged, and affirmed or qualified by reflection; and in which finally a judgment is made about what God is enabling and requiring. This reflection will illumine the discernment of God's will; it will never have clear and unambiguous authority so that the reflecting man will equate his serious judgment with God's will itself. Indeed, careful reflection is necessary in discernment because of the partialities of men, and the tendency to discern what is fit and acceptable for one's own gratification or the gratification of one's own group rather than fit and acceptable to God. Reflection is necessary because Christians, like others, tend to be conformed to the expectations of their own desires and to the ethos of the time in which they live, rather than remembering that they are not to be conformed to this world.

Moral discernment always takes place within communities; the moral discernment of Christians takes place within the Christian community. The community is in part the present gathering of Christians, in a congregation or some other group, that engages in the moral discourse that informs the conscientiousness of its members through participation in moral deliberation.[2] Through moral discourse in the Christian community, both the minds and hearts of men can be trained to discernment; their capacities to make discerning moral judgments can be deepened, broadened, and extended. Such training is not an automatic accrual from hearing sermons or receiving the sacraments; if the Holy Spirit is at work in the community to make men better discerners of God's will he is present in and through the moral deliberations that occur, as well as the preached word and the bread and wine.

But the community is not only the present gathering at this time and place. Those presently gathered are part of a historical community that has lived the moral life as Christians in the past, that has reflected upon situations comparable to the present ones with references to the same gospel, and the same intention to discern God's will. This does not mean that an answer from the fourth century is the answer to the twentieth century, but it does mean that in present reflection the community does not have to begin *de novo* as if God's will for present and future had no consistency with God's will for the past. Certain values, or principles, or points for consideration that were arranged in one combination with reference to a past situation might be rearranged and added to with reference to a present situation to the illumination and accuracy of the present community. John Noonan's *Contraception*,[3] the greatest book yet published on the

2. I have developed this theme in several other places, most concisely in "The Church: A Community of Moral Discourse," *Crane Review* 7 (Winter 1964): pp. 75–85, and in "The Voluntary Church: A Moral Appraisal," *Voluntary Associations,* ed. D. B. Robertson (Richmond, Va.: John Knox Press, 1966), especially pp. 313–322.

3. John T. Noonan, Jr., *Contraception* (Cambridge, Mass.: Harvard University Press, 1966).

history of an issue in Christian ethics, makes this point clear. Moral discernment is in continuity with the past, not discontinuity; it learns from, and is thus informed and directed without being determined by, the past. (The current celebration of the openness toward the future is proper insofar as it recognizes that the God whose will one seeks to discern for the future is the God who has willed in the past. Much of this celebration refers primarily to human *attitude* in any case, and as such is insufficient to determine what men ought to be doing in particular instances. Attitude alone does not determine act. To be open to the future is not to discern what one ought to do in it.)

Perhaps all that has been said about moral discernment in this chapter is only another way of talking about the virtue of prudence. Prudence is the virtue that is both intellectual and moral; it involves reason, sensibilities, and the will. It is a virtue: it is a lasting disposition of the self that comes into being not in the moment by some inspiration of the Spirit or by some visceral response to a narrowly defined situation, but by experience, training, reflection, and action. It does not exist independent from law, although it is the capacity to perceive what law might require in a particular case, and to perceive what might be required that is more than the law demands. It is open to the concrete situation, but not in such a way that the past is ignored, as if similar situations have never occurred before. It is an exercise of character that has been formed; the formation of character is important in the whole of the moral life of which a particular discernment is but a moment in time. It is formed and informed by love, trust, hope, and other gifts of the Spirit. But it is never simply an attitude; it is a capacity to discern that uses reason and intellectual discrimination.

Prudence in the Christian life refers to the fitting judgment, response, and act. But the fitting in turn refers to what God is enabling and requiring, not just what seems to be pleasing to men. Thus the exercise of prudence, of discernment, in the Christian life is intricate and complex; it can never be programed for all men, for some are gifted in different ways from others, and some have different roles from others. Its exercise is not only in moral discrimination; it is itself offered to God in praise and devotion, in reliance upon the grace of God to empower and inform it. But it is human; man is the exerciser of prudence in reliance upon God, and in discernment of God's will.

At best, however, the Christian who is morally discerning, who has the capacity to be perceptive, discriminating, accurate, and sensitive, probably has to modify his acceptance of the words of St. Paul. He said with assurance, "Then you *will* be able to discern the will of God." I suspect that more modest claims would be more precise. By offering oneself up to God, and by formation in prudence informed by love and faith and hope, "Then you *might* discern the will of God."

Chapter 3

The Relation of the Gospels to the Moral Life

The Gospels can be related to morality in three important ways. First, they can be interpreted to provide a theological justification for the moral life. For example, the Farewell Discourses in the fourth Gospel can be interpreted to provide a Christological justification for a morality of love and self-sacrificial service. This can be seen in the author's understanding of the relationship of the love of the Father for the Son, the love of the Son for the disciples, and the Son's commandment that the disciples should love one another.[1] One finds in the fourth Gospel a reason for being moral that is present throughout the scriptures, namely, that in response to the love of God for his creation and redemption, the people ought to be grateful and ought to walk in his way, follow him, and, indeed, imitate his loving deeds in their actions toward one another. The ultimate reason for being moral is that God has shown his love toward man, and thus man, both out of joyous gratitude and out of obligation to God, is to be concerned for the well-being of others.

---

1. "As the Father has loved me, so have I loved you; abide in my love. If you keep my commandments, you will abide in my love" (John 15:9–10); "This is my commandment, that you love one another as I have loved you. Greater love has no man than this, that a man lay down his life for his friends. You are my friends if you do what I command you" (15:12–14).

The second way in which the Gospels can be related to moral life is by interpreting them to provide moral commands, rules, and principles to be applied to particular moral acts. Here I wish to accent not the theological justifications for these commands, rules, and principles, but their function in the determination of particular acts of the members of the community. Theologians, biblical scholars, and others continue to have interminable arguments about how the moral contents of the precepts in the Q materials, for one example, are to be understood, both from the point of view of the intention of the author and from that of the community which responds to them. Are they to be read as a new Torah? Or are they "prominent lines" which give some guidance to the Christian in his choices? Is one to read them as proposing an important but impossible ideal?[2] The authority of these teachings has been defined by scholars in various ways: the Christian community has responded to them in different ways. With all the divergence, however, there has remained a persistent history of receiving them seriously as in some sense important (if not decisive) in the determination of the conduct of the community and its members.

A third way in which the Gospels can be related to the moral life is by interpreting them to influence the development of the "sort of persons" members of the community become. Here I wish to accent not the impact that moral precepts have on the determination of particular acts, but the impact that the Gospels have on the formation of the agent, the person, who acts. The question to be explored is "In what ways do, can, and should the Gospels qualify or accent the persisting characteristics of the person as a moral agent? In what ways do they affect his attitudes, his dispositions, his basic orientation of intentionality toward the world and other persons?"

It is this third way of looking at the relation of the Gospels to moral life that I shall discuss in this chapter. By concentrating on it, I do not intend to suggest that it is either more important than the other two ways or that in itself it is sufficient to exhaust the moral significance of the Gospels. I am also very much aware of the philosophical and theological difficulties, not to mention those that range into psychology, that inhere in dealing with this subject.

I. A NEW TESTAMENT WARRANT FOR THE TASK

I believe that there is warrant in the New Testament itself for engaging in this sort of exploration. Two passages in Philippians, each of which poses difficulties in English renderings, have struck me as worth attending to in finding a warrant for the work of this chapter. They are Philippians 1:27 and 2:5.

Writing to the Christians in Philippi, with the intention of encouraging them to maintain unity and strength in the face of opposition, Paul says in 1:27: "Only

---

2. I have examined some of these proposals more fully in *Christ and the Moral Life* (New York: Harper and Row, 1968), Chap. 6.

let your manner of life be worthy of the gospel of Christ." The textual difficulty for my purposes lies in the translation of *politeuesthè*. The Revised Standard Version fixes on "manner of life," which is, for my intentions, convenient, for it suggests not simply individual instances of conduct, but persisting characteristics of life. The King James Version uses "conversation" and *The New English Bible* uses "conduct," both of which are more action-oriented than agent-oriented references, and thus are less useful. Marvin Vincent, in the International Critical Commentary, suggests alternative renderings, "be citizens" or "exercise your citizenship"; the former is agent-oriented, the latter action-oriented. In his translation of the whole passage, however, Vincent says, "I exhort you to bear yourselves as becomes members of the Christian community," which appears to be more agent-oriented.[3] Ernst Lohmeyer uses the German *wandelt,* which is clearly action-oriented.[4] Joachim Gnilka, in the Herder commentary, uses *"Fuhrt euer Gemeindeleben."*[5] This makes clear that it is a corporate manner of life. Karl Barth, in his 1926–27 lectures on the epistle, uses the word "state," which is expounded in the following way: "Their state, their 'form', their bearings must therefore here and now already be under the invisible discipline of that kingdom, must in fact be in accordance with *the* 'state' which is to be reflected in their conduct, 'worthy' of the Gospel."[6] Thus, he also supports an agent-oriented interpretation.

For purposes of this chapter, the point is best made in the Revised Standard Version rendition: the apostle is stating an imperative: "Only let your *manner of life* be worthy of the gospel of Christ."

Philippians 2:5, while perhaps textually more ambiguous, in all renditions seems to be agent-oriented. The King James Version records it: "Have this mind in you which was also in Christ Jesus." The Revised Standard Version says: "Have this mind among yourselves, which you have in Christ Jesus"; this rendition makes the reference more corporate in character. Vincent translates it: "Cherish the disposition which dwelt in Christ Jesus."[7] *The New English Bible* reads: "Let your bearing towards one another arise out of your life in Christ Jesus." Lohmeyer puts it: *"Also seid gesinnt."*[8] The English terms "mind," "bearing toward one another," and "disposition" all suggest aspects of the agent. As in 1:27, the gospel provides a norm for the sorts of persons Christians are to be. Their manner of life, their dispositions, their bearing toward one another is to arise out of their life in Christ Jesus, and is to be worthy of that gospel.

The manner of life, the bearing, the disposition, clearly refer not only to individual members of the community, but also they are to characterize the relations of

3. Marvin R. Vincent, A *Critical and Exegetical Commentary on Epistles to the Philippians and to Philemon,* International Critical Commentary (New York: Scribner, 1903), pp. 32, 31.

4. Ernst Lohmeyer, *Die Briefe an die Philipper, an die Kolosser und an Philemon,* Meyer Series (Göttingen: Vandenhoeck und Ruprecht, 1954), p. 72.

5. Joachim Gnilka, *Der Philipperbrief* (Freiburg: Horden, 1968), p. 96.

6. Karl Barth, *The Epistle to the Philippians* (London: SCM Press, 1962), pp. 45–46.

7. Vincent, op.cit., p. 57.

8. Lohmeyer, op.cit., p. 90.

the members of the community to each other, and thus characterize the manner of life of the community itself. Thus, the individual members of the community participate in a manner of life that is both gift and task (the well-worn German *Gabe und Aufgabe*). The community, however, could not bear the marks of a particular manner of life without its individual members having certain characteristics.

In the context of the letter to the Philippians the manner or bearing that is counseled is one of humility, self-abnegation, self-emptying. We have one of the most striking passages for an *imitatio Christi* ethic that there is in the New Testament. It is not my intention in this chapter to focus on a single mark of the "bearing" toward one another, such as humility, but rather to indicate that there is warrant in the New Testament for examining the relation of the gospel to the persisting tendencies, dispositions, and intentions of members of the community.

Our interest is not only in finding a New Testament warrant, however, but it is also in addressing the questions raised from the point of view of ethics about the significance of the characteristics of the moral agent for his moral actions. Extensive theological and philosophical justification for such interest cannot be developed in this chapter.[9]

II. THE GOSPEL AND THE GOSPELS

If it can be granted that the Philippians texts give warrant for discussing a "manner of life" that is "worthy of the gospel of Christ," or a "bearing toward one another" that "arises out of your life in Christ Jesus," we face, for our purposes here, the question of the relation of the gospel to the Gospels. Such a persistent and difficult theological problem, however, has to receive brief attention here, pivotal though it is. I would make the following assertion: the *gospel* provides a new and characteristic orientation toward God, toward the world, and toward other persons. It provides a fundamental intentionality, or directionality for the person and community of faith. The *Gospels,* in their literary unity as well as variety, provide the engendering provocation, the efficient cause, which brings this new orientation into being, and also provide in the narratives of deeds, in the language of commands, in the illustrative and parabolic discourses, a depiction of the manner of life and the bearing toward one another that arises out of and is worthy of the gospel. The Gospels function in the formation of the Christian as a person in the way that Sallie TeSelle suggests that all literature does: they provide "concrete, varied, and creative depictions of the basic structure of human experience," they create a "vision of life" in relation to God, to the world, and to other persons.[10]

9. The issues and the literature pertinent to this point have been explored in a very fruitful way in Stanley M. Hauerwas, "Moral Character as a Problem for Theological Ethics," unpublished Yale Ph.D. dissertation, 1968.

10. Sallie McFague TeSelle, *Literature and the Christian Life* (New Haven: Yale University Press, 1966), p. 114.

It is increasingly common in contemporary moral philosophy to write about a "way of life," which is beyond full rational justification, and about which, for some persons, decision is king. For example, R. M. Hare, in discussing the justifications for moral decisions, writes:

> Thus, if pressed to justify a decision completely, we have to give a complete specification of the way of life of which it is a part. This complete specification is impossible in practice to give; the nearest attempts are those given by the great religions, especially those which can point to historical persons who carried out the way of life in practice.[11]

What I am suggesting here is that the gospel enables a "way of life," an orientation, intentionality, or directionality toward God, the world, and other persons. Depictions of that way of life are given in the Gospels, which also depict the "engendering deed" (to use Joseph Sittler's term) that makes the way of life possible. There is a significant coherence or consonance between the patterns of life that are depicted and the gospel, the event which brings about the fundamental orientation. The varieties of literature in the Gospels, the Beatitudes and the commands, the parables, the narrations of the actions of Jesus, line out the manner of life that is worthy of the gospel of Christ, the bearing toward one another that arises out of life in Christ Jesus. Since the coherence or consonance exists between the engendering or enabling deed on the one hand and the depiction of the manner of life on the other, there is also a normative or obligatory character to the way of life. Persons whose intentionality is reoriented by the gospel ought to have its marks on their manner of life, their bearing toward one another. Thus, in the scheme, there are three ways that characterize the relation of the Gospels to the manner of life: (1) they enable or engender it (not as final, but as efficient cause); (2) they depict it; and (3) this depiction is, in some sense, normative or obligatory.

To launch into these waters is, I recognize, historically, theologically, and philosophically treacherous. Research on the Gospels by biblical scholars has achieved a high degree of precision and refinement in analysis; yet on crucial points for our purposes, such as the interpretation of particular parables, consensus is limited. How this research is to govern the uses of the Gospels by theologians and Christian ethicians remains a disputed question. Also, in recent decades Protestants have been particularly fearful of saying too much about the manner of life that is worthy of the gospel for fear that the gospel becomes limited to, or primarily an account of, a particular kind of morality. There is an understandable revulsion against those less historically and theologically sophisticated treatments of "Christlike character" or "qualities of life" that are presumably enjoined by the Gospels which had wide popular appeal earlier in the

11. R. M. Hare, *The Language of Morals* (Oxford: Oxford University Press, 1952), p. 69. See also Paul Taylor, *Normative Discourse* (Englewood Cliffs, N.J.: Prentice-Hall, 1961), pp. 151–58. Antonio S. Cua has written an interesting article, "Morality and the Paradigmatic Individuals," *American Philosophical Quarterly,* VI, pp. 3224–39, in which he takes a cue from Karl Jaspers and reflects on the significance of individuals in developing a "way of life."

century. Catholic theologians properly raise the question of whether the "manner of life" that is depicted has its authorization only on positivistic historical grounds, that is, on the grounds that Jesus was the founder of a historical community to whose "ethos" Christians bear a loyalty for only historical religious reasons. They are rightly concerned about whether that manner of life does not have to be grounded in "true humanity," in the ontological structures of human existence. And certainly many efforts to delineate a Christian bearing have excessively concentrated on particular characteristics, even as particular New Testament books seem to concentrate on those characteristics that were appropriate under particular circumstances, such as humility in the situation of the church in Philippi, or submissiveness at the time in which 1 Peter was written. Granting the problematics involved, the journey on which we have begun is important to take.

III. MANNER OR BEARING; DISPOSITIONS AND INTENTIONS

To provide some specification to the terms "manner of life" and "bearing toward one another," I shall concentrate on two terms: disposition and intention. The discussion of the nature of the person as moral agent that is involved in this explication is derived from contemporary philosophical literature that deals with the questions of the person as an agent and with the questions of the nature of human acts, though I do not follow any particular philosopher in the way in which I am here working.[12] Simply put, my point is that when one chooses to generalize empirically about a person's or community's manner or bearing, one is likely to point to certain characteristic intentions of their activities and to certain dispositions to act in these particular ways. Generalizations about a manner of life are inferred from characteristic actions, actions are governed by dispositions and intentions.

For purposes of this chapter, I am using the term "disposition" to refer to a readiness or tendency to act in a certain way. A disposition is a qualification of a person which makes him tend to act in one way rather than in another. There are obvious affinities between my use of the term disposition and the concept of "habitus" in the

---

12. Some of the literature that has contributed to my thinking are:

John MacMurray, *The Self as Agent* (New York: Harper and Bros., 1957)
John MacMurray, *Persons in Relations* (New York: Harper and Row, 1961)
H. R. Niebuhr, *The Responsible Self* (New York: Harper and Row, 1963)
G. E. M. Anscombe, *Intention* (2d ed.; Oxford: B. Blackwell, 1963)
S. Hampshire, *Thought and Action* (New York: Viking Press, 1960)
E. D'Arcy, *Human Acts* (Oxford: Clarendon Press, 1963)
R. Taylor, *Action and Purpose* (Englewood Cliffs, N.J.: Prentice-Hall, 1966)
R. S. Peters, *The Concept of Motivation* (London: Routledge and Kegan Paul, 1958)
A. I. Melden, *Human Acts* (London: Routledge and Kegan Paul, 1961)
A. Kenny, *Action, Emotion and Will* (London: Routledge and Kegan Paul, 1963)
P. Ricoeur, *Freedom and Nature: The Voluntary and the Involuntary* (Evanston: Northwestern University Press, 1966).

theology of Thomas Aquinas, particularly when it is recalled that a distinction is drawn between an automatic motor habit that appears to determine an action on the one hand, and those habits which maintain a dependence on consciousness and volition on the other. By disposition I do not intend to suggest an automatic determination of particular acts, but a preferential readiness to act in a certain way, a readiness which requires confirmation and specification by practical moral reasoning.

I am using the term "intention" with two different references: one is the fundamental directionality of intentiveness which gives coherence and "identity" to a particular person or to a community. The other reference is to the specification of purposes, ends, or directions of particular actions under specific circumstances. As some philosophers put it, intentions are one's "forward-looking reasons" for acting, for exercising one's capacities and powers in a particular way. We shall use primarily the second reference in this chapter, and will note particularly when it is the first, more general reference, that is intended.

IV. THE GOSPELS AND MAN'S DISPOSITIONS AND INTENTIONS

How do the Gospels affect the Christian's dispositions and intentions? What sorts of dispositions and intentions do the Gospels form? In our exposition of the ways in which the Gospels affect the "sort of persons" Christians become, we will keep these two questions in mind. Underlying this exploration is the assumption that Christian faith is properly, though only partially, spelled out in terms of trust in and fidelity to God through Jesus Christ.

The person of Jesus Christ is the paradigm for the life of the Christian community and of individual members of the community. It appears to me that this is what Paul assumes in the letter to the Philippians, and what other occurrences of the motif of Christ as pattern or example in the New Testament also assume. Thus, in a sense, the Gospels portray the paradigmatic person, not by stipulating a set of virtue-adjectives for his character, but by depicting the sorts of actions and relations that were thought to be characteristic of him in the community's memory and imagination, and by recording the teachings he was remembered to have delivered. In him there was the embodiment of a way of life, a coherence between his teachings on the one hand, and his person and his actions on the other, that depicts what man is meant to be in his faithfulness and love to God and to others. He was one of those "historical persons who carried out a way of life in practice."[13]

13. R. M. Hare, op.cit. The term "paradigmatic individual" was used by Karl Jaspers in *The Great Philosophers: The Foundations* (New York: Harcourt, Brace, 1962) with reference to Socrates, Buddha, Confucius, and Jesus. My development has affinities with, and is no doubt dependent upon, two suggestive discussions by H. Richard Niebuhr: "Toward a Definition of Christ," *Christ and Culture* (New York: Harper and Bros., 1951), pp. 11–29; and "Metaphor and Morals" and "Responsibility and Christ," *The Responsible Self* (New York: Harper and Row, 1963), pp. 149–78. It is also dependent upon Sallie TeSelle, op.cit., pp. 153ff.

Some attention must be given to the use of the notion of paradigm. In the context of this chapter paradigms refer primarily to examples of a way of life.[14] Paradigms are basic models of a vision of life and of the practice of life, from which follow certain consistent attitudes, outlooks (or "on-looks"), rules or norms of behavior, and specific actions. As I am using the term, the function of a paradigm is not to provide an extrinsic *goal* for a "style of life" toward which one strives in order to embody an increasingly perfect approximation of it in the course of the self-development of his character. Nor is it to provide a timeless *ideal* to which particular actions, dispositions, and intentions are to be conformed. Nor does it function as a universal *rule* of conduct. Rather, the paradigm *in*-forms and *in*-fluences the life of the community and its members as they become what they are under their own circumstances. By *in*-form I wish to suggest more than giving data or information; I wish to suggest a flowing into the life of the community and its members. A paradigm allows for the community and its members to make it their own, to bring it into the texture and fabric of life that exists, conditioned as that is by their historical circumstances, by the sorts of limitations and extensions of particular capacities and powers that exist in persons and communities.

Thus, the paradigm of Christ does not require uniformity among all members of the community; it does not create perfect copies of itself, as if Christians are clones from the genotype of Jesus Christ. Rather, individuals, with their uniqueness and particularity, are informed and influenced by the paradigm of Christ as they live out and develop the capacities that they have acquired through the processes of natural and cultural development. Similarly, the paradigm does not require uniformity in persons or in the community in its attitudes and actions through all times and in all places. For example, there are conditions in which the paradigm informs a response of boldness and those in which it informs humility and even submissiveness. The paradigm does not function as a totally self-sufficient reality which dictates precisely which actions, intentions, and dispositions are right and good under any or all sets of circumstances. Rather, Christ as paradigm, the paradigm of true humanity, of life as its creator and redeemer intends it to be, of life which is lived in perfect trust and obedience to God, *in*-forms and flows into actions, intentions, and dispositions which are governed also by many other specific and situated realities of human experience.

To make a case for Christ as the paradigm of the way of life of the Christian community and its members does not require one to make a case for the *absolute* uniqueness of his teachings relative to rabbinic teachings of his time, or the *absolute* uniqueness of his actions relative to actions of prophets and other religious leaders, or the *absolute* uniqueness of his virtues or dispositions relative to

---

14. Cf. the use of the notion as a tool for interpreting developments in scientific thought in Thomas S. Kuhn, *The Structure of Scientific Revolutions* (Chicago: University of Chicago Press, 1962), esp. p. 10. "By choosing (the term paradigms), I mean to suggest that some accepted examples of actual scientific practice—examples which include law, theory, application, and instrumentation together—provide models from which spring particular coherent traditions of scientific research."

those of other "paradigmatic individuals" in history. The scientific establishment of the absolute historical uniqueness of Christ is not necessary in order for the Gospels to provide paradigms of actions, intentions, and dispositions for the community and its members. Nor is it necessary to depict a single, total portrait of Christ out of the several Gospel accounts, though the imagination is prone to develop certain generalizations drawn from his separate deeds and teachings.[15]

It remains for me to attempt to show how the Gospels provide three sorts of paradigms for the moral life of the Christian community and its members: paradigms of action, intention, and disposition.

The narratives of the deeds of Jesus provide the community examples of the sorts of actions under particular circumstances that are consonant with complete trust in God. Thus, they have a normative force for the community whose own trust is evoked by the gospel. Through sensitivity to the specificity of the narratives, and through the exercise of imagination evoked and guided by them, the members of the community are informed and influenced in the determination of their own actions by the records of the deeds of Jesus. The form of their actions is *in*-formed by the actions of Jesus.

This can be illustrated by one of the Gospel narratives that is read during Holy Week in the church, namely, the account of the foot-washing in John 13. The action and dialogue in the story of Jesus' washing of the disciples' feet is at one and the same time a paradigm of three interlocking actions. They depict God's own love for man, his giving of himself for the salvation and well-being of his people. That depiction is at the same time a paradigm of the *kind of action that reveals* God's love through his Son; it is an account of Jesus in word and deed that reveals him to be the agent of God's love. It also, at the same time, provides a paradigm of action for members of the community who know the love of God through the words and deeds of the Son in this very earthy activity. The love of God enacted in the deeds of the Son provides the form of action for those who know God's love through the Son.

The account in John 13 is not primarily written for a moral purpose. Yet it is an account that flows into and informs the bearing toward one another that arises out of life in Christ Jesus and the manner of life that is worthy of the gospel of Christ. It is one of the most beautiful accounts in the Gospels, evoking an enabling and compelling power in those who read it and participate in its dramatic reenactments. It depicts the sort of action that those whose lives are oriented by the gospel ought to be engaged in, not only in relation to each other in the community's liturgical life, but in relation to others in the world.

From the action and dialogue, one infers the appropriateness of a basic intentionality or direction that is consistent with God's love. Christians ought to have

---

15. It might be suggested that Jesus functioned already as a paradigm in the writing of the Gospels. His actions and teachings inform the individual accounts of the writers as his significance flows into and through their several intentions in writing the Gospels. Each writer's compilation and redaction takes place with reference to his context and purposes; the paradigm informs the individuality of the Gospels without creating uniformity among them.

an orientation toward others that issues in actions which meet the needs of men through humble and loving service. As a paradigm of action, the narrative makes its point more concretely than does a statement of the command to love the neighbor. Not only is the appropriate intention pointed to, but an example of what that intention might require under particular circumstances is portrayed. This paradigmatic intentionality can be distinguished in its function in the determination of actions from the provision of a precise rule of conduct. Rather than binding the community and its members to precise rules of behavior, the paradigm flows into and informs them as they are in their own bodily and social particularity, as particular moral agents with particular capacities and limitations, existing in different particular circumstances. Its function can also be distinguished from a strict process of analogical reasoning; it is not as if one can move by analogy (in a strict sense) from the account of John 13 to the particular intentions that are appropriate for the community in its own present circumstances. Rather, moral sensibility and the imagination are exercised in the movement from this paradigm to other occasions of action. The intention inferred from the narrative flows into both the basic orientation of the community and its members and into the formation of their particular purposes or intentions, their "forward-looking reasons" for action under other specific circumstances. It bears upon the decision of what goals are to direct action, and what sorts of consequences ought to be sought in the course of events or the state of affairs in which the action takes place.

From the action and dialogue one also infers the appropriateness of certain dispositions for members of the community. The gospel both enables and requires a readiness to act in the manner exemplified in the account of the foot-washing. The account depicts, evokes, and even commands a qualification of the sorts of persons that those who follow Jesus are to be. Jesus, in his speech and action, expresses dispositions which are consistent with God's love for the world and which are exemplary for those who know the love of God through the Son.

From this narrative a case can be made for at least two of the "virtues of Christ," as H. Richard Niebuhr calls them in a section of his *Christ and Culture* that has rarely been discussed.[16] These are love and humility. "Having loved his own who were in the world, he loved them to the end (John 13:1)." The actions are expressions of a loving disposition, of a tendency in Jesus as a person to do that which makes specific the meaning of love. "If I then, your Lord and Teacher, have washed your feet . . . (vs. 14)." "Jesus, knowing that the Father had given all things into his hands, and that he had come from God and was going to God (vs. 3)," is the sort of person who washes the feet of his followers. The disposi-

16. Cf. pp. 15–16: "By virtues of Christ we mean the excellences of character which on the one hand he exemplifies in his own life, and which on the other he communicates to his followers. For some Christians they are virtues his example and law demand; for others they are gifts he bestows through regeneration, the dying and rising of the self in him, the first-born of many brothers. But whether Christians emphasize law or grace, whether they look to the Jesus of history or to the preexistent and risen Lord, the virtues of Jesus Christ are the same." Niebuhr goes on to develop love, hope, obedience, faith, and humility.

tions of love and humility that are pointed to in the actions and dialogue are paradigms both of God's own readiness to loving and humble service and of the manner of life, the bearing toward one another that is to characterize the community and its members. "For I have given you an example, that you also should do as I have done to you (vs. 15)."

The crucifixion of Jesus can be shown to function as a paradigmatic action in a way that is parallel to what I have done with the story of the Passover meal. Jesus acts in perfect obedience to the Father, in perfect fidelity, and in love. To live by the form of the cross is to be enabled to be oriented toward God, the world, and others in a characteristic way. The gospel is, in part, the gospel of the crucifixion. The accounts of the crucifixion are also paradigms of intentions and dispositions that ought to characterize the manner of life, the bearing of the community and its members. They are called to fulfil those purposes which are faithful to the love and purposes of God, to give themselves sacrificially for the sake of the well-being of others and the world. The cross stands as a paradigm which flows into and informs the purposes of the community and its members in their own capacities and in their own circumstances. They are to have a readiness to be faithful to God and to others, to be loving and merciful toward others, to sacrifice their own interests and even lives. Indeed, the apostle Paul suggests the meaning of the paradigm of the cross in his explication of the content of the "mind of Christ." Philippians 2:5–8 in the Revised Standard Version reads:

> Have this mind among yourselves, which you have in Christ Jesus, who, though he was in the form of God, did not count equality with God a thing to be grasped, but emptied himself, taking the form of a servant, being born in the likeness of men. And being found in human form he humbled himself and became obedient unto death, even death on a cross.

Further development of the thesis of this chapter would require an exploration of various teachings of Jesus—commands, parables, his teaching about the kingdom of God—as paradigms which suggest the appropriateness of certain intentions and dispositions among the community and its members. Time does not permit extension at this point. I hope that at least I have provided a plausible and discussible thesis, namely, that the Gospels provide paradigms of action, intention, and disposition which flow into and inform the manner of life, the bearing toward one another that arises from and is worthy of the gospel.

Chapter 4

Down Syndrome, Parental Desires, and the Right to Life

THE PROBLEM

The Family Setting

Mother, 34 years old, hospital nurse.

Father, 35 years old, lawyer.

Two normal children in the family.

In late fall of 1963, Mr. and Mrs.——gave birth to a premature baby boy. Soon after birth, the child was diagnosed as having Down syndrome with the added complication of an intestinal blockage (duodenal atresia). The latter could be corrected with an operation of quite nominal risk. Without the operation, the child could not be fed and would die.

Editors' note: This essay was originally titled "Mongolism, Parental Desires, and the Right to Life." At the time of its drafting in the early 1970s, "mongolism" was the standard designation for the condition that is known today as Down syndrome. The title has been changed and throughout the essay the older terminology has been replaced with current usage.

At the time of birth Mrs.——overheard the doctor express his belief that the child had Down syndrome. She immediately indicated she did not want the child. The next day, in consultation with a physician, she maintained this position, refusing to give permission for the corrective operation on the intestinal block. Her husband supported her in this position, saying that his wife knew more about these things (i.e., children with Down syndrome) than he. The reason the mother gave for her position—"It would be unfair to the other children of the household to raise them with a child who has Down syndrome."

The physician explained to the parents that the degree of mental retardation cannot be predicted at birth—running from very low mentality to borderline subnormal. As he said: "Down syndrome, it should be stressed, is one of the milder forms of mental retardation. That is, the IQs of persons with Down syndrome are generally in the 50–80 range, and sometimes a little higher. That is, they're almost always trainable. They can hold simple jobs. And they're famous for being happy children. They're perennially happy and usually a great joy." Without other complications, they can anticipate a long life.

Given the parents' decision, the hospital staff did not seek a court order to override the decision (see "Legal Setting" below). The child was put in a side room and, over an 11-day period, allowed to starve to death.

Following this episode, the parents undertook genetic counseling (chromosome studies) with regard to future possible pregnancies.

The Legal Setting

Since the possibility of a court order reversing the parents' decision naturally arose, the physician's opinion in this matter—and his decision not to seek such an order—is central. As he said: "In the situation in which the child has a known, serious mental abnormality, and would be a burden both to the parents financially and emotionally and perhaps to society, I think it's unlikely that the court would sustain an order to operate on the child against the parents' wishes." He went on to say: "I think one of the great difficulties, and I hope [this] will be part of the discussion relative to this child, is what happens in a family where a court order is used as the means of correcting a congenital abnormality. Does that child ever really become an accepted member of the family? And what are all of the feelings, particularly guilt and coercion feelings that the parents must have following that type of extraordinary force that's brought to bear upon them for making them accept a child that they did not wish to have?"

Both doctors and nursing staff were firmly convinced that it was "clearly illegal" to hasten the child's death by the use of medication. One of the doctors raised the further issue of consent, saying: "Who has the right to decide for a child anyway? . . . The whole way we handle life and death is the reflection of the long-standing belief in this country that children don't have any rights, that they're not citizens, that their parents can decide to kill them or to let them live, as they choose."

The Hospital Setting

When posed the question of whether the case would have been taken to court had the child had a normal IQ, with the parents refusing permission for the intestinal operation, the near unanimous opinion of the doctors: "Yes, we would have tried to override their decision." Asked why, the doctors replied: "When a retarded child presents us with the same problem, a different value system comes in; and not only does the staff acquiesce in the parent's decision to let the child die, but it's probable that the courts would also. That is, there is a different standard. . . . There is this tendency to value life on the basis of intelligence. . . . [It's] a part of the American ethic."

The treatment of the child during the period of its dying was also interesting. One doctor commented on "putting the child in a side room." When asked about medication to hasten the death, he replied: "No one would ever do that. No one would ever think about it, because they feel uncomfortable about it. . . . A lot of the way we handle these things has to do with our own anxieties about death and our own desires to be separated from the decisions that we're making."

The nursing staff who had to tend to the child showed some resentment at this. One nurse said she had great difficulty just in entering the room and watching the child degenerate—she could "hardly bear to touch him." Another nurse, however, said: "I didn't mind coming to work. Because like I would rock him. And I think that kind of helped me some—to be able to sit there and hold him. And he was just a tiny little thing. He was really a very small baby. And he was cute. He had a cute little face to him, and it was easy to love him, you know?" And when the baby died, how did she feel? "I was glad that it was over. It was an end for him."

THE RESOLUTION

This complex of human experiences and decisions evokes profound human sensibilities and serious intellectual examination. One sees in and beyond it dimensions that could be explored by practitioners of various academic disciplines. Many of the standard questions about the ethics of medical care are pertinent, as are questions that have been long discussed by philosophers and theologians. One would have to write a full-length book to plow up, cultivate, and bring to fruition the implications of this experience.

I am convinced that, when we respond to a moral dilemma, the way in which we formulate the dilemma, the picture we draw of its salient features, is largely determinative of the choices we have. If the war in Vietnam is pictured as a struggle between the totalitarian forces of evil seeking to suppress all human values on the one side, and the forces of righteousness on the other, we have one sort of problem with limited choice. If, however, it is viewed as a struggle of oppressed people to throw off the shackles of colonialism and imperialism, we have another sort of problem. If it is pictured as more complex, the range of choices is wider, and the factors to be considered are more numerous. If the population problem is depicted as a race against imminent self-destruction of the human race, an ethics of survival seems to be legitimate and to deserve priority. If, however, the population problem is depicted more complexly, other values also determine policy, and our range of choices is broader.

One of the points under discussion in this medical case is how we should view it. What elements are in the accounts that the participants give to it? What elements were left out? What "values" did they seem to consider, and which did they seem to ignore? Perhaps if one made a different montage of the raw experience, one would have different choices and outcomes.

Whose picture is correct? It would not be difficult for one moral philosopher or theologian to present arguments that might undercut, if not demolish, the defenses made by the participants. Another moralist might make a strong defense of the decisions by assigning different degrees of importance to certain aspects of the case. The first might focus on the violation of individual rights, in this case the rights of the infant. The other might claim that the way of least possible suffering for the fewest persons over the longest range of time was the commendable outcome of the account as we have it. Both would be accounts drawn by external observers, not by active, participating agents. There is a tradition that says that ethical reflection by an ideal external observer can bring morally right answers. I have an observer's perspective, though not that of an "ideal observer." But I believe that it is both charitable and intellectually important to try to view the events as the major participants viewed them. The events remain closer to the confusions of the raw experience that way; the passions, feelings, and emotions have some echo of vitality remaining. The parents were not without feeling, the nurses not without anguish. The experiences could become a case in which x represents the rights of the infant to life, y represents the consequences of continued life as a person with Down syndrome, and z represents the consequences of his continued life for the family and the state. But such abstraction has a way of oversimplifying experience. One would "weigh" x against y and z. I cannot reproduce the drama even of the materials I have read, the interviews with doctors and nurses, and certainly even those are several long steps from the thoughts and feelings of the parents and the staff at that time. I shall, however, attempt to state the salient features of the dilemma for its participants; features that are each value laden and in part determinative of their decisions. In the process of doing that for the participants, I will indicate what reasons might justify their decisions. Following that I will draw a different picture of the experience, highlighting different values and principles, and show how this would lead to a different decision. Finally, I shall give the reasons why I, an observer, believe they, the participants, did the wrong thing. Their responsible and involved participation, one must remember, is very different from my detached reflection on documents and interviews almost a decade later.

The Mother's Decision

Our information about the mother's decision is secondhand. We cannot be certain that we have an accurate account of her reasons for not authorizing the surgery that could have saved the infant's life. It is not my role to speculate whether her given reasons are her "real motives"; that would involve an assessment of her "unconscious." When she heard the child was probably afflicted with Down syndrome, she "expressed some negative feeling" about it, and "did not want a retarded child." Because she was a nurse she understood what Down syndrome indicated. One reason beyond her feelings and wants is given: to raise a child with Down syndrome in the family would not be "fair" to the other children. That her decision was anguished we know from several sources.

For ethical reflection, three terms I have quoted are important: "negative feeling," "wants" or "desires," and "fair." We need to inquire about the status of each as a justification for her decision.

What moral weight can a negative feeling bear? On two quite different grounds, weight could be given to her feelings in an effort to sympathetically understand her decision. First, at the point of making a decision, there is always an element of the rightness or wrongness of the choice that defies full rational justification. When we see injustice being done, we have strong negative feelings; we do not need a sophisticated moral argument to tell us that the act is unjust. We "feel" that it is wrong. It might be said that the mother's "negative feeling" was evoked by an intuition that it would be wrong to save the infant's life, and that feeling is a reliable guide to conduct.

Second, her negative response to the diagnosis of Down syndrome suggests that she would not be capable of giving the child the affection and the care that it would require. The logic involved is an extrapolation from that moment to potential consequences for her continued relationship to the child in the future. The argument is familiar; it is common in the literature that supports abortion on request—"no unwanted child ought to be born." Why? Because unwanted children suffer from hostility and lack of affection from their mothers, and this is bad for them.

The second term is "wants" or "desires." The negative feelings are assumed to be an indication of her desires. We might infer that at some point she said, "I do not want a retarded child." The status of "wanting" is different, we might note, if it expresses a wish before the child is born, or if it expresses a desire that leads to the death of the infant after it is born. No normal pregnant woman would wish a retarded child. In this drama, however, it translates into: "I would rather not have the infant kept alive." Or, "I will not accept parental responsibilities for a retarded child." What is the status of a desire or a want as an ethical justification for an action? To discuss that fully would lead to an account of a vast literature. The crucial issue in this case is whether the existence of the infant lays a moral claim that supersedes the mother's desires.

If a solicitor of funds for the relief of refugees in Bengal requested a donation from her and she responded, "I do not want to give money for that cause," some persons would think her to be morally insensitive, but none could argue that the refugees in Bengal had a moral claim on her money which she was obligated to acknowledge. The existence of the infant lays a weightier claim on her than does a request for a donation. We would not say that the child's right to surgery, and thus to life, is wholly relative to, and therefore exclusively dependent upon, the mother's desires or wants.

Another illustration is closer to her situation than the request for a donation. A man asks a woman to marry him. Because she is asked, she is under no obligation to answer affirmatively. He might press claims upon her—they have expressed love for each other; or they have dated for a long time; he has developed his affection for her on the assumption that her responsiveness would lead to marriage. But none of these claims would be sufficient to overrule her desire not to marry him. Why? Two sorts of reasons might be given. One would refer to potential consequences: a marriage in which one partner does not desire the relationship leads to anxiety and suffering. To avoid needless suffering is obviously desirable. So in this case, it might be said that the mother's desire is to avoid needless suffering and anxiety: the undesirable consequences can be avoided by permitting the child to die.

The second sort of reason why a woman has no obligation to marry her suitor refers to her rights as an individual. A request for marriage does not constitute a moral obligation, since there is no prima facie claim by the suitor. The woman has a right to say no. Indeed, if the suitor sought to coerce her into marriage, everyone would assert that she has a right to refuse him. In our case, however, there are some differences. The infant is incapable of expressing a request or demand. Also, the relationship is different; the suitor is not dependent upon his girl friend in the same way that the infant is dependent upon his mother. Dependence functions in two different senses; the necessary conditions for the birth of the child were his conception and *in utero* nourishment—thus, in a sense the parents "caused" the child to come into being. And, apart from instituting adoption procedures, the parents are the only ones who can provide the necessary conditions for sustaining the child's life. The infant is dependent on them in the sense that he must rely upon their performance of certain acts in order to continue to exist. The ethical question to the mother is, Does the infant's physical life lay an unconditioned moral claim on the mother? She answered, implicitly, in the negative.

What backing might the negative answer be given? The most persuasive justification would come from an argument that there are no unconditioned moral claims upon one when those presumed claims go against one's desires and wants. The claims of another are relative to my desires, my wants. Neither the solicitor for Bengal relief nor the suitor has an unconditioned claim to make; in both cases a desire is sufficient grounds for denying such a claim. In our case, it would have to be argued that the two senses of dependence that the infant has on the mother are not sufficient conditions for a claim on her that would morally require the needed surgery. Since there are no unconditioned claims, and since the conditions in this drama are not sufficient to warrant a claim, the mother is justified in denying permission for the surgery.

We note here that in our culture there are two trends in the development of morality that run counter to each other: one is the trend that desires of the ego are the grounds for moral and legal claims. If a mother does not desire the fetus in her uterus, she has a right to an abortion. The other increasingly limits individual desires and wants. An employer might want to hire only white persons of German ancestry, but he has no right to do so.

The word "fair" appeals to quite different warrants. It would not be "fair" to the other children in the family to raise a child who has Down syndrome with them. In moral philosophy, fairness is either the same as justice or closely akin to it. Two traditional definitions of justice might show how fairness could be used in this case. One is "to each his due." The other children would not get what is due them because of the inordinate requirements of time, energy, and financial resources that would be required if the child with Down syndrome lived. Or, if they received what was due to them, there would not be sufficient time, energy, and other resources to attend to the particular needs of the child with Down syndrome; his condition would require more than is due him. The other traditional definition is "equals shall be treated equally." In principle, all children in the family belong to a class of equals and should be treated equally. Whether the child with Down syndrome belongs to that class of equals is in doubt. If he does, to treat him equally with the others would be unfair to him because of his particular needs. To treat him unequally would be unfair to the others.

Perhaps "fairness" did not imply "justice." Perhaps the mother was thinking about such consequences for the other children as the extra demands that would be made upon their patience, the time they would have to give the care of the child, the emotional problems they might have in coping with a retarded sibling, and the sense of shame they might have. These consequences also could be deemed to be unjust from her point of view. Since they had no accountability for the existence of the child with Down syndrome, it was not fair to them that extra burdens be placed upon them.

To ask what was due the infant with Down syndrome raises harder issues. For the mother, he was not due surgical procedure that would sustain his life. He was "unequal" to her normal children, but the fact of his inequality does not necessarily imply that he has no right to live. This leads to a matter at the root of the mother's response which has to be dealt with separately.

She (and as we shall see, the doctors also) assumed that a factual distinction (between a normal child and a child with Down syndrome) makes the moral difference. Factual distinctions do make moral differences. A farmer who has no qualms about killing a runt pig would have moral scruples about killing a deformed infant. If the child had not been born with Down syndrome and had an intestinal blockage, there would have been no question about permitting surgery to be done. The value of the infant is judged to be relative to a quality of its life that is predictable on the basis of the factual evidences of Down syndrome. Value is relative to quality: that is the justification. Given the absence of a certain quality, the value is not sufficient to maintain life; given absence of a quality, there is no right to physical life. (Questions about terminating life among very sick adults are parallel to this instance.)

What are the qualities, or what is *the* quality that is deficient in this infant? It is not the capacity for happiness, an end that Aristotle and others thought to be sufficient in itself. The mother and the doctors knew that children with Down syndrome can be happy. It is not the capacity for pleasure, the end that the hedonistic utilitarians thought all men seek, for persons with Down syndrome can find pleasure in life. The clue is given when a physician says that the absence of the capacity for normal intelligence was crucial. He suggested that we live in a society in which intelligence is highly valued. Perhaps it is valued as a quality in itself, or as an end in itself by some, but probably there is a further point, namely that intelligence is necessary for productive contribution to one's own well-being and to the well-being of others. Not only will a person with Down syndrome make a minimal contribution to his own well-being and to that of others, but also others must contribute excessively to his care. The right of an infant, the value of his life, is relative to his intelligence; that is the most crucial factor in enabling or limiting his contribution to his own welfare and that of others. One has to defend such a point in terms of the sorts of contributions that would be praiseworthy and the sorts of costs that would be detrimental. The contribution of a sense of satisfaction to those who might enjoy caring for the child with Down syndrome would not be sufficient. Indeed, a full defense would require a quantification of qualities, all based on predictions at the point of birth, that would count both for and against the child's life in a cost-benefit analysis.

The judgment that value is relative to qualities is not implausible. In our society we have traditionally valued the achiever more than the nonachievers. Some hospitals have sought to judge the qualities of the contributions of patients to society in determining who has access to scarce medical resources. A person with Down syndrome is not valued as highly as a fine musician, an effective politician, a successful businessman, a civil rights leader whose actions have brought greater justice to the society, or a physician. To be sure, in other societies and at other times other qualities have been valued, but we judge by the qualities valued in our society and our time. Persons are rewarded according to their contributions to society. A defense of the mother's decision would have to be made on these grounds, with one further crucial step. That is, when the one necessary condition for productivity is deficient (with a high degree of certitude) at birth, there is no moral obligation to maintain that life. That the same reasoning would have been sufficient to justify overtly taking the infant's life seems not to have been the case. But that point emerges later in our discussion.

The reliance upon feelings, desires, fairness, and judgments of qualities of life makes sense to American middle-class white families, and anguished decisions can very well be settled in these terms. The choice made by the mother was not that of an unfeeling problem-solving machine, nor that of a rationalistic philosopher operating from these assumptions. It was a painful, conscientious decision, made apparently on these bases. One can ask, of course, whether her physicians should not have suggested other ways of perceiving and drawing the contours of the circumstances, other values and ends that she might consider. But that points to a subsequent topic.

The Father's Decision

The decision of the father is only a footnote to that of the mother. He consented to the choice of not operating on the infant, though he did seek precise information about Down syndrome and its consequences for the child. He was "willing to go along with the mother's wishes," he "understood her feelings, agreed with them," and was not in a position to make "the same intelligent decision that his wife was making."

Again we see that scientific evidence based on professional knowledge is determinative of a moral decision. The physician was forthright in indicating what the consequences would be of the course of action they were taking. The consequences of raising a child with Down syndrome were presumably judged to be more problematic than the death of the child.

The Decision of the Physicians

A number of points of reference in the contributions of the physicians to the case study enable us to formulate a constellation of values that determined their actions. After I have depicted that constellation, I shall analyze some of the points of reference to see how they can be defended.

The constellation can be stated summarily. The physicians felt no moral or legal obligation to save the life of an infant with Down syndrome by an ordinary surgical procedure when the parents did not desire that it should live. Thus, the infant was left to die. What would have been a serious but routine procedure was omitted in this instance on two conditions, both of which were judged to be necessary, but neither of which was sufficient in itself: the Down syndrome and the parents' desires. If the parents had desired the infant to be saved, the surgery would have been done. If the infant had not been born with Down syndrome and the parents had refused permission for surgery to remove a bowel obstruction, the physicians would at least have argued against them and probably taken legal measures to override them. Thus, the value-laden points of reference appear to be the desires of the parents, the Down syndrome of the infant, the law, and choices about ordinary and extraordinary medical procedures.

One of the two most crucial points was the obligation the physicians felt to acquiesce to the desires of the parents. The choice of the parents not to operate was made on what the physicians judged to be adequate information: it was an act of informed consent on the part of the parents. There is no evidence that the physicians raised questions of a moral sort with the parents that they subsequently raised among themselves. For example, one physician later commented on the absence of rights for children in our society and in our legal system and on the role that the value of intelligence seems to have in judging worthiness of persons. These were matters, however, that the physicians did not feel obligated to raise with the distressed parents. The physicians acted on the principle that they are only to do procedures that the patient (or crucially in this case, the parents of the patient) wanted. There was no overriding right to life on the part of an infant with Down syndrome that led them to argue against the parents' desires or to seek a court order requiring the surgical procedure. They recognized the moral autonomy of the parents, and thus did not interfere; they accepted as a functioning principle that the parents have the right to decide whether an infant shall live.

Elaboration of the significance of parental autonomy is necessary in order to see the grounds on which it can be defended. First, the physicians apparently recognized that the conscientious parents were the moral supreme court. There are grounds for affirming the recognition of the moral autonomy of the principal persons in complex decisions. In this case, the principals were the parents: the infant did not have the capacities to express any desires or preferences he might have. The physicians said, implicitly, that the medical profession does not have a right to impose certain of its traditional values on persons if these are not conscientiously held by those persons.

There are similarities, but also differences, between this instance and that of a terminal patient. If the terminally ill patient expresses a desire not to have his life prolonged, physicians recognize his autonomy over his own body and thus feel under no obligation to sustain his life. Our case, however, would be more similar to one in which the terminally ill patient's family decided that no further procedures ought to be used to sustain life. No doubt there are many cases in which the patient is unable to express a preference due to his physical conditions, and in the light of persuasive medical and familial reasons the physician agrees not to sustain life. A difference between our case and that, however, has to be noted in order to isolate what seems to be the crucial point. In the case of the infant with Down syndrome, a decision is made at the beginning of his life and not at the end; the effect is to cut off a life which, given proper care, could be sustained for many years, rather than not sustaining a life which has no such prospects.

Several defenses might be made of their recognition of the parents' presumed rights in this case. The first is that parents have authority over their children until they reach an age of discretion, and in some respects until they reach legal maturity. Children do not have recognized rights over against parents in many respects. The crucial difference here, of course, is the claimed parental right in this case to determine that an infant shall not live. What grounds might there be for this? Those who claim the moral right to an abortion are claiming the right to determine whether a child shall live, and this claim is widely recognized both morally and legally. In this case we have an extension of that right to the point of birth. If there are sufficient grounds to indicate that the newborn child is significantly abnormal, the parents have the same right as they have when a severe genetic abnormality is detected prenatally on the basis of amniocentesis. Indeed, the physicians could argue that if a mother has a right to an abortion, she also has a right to determine whether a newborn infant shall continue to live. One is simply extending the time span and the circumstances under which this autonomy is recognized.

A second sort of defense might be made: that of the limits of professional competence and authority. The physicians could argue that in moral matters they have neither competence nor authority. Perhaps they would wish to distinguish between competence and authority. They have a competence to make a moral decision on the basis of their own moral and other values, but they have no authority to impose this upon their patients. Morals, they might argue, are subjective matters, and if anyone has competence in that area, it is philosophers, clergymen, and others who teach what is right and wrong. If the parents had no internalized values that militated against their decision, it is not in the province of the physicians to tell them what they ought to do. Indeed, in a morally pluralistic society, no one group or person has a right to impose his views on another. In this stronger argument for moral autonomy no physician would have any authority to impose his own moral values on any patient. A social role differentiation is noted: the medical profession has authority only in medical matters—not in moral matters. Indeed, they have an obligation to indicate what the medical alternatives are in order to have a decision made by informed consent, but insofar as moral values or principles are involved in decisions, these are not within their professional sphere.

An outsider might ask what is meant by authority. He might suggest that surely it is not the responsibility (or at least not his primary responsibility) or the role of the physician to make moral decisions, and certainly not to enforce his decisions on others. Would he be violating his role if he did something less determinative than that, namely, in his counseling indicate to them what some of the moral considerations might be in choosing between medical alternatives? In our case the answer seems to be yes. If the principals desire moral counseling, they have the freedom to seek it from whomsoever they will. In his professional role he acknowledges that the recognition of the moral autonomy of the principals also assumes their moral self-sufficiency, that is, their capacities to make sound moral decisions without interference on his part, or the part of any other persons except insofar as the principals themselves seek such counsel. Indeed, in this case a good deal is made of the knowledgeability of the mother particularly, and this assumes that she is morally, as well as medically, knowledgeable. Or, if she is not, it is still not the physician's business to be her moral counselor.

The physicians also assumed in this case that the moral autonomy of the parents took precedence over the positive law. At least they felt no obligation to take recourse to the courts to save the life of this infant. On that issue we will reflect more when we discuss the legal point of reference.

Another sort of defense might be made. In the order of society, decisions should be left to the most intimate and smallest social unit involved. That is the right of such a unit, since the interposition of outside authority would be an infringement of its freedom. Also, since the family has to live with the consequences of the decision, it is the right of the parents to determine which potential consequences they find most desirable. The state, or the medical profession, has no right to interfere with the freedom of choice of the family. Again, in a formal way, the argument is familiar; the state has no right to interfere with the determination of what a woman wishes to do with her body, and thus antiabortion laws are infringements of her freedom. The determination of whether an infant shall be kept alive is simply an extension of the sphere of autonomy properly belonging to the smallest social unit involved.

In all the arguments for moral autonomy, the medical fact that the infant is alive and can be kept alive does not make a crucial difference. The defense of the decision would have to be made in this way: if one grants moral autonomy to mothers to determine whether they will bring a fetus to birth, it is logical to assume that one will grant the same autonomy after birth, at least in instances where the infant is abnormal.

We have noted in our constellation of factors that the desire of the parents was a necessary but not a sufficient condition for the decisions of the physicians. If the infant had not been born with Down syndrome, the physicians would not have so readily acquiesced to the parents' desires. Thus, we need to turn to the second necessary condition.

The second crucial point is that the infant was afflicted with Down syndrome. The physicians would not have acceded to the parents' request as readily if the child had been normal; the parents would have authorized the surgical procedure if the child had been normal. Not every sort of abnormality would have led to the same decision on the part of the physicians. Their appeal was to the consequences of the abnormality of Down syndrome: the child would be a burden financially and emotionally to the parents. Since every child, regardless of his capacities for intelligent action, is a financial burden, and at least at times an emotional burden, it is clear that the physicians believed that the quantity or degree of burden in this case would exceed any benefits that might be forthcoming if the child were permitted to live. One can infer that a principle was operative, namely, that infants with Down syndrome have no inherent right to life; their right to life is conditional upon the willingness of their parents to accept them and care for them.

Previously we developed some of the reasons why an infant with Down syndrome was judged undesirable. Some of the same appeals to consequences entered into the decisions of the physicians. If we are to seek to develop reasons why the decisions might be judged to be morally correct, we must examine another point, namely, the operating definition of "abnormal" or "defective." There was no dissent to the medical judgment that the infant had Down syndrome, though precise judgments about the seriousness of the child's defect were not possible at birth.

Our intention is to find as precisely as possible what principles or values might be invoked to claim that the "defectiveness" was sufficient to warrant not sustaining the life of this infant. As a procedure, we will begin with the most general appeals that might have been made to defend the physician's decision in this case. The most general principle would be that any infant who has any empirically verifiable degree of defect at birth has no right to life. No one would apply such a principle. Less general would be that all infants who are carriers of a genetic defect that would have potentially bad consequences for future generations have no right to life. A hemophiliac carrier would be a case in point. This principle would not be applicable, even if it were invoked with approval, in this case.

Are the physicians prepared to claim that all genetically "abnormal" infants have no claim to life? I find no evidence that they would. Are they prepared to say that where the genetic abnormality affects the capacity for "happiness" the infant has no right to live? Such an appeal was not made in this case. It appears that "normal" in this case has reference to a capacity for a certain degree of intelligence.

A presumably detectable physical norm now functions as a norm in a moral sense, or as an ideal. The ideal cannot be specified in precise terms, but there is a vague judgment about the outer limits beyond which an infant is judged to be excessively far from the norm or ideal to deserve sustenance. Again, we come to the crucial role of an obvious sign of the lack of capacity for intelligence of a certain measurable sort in judging a defect to be intolerable. A further justification of this is made by an appeal to accepted social values, at least among middle- and upper-class persons in our society. Our society values intelligence; that value becomes the ideal norm from which abnormality or deficiencies are measured. Since the infant is judged not to be able to develop into an intelligent human being (and do all that "normal" intelligence enables a human being to do), his life is of insufficient value to override the desires of the parents not to have a retarded child.

Without specification of the limits to the sorts of cases to which it could be applied, the physicians would probably not wish to defend the notion that the values of a society determine the right to life. To do so would require that there be clear knowledge of who is valued in our society (we also value aggressive people, loving people, physically strong people, etc.), and in turn a procedure by which capacities for such qualities could be determined in infancy so that precise judgments could be made about what lives should be sustained. Some members of our society do not value black people; blackness would obviously be an insufficient basis for letting an infant die. Thus, in defense of their decision the physicians would have to appeal to "values generally held in our society." This creates a different problem of quantification: what percentage of dissent would count to deny a "general" holding of a value? They would also have to designate the limits to changes in socially held values beyond which they would not consent. If the parents belonged to a subculture that value blue eyes more than it valued intelligence, and if they expressed a desire not to have a child because it had hazel eyes, the problem of the intestinal blockage would not have been a sufficient condition to refrain from the surgical procedure.

In sum, the ideal norm of the human that makes a difference in judging whether an infant has the right to life in this case is "the capacity for normal intelligence." For the good of the infant, for the sake of avoiding difficulties for the parents, and for the good of society, a significant deviation from normal intelligence, coupled with the appropriate parental desire, is sufficient to permit the infant to die.

A third point of reference was the law. The civil law and the courts figure in the decisions at two points. First, the physicians felt no obligation to seek a court order to save the life of the infant if the parents did not want it. Several possible inferences might be drawn from this. First, one can infer that the infant had no legal right to life; his legal right is conditional upon parental desires. Second, as indicated in the interviews, the physicians believed that the court would not insist upon the surgical procedure to save the infant since it had Down syndrome. Parental desires would override legal rights in such a case. And third (an explicit statement by the physician), if the infant's life had been saved as the result of a court order, there were doubts that it would have been "accepted" by the parents. Here is an implicit appeal to potential consequences: it is not beneficial for a child to be raised by parents who do not "accept" him. The assumption is that they could not change their attitudes.

If the infant had a legal right to life, this case presents an interesting instance of conscientious objection to law. The conscientious objector to military service claims that the power of the state to raise armies for the defense of what it judges to be the national interest is one that he conscientiously refrains from sharing. The common good, or the national interest, is not jeopardized by the granting of a special status to the objector because there are enough persons who do not object to man the military services. In this case, however, the function of the law is to protect the rights of individuals to life, and the physician-objector is claiming that he is under no obligation to seek the support of the legal system to sustain life even when he knows that it could be sustained. The evidence he has in hand (the parental desire and the diagnosis of Down syndrome) presumably provides sufficient moral grounds for his not complying with the law. From the standpoint of ethics, an appeal could be made to conscientious objection. If, however, the appropriate law does not qualify its claims in such a way as to (a) permit its nonapplicability in this case or (b) provide for exemption on grounds of conscientious objection, the objector is presumably willing to accept the consequences for his conscientious decision. This would be morally appropriate. The physician believed that the court would not insist on saving the infant's life, and thus he foresaw no great jeopardy to himself in following conscience rather than the law.

The second point at which the law figures is in the determination of how the infant should die. The decision not to induce death was made in part in the face of the illegality of overt euthanasia (in part, only, since also the hospital staff would "feel uncomfortable" about hastening the death). Once the end or purpose of action (or inaction) was judged to be morally justified, and judged likely to be free from legal censure, the physicians still felt obliged to achieve that purpose within means that would not be subject to legal sanctions. One can only speculate whether the physicians believed that a court that would not order an infant's life to be saved would in turn censure them for overtly taking the life, or whether the uncomfortable feelings of the hospital staff were more crucial in their decision. Their course of decisions could be interpreted as at one point not involving obligation to take recourse to the courts and at the other scrupulously obeying the law. It should be noted, however, that there is consistency of action on their part; in neither instance did they intervene in what was the "natural" course of developments. The moral justification to fail to intervene in the second moment had to be different from that in the first. In the first it provides the reasons for not saving a life; in the second, for not taking a life. This leads to the last aspect of the decisions of the physicians that I noted, namely, that choices were made between ordinary and extraordinary means of action.

There is no evidence in the interviews that the language of ordinary and extra-ordinary means of action was part of the vocabulary of the medical staff. It is, however, an honored and useful distinction in Catholic moral theology as it applies to medical care. The principle is that a physician is under no obligation to use extraordinary means to sustain life. The difficulty in the application of the principle is the choice of what falls under ordinary and what under extraordinary means. Under one set of circumstances a procedure may be judged ordinary, and under another extraordinary. The surgery required to remove the bowel obstruction in the infant was on the whole an ordinary procedure; there were no experimental aspects to it, and there were no unusual risks to the infant's life in having it done. If the infant had had no other genetic defects, there would have been no question about using it. The physicians could make a case that when the other defect was Down syndrome, the procedure would be an extraordinary one. The context of the judgment about ordinary and extraordinary was a wider one than the degree of risk to the life of the patient from surgery. It included his other defect, the desires of the family, the potential costs to family and society, etc. No moralists, to my knowledge, would hold them culpable if the infant were so deformed that he would be labeled (non-technically) a monstrosity. To heroically maintain the life of a monstrosity as long as one could would be most extraordinary. Thus, we return to whether the fact of Down syndrome and its consequences is a sufficient justification to judge the lifesaving procedure to be extraordinary in this instance. The physicians would argue that it is.

The infant was left to die with a minimum of care. No extraordinary means were used to maintain its life once the decision not to operate had been made. Was it extraordinary not to use even ordinary procedures to maintain the life of the infant once the decision not to operate had been made? The judgment clearly was in the negative. To do so would be to prolong a life that would not be saved in any case. At that point, the infant was in a class of terminal patients, and the same justifications used for not prolonging the life of a terminal patient would apply here. Patients have a right to die, and physicians are under no moral obligation to sustain their lives when it is clear that they will not live for long. The crucial difference between a terminal cancer patient and this infant is that in the situation of the former, all procedures which might prolong life for a goodly length of time are likely to have been exhausted. In the case of the infant, the logic of obligations to terminal patients takes its course as a result of a decision not to act at all.

To induce death by some overt action is an extraordinary procedure. To justify overt action would require a justification of euthanasia. This case would be a good one from which to explore euthanasia from a moral point of view. Once a decision is made not to engage in a life-sustaining and lifesaving procedure, has not the crucial corner been turned? If that is a reasonable and moral thing to do, on what grounds would one argue that it is wrong to hasten death? Most obviously it is still illegal to do it, and next most obviously people have sensitive feelings about taking life. Further, it goes against the grain of the fundamental vocation of the medical profession to maintain life. But, of course, the decision not to operate also goes against that grain. If the first decision was justifiable, why was it not justifiable to hasten the death of the infant? We can only assume at this point traditional arguments against euthanasia would have been made.

The Decision of the Nurses

The nurses, as the interviews indicated, are most important for their expressions of feelings, moral sensibilities, and frustrations. They demonstrate the importance of deeply held moral convictions and of profound compassion in determining human responses to ambiguous circumstances. If they had not known that the infant could have survived, the depth of their frustrations and feelings would have not been so great. Feelings they would have had, but they would have been compassion for an infant bound to die. The actual range of decision for them was clearly circumscribed by the role definitions in the medical professions; it was their duty to carry out the orders of the physicians. Even if they conscientiously believed that the orders they were executing were immoral, they could not radically reverse the course of events; they could not perform the required surgery. It was their lot to be the immediate participants in a sad event but to be powerless to alter its course.

It would be instructive to explore the reasons why the nurses felt frustrated, were deeply affected by their duties in this case. Moral convictions have their impact upon the feelings of persons as well as upon their rational decisions. A profound sense of vocation to relieve suffering and to preserve life no doubt lies behind their responses, as does a conviction about the sanctity of human life. For our purposes, however, we shall leave them with the observation that they are the instruments of the orders of the physicians. They have no right of conscientious objection, at least not in this set of circumstances.

Before turning to another evaluative description of the case, it is important to reiterate what was said in the beginning. The decisions by the principals were conscientious ones. The parents anguished. The physicians were informed by a sense of compassion in their consent to the parents' wishes; they did not wish to be party to potential suffering that was avoidable. Indeed, in the way in which they formulated the dilemma, they did what was reasonable to do. They chose the way of least possible suffering to the fewest persons over a long range of time, with one exception, namely, not taking the infant's life. By describing the dilemma from a somewhat different set of values, or giving different weight to different factors, another course of action would have been reasonable and justified. The issue, it seems to me, is at the level of what is to be valued more highly, for one's very understanding of the problems he must solve are deeply affected by what one values most.

The Dilemma from a Different Moral Point of View

Wallace Stevens wrote in poetic form a subtle account of "Thirteen Ways of Looking at a Blackbird." Perhaps there are 13 ways of looking at this medical case. I shall attempt to look at it from only one more way. By describing the dilemma from a perspective that gives a different weight to some of the considerations that we have already exposed, one has a different picture, and different conclusions are called for. The moral integrity of any of the original participants is not challenged, not because of a radical relativism that says they have their points of view and I have mine, but out of respect for their conscientiousness. For several reasons, however, more consideration ought to have been given to two points. A difference in evaluative judgments would have made a difference of life or death for the infant, depending upon: (1) whether what one ought to do is determined by what one desires to do and (2) whether an infant with Down syndrome has a claim to life.

To restate the dilemma once again: If the parents had "desired" the infant with Down syndrome, the surgeons would have performed the operation that would have saved its life. If the infant had had a bowel obstruction that could be taken care of by an ordinary medical procedure, but had not been born with Down syndrome, the physicians would probably have insisted that the operation be performed.

Thus, one can recast the moral dilemma by giving a different weight to two things: the desires of the parents and the value or rights of an infant with Down syndrome. If the parents and the physicians believed strongly that there are things one ought to do even when one has no immediate positive feelings about doing them, no immediate strong desire to do them, the picture would have been different. If the parents and physicians believed that children with Down syndrome have intrinsic value, or have a right to life, or if they believed that Down syndrome is not sufficiently deviant from what is normatively human to merit death, the picture would have been different.

Thus, we can redraw the picture. To be sure, the parents are ambiguous about their feelings for an infant with Down syndrome, since it is normal to desire a normal infant rather than an abnormal infant. But (to avoid a discussion of abortion at this point) once an infant is born its independent existence provides independent value in itself, and those who brought it into being and those professionally responsible for its care have an obligation to sustain its life regardless of their negative or ambiguous feelings toward it. This probably would have been acknowledged by all concerned if the infant had not been born with Down syndrome. For example, if the pregnancy had been accidental, and in this sense the child was not desired, and the infant had been normal, no one would have denied its right to exist once it was born, though some would while still *in utero,* and thus would have sought an abortion. If the mother refused to accept accountability for the infant, alternative means of caring for it would have been explored.

To be sure, an infant with Down syndrome is genetically defective, and raising and caring for it put burdens on the parents, the family, and the state beyond the burdens required to raise a normal infant. But an infant with Down syndrome is human, and thus has the intrinsic value of humanity and the rights of a human being. Further, given proper care, it can reach a point of significant fulfillment of its limited potentialities; it is capable of loving and responding to love; it is capable of realizing happiness; it can be trained to accept responsibility for itself within its capacities. Thus, the physicians and parents have an obligation to use all ordinary means to preserve its life. Indeed, the humanity of mentally defective children is recognized in our society by the fact that we do not permit their extermination and do have policies which provide, all too inadequately, for their care and nurture.

If our case had been interpreted in the light of moral beliefs that inform the previous two paragraphs, the only reasonable conclusion would be that the surgery ought to have been done.

The grounds for assigning the weights I have to these crucial points can be examined. First, with reference simply to common experience, we all have obligations to others that are not contingent upon our immediate desires. When the registrar of my university indicates that senior grades have to be in by May 21, I have an obligation to read the exams, term papers, and senior essays in time to report the grades, regardless of my negative feelings toward those tasks or my preference to be doing something else. I have an obligation to my students, and to the university through its registrar, which I accepted when I assumed the social role of an instructor. The students have a claim on me; they have a right to expect me to fulfill my obligations to them and to the university. I might be excused from the obligation if I suddenly became too ill to fulfill it; my incapacity to fulfill it would be a temporarily excusing condition. But negative feelings toward that job, or toward any students, or a preference for writing a paper of my own at that time, would not constitute excusing conditions. I must consider, in determining what I do, the relationships that I have with others and the claims they have on me by virtue of those relationships.

In contrast to this case, it might be said that I have a contractual obligation to the university into which I freely entered. The situation of the parents is not the same. They have no legal contractual relationship with the infant, and thus their desires are not bound by obligations. Closer to their circumstances, then, might be other family relationships. I would argue that the fact that we brought our children into being lays a moral obligation on my wife and me to sustain and care for them to the best of our ability. They did not choose to be; and their very being is dependent, both causally and in other ways, upon us. In the relationship of dependence, there is a claim of them over against us. To be sure, it is a claim that also has its rewards and that we desire to fulfill within a relationship of love. But until they have reached an age when they can accept full accountability (or fuller accountability) for themselves, they have claims upon us by virtue of our being their parents, even when meeting those claims is to us financially costly, emotionally distressing, and in other ways not immediately desirable. Their claims are independent of our desires to fulfill them. Particular claims they might make can justifiably be turned down, and others can be negotiated, but the claim against us for their physical sustenance constitutes a moral obligation that we have to meet. That obligation is not conditioned by their IQ scores, whether they have cleft palates or perfectly formed faces, whether they are obedient or irritatingly independent, whether they are irritatingly obedient and passive or laudably self-determining. It is not conditioned by any predictions that might be made about whether they will become the persons we might desire that they become. The infant in our case has the same sort of claim, and thus the parents have a moral obligation to use all ordinary means to save its life.

An objection might be made. Many of my fellow Christians would say that the obligation of the parents was to do that which is loving toward the infant. Not keeping the child alive was the loving thing to do with reference both to its interests and to the interests of the other members of the family. To respond to the objection, one needs first to establish the spongy character of the words "love" or "loving." They can absorb almost anything. Next one asks whether the loving character of an act is determined by feelings or by motives, or whether it is also judged by what is done. It is clear that I would argue for the latter. Indeed, the minimal conditions of a loving relationship include respect for the other, and certainly for the other's presumption of a right to live. I would, however, primarily make the case that the relationship of dependence grounds the claim, whether or not one feels loving toward the other.

The dependence relationship holds for the physicians as well as the parents in this case. The child's life depended utterly upon the capacity of the physicians to sustain it. The fact that an infant cannot articulate his claim is irrelevant. Physicians will struggle to save the life of a person who has attempted to commit suicide even when the patient might be in such a drugged condition that he cannot express his desire—a desire expressed already in his effort to take his life and overridden by the physician's action to save it. The claim of human life for preservation, even when such a person indicates a will not to live, presents a moral obligation to those who have the capacity to save it.

A different line of argument might be taken. If the decisions made were as reliant upon the desires of the parents as they appear to be, which is to say, if desire had a crucial role, what about the desire of the infant? The infant could not give informed consent to the non-intervention. One can hypothesize that every infant desires to live, and that even a defective child is likely to desire life rather than death when it reaches an age at which its desires can be articulated. Even if the right to live is contingent upon a desire, we can infer that the infant's desire would be for life. As a human being, he would have that desire, and thus it would constitute a claim on those on whom he is dependent to fulfill it.

I have tried to make a persuasive case to indicate why the claim of the infant constitutes a moral obligation on the parents and the physicians to keep the child alive. The intrinsic value or rights of a human being are not qualified by any given person's intelligence or capacities for productivity, potential consequences of the sort that burden others. Rather, they are constituted by the very existence of the human being as one who is related to others and dependent upon others for his existence. The presumption is always in favor of sustaining life through ordinary means; the desires of persons that run counter to that presumption are not sufficient conditions for abrogating that right.

The power to determine whether the infant shall live or die is in the hands of others. Does the existence of such power carry with it the moral right to such determination? Long history of moral experience indicates not only that arguments have consistently been made against the judgment that the capacity to do something constitutes a right to do it, or put in more familiar terms, that might makes right. It also indicates that in historical situations where persons have claimed the right to determine who shall live because they have the power to do so, the consequences have hardly been beneficial to mankind. This, one acknowledges, is a "wedge" argument or a "camel's nose under the tent" argument. As such, its limits are clear. Given a culture in which humane values are regnant, it is not likely that the establishment of a principle that some persons under some circumstances claim the right to determine whether others shall live will be transformed into the principle that the right of a person to live is dependent upon his having the qualities approved by those who have the capacity to sustain or take his life. Yet while recognizing the sociological and historical limitations that exist in a humane society, one still must recognize the significance of a precedent. To cite an absurd example, what would happen if we lived in a society in which the existence of hazel eyes was considered a genetic defect by parents and physicians? The absurdity lies in the fact that no intelligent person would consider hazel eyes a genetic defect; the boundaries around the word "defect" are drawn by evidences better than eye color. But the precedent in principle remains; when one has established that the capacity to determine who shall live carries with it the right to determine who shall live, the line of discussion has shifted from a sharp presumption (of the right of all humans to live) to the softer, spongier determination of the qualities whose value will be determinative.

Often we cannot avoid using qualities and potential consequences in the determination of what might be justifiable exceptions to the presumption of the right to life on the part of any infant—indeed, any person. No moralist would insist that the physicians have an obligation to sustain the life of matter born from human parents that is judged to be a "monstrosity." Such divergence from the "normal" qualities presents no problem, and potential consequences for its continued existence surely enter into the decision. The physicians in our case believed that in the absence of a desire for the child on the part of the parents, Down syndrome was sufficiently removed from an ideal norm of the human that the infant had no overriding claim on them. We are in a sponge. Why would I draw the line on a different side of Down syndrome than the physicians did? While reasons can be given, one must recognize that there are intuitive elements, grounded in beliefs and profound feelings, that enter into particular judgments of this sort. I am not prepared to say that my respect for human life is "deeper," "profounder," or "stronger" than theirs. I am prepared to say that the way in which, and the reasons why, I respect life orient my judgment toward the other side of Down syndrome than theirs did.

First, the value that intelligence was given in this instance appears to me to be simplistic. Not all intelligent persons are socially commendable (choosing socially held values as the point of reference because one of the physicians did). Also, many persons of limited intelligence do things that are socially commendable, if only minimally providing the occasion for the expression of profound human affection and sympathy. There are many things we value about human life; that the assumption that one of them is the *sine qua non,* the necessary and sufficient condition for a life to be valued at all, oversimplifies human experience. If there is a *sine qua non,* it is physical life itself, for apart from it, all potentiality of providing benefits for oneself or for others is impossible. There are occasions on which other things are judged to be more valuable than physical life itself: we probably all would admire the person whose life is martyred for the sake of saving others. But the qualities or capacities we value exist in bundles, and not each as overriding in itself. The capacity for self-determination is valued, and on certain occasions we judge that it is worth dying, or taking life, for the sake of removing repressive limits imposed upon persons in that respect. But many free, self-determining persons are not very happy; indeed, often their anxiety increases with the enlargement of the range of things they must and can determine for themselves. Would we value a person exclusively because he is happy? Probably not, partly because his happiness has at least a mildly contagious effect on some other persons, and thus we value him because he makes others happy as well. To make one quality we value (short of physical life itself, and here there are exceptions) determinative over all other qualities is to impoverish the richness and variety of human life. When we must use the sponge of qualities to determine exceptions to the presumption of the right to physical life, we need to face their variety, their complexity, the abrasiveness of one against the other, in the determination of action. In this case the potentialities of a person with Down syndrome for satisfaction in life, for fulfilling his limited capacities, for happiness, for providing the occasions of meaningful (sometimes distressing and sometimes joyful) experience for others are sufficient so that no exception to the right to life should be made. Put differently, the anguish, suffering, embarrassment, expenses of family and state (I support the need for revision of social policy and practice) are not sufficiently negative to warrant that the life of a child with Down syndrome not be sustained by ordinary procedures.

Second, and harder to make persuasive, is that my view of human existence leads to a different assessment of the significance of suffering than appears to be operative in this case. The best argument to be made in support of the course of decisions as they occurred is that in the judgment of the principals involved, they were able to avoid more suffering and other costs for more people over a longer range of time than could have been avoided if the infant's life had been saved. To suggest a different evaluation of suffering is not to suggest that suffering is an unmitigated good, or that the acceptance of suffering when it could be avoided is a strategy that ought to be adopted for the good life, individually and collectively. Surely it is prudent and morally justifiable to avoid suffering if possible under most normal circumstances of life. But two questions will help to designate where a difference of opinion between myself and the principals in our drama can be located. One is, At what cost to others is it justifiable to avoid suffering for ourselves? On the basis of my previous exposition, I would argue that in this instance the avoidance of potential suffering at the cost of that life was not warranted. The moral claims of others upon me often involve emotional and financial stress, but that stress is not sufficient to warrant my ignoring the claims. The moral and legal claim of the government to the right to raise armies in defense of the national interest involves inconvenience, suffering, and even death for many; yet the fact that meeting that claim will cause an individual suffering is not sufficient ground to give conscientious objection. Indeed, we normally honor those who assume suffering for the sake of benefits to others.

The second question is, Does the suffering in prospect appear to be bearable for those who have to suffer? We recognize that the term "bearable" is a slippery slope and that fixing an answer to this question involves judgments that are always hypothetical. If, however, each person has a moral right to avoid all bearable inconvenience or suffering that appears to run counter to his immediate or long-range self-interest, there are many things necessary for the good of other individuals and for the common good that would not get done. In our case, there appear to be no evidences that the parents with assistance from other institutions would necessarily find the raising of a child with Down syndrome to bring suffering that they could not tolerate. Perhaps there is justifying evidence to which I do not have access, such as the possibility that the mother would be subject to severe mental illness if she had to take care of the child. But from the information I received, no convincing case could be made that the demands of raising the child would present intolerable and unbearable suffering to the family. That it would create greater anguish, greater inconvenience, and greater demands than raising a normal child would is clear. But that meeting these demands would cause greater suffering to this family than it does to thousands of others who raise children with Down syndrome seems not to be the case.

Finally, my view, grounded ultimately in religious convictions as well as moral beliefs, is that to be human is to have a vocation, a calling, and the calling of each of us is "to be for others" at least as much as "to be for ourselves." The weight that one places on "being for others" makes a difference in one's fundamental orientation toward all of his relationships, particularly when they conflict with his immediate self-interest. In the Torah we have that great commandment, rendered in *The New English Bible* as "you shall love your neighbour as a man like yourself" (Lev. 19:18). It is reiterated in the records we have of the words of Jesus, "Love your neighbor as yourself" (Matt. 22:39, and several other places). Saint Paul makes the point even stronger at one point: "Each of you must regard, not his own interests, but the other man's" (1 Cor. 10:24, NEB). And finally, the minimalist saying accredited both to Rabbi Hillel and to Jesus in different forms, "Do unto others as you would have others do unto you."

The point of the biblical citations is not to take recourse to dogmatic religious authority, as if these sayings come unmediated from the ultimate power and orderer of life. The point is to indicate a central thrust in Judaism and Christianity which has nourished and sustained a fundamental moral outlook, namely, that we are "to be for others" at least as much as we are "to be for ourselves." The fact that this outlook has not been adhered to consistently by those who professed it does not count against it. It remains a vocation, a calling, a moral ideal, if not a moral obligation. The statement of such an outlook does not resolve all the particular problems of medical histories such as this one, but it shapes a bias, gives a weight, toward the well-being of the other against inconvenience or cost to oneself. In this case, I believe that all the rational inferences to be drawn from it, and all the emotive power that this calling evokes, lead to the conclusion that the ordinary surgical procedure should have been done, and this infant's life saved.

Chapter 5

A Theocentric Interpretation of Life

In my circumstances, the title "How My Thinking Has Been Developing" would be preferable for this series to "How My Mind Has Changed." The latter assumes that an author had "made up his mind" and is interested in checking carefully what he or she said in the past and, like St. Augustine, in making retractions. The notion of making retractions seems to require that at a later stage one has arrived at Truth, and that thus there is a clear standard for judging earlier errors. Perhaps the editors were not expecting that to occur. I shall not cite quotations from my previous work which are no longer accurate expressions of my present thinking; I have no interest in doing so.

This article has a pattern. The form is somewhat like the plan of the city of New Delhi. The British planned a good bit of the city around the huge Connaught Circle, into which arteries of traffic flow from all directions. In this article I initially take one artery after another to the outer rim of the circle. Then I go around the circle a few times, and in the end indicate how I, at least, take my bearings. The circle we might call theocentricity.

Some recollection is required even to respond to my revision of the series title. Certainly it is the case that I was very interested for a number of years in trying to develop methods for Christian ethics that would correct the simplistic Christian moralisms to which Protestantism has been addicted for a long time. There were at least two fronts being attended to in this enterprise: the importance of taking very seriously the kinds of precise and technical information required to make particular judgments and choices (while not losing sight of the difficulties in getting accurate information and ideologically unbiased interpretation), and the importance of making the moral arguments of Christians more rigorous both philosophically and theologically. I was attracted to Paul Ramsey's work because he clearly shared these purposes, though we have worked them out differently; I was interested in Roman Catholic moral theology and social ethics for similar reasons, though again the execution of a similar purpose is different.

I do not regret the attention I gave to those matters, and I admire many of my colleagues who have pursued similar purposes with rigor and diligence beyond my capacities to achieve. Many of them now call themselves "religious ethicists," and therein lies a clue to some dissatisfaction. Those who have taken the garb of "religious studies," and who have either left behind any serious personal religious interests or valiantly hold them in abeyance, are doing important analytical work on religious ethics—work that I continue to do in seminars. Some, however, have become practical moral philosophers, moral problem-solvers, and it is not clear to what the adjective "religious" refers. Against my friends and colleagues, and even against myself, I have fired this arrow previously in an article published in *Commonweal,* and I shall not use another arrow on the same target.

The issue, however, persists: What makes ethics religious? Several things can be said to do so: the fact that one is working from the lore of a particular religious tradition; the seriousness of the attention and intention with which one is concerned about morality; the openness to larger dimensions that affect morality, like world views, metaphysics or ontology. Or it might be that moral life is related to God, and ethics to theology.

ETHICS AND ANTHROPOCENTRISM

For more than a decade the practical area that primarily occupied my attention was that of biological research and medicine. I believe it was in 1960 that I first delivered lectures on ethics to medical students at Yale. That interest was substantive and real, though its lasting benefits to me might well be the problems which most work in that area comes up to and then ignores. I have tried to encourage the casuists—whether physicians, scientists, philosophers, ex-theologians or continuing theologians—to take some of these problems into account.

For example, every particular question in critical cases of medical ethics involves some choices regarding what we value about human life. What is it we value? What is the normatively human? Why do we value what we value? Why do we say that persons have rights? What is the ground of these rights? If these questions do not drive one to theology, they at least drive one to the secular first cousins of theology. And if traditional ways of answering these questions—for instance, in classic natural-law theory—are not sufficient, how do we go about finding better answers? And why are they better?

Developments of Western culture have increasingly tended toward anthropocentrism. That history has been written by a number of scholars. One line of argument goes that it is biblical faith that has contributed to the demystification of nature, robbing it of the religious or spiritual significance it had not only in primitive animistic cultures, but also in ancient Greek and Roman cultures, and has yet in Asian cultures. This liberation of nature, a necessary effect of the Bible's transcendent God, enabled humanity to "thingify" it, to see its utility value, to take from it any inherent teleology, not to mention an ultimate purpose in relation to God other than its meeting of human needs.

Certain interpretations of the Bible, and certain interpretations of the hierarchy of beings in our culture, have reinforced the notion that the rest of the creation exists for the benefit of our species—a species that has evolved relatively recently in paleontological perspectives. The increase of human capacities to describe and explain the operations of nature and of human society has been turned to instrumental usage, and we have seen the ascendance of "technical reason." The time and space scopes of the consequences of human interventions into nature and into social processes have expanded without the commensurate increase in humility that is proper, given the continuing remarkable limitations of foreknowledge of long-range consequences and of the capacity to control them. The human being becomes both the measurer of all things and the measure of all things—at humankind's own peril, we need to add, and to the peril of the creation of which humankind is a minuscule part.

"All traditional ethics is anthropocentric," wrote that wise first cousin of theologians, Hans Jonas; at least traditional Western ethics has had a strong tendency toward anthropocentrism. Teleologies have been in focus on what is the good for humans, and not for the whole of the creation; frequently they have been in focus on what is the good for individuals, and not even the common good of the human community. The difficulty of knowing the latter itself becomes an excuse for not seeking to find it, and the historical evidences of injustices and tyrannies that have occurred when persons who thought they knew it gained power warn us properly against its perils. Modern secular ethics has had good epistemological reasons for doubting whether we could know an objective moral order even if there is one, and has devised sophisticated techniques for formulating the principles of moral action without recourse to "metaphysics" or anything that looks remotely like it.

Yet it is events that move many of our contemporaries to what might well be intellectually primitive impulses toward recognition of the need to enlarge the range of considerations involved in ethics, to see individuals in relation not only to other individuals but also to communities, to see our actions in relation not only to historical events, but also to the wider natural world. While I am not persuaded that we can know the moral order of nature with the certainty that some

Roman Catholic philosophers and moral theologians have thought we could, I am persuaded that a turn in ethical thinking is required, if not from humanity to God, at least from humanity to the signs of an ordering of life which is objective to individuals, objective to communities of persons, and objective to our species.

A THEOCENTRIC ORIENTATION

During this period I have found myself making a move that the generation of my teachers made in the 1920s and 1930s. Religion had become terribly subjective; its object, God, seemed to be left out. My perceptions of a great deal of religious activity in the past two decades is that it is highly instrumental—not for the purpose of honoring God and offering gratitude to him, but for the purpose of inducing subjective states in humans. Even the great Christian theme of redemption has been reduced to a psychological principle: you are accepted. By whom? On what basis?

And, as has been the case so often in Christian history, religion becomes instrumental to moral ends chosen for other than religious reasons. When we give the examples of anticommunism and nationalism, all of us cheer and say Amen. But the same principle has been at work in movements for radical social change. The most vulgar form is the "pray-in"; the sophisticated forms are more profoundly theological: a moral end or a moral interest becomes the hermeneutical device for interpreting the Bible or theological themes that can be grounded in the Bible. If we can find a way to make religion or God serve our subjective ends, whether they be to help us feel better or to change the world, we use them.

Certainly religion in all times and all cultures has had utility value; in the biblically grounded religions of the West, however, the ultimate end has been theocentrically oriented, turned toward an objective reality. Moses and the prophets, Jesus and Paul, Augustine and Thomas Aquinas, the great 16th century Reformers, the Puritans, Jonathan Edwards and others—they were correct in the primary intuition that religion deals with the relations of humans and the world to God and to his purposes. Those rebels against religious subjectivism earlier in our century—Barth and Brunner, Wieman and H. Richard Niebuhr and others—had a similar primary intuition, and it was correct.

I have, since adolescence, been persuaded that cultural and historical relativism was more valid than the efforts to shed our various layers of skin so that we could achieve pure disinterestedness, rational autonomy in morality, and pure objectivity in other areas of knowledge. No doubt my growing up in an immigrant sectarian religious community contributed to that opinion, as did my service in Burma and India during World War II, studies of sociology and anthropology as an undergraduate, my reading of Troeltsch under the aegis of a great teacher, James Luther Adams, and other things. It was H. Richard Niebuhr's *The Meaning of Revelation* that made more theological sense to me than the process theology that dominated the Federated Theological Faculty of the University of Chicago in my years as a Bachelor of Divinity student.

I am somewhat amused that Roman Catholic theologians, a lot of Protestants, and sociologists of religion are only now learning about sociology of knowledge and its significance for theology, about "historical" mentalities and such things. Different persons and different groups are not, in that terrible current term, "in phase" because they are the bearers of the cultures and beliefs from which they come. But when persons begin to call any set of symbols—any beliefs which give meaning and coherence to life—a "theology," I wish they would instead talk about the functional equivalents to theology. (I suppose, though, that if philosophers are no longer lovers of wisdom, theologians no longer should be expected to be thinking about God.)

Surely all religions do function to provide meaning to experience; descriptively there is nothing wrong with that. But surely in the Western religious traditions those meanings relate all things to God, and when the properly descriptive becomes the basis for prescriptions for religious life, the reduction transforms Christianity and Judaism almost to the point of unrecognizability. Relativism without relation to an ultimate object degenerates into religious subjectivism; i.e., there are no bases for making judgments about the adequacy of religious views other than how satisfying they are to those who share them. When relative traditions do not test themselves by more generalizable criteria, they become defensive, smug and incorrigible.

HONEST IN REGARD TO CULTURE

The work of Stephen Toulmin and others has given me strong bases for believing what I always suspected as a relativist—namely, that the development of the sciences as historical movements is not unlike the development of theology, and that while the sciences have different and more satisfactory ways to adduce evidences that sustain their theories than does theology, the truth claims they make are not as "hard" as sometimes was thought to be the case. A theologian can respond to this work in two ways: one can say with satisfaction and glee that the sciences are in their own way relativistic and even "confessional" and so theology is liberated from its presumed archaism. But one can also say that theology, like the developments in particular sciences, has to be prepared to make its own revisions of those theories that have provided past ways of construing the world— ways that are no longer tenable.

The previous paragraph is not without its point with reference to the outcome of several of the paragraphs prior to it. Religion has an "objective reference," in piety called God. But the kind of retreat into biblical theology that some of the generation of my teachers made in order to recover the object of love and faith, the ultimate limiter and the condition of possibilities for life, is not a defensible retreat for me. At the same time it is the case that I am a religious thinker in the Christian tradition; I could not chuck that out if I tried. So the theological problem is the one that has been present since at least the Apologists (and really, in the Scriptures also); namely, how does a community working for good reasons within a historically particular tradition think about the object of its reverence, respect and gratitude in ways that can be honest with reference to its own culture and time?

Theological ethics has consistently been the area that I have most relished. I have taken generations of graduate students through classic texts and through important contemporary texts that have related God to morality, theology to ethics. We have together worked through these texts with systematic issues in view: Christian love; sin as a religious and moral term; love and justice; persons as moral agents; and the like. We have worked through Karl Barth and Thomas Aquinas side by side—to historians a scandalous way to teach—to sort out the fundamental options for relating theology to ethics. We have worked through important texts in a given period for comparative purposes, such as the Reformation (the Anabaptists get "equal time"); we have analyzed developments in Roman Catholic ethics in the modern period to see how and why they have changed; we have looked carefully at the works of a single author—for example, Jonathan Edwards. We have examined the ethics in the Bible, writings about the ethics in the Bible, and constructive biblical ethics with the same analytical agenda. We have studied various moral philosophers in conjunction with theologians. My route to theology has been and is the route of ethics. But that route always leads to theology.

Classic religious texts provide for me more joy and more use than most contemporary writings. It is more difficult, more fun and more profitable to think about my agenda for theology and ethics by reading the Bible, Augustine, Thomas Aquinas, Calvin, Luther, Edwards, Schleiermacher and Barth than it is to keep up with all the good books published by Orbis, Paulist, Westminster, Fortress, Abingdon, Eerdmans and Seabury presses. There are novel circumstances in the relations of theology and ethics, but no novel issues.

My attention has not been as parochial as the preceding paragraphs might suggest. For some years I worked with significant concentration on the Jewish legal and ethical tradition; in preparation for lectures delivered in various Indian universities I spent a year attempting to grasp some of the major features of religion, morality and history in that complex culture. To read again the classic tradition from Homer forward, and to be stimulated in my reflections about it by the work of Arthur W. H. Adkins and others, has been enormously beneficial. To have had the personal intellectual companionship of some colleagues from genetics, clinical medicine, psychiatry, philosophy, law, literature, social sciences and other fields has been a valuable gift that the University of Chicago and the professional communities of the city have provided. Similar contacts of comparable length and depth took place during the years of my more intimate participation in the work of the Hastings Center. My convictions about theology and ethics are being forged not only on the anvil of classics of the Christian tradition, but also by the hammers of pleasant and sometimes intensive cross-disciplinary contacts.

ITEMS FOR AN AGENDA

I have rather cryptically referred to the agenda for theology and ethics. What are its items? I have worked it out most systematically in the last chapter of *Protestant and Roman Catholic Ethics: Prospects for Rapprochement* (University of Chicago Press, 1978). Briefly and in summary, it includes the following theses and items: Any systematic and comprehensive account of theological ethics has to have an organizing perspective, metaphor or principle. That "discremen" (to use Robert Clyde Johnson's term for such) must relate coherently four base points: theology in the restricted sense of an understanding of God and his purposes in relation to the world; an interpretation of the meaning and significance of "the world"; an interpretation of persons as moral agents and of their acts; and an interpretation of how persons ought to make moral choices and moral judgments. In doing this, the author must make judgments about the adequacy of a proposed position with reference to four sources: the historically identifiable Christian tradition; philo-sophical methods, insights and principles; scientific information that is relevant and reasonably solid; and human experience broadly conceived.

Just as the "discremen" makes a critical difference in how the base points are ordered, so does the preference for one of the base points as being most signifi-cant. Another critical choice is which of the four sources is most important and finally determinative when resolutions of issues between the four sources are made. Systematic and comprehensive theological ethics, I have argued, touches all the base points and uses all the sources in one way or another.

I am confident that this agenda and its items provide a very useful analytical framework for studying the theological ethics of a religious tradition. I am not nearly so confident that it is within my powers to develop a cogent, persuasive, constructive account of theological ethics that meets the tests of adequacy and coherence that the agenda requires. Nonetheless, that is the task to which I have turned my attention.

A NATURAL PIETY

This all sounds terribly cerebral and abstract, as if one were arranging informa-tion according to concepts, and interpreting them with some basic principle or metaphor. And so it would be if another deep conviction were not introduced—namely, that religion is basically a matter of the affections, in that rich 18th cen-tury sense of the term that Jonathan Edwards used; that it is a matter of piety (not piousness or pietism), in the rich sense that both St. Augustine and Calvin affirmed. Religion is an aspect or dimension of experience, and while that aspect can be described to a considerable extent, and some reasons be given to explain it, it is never susceptible to the kind of full, disinterested, rational justification that would be desirable for some apologetic purposes.

On this critical item for my current work I have already declared myself in *Can Ethics Be Christian?* (University of Chicago Press, 1975). That this assertion sounds "spooky" and esoteric to a number of my distinguished contemporaries, I know; that there is a natural piety in many persons similar to that about which Calvin was certain, I am willing to argue. (Indeed, I find four significant impulses to be present in many of my "secularized" friends: a natural piety in the sense of a gratitude and respect for the givenness of "the world," a recognition that there are some dimly perceived orderings of life to which human activity must in some sense be conformed, an awareness of a human defect, and a muted honoring of Another about which not much is said.)

It is not only the acknowledgment of the priority of piety or affections in religion that leads me back to such classic theologians as Augustine, Calvin, Edwards and Schleiermacher; it is also their intimations and declarations of a very sovereign power who sustains and limits us as humans. It is their powerful portrayals of a shared theme—namely, that the destiny of the worlds is not in human hands—that makes them theologically important to me, though with some critical themes that they generally share I have deep disagreements. And with the first three named I share a deep sense of the miseries and defects of human life. (A psychiatrist friend attributes much of this to a north Scandinavian view of the world, and wonders how Christian it really is.)

What in very general terms these theologians share which I find persuasive for many reasons is the primacy of piety, evoked by the powers of the Deity, and a sense that there are no clear resolutions of human ambiguities and, in the strongest technical sense, human tragedies in our temporal lives. They all sense that the conduct of human affairs requires conformity to an ordering of both possibilities and constraints ultimately grounded in the purposes of God. While Christian faith and life had for all of them its benefits, and while they did not hesitate to seek to persuade persons to take the Christian faith seriously because it guaranteed what they thought was in the best self-interests of humans (thus instrumentalizing Christianity), each in his own way proclaimed that the chief end of humanity, and indeed of the whole of the creation, was to honor, celebrate, glorify God.

HOW GOD IS PROPERLY HONORED

There is a lot of celebration going on in Christian circles. I suppose it is those who have most deeply felt the inhibitions of moralistic Christianity, in Protestant or Catholic forms, who insist on religion's making one feel good, and who want Christians to enjoy life. There is a lot of "piety" around that is also unrelated to morality in any effective and serious way. What a selective retrieval of theological tradition can express and enable us to see is that gratitude and honor to God, the forms of piety, require that we relate to all things appropriate to their relations to God—a phrase I have taken and slightly revised from the writings of my close friend Julian N. Hartt. The honoring of God is not the emotive impulse for taking morality seriously; God is properly honored only as humans seek in their actions and their relations to relate to all things appropriate to their relations to God.

Piety in my theological "construing of the world" (another turn of phrase which I owe to Hartt) does not take one beyond morality; the Deity whose majesty evokes piety is the ultimate power that sustains and orders the universe. And there is no guarantee that facing the limits of my finitude, ordering life according to some principles which are grounded in God's governance, will make me feel good, meet my short-range or even long-range interests, keep suffering from my doorstep or anyone's, or adequately explain it away, or bring compensatory justice to bear in some world to come. Piety—gratitude, honor, reverence and respect to God—demands from its most interior wellsprings the disciplining of life, the ordering of human communities, the relating of human activity and culture to the natural world in ways that recognize both human finitude and the human defect, and recognizes that life must be conformed to that ordering activity of God which we cannot fully know.

To state these interests, and to work out a coherent position that reflects them, requires selectivity with reference to the materials from the Christian tradition. But then, what theologian has not been selective? It requires selection of themes even from those theologians who most deeply inform one's thought and experience. E. R. Dodds, in *The Greeks and the Irrational* (University of California Press, 1951), cites an apt passage from an article by W. H. Auden:

> If we talk of tradition today we no longer mean what the eighteenth century meant, a way of working handed down from one generation to the next; we mean a consciousness of the whole of the past in the present. Originality no longer means a slight modification of one's immediate predecessors; it means the capacity to find in any other work of any date or locality clues for the treatment of one's own subject matter [pp. 237–38].

ADEQUACY TO HUMAN EXPERIENCE

If one emended the presumption that any of us can have a consciousness of the whole of the past, and the intimation that originality seems to be desirable, this statement expresses well my own response to the traditions to which I have sought to expose myself. It is one's own subject matter, and the attempt to deal with it responsibly in one's own time and place, that determines one's selection and use of materials from the Christian and other traditions. When the chips are down, it is adequacy to human experience—not just individual, but that of those whose experience is similar to one's own—that is decisive. That experience is deeply informed by traditions, by contemporary events in culture and society, by scientific and other intellectual enterprises of the modern world; one is not talking about minimal sensations. The best one can expect to do is speak honestly for oneself, with some confidence that one's own experience is not utterly unique but similar to that of a significant number of persons.

During my three years as a graduate student at Yale I was pastor of a small Congregational church; it was a rich and formative experience. When one sat up most of a night with a family that was bearing the grief of a suicide, or when one was responsible to preach to a group of people in the village, all of whom one knew very well, theological studies had to be forged into an honest way of interpreting not only the experiences of human suffering, but the threats of McCarthyism and the cold war, and the proposals to rezone a rural village in the face of the coming suburbanization. Such coherence as my theological and ethical thinking had then, has ever had, and has now, has come in significant measure from trying to make sense of human life in the light of that measure of the knowledge of God that can be affirmed. Although I seldom preach or conduct public worship, it continues to be the case that my most generalized thought comes in relation to a broad range of quite specific human experiences. And so at this stage, toward the end of my career, I continue to work at expressing and defending a theocentric interpretation of life, and particularly of moral activity. To this task I am by now fated.

Chapter 6

Say Something Theological!

Ten years ago I was co-chairman of an interdisciplinary research group that worked intensively on the applications of new developments in human genetics, and particularly their social, moral, legal, and political implications. The group met monthly; papers were circulated, criticized, revised, and rewritten several times. The final stage was the circulation of the papers to distinguished scholars and other professional persons whose work was related to ours. Among those gathered for the final review was an eminent biologist.

At the end of a day of rigorous and exhausting discussion, the group adjourned to a temple of the god of wine. As the effects of the spirits grew, I was approached by this biologist.

First he told me about his childhood and youthful experiences in a Protestant church.

Secularized intellectuals are prone to do that to a theologian when they become friendly—or slightly intoxicated.

Then he went on to tell me that for his whole professional life he had felt embarrassed in the presence of theologians.

We talked about various theologians he had met from time to time, and then he said that these hours were the longest time he had spent in the same room with a theologian in his whole life!

He survived!

Finally, with great sentiment he put his left arm around my shoulder and said, "Gustafson, say something theological!"

I had the presence of mind to say, "God."

When I was invited to deliver the Ryerson Lecture, among many thoughts that crossed my mind was this: the Committee must be trying to show what a truly liberal university we are by inviting a theologian to deliver the lecture in the 1980s. It's a little like inviting Charles Darwin to lecture to a church group in the 1860s.

The University of Chicago is hardly a community that is famous for its religious interests, though many of its scholars are interested in religion from historical, philosophical, anthropological, psychological, sociological, and other perspectives.

Some among us no doubt believe that theological proposals are too soft to warrant a place in university studies and teaching. To some they deserve no more respect than alchemy or astrology.

Some of us are suspicious of any effort to grasp the significance of particulars in the context of any larger whole, not to mention theology. We are all adept at dividing reality into segments that our special disciplines can manage. This is as true of the Divinity School faculty as any other part of the University, as a theologian is likely to find out when he or she has the audacity to step into the territory of the biblical scholars or the historians. Yet most of us are forced to attend to the margins of our specializations, since one object under investigation impinges upon others.

Some of us probably still perceive theology to be a discipline based upon authority, rather than one that provides reasons for believing.

There might even be someone around who worries that theology will again try to assert itself as the queen of the sciences—but this is hardly a practical problem in this university.

My conversation with the biologist perhaps symbolizes how theology is viewed in secular universities.

Nonetheless: "Gustafson, say something theological!"

To say something theological is to say something religious. Theology has its deepest significance within the context of piety, and in the context of a historic religious tradition.

This is not to say that theology is uninteresting to many scholars who have no obvious religious interest. Anselm's ontological argument for the existence of God, for example, continues to generate literature, some of which is in the service of sophisticated and even recondite philosophical interests. (I once participated in an oral examination of a student who interpreted and defended Charles Hartshorne's version of the ontological argument. In the course of it I received a vivid cram course in modal logic from our colleague Leonard Linsky. Clearly the logical problems in the ontological argument are interesting in themselves, at least to a logician!) Nor is it to say that defenders of the realistic epistemology and metaphysics that ground classic natural theology no longer exist. Historians of the intellectual life of Western culture cannot avoid theology, and theologians are often indebted to them for their work. Nonetheless, the principal context for theology is religion.

Theology is reflection on the object of piety. Piety is a fundamental stance toward what is given in the world and human life: it is an attitude or disposition of respect, awe, and even devotion that is evoked by human experiences of dependence on powers we do not create and cannot fully master. Piety is not something esoteric; it is not to be confused with piousness—that pretentious display of religiosity that offends all of us, nor with pietism—that movement of religious life that strives to engender and sustain a high pitch of emotions. Piety is not self-stimulated; it is a response to the powers, objective to ourselves, that bring life into being and sustain it, that bear down upon us, and threaten us.

I use the term piety rather than faith. To be sure, there is a long history of theology as "faith seeking understanding." This expression can create what are, from my point of view, erroneous perceptions of theology. Faith often is construed to be trust in the ultimate powers, and particularly a confidence that God guarantees the ultimate well-being of the human species, and even my ultimate well-being. Piety, in contrast with this, does not assume that a divine beneficence guarantees human fulfillment; it includes the possibilities of not only trust and love toward God, but also dread and anger.

Faith is sometimes construed as a deposit of revelation, a kind of knowledge that is authorized by God in such a way that it is exempt from critical scrutiny. Piety, in contrast with this, is an attitude and disposition toward a wide range of objects of human experience, and thus theology must be open to learning from data and theories about the powers that order life which come from many areas of human investigation.

Faith is sometimes contrasted with reason; the polarity invites the opinion that theology is fundamentally unreasonable, its authorization secure from critical evaluation, and that it is futile to develop arguments for the object of theological investigation. Piety, in contrast, invites rational justification. To be sure, since its ultimate object is not a phenomenon like DNA, theological investigation does not use the methods of scientific investigation, and its conclusions are not susceptible to the same tests of validity. But the attitude and disposition of piety is not an unreasonable one; rational activity can provide backing and warrants for it, and can point to some features of its ultimate object.

Piety involves human affections. "True religion," Jonathan Edwards wrote, "in great part consists in holy affections."[1] This assertion, born in the turmoil of the

---

1. Jonathan Edwards, *Religious Affections*, ed. John E. Smith (New Haven: Yale University Press, 1959), p. 59.

emotionalism of the religious revivals of eighteenth century New England, was developed into signs and tests of true and false religious affections. While its elaboration was time and culture-bound, and led to an almost nauseating introspection, the fundamental perception is correct. Religion is a matter of the affections. It is not a matter of fleeting emotions evoked by the glory of a sunset over New Mexican mesas, or by the failure to fulfill an obligation that leads to anguished guilt, though these can be religiously and theologically construed. Piety expresses deeper, more settled affections.

It takes the form of a profound sense of dependence that comes with the recognition that, for all our human achievements, the world was brought into being by powers long before the emergence of our species; that the continuation of life relies upon powers that are not fully in human control; and that the destiny of the universe is not in human hands.

Piety takes the form of a sense of gratitude. Many possibilities for human flourishing come from achievements of human culture, but the deepest necessary conditions for human flourishing are not created by man, but given. Indeed, in religious terms they are a gift, and evoke gratitude. To be sure, much human pain and suffering is caused by forces beyond human control; God is the source of human good, but God does not guarantee it. The measure of flourishing we have, the human good that we experience, has a source beyond our capacities to create. For this, gratitude is an appropriate affection.

Piety takes the form of a sense of obligation. To acknowledge our dependence on processes of life beyond full human control, to recognize that we are sustained by the care of others and that others (including the natural world) are in our care—these are aspects of experience out of which a sense of obligation arises. In biblical imagery, we are called to be responsible stewards of what is given us in nature and in society; we have obligations to discern what human actions and relationships fit our place in the larger scheme of things.

From time to time piety takes the form of a sense of remorse, which can lead to a sense of repentance. Failure to recognize our dependence on the powers that sustain and bear down upon us can lead to claims for human self-sufficiency which erode or destroy human relationships and the proper relations between human life and the natural world of which we are a part. Traditional religious language terms this "pride." Failure to participate actively in the conduct of the affairs of our communities, to share in the nurture of our world is equally a fault. Traditional religious language terms this "sloth." For these, and other forms of "sin," we feel remorse.

Piety takes the form of a sense of possibilities, the form of hope. Except for the darkest nights of despair, and the most disastrous catastrophes, human beings see, or seek for, possibilities to alter those conditions that oppress them, to protect themselves against destructive forces, and to sustain the conditions that support them. We have capacities of human agency; we can intentionally intervene into the course of events. Within limits we, as individuals, can strive to become what we now are not. Some of the external conditions in which we live are alterable. The powers that rule the world do not fate us; they provide conditions of possibility for human activity: for the achievements of the arts, the sciences and technology, for justice and peace.

Piety takes the form of a sense of direction. The end might be as general as human happiness; it might have the particularly religious qualities of a vision of God, of communion with God, or of honoring God. To be sure, there are many persons whose lives are impulsive, wandering, self-contradictory, reactive, and in other ways aimless. But piety opens us to vision of the place of human life in the whole of creation, and of larger ends and purposes that human life can serve.

To say something theological is to say something religious—in the sense that what we say about the ultimate power is moved and informed by piety, by affections. To play on words of John Calvin, piety is the awe and reverence induced by the acknowledgment of the powers that bring the world into being and control its destiny.[2] Theology seeks to construe the meaning of those powers, and ultimately *the* power that induces piety.

To say something theological is to say something religious in a second sense. It is to speak from a religious tradition, while also being open to its alteration and revision. Religions are historical phenomena. Like other aspects of culture, they undergo change. Theology is historical; how the Deity is understood, and how the world is construed theologically undergo alteration in the light of other developments of knowledge. Nonetheless, theologians speak from traditions. Even the various "natural theologies" of philosophers develop from historical traditions of thought. The natural theology that developed from Aristotelian philosophy is different from that based on the philosophy of Alfred North Whitehead, which in turn has its own antecedents in the Western philosophical tradition. Even the sciences are not exempt from grounding in a tradition. The work of historians and philosophers of science shows how received theories and methods predispose investigators to construe their objects of study in certain ways, and how the process of development in the sciences involves selective retrieval from the past, an abandonment of certain theories and methods, and a reordering of the salience of certain features, as well as genuine novelty of perception, understanding, and verification. Theology is not unique in the fact that it develops within an identifiable historical tradition.

To be sure, theologians show greater reverence for the received tradition than do most other scholars. Particularly in the historic religions of the Book, the past has authority, though what it is and how binding it is elicits continuing debate. Even within the charter document of Western theologies, the Bible, there are many strands of thought, many types of literature, many theological interpretations of natural and historic events. Any theologian, even as he or she grounds theology in the Bible and in the tradition, selects certain features from the past to be more worthy of defense and development than others. Choices are made

2. John Calvin, *Institutes of the Christian Religion* 1.2.1; 2 vols., ed. John T. McNeill, trans. Ford Lewis Battles (Philadelphia: Westminster, 1960), 1:41.

from the tradition, and where there are choices there are principles that determine them. Those principles might derive from the tradition itself; one strand of biblical thought, such as eschatology (the doctrine of last things), for example, is judged by some theologians to be the essential clue to the whole of the biblical material, or to be the strand that can best organize many others into a comprehensive whole. Or, the principles might be derived from a philosophical movement in the culture; on the basis of a philosophical perspective the traditional materials are ordered and arranged to provide a coherent understanding of the Deity and its relations to the world. The adequacy of a received tradition might be challenged by horrendous historical events; the Holocaust has had this effect in both some Jewish and some Christian theologies. And, indeed, as Ernst Troeltsch noted early in this century, at some point in the process of selection from, and interpretation of, a received tradition the result might well become so novel that a different religion is being proposed.[3]

But it is always a tradition that is being revised and reordered. By this time in the history of religious thought it is quite likely that at one time or another all possible proposals for understanding God or the gods, and for interpreting the relations of the Deity to the world, have been made. No contemporary theologian begins *de novo;* each begins with an exploration of the resources of a tradition to determine what is to be sustained or retrieved, what is to be abandoned and for what reasons, what concepts and ideas are deemed most important to bring other concepts and ideas into some coherence, what rearrangement of traditional themes is defensible, and by what criteria of adequacy, if not of validity or truth, his or her own proposals are to be tested. It is intellectually naive to assume that such a process has not always occurred in theology; it is intellectually irresponsible to think that such a process must not continue to be the case. Those who think otherwise, whether secular persons in universities or pious persons in religious institutions, have simply fixed some historical point in the development of a tradition to be normative. It is equally naive and irresponsible for any novice theologian to assume that he or she can begin to think about God without learning first what others have thought about God.

To say something theological is to say something religious—in the sense that what we say about the ultimate power is informed by the experience and thought of our predecessors in a tradition, by those who have thought carefully about the Deity and its relations to the world. It is to say something, no matter how innovative, that draws on strands of a historic religious heritage. It is also, one must add, to say something that helps a religious community to grasp both what has continuing validity and what needs reformulation in its historic tradition.

To say something theological is to say something about how things really and ultimately are.

3. "What Does 'Essence of Christianity' Mean?" in *Ernst Troeltsch: Writings on Theology and Religion*, ed. Robert Morgan and Michael Pye (Atlanta: John Knox, 1977), p. 169.

This aspect of the theological enterprise is always the most troublesome. Historically, theologians have often said too much with too great certainty about how things really and ultimately are. Some have been dogmatic about the Scriptures; they have been certain that in them there is a sufficient basis for knowing the beginning and the end of the universe, the meaning and intention of the divine activity in history, the true understanding of the human situation, the cure of the ills of human life, and the beliefs and rules that must guide moral activity. Some have been dogmatic about their descriptions as a result of their uncritical and excessive reliance on time-bound interpretations of nature, only to have the pillars of their theology collapse under subsequent developments in science and philosophy. Some have resorted to a theory of several truths: the knowledge derived from the sciences is conveniently confined to its own sphere, and the language of religion is conveniently confined to a realm of faith, or of the interior condition of persons. Since the spheres are deemed incommensurable, no conflicts can arise.

In the face of having said too much with too great certainty, some theologians take recourse to other alternatives. For some, religion simply provides stories and myths which help persons to cope with the complexities and possibilities of life. Theology becomes storytelling; a pragmatic criterion of truth is deemed sufficient. Others quickly take recourse to the language of "absolute mystery"; the word God is "the final word before wordless and worshipful silence in the face of the ineffable mystery."[4]

But throughout the Western theological tradition there have always been those wise persons who have felt obliged to say as much as they could and dared to say on the basis of rational reflection on nature and experience, or on the basis of the accounts given in the biblical materials, or a combination of the two. Then they have properly and candidly admitted the final inadequacy of human words about God, and warn themselves and others about the presumptuousness of theology while defending its necessity.

If piety is induced by the experience of powers that brought the world into being, sustain it, and control its destiny, then a theologian must say what he or she can about those powers, and propose a way of construing the world in their light. If the religious tradition is the distillation of how people have understood the relations of those powers to nature, history, society, culture, and individuals, then the contemporary theologian must learn from their accounts while being open to revising them in the light of contemporary knowledge and experience. The theologian does so in consciousness of his or her own limitations, and the limitations of the culture in which proposals are made. Our colleague Stephen Toulmin asks, by implication, with reference to many investigations: Must truth be historically invariant?[5] Can it not be the case in theology, as in other investigations, that one

4. Karl Rahner, *Foundations of the Christian Faith*, trans. William V. Dych (New York: Seabury, 1978), p. 51.

5. Stephen Toulmin, *Human Understanding*, vol. 1 (Princeton: Princeton University Press, 1972), p. 45 and p. 51.

conscientiously and critically says something about how things really and ultimately are within the constraints of our time and place in culture and history, and yet with the awareness that new interpretations will follow? To be sure, the investigations of theology are not into phenomena like DNA; God is not such a phenomenon. The theologian will never come forward with a verification for his views of the Deity like Watson and Crick did for the double helix structure of the DNA molecule. But the theologian's interpretation of the powers needs to be informed by, and cannot be incongruous with, the most reliable knowledge we have from other investigations of how some things really and ultimately are.

I want briefly to illustrate this point. Western theology has dominantly viewed human life, and often each individual, to be the end and object of the divine purposes. John Calvin was quite typical of the tradition when he wrote that "God himself has shown by the order of Creation that he created all things for the sake of man."[6] His all-powerful Deity was finally construed to be in the service of man. It is almost as if God exists to glorify man; as if among all the stars and planets, the earth was the center of the divine interest; as if among all the forms of life on earth our species was the final object of the divine will and concern; as if among all the human beings who populate the earth God is supremely concerned about me. Calvin's perception of a powerful Deity, in whose "hands" is the ultimate destiny of all of us, and of all of the creation, has merit, and some things can be retrieved from it. But in the light of other things we know, a different construal of the Deity, and its relations to man and the world, is required.

Obviously I am not a scientist, and thus cannot defend one or another theory to which I appeal for a theological reconsideration of the place of man in the universe. I shall, however, offer a sketchy account, the main lines of which are defended by persons from various sciences, to make my point.

If the Big Bang theory of the origin of our universe is correct, it all began with a cosmic fireball some ten to fifteen billion years ago. (This is, of course, subject to revision by Professors Chandrasekhar, David Schramm, and our other colleagues in astrophysics!) The sun, indispensable for the development of the kind of life we have on this planet, and our planetary system probably began about four and one half billion years ago. Some scholars judge that the total history of our universe will be about sixty billion years, of which ten to fifteen have passed. If the universe ends in a gravitational collapse, that will probably occur billions of years after the end of our solar system. Our species will no longer be.

Life as we know it could not exist without carbon, oxygen, nitrogen, and phosphorous, which took billions of years to come into being. Within our planetary system, the earth is unique; it alone provides the conditions necessary for life to have developed as we know it. While all living organisms have the same complex chemical system (DNA and RNA), the development of the forms of life as we know them took place over millions of years during which countless forms failed

6. Calvin, *Institutes*, 1.14.22; 1:181–82.

to survive. The evidences for the development of our species continue to be found, and with increasing accuracy its biological evolution is being traced. Through natural selection have come the combinations of genes that have enabled present species, including our own, to survive. Relative to the time span of the universe, and even of our own solar system, our species, with its highly developed brain and nervous system, is a newcomer.

We have developed culture, which alters the immediacy of interactions between us and the natural forces that so long determined the course of development of nature. We can now intervene in nature in ways more dramatic than at any other time even in the brief residence of man on this little planet, minuscule in the "space" of the universe. We are the only species known to be able to gather the data and formulate the theories that give us knowledge of how some things really and ultimately are. But had a few developments been different in the history of our planetary system and in the survival of the mammalian strain among motile creatures, we would not be. Not only is human history but a speck in the span of time, but our continued existence depends on countless forms of interdependence of our planet with its system, and of our lives with the rest of the natural world.

It is understandable that members of our species have come to believe that all these developments have occurred for our sakes; that, as John Calvin put it with reference to the Genesis creation accounts, God did not bring us into being until he had prepared the earth with the necessities for our survival and flourishing.[7] It is obviously in our self-interest to believe such an interpretation. It is, indeed, highly geocentric and anthropocentric to think in these terms. It is very *un-theocentric* to think in these terms.

The British historian of science Herbert Butterfield (who was also a Methodist lay preacher) remarks on the change of perspective that seventeenth century science brought to the Western world. He notes that from many sources came support for a thesis found in Galileo's writings, "namely, the assertion that it is absurd to suppose that the whole of this . . . colossal universe was created by God purely for the sake of man, purely to serve the purposes of earth."[8] There is an implied indictment of Western theology in this observation; while no modern theologian defends a Ptolemaic view of the universe on scientific grounds, most theologians continue to support a geocentric and anthropocentric interpretation of the purposes of the Deity.

Ernst Troeltsch, in 1911, called attention to this matter in an essay on the significance of Jesus. He wrote, using the knowledge of his time, "Man's age upon earth amounts to several hundred thousand years or more. His future may come to still more. It is hard to imagine a single point of history along this line, and

---

7. Ibid., 1.14.13; 1:161–62.
8. Herbert Butterfield, *The Origins of Modern Science*, rev. ed. (New York: The Free Press, 1965), p. 69.

that the centre-point of our own religious history, as the sole center of humanity. That looks far too much like absolutizing our contingent area of life. That is
in religion what geocentrism and anthropocentricism are in cosmology and metaphysics. . . . We have only to think of past ice-ages which will presumably recur,
and the effects of the minutest polar variations and the rise and fall of great cultural systems, to judge the absolute and eternal position improbable."[9] In another
place Troeltsch calls theologians' attention to the import of modern views of the
universe with a chilling starkness: "At a certain point we emerged from development, at a certain point we will disappear again. . . . As the beginning was without us, so will the end also be without us."[10] It is not that the theologian draws
rigorous deductions from the scientific materials that sustain such views to a tight
doctrine of the Deity. It is the case, however, that what one says theologically cannot be incongruous with such sources; it is the case that the place of man in the
universe, ultimately determined by powers beyond our control, is not what the
dominant strand of Western theology has claimed. Whatever is said about God,
and God's relations to the world, must take account of such sources.

Indeed, Charles Hartshorne, to whose writings one normally does not turn
for prophetic insight, wrote, "There has been a secret poison long working in religious thought and feeling, the poison of man's self service, not genuinely his service to God."[11] What can be retrieved and sustained from the tradition is the view
of an all-powerful Deity who ultimately controls the destiny of the world; what
must be revised in the light of what we are coming to know about that power is
the view that all that is exists for our sakes.

Put starkly, and perhaps too homiletically for a university lecture, God does
not exist solely to secure the interests and purposes of man; God does not exist
to glorify man. The place of man within the governance of God must be reconsidered. A theological construal of how things really and ultimately are must take
account of other sources of knowledge. Piety will alter in the face of this interpretation of the powers that induce it; aspects of the historic tradition will be
abandoned and revised, and others, long neglected, will be retrieved.

To say something theological is to say something about how things really and
ultimately are. It is to be informed not only by a religious tradition's perceptions
and accounts about how things are, but also by human experience and by the sciences. It is also to be informed by piety. Even John Calvin could write, "I confess, of course, that it can be said reverently, provided that it proceeds from a
reverent mind, that nature is God."[12] His further qualification warns that this

9. From "The Significance of the Historical Existence of Jesus for Faith" in *Ernst Troeltsch: Writ-ings*, p. 189.
10. Ernst Troeltsch, *Glaubenslehre*, p. 64, trans. and quoted by B. A. Gerrish, in "Ernst Troeltsch and the Possibility of Historical Theology" in John Powell Clayton, ed., *Ernst Troeltsch and the Future of Theology* (Cambridge: Cambridge University Press, 1976), p. 117.
11. Charles Hartshorne, *The Divine Relativity* (New Haven: Yale University Press, 1948), p. 58.
12. Calvin, *Institutes*, 1.5.5; 1:58.

bold statement might lead to confusion between God and "the inferior course of his works." And about that he is also correct.

To say something theological is to say something ethical. Note: I did not say, "To say something ethical is to say something theological." I am not proposing that in order to be moral one must be religious. This would simply be false, empirically. Nor am I proposing that in order to have a coherent and defensible ethical theory one must have a theology. The very distinguished recent works of two of our colleagues in philosophy, Alan Donagan and Alan Gewirth, certainly demonstrate that cogent moral theories can be developed without theological foundations.[13] There are in these works in my opinion, some judgments about how some things really are, for example, the nature of human beings as agents and the nature of human action, but it would be false to call these theological judgments. The purpose of theology is not to prop up ethics any more than the reason for being religious is to motivate moral behavior.

If the theological task is to perceive and conceive what finite human beings can of the ultimate power and the powers that bring life into being, sustain it, and ultimately destine it, then the ethical task is to discern what these powers are enabling and requiring us to be and to do. If there are good reasons to doubt that God has ordered the world so that all things exist for our sake, then from a theological perspective, human activity must be set in a broader and more complex context of relationships than most Western ethics, religious or non-religious, usually interprets it. Man must be seen as a participant in a larger whole.

The patterns of interdependence of things on each other, which are in theological terms the patterns of the divine governance of all things, become the bases or grounds from which more precise and particular ethical norms and values are inferred. I mean to indicate not only the interdependence of persons with each other in human communities as small as family, and as large as nations. On these we base our principles of just distribution of goods and resources; our concern for the common good of communities that requires restraints of our individual interests; our proscription of undue interference in the lives of others, both individuals and communities, which guards against tyranny. I mean also to indicate the interdependence of our species with the rest of the world. On these we base our judgments of the right and wrong uses of air and water, of forests and minerals. I mean also to indicate the dependence of future generations on what we bequeath to them: not only how we pass on the world of nature, but what social arrangements and cultural benefits they inherit.

The distinctive biological capacities of our species which enable us to choose our purposes and to act, to intervene in nature, and to develop culture, enlarge our opportunities and deepen our obligations. Unlike plants we are not immediately

---

13. Alan Donagan, *The Theory of Morality* (Chicago: University of Chicago Press, 1977), and Alan Gewirth, *Reason and Morality* (Chicago: University of Chicago Press, 1978).

susceptible to the effects of our natural environments. Like the animals, we are motile, and can enlarge the range of our activities. Unlike other animals we use nature to create a complex culture, to develop the sciences, the arts, and technology. We can make choices and exercise various forms of power to give some direction to the course of historical events, and even to the course of the development of nature.

The familiar eighth Psalm reads: "What is man, that thou art mindful of him? and the son of man, that thou visitest him? For thou hast made him a little lower than the angels, and hast crowned him with glory and honour. Thou madest him to have dominion over the works of thy hands; thou hast put all things under his feet." This is usually heard as a celebration of our unique value; it should also be heard as a call to unique accountability to the divine governor of all things.

What one says ethically when one says something theological obviously depends upon how the divine governance is perceived and conceived. It depends upon what is judged to be the *telos*, the end, both of human life and of the whole of creation of which it is a part. The theological ethical task can be pursued with almost absolute certainty when it is believed that every entity in nature, including the human species, has an eternal form that establishes its uniqueness, and from which its proper end in the whole scheme of things can be determined. It can be pursued with almost absolute certainty when it is believed that there is a pre-ordained harmonious moral order of the whole of creation. If sexuality has a single end in the purpose of the Deity, procreation, then of course every act of sexual intercourse must be open to the transmission of new life, as Pope Paul argues.[14] If the end, the ultimate purpose, of society is calm and peace, then of course there must be an ordering of activity in society in which stability is preferable to mobility and change, in which repression for the sake of order is preferable to conflict for the sake of justice. If a hierarchy of being unequivocally establishes a hierarchy of value, and with the demise of belief in angels we are at the pinnacle, then of course all things can be used to serve human ends.

The theological ethical task is more difficult, however, when we can no longer be certain about the end, or purpose, of man and of the whole of the creation, and if we perceive that there is no pre-established harmony of ends and purposes into which our cultural and moral activities can be fitted with precision. The ultimate power and powers create conditions for new developments in nature, and in human activities that become our culture. But all is not openness, flux, and creativity; there are restraints within which we must act and live, not merely for the sake of human survival and well-being but also for the sake of a larger whole of things. We live in what theologians like to call the conditions of finitude— with limitations as well as achievements of knowledge; with restricted capacities

14. Paul VI, *Humanae Vitae*, in Joseph Gremillion, ed., *The Gospel of Peace and Justice: Catholic Social Teaching since Pope John* (Maryknoll, N.Y.: Orbis Books, 1975), pp. 427–44. The crucial sentence is, "Nonetheless the Church, calling men back to observance of the norms of the natural law, as interpreted by constant doctrine, teaches that each and every marriage act must remain open to the transmission of life" (p. 433).

to control the consequences of well-intended interventions into human lives, the ordering of society, and the processes of nature. While it is our obligation to act with as much knowledge and foresight as possible, there is no avoidance of risk and possible harm. While we can and must establish moral principles and values to direct and judge our actions, their applications will always need to be extended to meet new circumstances; exceptions will be made to them in some emergencies; and sometimes they may need to be revised.

I must leave far more unsaid than I can say here about what it means to claim that to say something theological is to say something ethical. And a theology is not a sufficient basis for ethics. But, briefly, and in religious language, the practical moral question in a theological context is: What is God, the divine governance, enabling and requiring us to be and to do? The abstract answer to the question is: We are to relate ourselves and all things in a manner appropriate to their relations to God. But we "see through a glass darkly"; we are deprived of the absolute theological, and therefore absolute moral certainty that we deeply desire. We are human, and God is God. There is no guarantee that the ends of the power which controls the destiny of the world are the ends we perceive to fulfill our human good. Again: God is the source, but not the guarantor of the human good. The chief end of God is not to glorify man. It may be that the chief end of man is to honor God by seeing the place of man in the whole of creation, and by conducting life accordingly.

"Gustafson, say something theological!"
"God."
For some of us, at least, there is a name for the power and powers that brought the universe, our solar system, and life into being; for the power and powers that sustain life as well as threaten it; that create the necessary conditions for all that makes life worth living, and, in whose "hands" is the destiny of all that is. That name is God.

God is worthy of our awe and respect. God deserves our gratitude and service.
And—God is worthy of our disciplined thought.
A biblical ascription, much favored by Jonathan Edwards, sums up both the object of theological investigation and the spirit in which it is best done. "To the King of ages, immortal, invisible, the only God, be honor and glory for ever and ever."[15]

15. 1 Timothy 1:17, RSV.

Chapter 7

Nature, Sin, and Covenant:
Three Bases for Sexual Ethics

Sexual behavior is undergoing rapid changes in Western societies, and with changes in behavior come revisions of prescriptive sexual ethics. Behavior that was judged immoral by many persons several decades ago is not widely considered so today. Prescriptive moralists have revised traditional rules of behavior; this is most notable in religious circles that explicitly or implicitly judged masturbation, homosexual activity, and pre- or extramarital intercourse wrong and now have found reasons to remove prohibitions or mitigate the sanctions against them. The impression that revisions of sexual ethics have followed changes in behavior cannot be avoided.[1] Not only have standards changed; historical studies have also been undertaken which show that pluralism of judgment has occurred throughout history on several issues, and thus historical relativity weakens the fibers of traditional absolute

1. A. Kosnick, W. Carroll, and A. Cunningham, *Human Sexuality: New Direction in American Catholic Thought* (New York: Paulist, 1977); J. B. Nelson, *Embodiment: An Approach to Sexuality and Christian Theology* (Minneapolis: Augsburg, 1978); L. S. Cahill, "Sexual Issues in Christian Theological Ethics: A Review of Recent Studies," *Religious Studies Review* 4 (1978): 1–14. Nelson could not argue against the propriety of incest (the only topic he omits) in certain circumstances; his grounds for justifying other forms of sexual conduct can also justify incest.

prohibitions.[2] Persons who have not subscribed to "anything goes" are searching for a few solid out-croppings on a slippery slope on which to take a stand.

This article does not develop any prescriptive sexual ethics, but rather argues that there are fundamental bases in human nature and experience which necessarily must be taken into account in any more precise reformulation of sexual morality. These are our "nature" as humans, both biological and "personal"; the phenomenon that Western religions have traditionally called sin; and the social character of human experience. It is the further argument of this article that these three bases were the experiential foundations of traditional Christian ethics of marriage, as I shall demonstrate from an early Anglican service, "The Form of Solemnization of Matrimony." Such a service, it is argued, states comprehensive vindicating reasons for prescriptions; it states the necessary conditions for human well-being and moral accountability in the conduct of sexual life. While the language of the service might seem archaic and the specific Christian references sectarian, its perceptions continue to be sound. My procedure is to state five basic theses, each of which is elaborated and which cumulatively make and sustain the argument as a whole.

I

Morality is an aspect of our human nature and experience; it expresses in personal conduct, in society, and in culture ways to order our natural impulses and to guide and govern our actions and relations for the sakes of individual and collective well-being. Moral questions are of two types: What actions and relationships are right and which are wrong? And what intended ends and what consequences of our actions are good and which are bad? This thesis is simply descriptive; its stress on nature and experience will have continuing importance as the argument develops.

Sexual morality, then, arises out of our nature and experience as sexual beings, and indeed, as human sexual beings. Different sexual moralities are the accepted and approved modes of sexual behavior among different social and cultural groups. Their basic purposes, however, are similar if not the same; that is, to avoid various harmful consequences and to achieve various beneficial ones and to make clear which actions are morally wrong, morally excusable, morally permissible, and morally right.

We become aware of moral issues when dissonance occurs between actual conduct and customary morality or well-known prescriptions of conduct. Doubts are raised about traditional codes of conduct as a result of different events: a minority that has "closeted" its behavior comes into the open and demands the end of

---

2. J. T. Noonan Jr., *Contraception: A History of Its Treatment by Catholic Theologians and Canonists* (Cambridge, MA: Harvard University Press, 1963); J. Boswell, *Christianity, Social Tolerance, and Homosexuality* (Chicago: University of Chicago Press, 1980).

moral and other sanctions; a new technology, such as contraceptive drugs, reduces the possibility of harmful consequences that have supported traditional restrictions. Through various means, persons become acquainted with modes of conduct alternative to those they have internalized through family, religious communities, and other formative institutions. In relatively intact moral cultures, various rules and symbols of the good life sustain a common interpretation of the moral and human significance of sexual behavior. Certain rules and symbols—such as "Thou shalt not commit adultery" and the monogamous conjugal family as a worthy and stabilizing institution—have wide acceptance, and so disagreement about what persons ought to do arises less frequently. But when dissonance occurs between custom and prescriptive morality on the one hand and the behavior and experience of persons on the other, questions of ethics become open.

The significance of this can be seen in other areas of human experience where experience and custom or prescriptive morality are still quite consonant with each other. In matters of property rights and truth telling, for example, while there are many and serious infractions, there is no serious dissent about what is morally right. Experience confirms the presumptive validity of the rules and values that govern our actions. To permit theft would be to the disadvantage of all; rules about property sustain a necessary reliability in human relations that is experientially confirmed and rewarding. To speak the truth on all occasions except those in which there are exceedingly critical reasons for not doing so, and to be able to expect others to do the same, establishes in experience a necessary trustworthiness in human relations. Life becomes much more efficient; we are relieved of the need to be constantly skeptical or cynical about others, and human relations generally are facilitated. To be sure, the infractions of custom and codes of conduct are numerous enough to require safeguards. We lock our doors and otherwise protect our property; we require oaths and witnessed and notarized signatures. But on the whole experience confirms the customs and the rules, and they ease the conduct of ordinary human relations.

The dissonance between prescriptive rules and moral ideals of sexual conduct and actual behavior has been a continuous problem in cultures influenced by Christianity. While the moral culture is less intact on these matters now than in some previous times, the issues are not novel. Ancient biblical legal and moral codes attend in some detail to the conduct of sexual life. For various historical and theological reasons, sex became a matter of preoccupation in Christianity as the source of the greatest human temptations. Many of the early fathers of the Christian church wrote treatises on virginity as a high religious and moral ideal, and if virginity could not be kept, continence was counseled. Augustine and others argued that the only morally proper intention for sexual relations was to reproduce.[3] The stringency of moral ideals and moral rules ran deeply counter to human biological impulses, heeds, and experience. This leads to a second thesis.

---

3. "For intercourse of marriage for the sake of begetting hath not fault; but for the satisfying of lust, but yet with husband and wife, by reason of the faith of the bed, it hath venial fault: but adultery or fornication hath deadly fault, and through this, continence from all intercourse is indeed better even than intercourse of marriage itself, which takes place for the sake of begetting." Augustine,

II

Prescriptive ethics, while they can be tested and evaluated in several ways, are subject to tests of human experience. Various philosophical tests can be made: Are they internally coherent? Do the principles rest on solid metaphysical or other foundations? Is there a rational procedure for applying principles to the factual premises of particular cases? They are, however, also subject to the tests of experience. Certainly in sexual ethics this thesis is descriptively true. Examination of the evidences adduced and the reasons given to support alterations in traditional sexual ethics in Christianity makes this clear. The evidences and the reasons are usually drawn from different understandings of the causes and the consequences of certain actions, that is, from different understandings of biological and other processes and of experience.

Arguments of this sort for change are commonplace in recent Christian literature on masturbation, homosexuality, and pre- and extramarital sexual intercourse. I will illustrate the point in reference to masturbation. The principle by which it was judged to be morally wrong in traditional Christian ethics is that it is an act contrary to nature. Recourse to arguments from nature has long and interesting histories in ethics; what was judged to be in accord with nature and thus morally right depended, obviously, on the interpretation of nature.[4] With regards to masturbation, nature had a double reference, biological and moral. Masturbation was judged to be contrary to the biological nature of sexuality since the natural end of sexuality was deemed to lead to union between male and female. Indeed, on this principle fornication was a less grave sin than masturbation, for while it was morally illicit it did conform to the biological nature of sexuality.[5] The moral nature of sexuality was greatly determined by biological nature. Masturbation was morally wrong because it was biologically disordered. Masturbation was judged to be a mortal sin; many adolescents in Western culture went through deep disturbances of conscience and incurred deep senses of guilt because of this moral and religious description of the act.

Contemporary changes in the moral assessment of masturbation invoke various aspects of human experience. Important Roman Catholic moral theologians of our time have given careful attention to this issue.[6] Recourse is taken to a statistical generalization about the experience of adolescents; masturbation is "normal," statistically at least, during this period of physical and psychological development. Statistical normality, of course, is not sufficient to warrant a change in a moral rule. For an act to be morally wrong the agent must be accountable for it; the question of the degree of accountability for masturbation then must be

---

On the Good of Marriage, in *The Nicene and Post-Nicene Fathers*, 1st ser., vol. 3, ed. P. Schaff (Grand Rapids: Eerdmans, 1956), 401. (Reprint of 1887 ed.)

4. Boswell, *Christianity, Social Tolerance, and Homosexuality*, chap. 11.

5. Thomas Aquinas, *Summa theologiae* 2a-2ae, q. 154, a.12.

6. Kosnick, Carroll, and Cunningham, *Human Sexuality*, pp. 219–20; C. E. Curran, *A New Look at Christian Morality* (Notre Dame, IN: Fides/Clarentian, 1968), pp. 201–21.

assessed. Accountability becomes qualified in the light of interpretations of adolescent sexuality that are drawn from biology, adolescent psychology, and other human sciences. The morality of actions is assessed also in the light of their consequences. Studies of human experience show that there have been deep adverse consequences as a result of the stringent prohibitions of masturbation. Harm to the agent is not severe, as was thought to be the case, and great psychological harm to many persons can be demonstrated as a result of the stringent prohibition. Thus evidences from human experience are adduced to warrant alteration of a traditional moral prohibition. Indeed, the "nature" of masturbation has been reinterpreted in the light of experience and scholarly evidences, and while it is not condoned as morally proper sexual activity, it is more readily excused.

Certain high ideals and moral prohibitions are deemed so contrary to human nature and experience that they cannot be universally applied. Adverse human consequences have occurred, and the force of the ideals and prohibitions is mitigated by a different explanation and interpretation of experience. If the rules are not altered they are ignored; excusing conditions for infractions are readily established. Prescriptive ethics are tested by experience.

III

Three aspects of our experience as sexual beings are taken into account in actual sexual moralities and, as I shall argue later, must be taken into account as bases for any revisions of prescriptive sexual ethics. First, sexuality is part of our biological and personal natures. About the first there can be no dispute; by personal, I mean to suggest that our sexuality relates to our senses of identity, of human worth and fulfillment, and so forth. Human sexuality is never merely biological. Second, our experience of sin, of human moral fault, is deeply related to our sexuality. "Sin" may sound like something that modern secular persons have passed by, particularly in sexual experience. We do, however, take it into account under other names, such as exploitation, harassment, and betrayal. Third, sexuality is related to our experience as social beings, and particularly to our need for covenants. Like sin, "covenant" is an old religious term, referring to such things as the implicit or explicit commitments we make to one another and the acceptance of accountability for one another. I elaborate on each of these below.

Sexuality is part of our natures. Sexual activity is always biological, but the reduction of its significance to the biological is never quite successful. In humans as well as some other animals, sexual intercourse has more than reproductive significance. It expresses affection in most instances; it can express rage and domination as well. The historic ethical issue in Western culture influenced by Christianity has rather persistently been fixed on the relationship between human sexuality as a biological phenomenon and as a personal phenomenon. In both Judaism and Christianity, there have been different normative opinions about the human ends of sexuality and about the morally appropriate means of sexual activity. John T. Noonan Jr. demonstrates that the ascendance of procreation as the chief end of marriage did not occur without dissent and qualification.[7] Rabbi David Feldman's magisterial study lines out the intricate differences of opinion about sexual ethics in the Jewish tradition, and studies of teachings on abortion also show differences.[8] Ethical teachings on sexuality clearly are efforts to aid persons in directing their natural impulses in ways that avoid various harms, sustain various aspects of human well-being, and are morally accountable. Natural impulses in sexual relations cannot be reduced to reproductive functions. Ethics of sexuality are based in some sense upon our natures, and part of the argument about what is proper conduct is about what constitutes our human natures. Confinement of morally licit sexual activity to the intention to reproduce was never successful because it ran counter both to biological and personal natures of humans. Bonds of human affection, of love, can lead to physical sexual activity, and physical sexual activity can nourish the bonds of human affection. Unless affection can be reduced to a purely biological explanation, ethics has to take into account our capacities as human persons. There are meanings and feelings involved which are significant for our senses of well-being, individually and in relation to each other. Humans are agents; they can intend and choose the ends of their activities, including their affections and meanings, and they can restrain their activities. Affection does not necessarily lead to physical sexual activity. While the desire for affection or love is not fully mastered by the powers of intellect and will, it is not a blind urge and impulse either. Our capacities as agents complicate human sexual activity in a way that reduction to impulses to reproduce does not.

How aspects of our nature as humans have been sorted out in prescriptive sexual ethics can be seen, once again, in Roman Catholic documents. Reproduction became the chief end of marriage and, as we have noted, for some theologians the only morally licit justification for sexual intercourse. In effect, the principal biological and moral meaning of sexuality was judged to be reproduction. Obviously, for centuries this prescriptive teaching could not restrain sexual intercourse to this purpose. This was recognized, for example, in the encyclical *Casti Connubii,* issued by Pope Pius XI.[9] But any approved relaxation of the teaching also had to be in accord with nature, again in a strictly biological sense. To play on terms, it was acknowledged that the nature of human persons led to sexual relations without the intention to reproduce, but the licit expression of this personal nature had to be governed by biological nature. Thus the outcome was that the restriction of sexual intercourse in marriage to periods of the natural infertility of the wife was approved. The use of contraceptive devices, however, was condemned because

7. For a summary of the medieval discussions, see Noonan, *Contraception,* p. 300.

8. David Feldman, *Birth Control in Jewish Law* (New York: New York University Press, 1967); J. T. Noonan Jr., "An Almost Absolute Value in History," in *The Morality of Abortion,* ed. J. T. Noonan Jr. (Cambridge, MA: Harvard University Press, 1970); J. Connery, SJ, *Abortion: The Development of the Roman Catholic Perspective* (Chicago: Loyola University Press, 1977).

9. Pius XI, *Casti Connubii,* in *Seven Great Encyclicals* (New York: Paulist, 1963; originally published 1930), par. 59, p. 93.

they were deemed to be unnatural—clearly meant in a strictly biological sense. This teaching was basically reaffirmed in the encyclical *Humanae Vitae,* issued by Pope Paul VI in 1968, which includes in its proscriptions the use of pharmaceutical means of fertility control.[10]

The strict teaching hinges on the relations of three aspects of what we can call human nature. The first is biological; the primary natural (and therefore moral) function of sexual intercourse is to reproduce, and the most morally appropriate intention for it is governed by this. A second aspect is a richer and more complex notion of our nature as persons who desire and need companionship, affection, and the richness of interpersonal bonds. This is acknowledged with some reluctance as being related to sexuality, and while this cannot morally determine the chief end of marriage, it is admitted as a secondary end of sexual intercourse. The nature of persons is somehow personal and interpersonal; they are not mere means of species reproduction. The third aspect is human capacities as agents, the capacities to choose ends and to govern desires by restraints of human will governed by intentions. This is a clue to the reason why artificial means of contraception are judged morally illicit. They block the biological process of the act on an unnatural basis and surrender a highly regarded aspect of persons, namely, their capacities to be self-determining agents, to control desire by an act of will.

The critics of this conservative and traditional teaching counter it with appeals to nature and experience. The fundamental basis of their arguments involves a redescription of the distinctive features of human nature. To be human is to be interpersonally related to another in a rich and meaningful way, as well as to reproduce. This aspect of human nature is so significant that its sexual sustenance and expression need not be confined to periods of female infertility. Personal nature overrides biologically reproductive nature. Thus, for the critics of the encyclicals, it is morally licit to use modern means of contraception. A redescription of human nature, a reordering of the importance of aspects of it, leads to a change in prescriptive ethics. But it is still based on our natures as sexual human beings. Although I shall not develop what from the official perspective are the moral sequelae of the modern position, it leads to a reconsideration of the traditional proscriptions on homosexual and extramarital sexual intercourse.[11] My point is that any revision of traditional prescriptive sexual ethics involves a different understanding of our experience and nature as sexual beings.

The second aspect of experience can be indicated by an old-fashioned religious word, "sin." Theologians have always adduced evidence from experience in mounting arguments about a human fault. The fundamental character of the fault and the forms of misconduct that manifest it have been matters under debate. Disobedience to traditional rules is only one of its forms. In the early phases of the

---

10. Paul VI, *Humanae Vitae,* in *The Gospel of Peace and Justice: Catholic Social Teaching since Pope John,* ed. J. Gremillion (Maryknoll, NY: Orbis, 1975).

11. Kosnick, Carroll, and Cunningham, *Human Sexuality,* pp. 152–69, 186–218; J. G. Milhaven, *Toward a New Catholic Morality* (Garden City, NY: Doubleday, 1970), pp. 59–68; C. E. Curran, *Catholic Moral Theology in Dialogue* (Notre Dame, IN: Fides/Clarentian, 1972), pp. 184–219.

recent sexual liberation it appeared that sexual behavior had to be emancipated from repressive notions of sin that were thrust on persons by rigid proscriptions. The idea of sin seemed responsible for the sense of guilt that many persons incurred. This experience of liberation from rules is no doubt repeated by persons even in later phases of the sexual revolution. We have come to see, however, that liberation exposes persons to sexual exploitation, often an exploitation that formerly was protected against by rules. One does not need arcane explanations of the phenomenon of sin to recognize its presence in human sexual experience.

"Exploitation" and "harassment" are terms currently most used to describe the sins of human sexual conduct. They both refer to what is close to one of the most profound traditional meanings of immorality—to use another person for purely selfish ends, to fail to recognize that respect is due another person as a human agent with capacities to determine his or her own sense of purpose and well-being. It is to make another instrumental to one's own end, and to manipulate others to consent to fulfilling that end. The other becomes an object rather than a person. Sexuality, like other aspects of human relations, is deeply subject to exploitation, and exploitation of others is immoral.

Another aspect of the human fault is the propensity to deceive others. Being deceived no doubt leads to some of the deepest resentments that persons experience. We know this from human speech; profound human relations are ruptured by evidence that someone we trusted has deceived us by lying, for example. Sexual relations are no less occasions for deception. Tacit or explicit commitments to some forms of human faithfulness induce consent to sexual relations and often are not made in good faith, so expectations of the trustworthiness and loyalty of others are violated, which leads to resentment. It is not only that vows and promises are broken, it is that persons whom we trusted have violated our confidence in them. Betrayal is closely related. Loving relationships are highly vulnerable to betrayal; they involve an offering of one to another in many ways (not just sexually); they involve a deep confidence in the trustworthiness of another. When that trust is violated, deep senses of disaffection, resentment, and alienation occur. The intimacy and multifaceted meanings of sexual relations as expressions of self-offering to another—as expressions of love—are delicately subject to deception and betrayal.

The experience of sin in sexual relations does not wither away even for those who are emancipated from restrictive rules of conduct. Indeed, the deeper bases of some of the rules become exposed in painful ways: exploitation, harassment, and betrayal of trust. Any revision of prescriptive sexual ethics has to take into account these human propensities and faults.

A third aspect of human experience that has to be taken into account in any sex ethics is that of covenants. I use the term to refer to the commitments persons make to one another, implicit ones that are subject to deception and self-deception and exploitation, and explicit ones such as marriage vows. It refers to acceptance of accountability for one another and for the consequences of our human relations, including sexual ones. Some forms of commitment emerge from our interpersonal relations, including sexual, and are necessary for the conduct of them. In part they follow from love and affection and thus are nourished. In part they follow from the distinctive bonding that brings sometimes vague and sometimes precise obligations to one another. Covenants arise out of our experience as sexual beings and can foster our human well-being; they are not merely heteronomous, extrinsic contracts forced on persons by state or church. They, like other aspects of sex ethics, are based in human nature and experience.

An interesting bit of the history of Christian ethics illustrates the significance of covenants. A debate about Christian marriage ethics in the sixteenth and seventeenth centuries between Anglicans and Puritans was conducted in part over the primacy of two texts from Genesis.[12] In Genesis 1:28, God says to Adam and Eve, "Be fruitful and multiply, and fill the earth and subdue it. . . ." This was the Anglican emphasis. In Genesis 2:18, God says, "It is not good that the man should be alone; I will make him a helper fit for him." This was the Puritan emphasis. The primacy of the first makes reproduction the chief end of marriage, of the second, an interpersonal relationship or covenant. Both are based on our natures as humans.

Covenants are not "contrary to nature." They are based on a profound human need: the need to be related to another over time in such a way that the well-being of each and the well-being of both together are sustained. They provide conditions of mutual trust and confidence, of reliability in relationships, and explication of duties and obligations that are essential to human well-being. To be sure, they are also "dikes against sin"; in explicit contracts they guard against betrayal and exploitation. But they arise out of and express personal (and not merely sexual) fidelity and thus sustain mutual love. Within the allegiances of covenants persons are freed from certain anxieties, and human relations can flourish. To be sure, covenants do not guarantee mutual love; their meaning can wither, and they can be broken. Keeping covenants requires a process of what Gabriel Marcel calls "creative fidelity," of alteration and development through changes over time. There are often good reasons for breaking them, especially in modern societies. But on such occasions stress nonetheless occurs in those who undergo ruptures of covenanted relationships.

Covenants of some sort, implied or explicit, are functional requisites of satisfactory human sexual relations. They are not extrinsic, heteronomous impositions forced upon persons by arbitrary authorities with oppressive and repressive intentions. They are based upon human experience, biological, social, and personal.

IV

The traditional prescriptive sexual ethics of our culture are based on comprehensive vindicating reasons that continue to be valid. (The general points hold not

12. J. T. Johnson, *A Society Ordained by God: English Puritan Marriage Doctrine* (Nashville: Abingdon, 1970).

only for Christian tradition but others as well.) These vindicating reasons ground prescriptions for the forms of conduct and human relations that are necessary for human well-being and for moral accountability of persons to each other.

The profoundest bases and reasons for traditional rules and relations are quite unassailable. Historically, of course, the rules certainly have sometimes not been congruent with their vindicating reasons, and have often been counterproductive to their proper ends. Any revisions of sexual ethics will have to be based on nature and experience in the way that traditional ethics have been and will have a similar, if not the same, basic purpose: to sustain well-being and to develop the conditions of moral accountability (which is also necessary for well-being).

I shall establish this thesis by commenting on a very old marriage service from the Church of England.[13] Space does not permit full commentary on all aspects of the service, but brief comment on its major parts is in order:

1. Publication of the banns on Sundays prior to the service. The intent is sound, namely, to inquire whether there are serious impediments to the marriage becoming a reasonably satisfactory one.
2. The address to the congregation gathered for the service. On this portion I develop an extended commentary below.
3. The question to the couple inquiring about any impediments they might know; this is a public acknowledgment of their own conscientiousness in undertaking a time-binding commitment.
4. Questions to each of the couple, stating agreed-upon conditions for a reasonably good relationship: love, comfort of one another, giving honor or respect to each other, caring for each other in sickness and adversity, and a pledge of personal fidelity to one another.
5. The giving of the bride (which could be reasonably extended to a similar rite for the groom). This recognizes a break between the generations and announces a set of new, independent, accountable relations. It marks the transition of both persons from their families of procreation to a new nuclear relationship. There is social and moral wisdom in this rite.
6. The vows. These articulate the assumed obligations that express love and are conditions for its sustenance: to have and to hold, for better or worse, for richer or poorer, in sickness and in health, to love and to cherish. Note that there is an obligation to love, to sustain the creative and fulfilling wellsprings of a relationship.
7. The giving and receiving of rings, a publicly visible, nonverbal expression of mutual love and commitment.

At the end of the service comes an appropriate prayer, the blessing of the marriage, a declaration of marriage in the name of church and state, and the final

---

13. The Form for Solemnization of Matrimony, *The Book of Common Prayer* (Oxford: Oxford University Press, n.d.).

benediction. All of this is a public occasion; it recognizes the relatedness of the couple to a wider public and, in religious terms, to God.

This service, while it has archaic language and specific references to Christian beliefs and to God, nonetheless has its deepest vindication in the necessary bases for appropriate, intimate, and time-binding relations between man and woman. The precise formulations of vows and rules do not necessarily follow from the general vindicating reasons. There are, and can be, other precise expressions of the bases of this service, and clearly there are occasions on which covenants can be justifiably broken, when the stringent vows in this and other services are over-ridden. The main point is this: Traditional marriage services are authorized by bases in biological and personal nature, in human fault to which all persons are susceptible, and in the need for some form of covenant. The moral wisdom in the deepest reasons for traditional sexual ethics has not been superseded.

The address to the congregation assembled for the service illustrates these points more precisely. I choose selectively from the words read by the priest, words often parodied as they fall from the lips of silly otherworldly clergymen in movies and television shows and spoken with repulsive unctuousness. The address begins with the familiar, "Dearly beloved." After authorizations drawn from biblical materials, the priest says about marriage, "Therefore, [it] is not by any to be enterprised, nor taken in hand, unadvisedly, lightly, or wantonly, to sat-isfy men's carnal lusts and appetites, like brute beasts that have no understand-ing; but reverently, discreetly, advisedly, soberly, in the fear of God, duly considering the causes for which Matrimony was ordained."

The sobriety of this passage ignores the joys, satisfactions, and delights of rela-tions between a man and a woman. Its sobriety probably does not register in many auditors because of its familiarity, or because weddings are celebrative occa-sions. Perhaps the church thought that joys and delights came naturally enough and occupied itself with the moral conditions realistically necessary for a good and lasting relationship—thus, the tone of sobriety.

The passage properly and vividly calls attention to the morally serious quality of relations between a man and a woman. There is evidence, not adduced, that the depth and profundity of the relations are such that they ought not to be undertaken lightly; that those who undertake them without due consider-ation often suffer consequences that harm human well-being and denigrate human worth. There may be an implied forecast that those who enter into a relationship soberly and reverently are more likely to have a satisfactory one, in many ways.

One phrase in this passage has been dropped from the modern version, per-haps because it sounds indelicate to socially respectable ears. Marriage is not "to satisfy men's carnal lusts and appetites, like brute beasts that have no understand-ing." The good evidence for dropping the passage is that it reflects an exaggerated difference between beasts and humans that is deep in our culture, and that sexual relations among animals, while they "have no understanding," are better regulated than those among humans.[14] A dramatic point, however, is made. It shows the possibilities of sexual exploitation even within marriage, most dramatically occurring in rape within marriage, but also in the use of persons purely for gratification of sexual drives without regard to their personal natures. The meaning of sexual relations cannot be reduced to the satisfaction of "carnal lusts and appetites."

The service speaks of the ends of marriage. "First, it was ordained for the procreation of children to be brought up in the fear and nurture of the Lord. . . ." This recognizes the species' biological function of sexuality—reproduction—but also indicates a concern for responsible parenthood. The prescription for responsible parenthood, "the fear and nurture of the Lord," is not a sufficient guide for most modern persons and is for many no guide at all. It does indicate, however, that procreation does not have as its exclusive end the survival of the species. It has other ends, as in the nurture of children—caring, nourishing bodies and spirits, educating, loving, fulfilling natural duties toward them, restraining parental self-interests for their sakes at times—as well as enjoying their presence. Reproduction is a morally and humanly serious undertaking. It brings rich opportunities that are fulfilling and responsibilities that are not "to be taken in hand, unadvisedly, lightly, or wantonly" but "reverently, advisedly, and soberly."

"Secondly, it was ordained for a remedy against sin, and to avoid fornication: that such persons as have not the gift of continency might marry. . . ." This reflects the Pauline injunction that it is better to marry than to burn and is not persuasive to most persons in our culture. The "sin" that occupies current attention is not fornication per se, but the human fault, as I have indicated, is still expressed in sexual relations. A covenant of marriage, or any other covenant between persons, does not eradicate the fault. But covenants do establish conditions of accountability of man and woman to each other; they state the conditions of mutual trustworthiness and respect. These conditions are not repressions of individual freedom but bases for mutual trust and respect whose fruits are their own kind of inner freedom and security.

"Thirdly, it was ordained for mutual society, help, and comfort, that one ought to have of the other, both in prosperity and adversity." This reflects Gen. 2:18, the "helper" passage, and is an aspect of marriage more celebrated in some Victorian novels (such as Trollope's *Three Clerks*) than in any contemporary ones. Man and woman need each other; their relations are mutually supportive in more than biological ways. This may have particular poignancy in our time, when many persons believe that to acknowledge mutual need and comfort is a sign of human weakness and that the only truly beautiful and good relations are those that flow out of a superabundance of individual ego-strengths. To be sure, the "mutual society" end of marriage is open to personal exploitation; just as one is tempted to use one's friends, so one can use one's partner. It is the case, however,

14. M. Midgley, *Beast and Man: The Roots of Human Nature* (Ithaca, NY: Cornell University Press, 1978), pp. 39, 45.

that it profoundly recognizes the social character of human existence, the need to be related to another over time, to be sustained by another and to sustain another. Covenants express the nature of our humanity.

V

There is more moral wisdom in the religious traditions than many persons are ready to admit, and any new formulation of more precise prescriptive sexual ethics under changed conditions must take into account the vindicating reasons grounded in human nature and experience that the tradition recognizes. Any revised sexual ethics must recognize these bases. Sexual ethics need not be oppressive and repressive; they can establish more precise conditions necessary for human well-being and for mutual accountability that restrain exploitation and enable life to flourish.

A theological coda: Sexual ethics are based upon our nature and experience as humans. We can be sure, for example, that if the ratio of male to female births was 1:3 rather than nearly 1:1 monogamy would never have been judged to be morally normative. Nature does not provide a detailed moral blueprint for sexual ethics; it is too dynamic and diverse in its potentialities to become the sole basis for determining ethics. But ethics provide ways of ordering and governing our biological and personal natures, and the relationship between these two is more one of continuity than many moralists have been willing to recognize. Put in religious terms, there is no divine moral order that can simply be read off of nature from which to formulate detailed prescriptive sexual ethics. But there are necessary conditions that must be recognized, accepted, and met for the sake of human well-being. In this sense the religious consciousness can speak of a divine governance and ordering of life. Violations of certain conditions lead to human difficulties; acknowledgment of them can limit the difficulties and enhance human flourishing. Inferences drawn from these conditions will differ, relative to particular times and places, particular cultures, and natural conditions. In our time and culture there is great uncertainty about what the precise ordering of sexual relations ought to be. But this does not eliminate the necessity of the conditions, the bases for prescriptive sexual ethics. These necessary conditions cannot be ignored or defied without pain and harm, though acknowledgment of them does not guarantee happiness. Put homiletically, God will be God, and not, in the end, defied. Man must be man and take accountability for the more precise ordering of sexual relations, always in dependence on an ordering and governance that is given and not humanly created.

Chapter 8

Nature: Its Status
in Theological Ethics

The theme of this conference is "Biomedical Ethics: A Christian Perspective." The larger theme, running through the series of annual conferences is "Philosophical Issues in Christian Perspective." The title of my paper indicates that I shall address an issue that pertains both to biomedical ethics, and to the larger topic of the series of conferences.

The thesis of this paper is as follows. Modern Protestant theology, and therefore theological ethics as well, has been in focus almost exclusively on history, rather than nature, as the realm of divine activity and presence. Process theology is the major exception to this. Insofar as the biomedical ethics of modern Protestants has been theologically self-conscious, it has had difficulty in bringing "nature" as a source of norms into the ethical discussions. Insofar as it has not been theologically self-critical it has simply assumed that biomedical ethics has to be addressed from bases that do not rely upon indications from nature very heavily or directly. This has affected both the substance and the procedures of Protestant ethics. This tendency is theologically at fault, and ethically inadequate.

Roman Catholic biomedical ethics has traditionally been based on natural law theory. Nature has had, in the classic Roman Catholic tradition, theological status and a moral significance that certainly stands as a corrective to Protestant theology. Nature is the penultimate source, the mind of God being the ultimate, of knowledge of the proper ends of human interventions, and of the principles and rules that are to govern them. Roman Catholic moral theology has been able to provide great certitude in its judgments about biomedical matters because of its confidence that there is a telos in nature, and that various entities, including man, have essences that form their matter, and that fit their functions in the larger scheme of things. Happily, for our species, on the whole, all the rest of nature is seen to be in our service. A combination of theological and philosophical principles gives assurance that the fulfillment of man is a normative end of nature; certainty about this grounds traditional Roman Catholic biomedical ethics. There are good reasons, however, to question whether man is so exclusively the center of divine intention as this tradition believes. If these beliefs are no longer defensible, scientifically, philosophically, and theologically, the ethics they back are subject to significant criticism.

If Protestant ethics is at fault for not developing a theology of nature, and thus not providing sufficient theological background for biomedical ethics, and Roman Catholic theology is at fault in its interpretation of nature, theologically and ethically, the question to be addressed somewhat systematically is that of the status of nature in theological ethics. The final purpose of this paper is to note at least some lines of an answer to that question, and to suggest some of the inferences that can be drawn for ethics. The fuller development that is needed occurs in other of my current writing.

PROTESTANT THEOLOGY AND MEDICAL ETHICS

Few Protestant theologians who have written comprehensive and systematic accounts of theology have addressed issues of medical ethics; Karl Barth is the major exception to this, and in his remarks on these matters he does not get down to the hardest cases. His principal line of criticism is not so immediately ethical as it is religious and theological; he worries most about man usurping the place of God in determining what ought to be done, using human values and principles to decide. That he has a strong "pro-life" position is clear, whether on abortion, euthanasia or on matters of capital punishment and war. The word of grace is "Thou mayest live"; that is known not from nature but from the revelation of God's grace in Jesus Christ.[1]

Many Protestant theologians, however, have had a great deal more to say about "historical" events; political, economic, social and other circumstances are frequently addressed. Theological backing for this has varied, but one principal aspect of it has been the conviction that God "acts in history," and for many modern theologians this is substantiated by biblical interpretation that makes history dominant over nature as the arena of the divine presence. A related factor is personalism as a way of delineating God and God's relations to the world. A per-

---

1. Karl Barth, *Church Dogmatics*, III/4 (Edinburgh: T. and T. Clark, 1961), pp. 397–470.

sonal, or "interpersonal" view of the divine in relation to the world stresses that God is "an autonomous agent, capable of free acts (not merely, 'activity')," as Gordon Kaufman states the case.[2] The alternative to this is what Kaufman calls a "teleological" view of transcendence, which is developed in a theology of being, and which then views human life in a cosmic order that reduces its significance as historical, i.e., as being in the image of God as an autonomous agent capable of free acts. (Kaufman's view of God is Kant's view of a moral agent—writ large.) "Historical," then, has two referents: the arena of God's activity is history more than, or even rather than, nature; and a stress on history features both the divine and human capacities for radically free agency.[3]

If history is the primary arena of divine activity, and history is contingent and susceptible to change of course as a result of human choice, and if this entails less significance to nature as the arena of divine sovereignty, then theological ethics has to work out its principles in a way coherent with these basic themes. This might well predispose Protestant theology toward thinking ethically about historical events rather than those more dominated by physical and biological processes. It might predispose Protestant ethics to a basic Kantianism in its philosophical correlates, and thus in medical ethics to a bias against natural law. Since so few major systematic theologians have developed the implications of their theologies for ethics, however, we are left only to conjecture how theologies focused on history would back ethical theories, and these in turn back particular judgments about biomedical matters.

Few Protestant theologians who are interested in medical ethics have systematically and comprehensively addressed issues of theology. Indeed, it is quite safe to assert that for many Protestants who write about medical ethics, the word "Protestant" is more a social denominator than a theological adjective. They are interested in medical ethics, and happen to be Protestants. Paul Ramsey comes near to being an exception to this generalization, since his first book, *Basic Christian Ethics*, continues to be, thirty years after its first publication, a more coherent account of the theological bases of ethics than most others available.[4] Whether Ramsey can ground his subsequent concentrated work on medical ethics in the theology of that text is a matter of interpretation and dispute. That he has not undertaken anything in recent years of a similar scope is clear. This is not to fault him, since his contributions have been continuous and important in the areas in which he has written. Such specific signs as we have of the bases of his recent work, however, tend to bear out my contention that his theology is not concentrated on nature. His use of "covenant," a social metaphor, is adapted from Barth's basically interpersonal symbols for both the relation of God and man and human relations.[5] His use of *agape* as the basic Christian truth that is to be "in-principled" certainly

2. Gordon D. Kaufman, *God the Problem* (Cambridge, Mass.: Harvard Univ. Press, 1972), p. 78.
3. For a very interesting account of how "nature" has important effects on "historical" developments, see William H. McNeill, *Plagues and Peoples* (Garden City, N.Y.: Anchor Press, 1976).
4. Paul Ramsey, *Basic Christian Ethics* (New York: Scribners, 1950).
5. Paul Ramsey, *The Patient as Person* (New Haven: Yale Univ. Press, 1970), pp. xii–xiii.

comes from the historical revelation, and is not drawn from nature.[6] In my judgment, while he is enamored by certain facets of natural law theory, and has been
involved in almost interminable disputes with Richard McCormick about how
certain procedures of natural law ethics are to be used,[7] he has never undertaken
to defend natural law in its ontological or metaphysical dimensions, that is, those
that postulate some things about nature, per se.

These generalizations will have to stand for our purposes, without further
embellishment, substantiation by textual evidences, or nuanced qualifications. So
will my important inferences drawn from them, namely that Protestant biomedical ethics has had a predilection for developing relatively formal procedures
for dealing with particular issues, and insofar as they have substance it tends not
to be drawn from efforts to grasp the moral significance of natural processes. It
is not accidental, theologically, that Protestants in medical ethics have gravitated
toward Kantianisms, toward analytical moral philosophies, and toward making
procedures the substance of medical ethics. The neo-Kantian distinction between
facts and values, and the British and American literature on the is-ought question, have been bulwarks of defense against attempting to draw some moral
norms from the observations and theories of nature. If the bias toward procedures
has not grasped them, they can readily slip into a relatively uncritical utilitarianism, or consequentialism, as is the case of the celebrated Joseph Fletcher.[8]

One can ask Protestant theology, What happened to the divine sovereignty
over nature? As a historical question about theological developments we cannot
take time to offer answers here. But if God is in any sense controlling or ordering nature—from the creation of the universe to its prospective demise, from the
simplest forms of life to the complexity of the human organism—how can theological ethics avoid nature? If there is sound evidence that while we have capacities for action, they are grounded in not only our biomedical natures but also
sustained by the relationship between human life and other aspects of nature,
how can Protestant theology and ethics ignore nature? How can it be preoccu-
pied with history? Do Protestant theology and ethics not have to take into
account the insight expressed by John Calvin, "I confess, of course, that it can be
said reverently, provided that it proceeds from a reverent mind, that nature is
God."[9] While we ought not to confuse God with his "inferior works," as Calvin
goes on to warn, is it still not the case that nature has a status in the divine governance that theologically requires it to become one basis for theological ethics?
And, if this is the case, will this not require that the ordering of nature be more
significant in Protestant medical ethics? Should not Catholic hearts and minds

6. Paul Ramsey, "Faith Effective Through In-Principled Love," *Christianity and Crisis* 20 (1960):
76–78.

7. Richard McCormick and Paul Ramsey, eds., *Doing Evil to Achieve Good* (Chicago: Loyola Univ.
Press, 1978), is the culmination of the dispute, I hope!

8. Joseph Fletcher, *Situation Ethics* (Philadelphia: Westminster Press, 1966).

9. John Calvin, *Institutes of the Christian Religion* 1.5.5, 2 vols., ed. John T. McNeill, trans. Ford
Lewis Battles (Philadelphia: Westminster Press, 1960), 1:58.

rejoice, since they have consistently been insisting on something similar for centuries? Yes, but not too heartily, or for too long.

TRADITIONAL ROMAN CATHOLIC THEOLOGY
AND MEDICAL ETHICS

If we grant the theological principle of ultimate sovereignty of the ultimate power, God, then nature is at least as important a source for understanding the divine ordering as is history. If ethics are to be theological, one way in which the divine governance is perceived and conceived is in the ordering of nature. From a theological standpoint, then, a tradition which accepts these principles is more adequate than one, whether for "biblical" or philosophical reasons, which tends to interpret history as the exclusive, or at least most important, arena of divine activity. For purposes of this paper, then, two questions become very important. How is nature perceived and conceived? And, how does the concept of nature function in the ethics of a particular tradition? If a historical point can be granted, namely that the theology and philosophy of Thomas Aquinas have been the foundations of Roman Catholic ethics, it is proper to ask how these two questions are answered in that work.

How is nature perceived and conceived? My understanding of Thomas's answer to this question is as follows. The starting point for the process is quite empirical. Our first apprehension is of specific objects—trees, rocks, and human beings, for examples. A process of reflection occurs in which abstractions are developed from these specific observations. In this process certain distinctions are drawn, the major one being between substance and accidents. A child appears different from a mature person, but both share something that persists through change and distinguishes them as human, and different from dogs and trees. In the realm of the human, then, there is that which changes over time, and there are different particular characteristics of different persons, but there is the substantial form of the human; it is this that enables us to be classed in our species. Whatever that form is gives us knowledge of the essence of the human; this essence determines the qualities of our particularity to a significant degree. This essence is actualized in the existence of particular human beings; it acts to order and to direct the potentialities that are the matter we empirically observe in such a way that we can distinguish the class called human, for example, from the class called simians. From this the conclusion is drawn that there is an essence of the human, as there is an essence of the simian; there is a basically accurate interpretation, the key feature is what some have controversially called the "essentialism" which Thomas has taken over from Aristotle.

Before we continue to give Thomas's answers to our two questions, the critical question that will form the third part of this paper can be foreshadowed. What happens if, on the basis of observation, reflection and abstraction—and with the aid of modern sciences—we can no longer affirm that there is an essence of the human in Thomas's sense? What happens to the ethics that presupposes such an essence?

Before we get to such critical questions, however, it is necessary to describe how this "essentialism" functions in the ethics of Thomas. The essence of the human is our rational capacities. Other capacities we share with much of the animate world, such as appetites for food or for sexual activity. For purposes of this paper it is not necessary, I believe, to develop Thomas's conception of rationality, or as I prefer to say, his conception of human capacities for rational activity. But a bit more description of the human is required. All things in creation are ordained toward ends; there are biological ends so that our appetite for food directs us to the activity of eating, and there is an end that is distinctive to the human. That end of the human is happiness. This also is known on the basis of observations of human activity, reflection on them, and abstraction from them, as Aristotle makes clear in the *Nicomachean Ethics*. Given Thomas's theological purpose, he distinguishes between temporal happiness as attainable in this life, and perfect beatitude which is the vision of God, the very essence of goodness. The link between the perception and conception of the essence of the human, rationality, and the end of the human, happiness, is critical for Thomas's ethics.

If the description of the essence of man did not include, or was not in any significant way linked with, the end of man, a very different pattern of ethics could emerge. For a contrast we can hypothetically posit that what distinguishes the human is its developed brain and nervous system, and that there is no ultimate end that governs the ways in which the activity of this system is conducted. If this were the case, reflection on the "essence" of the human would give no particular or reliable clues as to how moral activity should be conducted. Ethics would have to come from somewhere else than "nature." Or again by contrast, let us suppose some theologian comes along who avers that there is something accurate about Thomas's description of the substantial form of the human, but that this has become totally perverse. Ethics then has to come from somewhere else than "nature" because Thomas did not take fully into account in his description of actual human nature the effects of the Fall.

A further aspect of Thomas's account of nature has to be brought into the picture to answer the question of how nature functions in ethics: the relationship between human nature and other aspects of the created world of which the human is a part. I believe one can say that Thomas's answer to Jonathan Edwards's question "concerning the end for which God created the world" is ultimately Edwards's answer, namely to glorify himself. If this is the case, then all created things somehow function not individually, but in their relations to each other to the glory of God. The questions to be asked are these: Is there a purposive order of the relations of all things to each other, and what is the place of man in that purposive order if there is one? My reconstruction of Thomas's answers is as follows. The answer to the first question is affirmative, and it is backed by evidences adduced in part from observations of objects in relation to each other, or reflections on these observations, and principles abstracted from this process. This can be illustrated from a limited area of the "creation," namely the human. Persons are related to each other in such a way that one has to take into account not only what brings them happiness as individuals, but also how their relations to each other affect the common good of a community. The good of the "whole," which is not simply the aggregate of the happiness of individuals, needs to be realized in part, if not totally, for the sake of the happiness of individuals. There is a purpose to the way persons are related to each other. This is not based simply on an abstract metaphysical theory, but on observation of and reflection on particular communities.

But what about the relationships between the human and the rest of the created order? Again, I believe, observation, reflection and abstraction are involved. There appears to be a purpose in these relations which dictates that the "lower" is in the service of the "higher." These terms are interesting, and obviously used metaphorically here; they entwine both descriptive and value judgments. The criterion for judging, it seems to me, is anthropocentric; humans are "descriptively" higher because of their rational capacities, and this makes them higher in the scale of values. Thus, while the ultimate end of "all things" is to glorify God, the penultimate end of all things is to be in the service of man; and, I take it, to be in the service of the essence and end of man. Put in terms used in moral theology, while the relations between man and the rest of the creation are such that it might appear that the "totality" of the creation backs the end of glorifying God, this is in fact not the case. Man, and individual persons, are totalities whose ends warrant pre-eminence of value.

This has quite immediate implications for some areas of medical ethics. For example, while the common good of a social unit like the family is an end to be considered, the family does not function as a morally significant totality when its common good is judged to warrant the abortion of a fetus whose coming to term will in high probability (though not with certainty) create havoc to the conditions necessary for the well-being of the family as a whole. For example, the "well-being" of large numbers of our species is threatened because the human interrelatedness with other aspects of the natural world upsets the prospects of sufficient nutrition; this is not a sufficient reason to warrant moral approval of artificial means of contraception. Not only is the penultimate purpose of the rest of nature to be in the service of humans, but because of the essence and telos or end of man, the value of the individual human is not to be overridden by concerns for a larger "totality." There are exceptions, of course. Thomas's discussion of taking the life of a sinner is interesting and important. On the basis of an analogy with the human body and the right to remove a diseased organ, it is licit to remove a threat to the community under specified conditions; also such a person has been so far deflected from realizing the human essence that he is no longer classed as human, and thus life can be taken.[10]

The general point that I believe is sustained is this: A concept of nature, and especially human nature, but also the relations between the human to other aspects

10. Thomas Aquinas, *Summa theologiae*, 2a-2ae, q. 64, a. 2.

of nature, is the crucial basis of traditional Roman Catholic ethics. That concept includes a judgment about the proper ends, which obviously is also crucial. And here is the critical question for this paper. These concepts are based on observations of, reflections on, and abstractions from the world we apprehend with our senses. What happens if, in modern culture, our observations, reflections, and abstractions lead to different conclusions? About man, about man's place in the universe, about whether there is a purpose, or at least a dominant purpose or end in creation? Roman Catholic ethics has been theologically correct in heavily basing its judgments about, what I prefer to call, the divine governance on nature. Since those judgments are based on observation, reflection, and abstraction from human experience, the interpretation of nature is critical when an ethics is backed by, or warranted by such an interpretation. Thus a different description and interpretation of nature leads to different conceptions of the divine governance. And if, theologically, ethics is grounded in the divine governance, different judgments both about more general matters and sometimes about particular issues, including medical ones, will follow. Only if the ethics of natural law are deductions from some a priori theological principles of even greater generality is it free from alteration that will occur with different description and interpretation of nature.

We have come thus far, in the argument of this paper. Traditional Roman Catholic theology is more adequate than modern Protestant theology because it attends much more seriously to the divine sovereignty over nature. It also then goes on to describe and interpret nature in such a way that nature provides clues to the divine governance of the creation. But, there are good reasons to question whether the interpretation of nature that backs Catholic moral theology and medical ethics can be sustained. To those reasons we now turn.

REINTERPRETATION OF NATURE

In the light of some modern knowledge from various sciences of nature, including human life, three questions are pertinent. 1) Is there an essence to the human (or to other species of life, for that matter) in the sense that Catholic "essentialism" has defended? 2) Is there an end not only of human activities but of other aspects of creation that can be clearly defined? 3) Is the assumed anthropocentric interpretation of man's relation to the rest of the creation correct? I believe that as theologians and ethicians we have to reconsider traditional answers to these questions. While what is said about the divine governance cannot simply be deductions from modern interpretations of nature drawn from various sciences, what we do say about the divine governance cannot be in sharp incongruity with well established contemporary interpretations. It must take them into account. If Roman Catholic moral theologians do not like, from a moral standpoint, the ethical inferences drawn from a theology of nature informed by modern sciences, they have two alternatives. Either they can choose to show that the new interpretations stem from inaccurate observations and illogical abstractions from them, or they must abandon nature as a basis for ethics and derive their theological justifications from some other source.

It is not possible in one paper to defend the answers I believe are more adequate to these three questions. My aspiration is to provide sufficient evidence to warrant, at least, a serious discussion of the issues.

1) Is there an essence to the human (or to other species of life, for that matter) in the sense that Catholic "essentialism" has defended? Certainly there are distinctive features to human life, and if the essence is merely the sum total of the distinctive features, the term may have utility value as a code word for those features. But whether the notion of a substantial form is still warranted is questionable. Evidences from two human sciences will point to the need for reconsideration: physical anthropology developed in evolutionary perspective, and brain research.

Even casual reading of the scientific press would be sufficient to raise questions about the adequacy of "essentialism." With reference to anthropology, I suppose the question is at what point in development did the essence of the simian become the essence of the human. In the language of the anthropologists the questions are, What are the characteristics of "hominid divergence"? and, At what stage in evolutionary development do they occur? It is important to get some sense of the language that these scholars use. In a recent article on "The Origin of Man," for example, C. Owen Lovejoy provides a summary statement of issues. "Four major character complexes are usually cited as distinguishing hominids from pongids. Hominids have remarkable brain expansion, a complex material culture, anterior dental reduction and molar dominance, and bipedal locomotion. Only bipedal locomotion and partial dental modifications can be shown to have an antiquity even approximating the earliest appearance of unquestioned, developed hominids."[11] That seems to leave brain expansion and complex material cultures as the distinguishing features of the human organism and activity. In popular presentations a great deal has been made of the fact that humans bury their dead, which seems commendable, but also that humans are the only species that looks at its feces after defecation—hardly flattering. If, as the physical anthropologists do, one thinks that the continuities of development of the human are as worthy of consideration as the distinctive aspects of the human it is not easy to state the essence of the human, at least not in the traditional manner, nor is it possible to isolate the event when the species was "ensouled." This does not, in the judgment of many scholars, warrant a flight into the arms of Teilhard de Chardin, since evidence for a course of development from past to present is not sufficient to project the course of development from present to future, and certainly not his. The point of this is whether the evidences and theories proffered by contemporary paleoanthropologists (and I do not assume that there is unanimity of judgment about many aspects of these evidences) require us radically to review the interpretation of human nature that has undergirded natural law ethics. For now, let me leave this

11. C. Owen Lovejoy, "The Origin of Man," *Science* 211 (23 Jan. 81): 343.

matter with some favorite quotations from Mary Midgley's *Beast and Man*, a book I find both persuasive and thought provoking. "Why should not our excellence involve our whole nature?" "Our dignity arises within nature, not against it." "We did not, personally and unassisted, invent every aspect of humanity. Much of it is drawn from a common source, and overlaps with dolphinity, beaverishness, and wolfhood."[12]

Brain research is a second area of important studies of man. I tend to agree with those who despair of arriving at consensus on the brain-mind problem, and it is clear that the biological investigators themselves differ about the inferences to be drawn from the best contemporary evidence of research. The spectrum of interpretation runs, as is widely known, from a radical dualism of brain and mind to the opinion that mental life is simply the effect of neurological processes in the brain and central nervous system. Between them, for example, is the judgment of Sir John Eccles who, in the first series of his Gifford Lectures, reflects on *The Human Mystery*. Eccles, who won his Nobel honors on the basis of his brain research, offers the following brief summary of his opinion: "The self-conscious mind is a self-subsistent entity that is actively engaged in reading out from the multifarious activities of the neuronal machinery of the cerebral cortex according to its attention and interest, and it integrates this selection to give the unity of conscious experience from moment to moment. It also acts back in a selective manner on the neuronal machinery. Thus it is proposed that the self-conscious mind exercises a superior interpretative and controlling role upon the neuronal events by virtue of a two-way interaction . . ."[13] This interpretation of the evidence keeps the way open for some traditional inferences about the human. He writes, "It is my thesis that we have to recognize the unique selfhood as being the result of a supernatural creation of what in the religious sense is called a soul," and promises that this theme will be developed in a second series of lectures, which have not yet been published.[14] I do not intend to offer a resolution of the brain-mind problem, but do wish to say that the evidence of research has to be taken into account, and that how it is interpreted has implications for how we understand the distinctiveness of the human. Eccles himself remarks on larger questions at the end of the book. "I attempt to build up a philosophy in which one's personal existence is central, but in which solipsism is rejected. There is recognition of the great mysteries in which we are immersed. Central to these mysteries is the fact of our personal existence as experiencing and creating being, our coming-to-be in life and our apparent ceasing-to-be in death. I repudiate philosophies and political systems which recognize human beings as mere things with a material existence of value only as cogs in the great bureaucratic machine of the state, which thus becomes the slave state."[15] There is a coherence between

12. Mary Midgley, *Beast and Man: The Roots of Human Nature* (Ithaca, N.Y.: Cornell Univ. Press, 1978). Quotations from p. 204, p. 196, and p. 160, respectively.
13. John Eccles, *The Human Mystery* (New York: Springer International, 1979), p. 226.
14. Ibid., p. 144.
15. Ibid., pp. 236–37.

his interpretation of the scientific evidence, his belief in the supernatural creation of the soul, and his moral-political preference. But what happens if his interpretation of the scientific evidence turns out to be false, or even inadequate? Or, to turn the question to moral theologians, what happens to a view of the essence of the human that undergirds ethics if the interpretation of human nature on which it rests is wrong?

If ethics is to rest on a theological interpretation of nature, which is in turn shaped by observation and abstraction from these observations, and if the determinists' account of mind by brain turns out to be accurate, its implications for ethics cannot be avoided.

2) Is there an end not only of human activities but of other aspects of creation that can be clearly defined? Certainly there are purposes to human actions, and certainly there are mutually interactive functions that can be discerned in the relations of aspects of nature to each other, and of persons to each other in society. Christianity as a whole, and not only its Roman Catholic strand, has assumed an end (both in terms of finis and telos) of all things. The biblical imagery of the Kingdom of God has had this role, and the notion of eternal life has also had it with reference to individual persons. The question of this section of the paper is whether the traditional formulations of the end, or indeed of various ends of various aspects of the creation, do not have to be reconsidered in the light of some contemporary observations of nature, and abstractions drawn from them.

In one area of great interest to moral theology at the present, namely sexuality, this general question is already a very practical question. Traditional Catholic, indeed, Christian thought about sexuality accurately observed that it has the obvious biological function of propagating any animal species, including the human. Many contrasts were drawn between "beasts of the field" and humans, with the denigrating tone that beasts were somehow lustier than man, when evidence can be adduced to suggest that the sexual activity of most animals is more completely governed by the purpose of propagation than that of the human animal. Recognition of more than a propagative function to sexuality was acknowledged in Christian thought, though with some reluctance. Augustine's *On the Good of Marriage* remains a classic document in this respect. In the Puritan tradition there was a clearer recognition of the legitimacy of the "second" end of marriage, and in part the discussion was over the primacy of texts from Genesis. Was it more significant that "The LORD God said, 'It is not good for the man to be alone. I will provide a partner for him'" (Genesis 2:18, NEB), or that he said to man, as he had earlier to the other animals, "Be fruitful and increase" (Genesis 1:28, NEB)? If the "partner" (or "helpmeet" [KJV] or "helper" [RSV]) text has equal significance or even greater significance than the "fruitful" text, or to make the point in different language, if the "covenant" view is of greater significance than the "creation" view, there are many implications for the ethics of marriage and sexuality.[16]

16. For an account of these matters, see James Johnson, *A Society Ordained by God* (New York: Abingdon, 1970).

Roman Catholic (and Protestant) revisers of sexual ethics make their appeals to aspects of "human experience" such as love. And in the light of many contemporary studies of the relations of "sexuality" (whatever that turns out to be) to all sorts of human behavior and activity—to aggression or pathological passivity, to creativity in the arts, etc.—it is recognized that the potency of sex naturally has many possible ends, and it is more difficult to determine which are proper.

In the area of the discussion of homosexuality, however, my main concern becomes clearer. Moralists who ground their substantive moral norms on "nature" have great stake in the confused and confusing "scientific" discussions of the causes or "nature" of homosexuality. It seems to me that the first step in the revision of the traditional absolute moral proscription was the acknowledgement that there might be excusing conditions for homosexual activity, and thus while blame was still laid forgiveness was more easily granted. But on down the road a short distance is the possibility that if there is an "essence" to human sexuality that defines its proper end, that essence has passed some persons by. Then if the "nature" of X's sexuality leads to homosexual activity, that is not simply excusable, deficient, and forgivable, but a proper end of his or her nature, X's activity is X's good. Basically my point is this: aspects of nature that were once thought to have a particular natural end from which moral inferences are drawn are now observed and understood to have not only a number of "natural" ends, but also that under certain conditions several of them might be judged to be morally excusable, or permissible, or legitimate, if not prescribed.

The issue of an end, and what that end is, also comes up in consideration of the projections made by geophysicists and astronomers about the destiny of the universe, and the destiny of our species within that. I have addressed this in other publications, but must briefly introduce it here since I think theologians as a whole, and moral theologians in particular, have not faced up to inferences that can reasonably be drawn. A quotation from John Calvin, with which the Roman Catholic tradition has basically been in agreement, makes the traditional point. "God himself has shown by the order of Creation that he created all things for the sake of man."[17] The lower serves the higher, and with the demise of much serious consideration of the angels, we are happily on top. But what is to be done with such evidences and hypotheses that suggest that the necessary conditions for the continuation of our species in the universe will atrophy long before the universe itself comes to its predicted end? All things, then, were not created for the sake of man. Another of my favorite quotations that pertains to this point can be offered here. Herbert Butterfield remarks on the change in perspective that seventeenth century science brought to the Western world. He notes that a thesis found in the writings of Galileo was supported by other sources, "namely, the assertion that it is absurd to suppose that the whole of this . . . colossal universe was created by God purely for the sake of man, purely to serve the purposes of earth."[18]

17. Calvin, *Institutes*, 1.14.22, McNeill ed., 1:181–82.
18. Herbert Butterfield, *The Origins of Modern Science*, rev. ed. (New York: The Free Press, 1965), p. 69.

I need not embellish the implications of this for Christian theology, and for theological ethics. The tradition has assumed to a great extent that God and nature were primarily focused on the service of our species as the temporal end. This, together with traditional Christian eschatologies, has backed many of our value preferences and valuations; it has been a larger vindication for many values and principles that are invoked to govern what is normally right and wrong, even in the realm of medical care. My general question of this paper can be raised once more. If, on the basis of observation and extrapolation—much more complex now than in the past as a result of developments in science and technology—it is hard to discern a telos, an end, of the creation, and if we continue to hold that the divine governance of nature is a source for moral norms, must we not be open to a reconsideration of some features of ethics? Insofar as particular orders of traditional valuation are dependent upon traditional teleological interpretations of theology and nature, and insofar as there is sufficient evidence to indicate that another interpretation is at least plausible, I believe such reconsideration is necessary, no matter how painful some particular conclusions of it might be for our traditional ethics, medical and other.

3) Is the assumed anthropocentric interpretation of man's relation to the rest of the creation correct? Certainly man has capacities purposively to relate to other aspects of the creation, and to use them, that are distinctive. Indeed those uses have led to culture, and in the present century to increasingly complex relationships to nature as a result of developments in science and technology. Man is not dependent upon nature in the way that immobile plants and even animals are. By creating culture man has established a distance from the immediate effects of nature. But this has not eliminated a more ultimate dependence on nature, not eliminated the many forms of interdependence with nature. Nature now "depends" on human activities in some respects, but man continues to depend upon nature.

From the previous stages of the argument of this paper it should be clear that I believe the traditional anthropocentrism must be significantly modified. If one construes the world in the following, perhaps odd, way, the case can at least be made hypothetically. In temporal terms one need only recall the billions of years it took for the rudiments of life, such as carbon, oxygen, nitrogen and phosphorous, to come into being; the uniqueness of our planet within our system in providing the conditions necessary for life to develop as we know it; and the evidences for the biological development of our species. If we should develop the order of "value" in relation to the order of necessary conditions for life, rather than in relation to the order of development from "lower" to "higher," the image of man's dependence on, and interdependence with the ordering of nature becomes sharper. Or, one reflects upon the prediction of the future of our planet and our universe, that the conditions necessary for human life will disappear long before the gravitational collapse, if that is how the end will be. It is not easy to claim that all things were created for our sakes as humans when there is considerable evidence that the destiny of our species is extinction.

In more "spatial" than temporal terms, one can call to attention the persistent forms of dependence and interdependence with natural processes in the environment, and the fact that human beings are not exempt from them. The evidences from problems of human population growth relative to nutritional resources, limited supplies of fossil fuels, air and water pollution, and other commonplace issues are sufficient to signal this. Man has to be construed in a context of relationships to the rest of nature in a way that qualifies the traditional Christian and Western (and not only Roman Catholic) anthropocentrism.

I need not embellish this point further in order to make my more general point. If on the basis of observation, reflection, and abstraction the place of man in the universe is not that assumed in traditional natural law theory, a modification of traditional valuations of man has to follow. That modification is bound to have some consequences for the ethics that are derived from nature. A different construal of the place of man in the universe will have implications for what are the proper ends of human action, and what forms of conduct most appropriately relate us to the rest of the world of which we are a part. Activity will have to be ordered by understanding our place in the universe as part of and participant in it, and not a view that all exists for our sakes.

I have dug myself, and I hope others, into a rather deep hole. As often is the case in writing a paper, the analysis of the issue has consumed the time and space allotted for the topic. I can only indicate a few lines—more threads than ropes—for getting us out of the hole. In general terms, the implications for theological ethics are these.

First, the ordering of nature does not sustain a morality that backs the homocentrism and the individualism that traditional natural law has warranted. Even in the interests of the future of the human species, not to mention the "interests" of conditions necessary for the sustenance and development of other forms of life, account must be taken of the relationships of man and culture to a larger "whole." Human continuities with other forms of life, and the continuities within the human between that which we share with all animals and that which distinguishes us have to be taken into account. The implications of this different construal of the world for ethics require careful study, since there are threats involved to the cherished values and principles that can be justified by good reasons.

Second, nature does not provide an unchanging order from which moral inferences can be drawn. Nature itself develops, and human activity involves participation in nature in such a way that some aspects of it are altered. Thus while the ordering of life in nature provides indications of what relationships are necessary between man and the rest of the world, and what ends are deemed to be desirable not only for man but also for the possibilities of development of life in the future, it does not provide moral certainty. Man is a *participant* in nature, and what is deemed right and desirable will be relative to the states of nature and culture in which we live, and to the understandings of nature that we have (and which are themselves developing through time). The recourse that theological ethics takes to nature necessarily will be much more complex and ambiguous than the traditional natural law theory provided.

Third, the ultimate destiny of the world is not in human hands, and it is not likely to be the Kingdom of God as that has been understood in the Christian tradition. But shorter range destinies are subject to the intentional interventions of man in our highly developed culture. There are proper considerations for the human good, but human interventions need to take into account the sustenance and preservation of the necessary conditions for life, and not merely human life, to flourish. Since both threats to and possibilities of these conditions come about by human understanding and action, moral ambiguity in some instances is unavoidable. While life may not be a "zero-sum game" there are few beneficial consequences that are not costly to other persons, to other aspects of nature, and to future generations of life—including human life. The tragedy of human choices, even when justified by good moral arguments, has to be faced.

I apologize for not being able here to draw inferences more precise than these, and particularly implications for medical ethics. I want to assure readers, however, that in other as yet unpublished writings, and in writings underway, I have gone, and shall go much further. If, however, as Calvin averred, "nature is God," and ethics is to be theological, then there is no way of avoiding the difficult task of finding out what clues, or indications, of the divine governance are present in nature. We cannot get even a glimpse of what the power that controls the destiny of the world is enabling and requiring us to be and to do without using the best understandings of nature that are available to us in our time. Thomas Aquinas did no less, and he is worthy of emulation in this respect. Some of the consequences might be uncomfortable, theologically and ethically. But who would defend the notion that God exists to glorify man? Not I, at least.

Chapter 9

Professions as "Callings"

We use several different words in our society to designate how a person makes his or her living: job, occupation, trade, vocation, profession, calling, and perhaps others. I want to "play" with some of these words to see what distinctions we make among their usages.

One of the distinctions we make is between the professional and the amateur. There seem to be two criteria used in this distinction. The professional person gets paid for what the amateur does without remuneration; but we also assume that the quality of skill and ability of the professional is greater than that of the amateur. This is adequate when we think about musicians, hockey players, and persons involved in a number of activities. But it is jolting to think about designating someone as an amateur lawyer or social worker or physician.

We hear professionals make reference to "real pros," those who have extraordinary skill or talent surpassing other professionals. And we have the "semipros" in athletics who earn part of their living by playing, and who presumably are not quite up to the capacities of those who can earn their full living that way. What makes a "professional" politician?

The use of the word "vocation" is just as confusing. I often wonder what students understand when they see the titles of the two famous essays by Max Weber,

"Science as Vocation" and "Politics as Vocation." Weber used the word *Beruf* in each, a word that can be better translated as "calling." Of course, vocation, *Beruf,* and calling share a common meaning: to have a vocation is to be "called." It still means that in Roman Catholic religious contexts. A candidate for the priesthood has to discern, or have discerned for him, whether he has a genuine vocation. In its religious dimensions, this is to say whether he has truly been called by God to be a priest. Of course, this judgment comes as a result of assessing other things— his various abilities, both learned and natural. It is not simply the result of adding various information from transcripts, course performance, and psychological tests.

The use of the term "vocational schools" is one reason why the word "vocational" is confusing. In comparison with a professional school or a liberal arts college, a vocational school is one where a "trade" is learned. This opens the issue of what distinguishes a trade from a profession, to which I shall return. Whether one is "called" to a trade is a separate issue from what skills one learns, if viewed from another perspective. In principle one can have a "vocation" for a trade, like becoming an auto mechanic, as readily as one can have a vocation for ministry or medicine or social work.

"Calling" is a word that, in my judgment, is rapidly moving toward obsolescence. One still hears it used in ecclesiastical institutions and life, but even there less and less. Ministers are, to the best of my knowledge, the only persons who are offered a "call" when they are offered employment. Even in ecclesiastical life the usage is not uniform; in some church polities a clergyman is appointed by a bishop; he or she has an appointment rather than a call. In our time when a minister is called by a congregation, he or she generally signs a contract which states the expectations of the congregation, compensation, fringe benefits such as continuing education time, and other things that other employment contracts stipulate.

CALLING

I want to dwell on the notion of calling to draw from it some religious elements that I shall later discuss in more secular terms. In the context of the ministry, John Calvin distinguished several aspects of a call. The first is what he called the "secret call" "of which each minister is conscious before God, and which does not have the church as a witness."[1] This, for Calvin, is the witness of the heart that one is without selfish ambition or avarice or any other selfish desire in receiving a "proffered office." Modern church bodies are given to requiring vocational aptitude tests, personality inventories, and other devices apparently to test even Calvin's "secret call." But there are some outer signs of that inward call that can be judged by others: whether a person is sound in doctrine and lives a holy life, and is in no way at fault so as to disgrace the ministry. This is part of what Calvin designates

---

1. John Calvin, *Institutes of the Christian Religion* 4.3.11; 2 vols., ed. John T. McNeill, trans. Ford Lewis Battles (Philadelphia: Westminster, 1960), 2:1063. This paragraph also draws from 2:1064–66.

the "churchly call," by which a person is set apart by the rite of ordination for the ministry. And then there is the call from a particular congregation for which the consent and approval of the people are necessary.

In the history of Christianity, the sixteenth-century reformers fostered the extension of the notion of a vocation or calling from those who were to become priests and ministers to all persons. To be sure, the "tests" of a call were not the same, but since any person could have a "calling," in some circles a calling became a synonym for an occupation. But that process, in a sense, cheapened the notion. To say that a shoemaker had a calling was not merely a statement of his role in the differentiation of labor in a community, or of how he earned his living. It meant that no matter how menial one's task, it was viewed both by the shoemaker and presumably by others as a service to persons and the community, and ultimately a service to God. Indeed, Martin Luther could speak of one's occupation as a "mask of God."[2] It was not only that one's service functioned for the common good and met individual human needs, and thus served God, but also that this was part of one's self-perception or self-understanding. It added dignity to quite ordinary work. One's work had almost cosmic significance, no matter how menial. Social status lines were not erased by this; in one respect they were intensified. A person was to stay within his or her calling. In another respect, however, the dignity of work was democratized.

There have been traces of this dignity, in some countries at least, until very recent times. I want to illustrate this by the very secular society of Sweden, a society whose secularism is as Lutheran as France's is Roman Catholic. First, one's listing in the telephone directory always included one's occupation. For example, my uncle's listing was "Gustavsson, Magni T., Railroad section hand." This uncle was no Christian; in fact, he was a communist until the Soviet invasion of Finland in 1940 and then he became a social democrat. He was also a union member all his life. From one perspective the occupational listing was judged to be part of what critical Swedes called the "title sickness" of Swedish society. It was undemocratic. From another perspective, his dignity was not demeaned but certified by the designation of his occupation. He had a sense of "calling."

My second illustration is from the social democratic and trade union daily paper published in Malmö. Frequently in Sweden persons have their photographs printed in papers on their fiftieth and some subsequent birthdays. In *Arbetet* there was a picture of a very proud woman. The caption was, "Toilet attendant Anna Andersson celebrates her sixtieth birthday." Even when there was no longer a consciousness that God might be served by attending toilets, there was pride and dignity in the occupation. And Anna Andersson probably kept the toilets very clean.

---

2. For example, "Thus the magistrate, the emperor, the king, the prince, the teacher, the preacher, the pupil, the father, the mother, the children, the master, the servant—all these are social positions or external masks. God wants us to respect and acknowledge them as His creatures, which are the necessity for this life." They are, however, only masks, and not to be confused with God. See Martin Luther, "Lectures on Galatians, 1535," trans. Jaroslav Pelikan, in *Luther's Works*, ed. Jaroslav Pelikan, 56 vols. (St. Louis: Concordia Publishing House, 1963), 26:95.

The point of this is to indicate that any occupation can be a calling in the particular sense I have been suggesting. There is both an outward and an inward significance to the idea. The outward is the larger context within which any person's contributions can be seen to have significance. It contributes to the meeting of human needs; it is an element, no matter how small, in the "common good" of the human community. It serves a purpose that is not simply self-referential in the object of its interests. The inward significance is twofold: there is a dignity to one's work that can be affirmed, and thus a dignity to the worker; and there is a sense of fulfillment and meaning that can come from being of service to others and to the common good. I never met Anna Andersson in Malmö, but I would infer that she was not ashamed to have her "title" in the caption under her photograph. Her title was as worthy as the title "professor." One can say these things about a calling without adding what Calvin believed was necessary for the "secret call" to the ministry, namely, that there are no elements of selfish ambition or avarice. Such purity of motives one does not need to have, or to claim. Put differently, there is a perception and interpretation of the significance of one's activities as contributing to human well-being and to a larger whole, and there is a self-perception and self-understanding that adds dignity and meaning to one's own life.

Such a view of calling is not without its weaknesses and perils, however. It is hard to find meaning in drudgery, and that was probably as true for slaves and serfs as it is for someone on an assembly line in a Ford plant. Kermit Eby, who was once the educational director for the United Auto Workers, used to say, "No one wants to put on nut number 999 until he becomes nut number 999." The view that human labor becomes an extension of machines and other technologies rather than machines becoming an extension of human activity, while it can be overdrawn, certainly contains a good bit of validity. The development of technology intensifies the difficulties of interpreting many occupations as callings. I am sure, however, that there are many things in common among a woodcutter in the sixteenth century, a sweeper in Bangalore, a factory line employee, or the operator of a word processor in Chicago today.

It is also the case that to view one's work as a calling can make a worker vulnerable to exploitation. I want to quote from an article about my maternal grandfather published in the *John Deere Magazine* in 1920. He was an immigrant blacksmith who began to work for John Deere in 1879. The reporter was looking for a "model employee" about whom to write. "During a protracted hot spell along about 1906, there were few men on the job in the blacksmith shop any day. On the hottest day of the period the men began dropping out at nine in the morning. At three in the afternoon the shop was practically deserted. At three-thirty the foreman walked through the shop to see that everything was all right before he shut down the plant for the day. He heard a noise emanating from the vicinity of Nels Moody's forge. He strolled over there and found Nels, unmindful of the heat, turning out work in the accustomed manner." The foreman was perplexed, for it was not cost effective to keep the shop running with only one man on the job. He inquired from the superintendent what he should do. "Keep the plant running as long as Moody wants to work," were the instructions from the superintendent. "Nels finished out the day and then walked home."

It is not hard to see why Nels Moody was a "model employee"! He had a profound sense of calling, which in his case included a deep sense of duty or obligation to his employer. It also included a sense of self-reliance that would make Ronald Reagan happy. Regarding the employee's pension plan, the report states, "Inasmuch as the pension is a gift of the company, [Moody] feels that he is not entitled to it." "He deems it a privilege to work."

With a sense of calling like that, Deere and Company did not have to worry about my grandfather agitating for a union! He was as vulnerable to exploitation as a blacksmith as many a social worker has been simply because of a profound sense of calling.

No doubt other weaknesses and perils are inherent in viewing work as a calling. I note only these because they are sufficient to suggest that one can become romantic about work from such a perspective, and one can permit oneself to have justifiable self-interests denied, even justice denied, because of a deep sense of vocation. But other notions are equally subject to perversions. Thus, I still want to make a case for continuing to interpret the professions as callings.

PROFESSION

What do I have in mind by a "profession"? I have in mind what still are named from time to time the "learned professions": the three that developed quite early in our culture—clergy, law, and medicine, as well as social service and other areas that have become differentiated in the course of more modern social developments. The literature of the professions suggests various marks that distinguish them from other occupations; I have found examples of a list of about fifteen items at one extreme and efforts to define the "essence" of a profession on the other. I shall delineate three characteristics that I judge to be important.

First, the professions are characterized by mastery of an extensive body of technical knowledge and concepts or theories that explain that knowledge and that guide its application to different circumstances. This characteristic has a graded relevance to a range of human activity, and I am not interested in drawing a precise line between the activity I would name professional and its next of kin that would be named something different. But certainly these features distinguish the professions from other occupations and from trades.

The professions do not simply apply rules and examples given in handbooks or manuals. To be a professional person is to learn to think in particular ways, and particularly to exercise practical reason in making judgments about specific courses of action. I am sure many of us have participated in formal or informal conferences about particular cases or policies. For example, in a medical setting in which a critical choice is to be made, the physician uses knowledge and concepts to explain the problem in its medical features; the social worker often sees features of the wider circumstances that the physician does not and interprets his or her vision of the case in the light of concepts distinctive to social work. Nurses, chaplains, and others might also be involved. Each has a way of thinking based not only on the mastery of relevant information but concepts, theories, and experiences distinctive to each profession. The purpose of such a conference is to come to a sound judgment about the best possible course of action, and to do that is to exercise practical reason.

Not only is mastery of information, concepts, and theories required; intelligence and reflectiveness are also essential. Exercising discretion, making judgments, and moving from the established and familiar to what is different in particular features distinguishes professions from most other occupations. Reliance on intelligence and learning within a sphere of discretionary judgment is important both to the practice of a profession and to the self-esteem of the professional person. This is why detailed regulations, detailed procedures, and extensive surveillance are often seen as impediments to good professional practice and insults to the practitioner. This is why confident professional persons prefer guidelines to rules; rules often seek to cover too many different cases and require strict compliance; guidelines give direction but permit the exercise of discretion in making judgments about fitting courses of action. The professional person who masters technical information and knows concepts and theories but cannot make sound applications or good judgments is not effective.

Second, the professions are institutionalized, and thus there are many social controls over professional activity. One is a "member" of a profession; one "belongs" to his or her profession. It is an important mark of one's personal and social identity. There are certification procedures, academic degrees from professional schools, certification by boards of one's peers, and often licensing by the state. Business school graduates are among the few whose university degrees alone are sufficient certification. Many others have to pass "state boards," get specialty certification on the basis of examinations set by experts, and so forth. Theological schools do not ordain clergy—churches do—and this normally requires examination and certification of fitness.

There are other forms of social control in the professions. In some instances, under both criminal and civil statutes, legal liability is present. In a litigious society this provides good business for lawyers and insurance companies; even the clergy have been sued for giving bad pastoral counsel. Codes of conduct have been written for most professions; they are quasi-legal devices which, in principle, subject practitioners to a judicial review process within a profession. Peer pressure functions informally; commendation for good performance and shame for poor clearly affect motivation and practice. Peer-review procedures, whether in universities, law firms, or hospitals, institutionalize peer pressure, and individuals have heavy stakes in their outcomes. In many professions the market system functions to some extent, though it does not drive out all incompetent persons, and tends to make the best services available to those who can afford to pay the highest fees and salaries. In one profession to which I belong, namely, the

Protestant ministry, being "called to a wider field of service" usually means being called to a more prestigious congregation for a higher salary; it certainly never means being called to Musselshell, Montana, a parish whose geographic area is half the size of the state of Connecticut! Continuing education, increasingly required by statute, is intended to maintain standards of competence in view of new developments in knowledge, theory, technology, and practice.

Increasingly professional persons are members of bureaucracies: a hospital staff or medical team, a social service agency, a law or architectural firm, a government research or service division, a public school or university system, or a staff of clergy. Rules and regulations, refined job descriptions within a pattern of division of responsibilities, effort reports, and hierarchies of authority and power must be taken into account. And finally, both specialization within professions and limited contact with the persons served lead to increasingly contracted, partial, and therefore often depersonalized relationships with clients and patients. Contracts for particular and precisely defined services take the place of relationships of mutual understanding and confidence between persons and often of a broader understanding of the circumstances and needs of those served. Anyone who has been shunted from clinic to clinic in a university hospital knows this to be the case. Seldom does one have just one lawyer any more; one has one lawyer for tax matters, others for real estate transactions, estate planning, divorce, courtroom litigation, and so forth. Contracts for highly specialized services are forms of social control.

Here I want to note something that is terribly obvious. The first characteristic of a profession that I described stresses intelligence, exercise of individual agency and capacities, and a range of permitted discretionary judgment. The second characteristic of a profession militates against that. Certification and licensing procedures presumably guarantee that the person has the capacities to exercise independent judgment within a particular frame of activity, but the bureaucratization and specialization of professions sharply inhibit that. The result is something also very obvious: a deep frustration or demoralization. With special reference to the ministry, a university colleague, Joseph Sittler, calls this a maceration of the professional person.

The third characteristic of the professions that I wish to note is that, at least traditionally, they are service oriented. Professions exist to meet particular human needs of individuals and communities. Certainly this was the case with the first learned professions in our culture: medicine, law, and clergy. I want to stress here that service to persons and communities is intrinsic to the professions as professions, and not a matter of adding a "calling" or a "vocation" to them. The professional institutions and those who participate in them have the end of benefiting patients, clients, and parishioners; they exist, trite as it is to say, to do good. And it is not only individuals whose needs are to be served, but human groups and even the larger common good of a society. The needs of individuals and communities are not in the service of the interests of a profession or a professional person. The profession and its members exist to meet the needs of others.

It might even be accurate to say that professions emerge in the course of the development of human communities in response to actual or felt needs of persons or groups. No one thought to establish a profession called "architecture" or "engineering" first, in the hope that if a profession developed a need would be generated to serve the profession. Illness preceded the development of physicians, settling disputes between parties existed before the development of lawyers, and perceived needs of the human spirit existed before the emergence of a priesthood that ministered to them. Certainly it was never necessary to establish social service agencies to create or even to discover individual, familial, and community needs out there. Social service agencies are instrumental to human needs.

I believe it was further understood in many times and places that the services of the professions would be available to all members of the communities they served. Even the needs of those who could not afford the services were to be met. Thus, those unable to pay for services were included in work done *pro bono publico*. Of course, probably at no time was *pro bono publico* time and effort available to large numbers of the sick, the unemployed, those needing legal services, and so forth. To a great extent the development of state-funded professional services has occurred to rectify the injustices of the voluntary and market systems. Few physicians do *pro bono publico* work, given Medicaid, Medicare, and private health insurance, though more may be called on to do it under the policies of the current regime and some was done in the sixties in free clinics.

An interesting question came to my mind in a conversation with a university colleague, physician Richard Landau. Has the development of institutionalized ways of meeting the needs of those who cannot afford services (done very properly, I want to stress, for the sake of distributive justice) altered the outlook and motivation of members of the professions? Does a profession which exists to meet human needs lose something of the sense of its intrinsic character as a profession when there are few occasions in which the exercise of the profession requires some self-denial on the part of the practitioner? This is not an implied moralistic criticism of the professions, but a possible line of inquiry. Certainly in terms of my interest in "callings," I can ask, While a profession fulfills its end of providing certain human services, is the motivation and the larger vision of purpose affected when every effort has guaranteed remuneration? Of course one can serve the needs of others and the common good without a deep motivation to fulfill those ends and without having those ends consciously in view. In Luther's terms, one can be a mask of God—that is, one can be in the service of others and the common good without being consciously motivated toward that end. Services to one another are simply a requirement of the human community.

PROFESSIONS AS "CALLINGS"

It now behooves me to discuss more directly the title of this article, "Professions as 'Callings,'" since I have attended to its principal terms. The strongest link between the two is in the third aspect of the professions, namely, the provision of services for the benefit to persons and communities. My grandfather pounding out plows on that John Deere forge for fifty years made a small contribution to farmers and to food production. But he did not interact with persons in the same way that a number of professions do. If one restricts one's interests to such professions as social service, law, medicine, and the clergy, a feature of personal relationships with patients and clients comes to the fore. At least in many professional activities of these sorts the effectiveness of one's work depends in a considerable measure on the qualities of interpersonal relationships that are developed: mutual confidence; recognition of aspects of the patient or client that are not fully articulated by him or her; metaphorically speaking, good peripheral vision so that the professional person can set the particular need or interest in the context of a larger and more complex whole. Such capacities are developed in professional schools through the kinds of technical information, concepts, and ways of thinking that I indicated earlier. But they also involve a capacity for empathy—a putting of oneself in the place of the other so that one can both imagine and feel what the client's views of the circumstances are. Indeed, refined exercise of practical reasoning is developed in part through natural and cultivated human sensibilities and sensitivities and not simply through quantified, computerized problem-solving methods and techniques, as important as these are. In critical situations I believe this might even involve a sense of suffering with the client or patient, virtually adopting the client's anguish, while at the same time maintaining the perspective of the disinterested observer and external agent who takes into account the client's perspective while interpreting the circumstances from his or her professional one.

Viewing a profession as a calling involves two distinguishable features: certain qualities of motivation, and a broader and deeper vision of the ends to be served. Commonly heard complaints about professions point to the absence of a sense of calling. It is sometimes said that a physician is more interested in the patient's disease than in the patient. The physician obviously had better be interested in the disease and be competent to make an accurate diagnosis and prescription for a course of action, but the particular disease is embodied in a person, and lack of concern for the person often evokes resentment. It is not uncommon to hear that many secondary school teachers view their jobs as a form of civil service; by that is meant that they put in their hours, meet the expectations of a contract, and receive their salaries just as trash collectors do. The element of complaint is that they are not deeply interested in their students as individuals, do not see them in relation to larger possibilities of intellectual and personal development, and often do not see their own subject matter in relation to a larger process of educational development. I was once genuinely shocked to see a course title in a theological school catalogue listed as "The Management of Grief Work." I inferred from it that persons do not grieve, but are objects who do grief work. The role of the minister is the external manipulator of some psychological processes, something like an engineer who knows the stress factors in bridge construction and gets the I-beams placed in such a way that possible dangers are avoided. There is merit in clergy learning about the psychology of grieving, but in a crisis I would want a pastor and not a manager. I think I could quickly tell the difference.

I suppose that studies have been made of the motives of persons going into the learned service professions; I have not attempted to search for such. My impression is that for many persons, especially those going into relatively low-salaried service professions, the incentive is a deeply moral one. The presence of poverty, social disorganization, disease, personal anguish, injustice in the distribution of human services, ignorance, and similar factors move persons to seek the education and training to relieve these impediments to human fulfillment. Incentive might well go beyond relief from suffering and avoidance of evil; persons see unfulfilled possibilities in the lives of individuals, groups, and communities which might be better realized by conscientious and competent professional activity. Such motives and incentives are not primarily self-interested; persons of great ability could certainly receive greater financial remuneration and status in other occupations. These moral motives are part of a "calling." Professional education and activity enable persons to competently exercise their callings, their moral motives.

The calling is not utterly dissimilar from what John Calvin saw as the "secret call." There is a sense that one's life experiences, one's capacities for sympathy and empathy, and one's moral beliefs and moral sensitivities make it reasonable to choose a certain profession. Professional training, certification, and employment are in the service of this moral calling. There are competence tests to prove one's fitness to pursue one's motives. A moral calling without professionalization can certainly be harmful. Some things not utterly dissimilar from Calvin's "churchly call" are necessary: assurance of adequate intelligence, knowledge, and experience to bear the responsibilities entailed in being agents whose activities have an important effect on the lives of persons and communities. But again, these exist to insure the effective fulfillment of a "calling." They not only provide a social license to practice but are specifications of the activities that give precision and direction to one's deepest motivation.

Not only subjective motives are involved; some vision of better lives for individuals, for groups, and even for the commonweal of the human community are part of a "calling." To be sure, such a vision might be idealistic to the point of utopianism; it might well need tempering by the recalcitrant realities of individual persons, institutions, politics, economics, and other factors that limit its realization. But such a vision draws persons forward in the hope that the lives of persons and groups can, with effective action by the professions, become better than they now are. Such a vision requires professional education. If a vision of a higher quality of life or of a better society is to be more than rhetoric, the requirements of technical knowledge, concepts, and training in thought processes must be met. If such a vision is not simply a call for revolution, but a guide to ends that can be approximated in quite specific conditions—in this body, this neighborhood, this psyche, this city—technical competence must be achieved. But apart from a "calling," professional competence becomes technique and manipulation, and the significance of one's partial contribution to a larger whole and larger good atrophies. Also, to have a larger vision sets one's own competence and effectiveness in a proper context; one sees what more must be done by others, and one sees how the larger context of the human need is related to the point of access that a particular profession has. Both "tunnel vision" and short-range thinking are altered by one's "calling."

A sense of calling is thus important for one's clients and for one's self. It can affect one's perspective on the particular needs that one seeks to meet; it can enable one to envision a contribution to a larger whole, a larger good, not only of individual clients but also of the community. It can affect one's sense of worth and well-being as a professional person not only by assuring some dignity but by nourishing and confirming the deep moral motives that lead persons to professions and that keep them alive in conditions of adversity and frustration.

I am not romantic about professions as callings. There are severe impediments to the realization of my concern, and the impediments are in a sense "structural"; they exist externally and not simply in the difficulties of keeping a sense of calling alive. They are objective to professional persons. Two impediments that I view as important are the following.

One is specialization within the profession. Recall my quotation from Kermit Eby, "No one wants to put on nut number 999 until he becomes nut number 999." I am not concerned here about the possible psychopathological consequences of specialization; Eby's words also suggest that it is difficult to find meaning and purpose in activity when the larger "product" is simply not in view. Even in industrial work, experiments are undertaken to overcome the ill effects on workers of specialization, such as team production of automobiles and other goods. In large law firms, as in medical clinics, referral to other experts is frequent; the requirements of technical specialization increase as both knowledge and institutional developments progress. No patient or client can complain in toto about this, for technical competence is the *conditio sine qua non* for a professional person. But "tunnel vision" and short-range thinking all too often accompany highly specialized competence; indeed, they seem to be demanded to achieve some kinds of competence. It is not easy to have a vision of a larger good, a common good, when one is a specialist in putting on nut number 999.

The second impediment is bureaucratization. I alluded to this earlier when I indicated that the first feature of a profession, that which requires initiative and capacities to make judgments, is in tension with the second, the institutionalization of the professions. The development of professional bureaucracies has been unavoidable and presents both possibilities and problems to any profession involved. It is not necessary to analyze the causes of the development of professional bureaucracies or their values in providing for division of labor, efficient use of resources, and so forth. Nor is it necessary to recite the charges made against them: inefficiency, depersonalization, and the like. These are often impediments of a sense of calling because of the demands they place on persons that are not immediately functional to the motives and intentions for professional activity. Specialization and bureaucracy go together to a considerable extent. Specialization narrows the range of professional competence of the individual; bureaucracies, even at their best, narrow the range of discretionary judgment of persons who rightly prize their intelligence, competence, and capacities to take initiative—all marks of a professional person.

In our culture and society there is no going back to a time when specialization and bureaucratization did not exist. If the professions are to be "callings," for many persons that sense of calling has to be sustained and nourished within the strictures of these social developments. Nor is there any turning back en masse to a religious view of the significance of work, if such a view was ever widely effective. Members of any professional group are not likely to find it very meaningful to hear that each is a "mask of God," that is, that each professional person is doing the work of the Deity in the world for the sake of the good of others, or of the common good of the human community. If professions are to be callings, for many persons the sense of calling has to be nourished outside of religious communities.

We ought not to succumb, however, to the notion that all of the impediments to sustaining a sense of calling are external, as if we as professional persons were simply passive flotsam and jetsam subject to institutional forces beyond our control. Certainly there are procedures and processes of participation in policy formation and decision making that can be developed within the contexts of specialization and bureaucracies which can sustain both motives and vision. One need not go to extreme "participatory democracy" to find ways in which contributions of individual professional persons can be made to the establishment of goals that are consonant with a vision of service and to a climate of mutual confidence that encourages the exercise of initiative and discretionary judgment. There are also, I believe, individual disciplines that professional persons can practice to sustain their own motives and outlooks. One can make the effort and take the time to read beyond the professional literature, to think and reflect about aims and purposes in the light of considerations that are marginal to one's specialization, to participate in extraprofessional activities that broaden one's perspective and nourish one's motives, and to converse with intelligent and learned persons from different fields of work. Indeed, one is likely to be a more effective professional person if one is not totally consumed by one's work and exercises self-disciplines that broaden one's horizons. No doubt many of us have experienced an alteration in our professional outlooks from the insights derived from a drama, a novel, a movie, a biography, a history, or the serious study of a text in social philosophy or some other field beyond our own. It would be a surrender of our integrity and human agency if we acted as if all the impediments to a sense of calling were external to our own characters and patterns of life.

I cannot prescribe for all persons in a given profession a way to keep the moral and humane wellsprings of motivation thriving for our work and a way to vitalize a vision of a larger whole to which we each contribute. A stubborn conviction remains, however, even if it is more asserted than substantially justified by evidences and argument. A "calling" without professionalization is bumbling, ineffective, and even dangerous. A profession without a calling, however, has no taps of moral and humane rootage to keep motivation alive, to keep human sensitivities and sensibilities alert, and to nourish a proper sense of self-fulfillment. Nor does a profession without a calling easily envision the larger ends and purposes of human good that our individual efforts can serve. The wider context of significance and meaning, both for ourselves and for others, easily withers away.

From a religious perspective there is meaning in the notion of professions as "masks of God," but I am not interested in promoting that idea. I do want to encourage the view, however, that professions are callings in the service of human needs—individual, social, and even for the sake of the common good of the human family. Professions ought to be "callings"; they exist to serve human needs. Needs do not exist to serve the interests of a profession.

Chapter 10

Death Is Not the Enemy

(coauthored with Richard L. Landau, MD)

Karl Barth, a 20th-century Protestant theologian, wrote, "Life is no second God, and therefore the respect due it cannot rival the reverence owed to God." On the other hand, for secularized persons in a secular society, there is no "first God" and thus nothing due more respect or reverence than life itself. Life and its preservation become more than the necessary conditions for the realization of a measure of self-fulfillment and for capacities to contribute to other persons and to society. They become virtually ends in themselves. The pursuit of health and the preservation of physical life seem to have replaced "salvation," the glorification of God, or the beatific vision as the chief end of man. To the secular person, what theologians call "the conditions of finitude," those inexorable restraints and limitations on human life of which the final one is death, seem repressive since there is nothing real or lasting beyond them. A kind of physical fundamentalism comes into being; the practical dogma is to preserve life as long as medically and technically possible. If God is functionally designated as one's "ultimate concern" (to use a term of another Protestant theologian, Paul Tillich), the preservation of life becomes one's God. If one's ultimate object of trust is fundamentally one's God, life becomes one's God—or one's idol.

We are not concerned to argue for the existence of God, or for some form of life after death. We do not claim that a religious outlook is necessary to avoid absolutizing the value of physical life. Secular persons can consent to the conditions of finitude, to the reality of death, to conceiving of death as sometimes friend as well as enemy at least as readily as the religious person. We are concerned, however, to reflect on some of the outcomes of the preoccupation with the preservation of physical life. The intensification of concern to sustain and preserve life is the other side of concern to avoid physical death. These concerns may have obvious benefits in most circumstances—the prevention of many risks through public health measures and educational activities directed toward preventive medicine and personal hygiene and the development of therapies for countless diseases.

An intense preoccupation with the preservation of physical life, however, seems sometimes to be based on an assumption that death is unnatural, or that its delay, even briefly, through medical and technical means is always a triumph of human achievement over the limitations of nature. It is as if death is in every case an evil, a kind of demonic power to be overcome by the forces of life, propped up by elaborate medical technologies. Dramatic medical interventions portrayed in the media become living "westerns." The powers of death are the bad guys, to be vanquished by the good guys, dressed in white coats, rather than white hats. Every delay of death is a victory by the forces of good. Or, to change the analogy, the development and use of costly and dramatic end-stage therapies are seen as the "arms" to be used in a "crusade," a war fought over "holy places" because they were occupied by an alien, and therefore enemy, power. A "crusading mentality" comes into being; almost any means is justified when it will delay the enemy, death.

We do not wish our position to be construed as being obstructive to scientific and technologic research, but we do believe medical scientists should be reminded that death is as integral an aspect of human life as it is of all other biologic species. The development of technologies with the prime aim of prolonging life should be seriously questioned if the ultimate result is destined to be a grotesque, fragmented, or inordinately expensive existence. We were not privy to the discussions of the institutional review board at the University of Utah that led to the news report that the board had refused to approve continuing human experiments with the artificial heart, but it is possible that such considerations contributed to that decision.

Today's practicing physicians have accepted—often without knowing it—a far greater priestly role than any of their predecessors. In part this is attributable to the diminished impact of religion in our civilization. To a greater extent, this phenomenon is due to the immense power that medical science has placed in physicians' hands. However, given the frequent announcements of scientific "breakthroughs," the limitations of their power to diagnose and control diseases are not always appreciated by the public. The emphasis on mortality statistics as a measure of medical care effectiveness has tended to obscure the fact that most of the time and effort of practicing physicians is devoted to improving the life of their patients. The real enemies are disease, discomfort, disability, fear, and anxiety. Sensitive, perceptive physicians attempt to guide their patients, those who are relatively healthy as well as those who are seriously handicapped and ill, to a perspective in which the preservation of life is not their God.

Chapter 11

The Sectarian Temptation: Reflections on Theology, the Church, and the University

I shall state in summary form the thesis of this lecture. It is very tempting in our cultural era to isolate Christian theology and ethics from critical external points of view in order to maintain the uniqueness or historic identity of Christianity. I call this a sectarian temptation, not because it is always associated with classic Anabaptist ecclesiologies, though in part it is, but because the separation of theology from other ways of construing the world in the culture is somewhat similar to the sharp separation of the Christian community from the world that has always characterized sectarianism.

In contemporary theology we have very sophisticated defenses of such a separation. I shall note and explain some of them all too briefly. The effect is that theology becomes a descriptive rather than normative discipline, and ethics becomes fidelity to the ethos of a particular historic community rather than participation in the patterns and processes of interdependence of life.

I shall then compare my account of contemporary proposals with what, to me, are better defended forms of "confessional" theology in the recent past to show where I think a critical difference lies in contemporary proposals.

Next I shall argue that assumptions underlying the new sectarianism in theology are untenable sociologically, philosophically, and theologically. Finally I shall briefly state what readers of my recent work already know, namely what I believe is necessary in theology and ethics, and the risks that are involved.

With this summary of the lecture in mind, I shall now proceed to develop my analysis and argument more fully, regretting that within the time constraints of one lecture it cannot be done with full adequacy.

1.

Christianity is a beleaguered religion. In the secularization of Western culture we have many alternative interpretations or construals of how things really and ultimately are—that is, functional equivalents to theology. We have, even in the West, a variety of moralities many of which are defended by modern ways of interpreting the nature of persons and the nature of morality itself. On the planet at large, as well as within Western countries, historic religious alternatives are practiced by vast numbers of people and new forms of religious life (or secular equivalents to religious life) appear. Religious pluralism is an inexorable fact. In this situation every *aggiornamento* in the Christian community poses threats to its historic uniqueness and identity, and every such move stimulates a conservative reaction. Pastors engaged in care of their parishioners are informed by theories of psychotherapy and begin to wonder what distinguishes them as Christians from their competitors down the street. Moralists become engaged in practical problems and social policy questions and wonder whether they are being faithful to their Christian commitments. Theologians take account of the learning provided by various nontheological disciplines in the university and are criticized for too much revisionism in their writings. Some lay persons feel that only a dogmatic preservation of "the old time religion" they learned as children provides an authentic basis for their beliefs and lives.

It is understandably tempting, if this brief description is somewhat accurate, to seek a position, theologically and ethically, that at least enables Christians to assert, "Here I stand, I can do no other." To entertain some revision in the received tradition is a threat psychologically to many individuals and sociologically to the community. To counter this threat some historic point gets frozen; it becomes the basis for contemporary faith and life. To waver from it is a threat. The line between true believers and others becomes a gulf of some depth, no matter how few are the true believers and how many find Christianity to be meaningless if not archaic. Reasons for believing are given, but tend to exclude what was classically the apologetic task of theology and ethics, that is, showing reasons for the plausibility of belief on grounds other than those drawn from within the historic tradition itself. Christian beliefs become subjectively meaningful, but their *truth* is not challenged.

Even secular persons who are cultural conservatives, worried about the drifts that occur in traditional values, speak respectfully only of some historically past form of religion. Vatican II is demeaned because a conservative cultural tradition is weakened; Orthodox Judaism is respected more than Reform Judaism because the reform compromises the marks of identity of a conservative force in culture. (A distinguished colleague of mine at the University of Chicago who was confirmed in a Lutheran Church in Germany does not darken a church door, but he is sure that any alteration in the use of Luther's Catechism is to be ridiculed.)

Sectarianism in theology and ethics becomes a seductive temptation. Religiously and theologically it provides Christians with a clear distinctiveness from others in beliefs; morally it provides distinctiveness in behavior. It ensures a clear identity which frees persons from ambiguity and uncertainty, but it isolates Christianity from taking seriously the wider world of science and culture and limits the participation of Christians in the ambiguities of moral and social life in the patterns of interdependence in the world.

Ironically, it seduces persons whose ecclesiologies were historically defined in part against sectarians. I shall later in this lecture comment on the very influential work in Christian ethics by Stanley Hauerwas; an ideal type of sectarian Christian ethics illumines much of what he writes. At the meetings of the British Society for the Study of Christian Ethics in September last, I found enthusiasm for his work from theologians from the Church of Scotland, the Church of England, and the Roman Catholic Church. I asked that some thought be given to possible incongruities between the ecclesiology that is necessary for the sectarian ethics and the ecclesiologies of these churches. I asked that some thought be given to the tension between the adherence of these churches to classic creeds on the Incarnation and the Trinity and the very particularistic historicist portrayal of Jesus in Hauerwas. A few days later at the conference on Reinhold Niebuhr at Kings College, London, I received an answer from a Scottish theologian. The sectarian ethic of discipleship is attractive because it made clear a historic confessional basis on which Christian morality could be distinguished from the culture, and how Christians could stand prophetically as Christians on matters of nuclear armaments and the like. Not every view that I put under a fairly large umbrella of the sectarian temptation becomes pacifist in its ethics, but my hypothesis is that assertive theological and moral confessionalism is a temptation offered in many forms.

2.

In contemporary theology we are offered some very sophisticated defenses for a sharp separation between Christian theology and ethics and their secular alternatives. Purely descriptive sectarian theology, on no matter what philosophical or institutional auspices, becomes isolated from the critical currents of the culture which might well call for a restatement and different apologetic defense of Christian theology. In my terms, purely descriptive theology becomes sectarian theology, isolated from other scientific endeavors which can rightly be seen to have implications for it.

One philosophical position that legitimates an isolation of theology has been espoused in Sweden by Anders Nygren and is espoused in the U.S. and Britain by writers whom the philosopher Kai Nielsen calls "Wittgensteinian fideists." D. Z. Phillips in England and Paul Holmer in the United States, in different ways, work from the same position. My reading of this position is as follows. There are various language games in culture: scientific, religious, aesthetic and moral. Among these it is clear that the language of science and the language of religion (including theology) are totally incommensurable. The language of religion is therefore exempt from critical assessment from any scientific perspective; it is free from criticism from all perspectives other than its own. The kind of theology that this sustains, Holmer writes, "seems by definition to be radically expressive, personalistic, confessional, illogical, and disorderly." Proper theological language "is everywhere permeated by an overpowering religious passion."[1] Theology then becomes incorrigible. "The Teachings do not have to change at all, for they are a kind of constant stretching through the ages."[2] I take it that one either has the correct religious passions or does not have them, and if one has correct ones "expressive, personalistic, confessional, illogical and disorderly" language is appropriate. Holmer stresses as does George Lindbeck (to whom I shall come shortly) that to become religious is to learn a language, and to learn to use that language properly. The incommensurability of scientific and religious language means that the same person and communities will have two very different ways of construing the reality of life in the world side by side. From this perspective of the division of languages one has no bearing upon the other. Theology and the morality of the Christian community necessarily become what I have called sectarian.

George Lindbeck has published very recently a book called *The Nature of Doctrine: Religion and Theology in a Post-Liberal Age.* I quote the final sentence: "Only in some younger theologians does one see the beginnings of a desire to renew in a posttraditional and postliberal mode the ancient practice of *absorbing the universe into the biblical world.* May their tribe increase."[3] The basis for the argument that sustains this hope is in some respects similar to his colleague Holmer's. Using the work of the cultural anthropologist, Clifford Geertz, Lindbeck defends what he calls "a cultural-linguistic" view of theology. "Religions are seen as comprehensive interpretive schemes, usually embodied in myths or narratives and heavily ritualized, which structure human experience and understanding of self and world."[4] "Stated more technically, a religion can be viewed as a kind of cultural and/or linguistic framework or medium that shapes the entirety of life and thought." "Like a culture or language, it is a communal phenomenon that shapes the subjectivities of individuals."[5] "One learns how to feel, act, and think *in conformity*

1. Paul Holmer, *The Grammar of Faith* (New York: Harper and Row, 1978), p. 63.
2. Ibid., p. 29.
3. George Lindbeck, *The Nature of Doctrine: Religion and Theology in a Post-Liberal Age* (Philadelphia: Westminster Press, 1984), p. 135. Italics added.
4. Ibid., p. 32.
5. Ibid., p. 33.

with a religious tradition."[6] The task of doctrine, then, is to maintain a distinctive language or culture, and to socialize persons (perhaps in an almost behavioristic psychological sense) into a particular form of life. It is not to carry on an interaction with other ways of viewing the world with any openness to what these other ways might require as alterations of the religion's own way of construing the world. The "Biblical mode" is not to be tampered with; rather one is to absorb "the universe into the Biblical world." The truth claims of theology are ignored, except insofar as they are *subjectively true* for persons socialized into the Christian culture and language.

It is difficult to see how one can make any critique of the tradition, internal or external. Interestingly, I think Lindbeck does not give us a powerful doctrine of the revelation of God in the Scriptures; one is left with the impression that the task of doctrine is to maintain an aspect of culture called Christianity. This, in my terms, becomes sectarian, and also defensive. Doctrine becomes ideology. It isolates theology from any correction by other modes of construing reality. Like Holmer, Lindbeck says that "Theology should therefore resist the clamor of the religiously interested public for what is currently fashionable and immediately intelligible. It should instead prepare for a future when continuing dechristianization will make greater Christian authenticity communally possible."[7] I agree that theology ought not to succumb to the immediately fashionable, but am alarmed by the denigration of the intelligible. It seems that the future of Christianity lies, for Lindbeck, in being a cognitively dissonant sectarian movement; its identity and authenticity demand this.

Scholars in the sociology of knowledge have contributed to what I harshly call a kind of sectarian tribalism in Christian theology and ethics. Their intentions, I take it, are descriptive and analytical; they attempt to show how the "social location" of scholars affects the ways in which they interpret reality. *The Social Construction of Reality* by Peter Berger and Thomas Luckman popularized and generalized the work of persons like Karl Mannheim and Robert Merton, and became important for theologians. Insofar as sociology of knowledge is a descriptive and analytical discipline its findings can be read as quite critical of knowledge claims made in any field of investigation, theology, sociology, or even the natural sciences. They are all socially relative. What is ironic to me is the following: rather than taking such interpretations as a challenge to the generality of truth claims in theology, as warnings about the limitations of such claims, and therefore as a matter for intellectual anxiety, some theologians accept these views as a basis for doing normative theology. If theology is the result of a social construction grounded in a historically relative community, then (it seems to me) many theologians say, "So be it." Proceed with confidence that the Christian community is a cultural linguistic community and, to repeat a counsel of Lindbeck's, absorb the universe into the biblical world. Historical relativism, rather than being something to worry

6. Ibid., p. 35. Emphasis added.
7. Ibid., p. 134.

about, to attempt to qualify, becomes a positive basis for virtually denying any cor-
rigibility of theology on the part of other ways of construing the world. Theology
becomes not concerned with its object, God, but rather with the perpetuation of
an ideology. A critical scholarly investigation, sociology of knowledge, becomes a
backing or warrant for sectarianism in theology.

Hermeneutics is another contributor to the possibility of sectarianism in theology. My reading, which is not thorough, of contemporary proposals is that the
term is now used not only with texts, but also for the interpretation of experience or any aspect of reality. I am uncomfortable with this expansion of the use
of the term. Here I confine myself to the ways in which hermeneutics can be used
to reinforce sectarian tendencies in theology and ethics. The theories I know
something about are quite formal; they are applicable to any sort of texts: biblical, theological, literary, and so forth. The possibility of sectarianism comes in
the choice of the text to be interpreted; that is, one can have rigorous principles
for interpreting a text without asking whether the text, for example, in theology,
refers to anything beyond itself. My point is that if theology asks first the question of the authority or truth value of a text for theology, it has to make that judgment on other grounds than hermeneutical theory. If it simply adopts a text, even
the Bible, without addressing what justifies the text as worthy of interpretation,
the interpretation is open to sectarianism. Hermeneutics can become a method
for purely descriptive theology, making a fideism. The Bible can become the only
text for the life of the Church, and the question of its authority and limits of
authority for theology can be bypassed. Theological hermeneutics is like Proteus;
its specific outcomes take different forms depending upon what text and who is
engaged in the task of interpretation. This charge is not equally applicable to all
hermeneutics in theology; my colleague David Tracy in *The Analogical Imagination* makes an argument for what constitutes what he calls a "classic" text based
on human experience and the Christian tradition. His notion rules out some texts
as theologically relevant although I find his choices of what to include in the modern period to be a bit quixotic. My point again is this: the acceptance of a text,
even the Bible, as that which is to be interpreted, can constrict the task of theology so that it avoids critical interaction with other "texts," that is, other ways of
interpreting how things really and ultimately are.

It is for reasons like this that I think what is called "narrative theology," something Lindbeck and many others applaud, is also in the end sectarian theology.
Stanley Hauerwas, whose impact in Christian ethics in North America and the
United Kingdom is considerable, is an example of this theology as it is expressed
in ethics. The general shape of his work is this: we grow up in communities in
which we share the narratives, the stories of the community. This, I would agree,
is partially true in a descriptive sense. The narratives and our participating in the
community, in his case the "Church" (very abstractly), give shape to our characters. Our characters are expressed in our deeds and actions. Further, the narratives of the community give shape to the way in which we interpret life in the
world. So far this is a description. A turn to the normative takes place. Since we

belong to the Christian community its narratives *ought* to shape the lives of its members. In Hauerwas's case, for example, this means that Christian morality is not based on a concern to be responsible participants in the ambiguities of public choices. It is rather based on its fidelity to the biblical narratives, and particularly to the gospel narratives. Thus the principal criterion for judging Christian behavior is its conformity to the stories of Jesus.[8] For Hauerwas this means, for example, that Christian morality must be pacifist because he reads the gospel narratives as pacifist. In this example, we have wedded a way of doing theology—narratives—to an ecclesiology—classically sectarian—and to an ethic which is also classically sectarian.

Among the things that get omitted is the doctrine of creation as in any way a basis for ethics. And if creation is important in theology and ethics contemporary ways of knowing nature are important. Fidelity to the narratives becomes virtually self-justifying in the sectarian temptation and both theology and ethics become incorrigible by anything outside of the community itself.

3.

Now I want to make some sketchy comparisons between what I judge to be sectarian tendencies and some theology of the recent past that was often called "confessional," and thus by implication also possibly sectarian in tendency. I must be brief, and cannot document my comparisons here. The main point is this: the confessional theologies of Barth and the Niebuhr brothers in America were given strong *theological* justifications for being confessional. I do not find those kinds of justification as strongly in some current writings.

One justification, that for Barth's theology, was a strong and well-defended view of Scripture as the Word of God, of the divine authorization of the covenant and the community given in the Bible, and of Christ as the revelation of the God who is for man. The theology had strong and widespread implications for ethics. Of course, Barth shared this view of the Word of God with Luther and Calvin and many other theologians. My impression is that the "sectarian" theologies currently promulgated do not back their claims with such a doctrine of biblical revelation. Lindbeck, for example, does not argue (though he may believe it—I do not know) that the cultural-linguistic community that bears the Christian doctrinal language was an especially chosen community by God through whose cultural-linguistic system God makes himself known to humankind. A powerful defense of biblical revelation could provide a backing for such theological proposals that I would find respectable even if I did not fully agree with it. Without such a backing theology seems to become the task of preservation of a tradition for the sake of preserving a tradition.

---

8. Stanley Hauerwas, *The Peaceable Kingdom* (Notre Dame: University of Notre Dame Press, 1983). My generalization is drawn from the argument of this book and other of his writings.

Whether the Niebuhr brothers were "confessional," or in what sense, is a matter that can be discussed. They certainly were more biblical theologians than they were speculative philosophical theologians. Each in a different way justified his use of the biblical themes on the basis of what they revealed about human life and the conditions of human life. Reinhold Niebuhr, for example, over and over argues that what he calls myths from the biblical material had extraordinary revelatory power—revealing the truth about life itself in the human community. There was a dialectic in his thought between biblical materials and human experience; the biblical materials, for example, the account of the fall, illumined the reality of human experience and the reality in turn confirmed the truth of the myth or the doctrine. Put crudely, the biblical material was extraordinarily useful because of what it helped to disclose about the human situation—a basis for hope, a need for mercy, and a wariness of human corruption.

H. Richard Niebuhr, in his classic little book *The Meaning of Revelation*, is one of the American sources for so-called narrative theology. But the biblical material for him was worthy of being called revelation because of the way in which it could make sense of the meaning of human life and provide an interpretation of the world in which we live in the light of its stories and its articulated beliefs that was confirmed in part by experience. What was known in a historically relative way was God, and thus ethics became the task of interpreting God's actions in the world—not the preservation of an ethos or fidelity to tradition. Theology was not self-justifying, but its truth and value was, as with his brother, confirmed in human experience.

Perhaps the disclosive power of the particular historical material, the fact that it was justified by its fruits, appears to some contemporaries to be moving away from a properly confessional stance; it appears to be apologetic. This is certainly the case with Stanley Hauerwas, who has argued that any effort to move beyond the particularistic historical tradition (as defined, in the end by him) either to justify it or to criticize and possibly alter it, is a move to what he calls "universalism." But apart from either a powerfully defended doctrine of revelation in the Bible and its accounts, as the particular history in which God chose to reveal himself, or apart from some confirmation of the revelatory power of the biblical material in human experience and what it discloses about life in the world, sectarian theologies become defensive efforts to sustain the historical identity of the Christian tradition virtually for its own sake. Ironically the sectarian position ends up not doing what it intends, namely, provide a critical religious vision of reality that can aggressively interact with other ways of construing the world. The marginalization of Christian faith is accepted and even praised; other confessional positions would hardly affirm this.

4.

In this section of the lecture I will indicate what I think are sociological, philosophical, and theological assumptions made by the new sectarians, and why I think these assumptions are incorrect.

Theologians who succumb to the sectarian temptation assume, *sociologically,* that the Church or the Christian community is socially and culturally isolable from the wider society and culture of which it is a part. They assume that there is, or can be, a kind of Christian tribe living in a kind of ghetto whose members are (or can be) shaped in their inner dispositions, their religious passions and their moral outlooks almost exclusively by the biblical or Christian language or narratives.

This assumption has always been false in the history of Christianity. Theology was shaped by the Hellenistic culture of the early Church; if the primitive Christian community had found its cultural home in India its theology and ethics would have been affected by Hinduism and Buddhism, and its history would have become very different from what it is. If Lindbeck's counsel to absorb the universe into the Biblical world is taken seriously, it perhaps follows earlier views of absorbing ideas of the universe into Christian thought—Platonic, Aristotelian, Kantian. But we live in a time when culture provides a different view of the universe, and just as previous views could not be absorbed without tension (if not contradiction) so contemporary ones cannot be absorbed without some possible revision of the "Biblical world."

Theologians or laity, people belonging to the churches and people educated in universities (or even people who read the science sections of the newspapers or watch television), are exposed to and share in alternative ways of construing the world and the place of human life in it—alternatives to the biblical narratives. Indeed, it is clear that these alternatives provide for many people a more adequate way of construing life, backed by theories and evidences which are strongly defended. And theologians and church people do find incongruities between certain historic claims of the Church and contemporary understandings.

I illustrate with an anecdote. Several years ago I was asked to meet with a denominational group that was writing a statement on "Death and Dying." The first part of the statement was on "Biblical background and basis." I noted that the section ignored a Biblical view that death was caused by the sin of Adam and Eve. I was told that it was not clear from the Bible whether that death was physical, or whether it was spiritual. I cited historic theologians, including Luther, who thought it was physical. Then I was told that the whole notion would have to be demythologized in the light of modern knowledge. I suggested that this group had two alternatives: either to say honestly that it no longer believed the tradition or try to demythologize the tradition so the laity would understand why they engage in such work. My point is this: In modern culture few persons with average education any longer believe that biological death is caused by the sins of Adam and Eve, including few who write theology or participate in the Church. A persuasive alternative way of explaining why we die exists. Neither theologians nor people in the churches can avoid it. The tradition, on this point, simply has to be revised because Christian theology and Christian churches are informed by the culture of which they are parts.

Sectarians might admit that the Christian community does not live in a cultural ghetto, but go on to propose that there are double, triple, or quadruple truths which are incommensurable with each other. Christians live in separable communities each with its own language. This seems to me to create problems of moral and intellectual integrity for Christians; they would have to interpret and explain the same events in different ways as they left the doors of the Church and went home to read the newspapers, the scientific journals, or watch television. Theologically Christianity becomes a modern and trivial form of gnosticism.

Sectarian tendencies in theology falsely assume that a cultural-linguistic community with a particular history and set of narratives is, can be, or ought to be isolated from the society and culture of which it is a part. Theologians in universities who succumb to the temptation have no right to accuse their colleagues in other fields of being excessively specialized, in-bred, and dogmatic if their own work is not open to correction and rethinking in the light of other disciplines which investigate life (life which is also construed theologically) from other perspectives. The sociological assumption of sectarian theology is at least weak if not false; to suppose that in our time the Christian community could become a tribal culture isolated from others is certainly false. Any normative proposals for theology that fail to address the weakness of errors of the sociological assumption are bound for frustration and eventual failure. Indeed, because of the power that other institutions in society and culture have to furnish symbols and constructs that interpret the same reality that Christian faith and theology does, the parish and congregational life of churches necessarily has to take these matters into account as it seeks to educate and form persons in Christian faith and life.

The sociological assumption also breaks on the rocks of the fact that Christians do (and ought to) participate in their professions, their political communities and other aspects of the social order. Their moral lives are not confined to some Christian community; they take place where choices have to be made that are not only moral but economic, political, medical, and so forth. If the test of the morality of Christians becomes its conformity to some version of the imitation of Christ, or some fidelity to the meaning of Biblical narratives, either Christians are put into positions of intense inner conflict or they must withdraw from participation in any structures which would presumably compromise their fidelity to Jesus. Again, this is not a novel problem in the history of Christianity; it is, however, intensified if theologically sectarian ethics demand withdrawal from participation in controverted moral and political situations during a cultural period when the destiny of life in the world is determined by secular centers of power. While the Anabaptist vision of Christian morality can be seductively appealing because it provides clear lines of distinction between Christ and culture, Church and world, it can also lead to isolation of Christians from participation in critical ambiguous choices in professional and public life. Even descriptively the sociological assumption of this is false. Christians, whether they choose to or not, are members of, and make choices in, other social communities.

The *philosophical* assumptions made by sectarian theologies are no doubt different for different authors. My remarks on this are general, but I believe pertain rather widely. For some authors, I think it is assumed that the ways of knowing religiously and theologically are radically distinct from other ways of knowing. No doubt there *are* differences; for example, religious knowing quite properly assumes a condition of piety if not faith, a readiness to move from that which is rationally established to acknowledgment of the divine reality. The logic of religious discourse is not the same as the logic of scientific discourse. But some sectarian theologies, insofar as they insist upon the view that Christianity is a separate cultural linguistic enterprise, and even more when they insist that the intent of this enterprise is to stimulate and shape subjective attitudes, isolate religious knowing from any effects of other ways of knowing. It would seem to stress excessively the distinctions between faith as subjective assent to positively given "truths" on the one hand and rational activity which is open to questions of the adequacy of the truths assented to on the other. To correct this assumption is not to claim that, for example, scientific ways of knowing can replace religious ways, or that there is an imperialism of science over theology and other areas of knowledge. But it is to claim that the rational activity of the religious community overlaps with and has similarities to the rational activities of other communities and therefore is subject to correction and revision by other ways of knowing.

In addition to the assumption of a radically different way of knowing, some sectarian theologies seem also to assume that the object of knowledge—God—is so unrelated to other objects of knowledge that there are no indications of God's reality from nature, human experience, and so forth. Of course it is the case that God is not an object like other objects, that God is not like the structure of a gene, and so forth. But if God is the source of how things really and ultimately are, if God is the sustainer and even destroyer of aspects of life in the world, if God is the determiner of the destiny of things, then whatever one says about how God is related to the world demands theological attention to ways in which nature, history and culture are interpreted and understood by investigations appropriate to them. Put boldly, if God is sovereign over all things, then knowledge of nature, and so forth, as informed by investigations proper to nature, have to be taken into account in order to say something about God. God is not nature without remainder, but the historic doctrine of creation certainly affirms that God orders life through nature. Thus knowledge of nature contributes to, but does not finally determine, what can be said about God. Sectarian assumptions seem to deny or underestimate this.

What I have briefly said about philosophical assumptions in some sectarian tendencies in theology has already been based on what might be a *theological* assumption, namely, that God is known *only* in and through history, and particularly the history of the Biblical people culminating in the events of Christ and their effects. Insofar as this describes an assumption it ignores a great deal of the Biblical witness itself. In Christian sectarian form God becomes a Christian God for Christian people; to put it most pejoratively, God is assumed to be the tribal God of a minority of the earth's population. Or, if God is not a tribal God there is only one community in the world that has access to knowledge of God because God has revealed himself only in the life of that community. Or still another possible assumption, and worse from my perspective than the other two, Christian theology and ethics really are not concerned so much about God as they are about maintaining fidelity to the biblical narratives about Jesus, or about maintaining the "Biblical view" as a historical vocation that demands fidelity without further external justification, or idolatrously maintaining a historic social identity.

The effect of such theological assumptions is sectarian. The sectarianism is particularly problematic in a historic time when technology brings not only various historic religions but also secular equivalents to theologies into intensive interaction. I do not believe that some agreement about the nature of God on the part of theologians of various faiths would provide a practical ground for a cooperative world culture; religions are rooted and expressed in particular cultures. Thus I am not as enthused as some are about finding a common theology as a result of interreligious conferences about God. I do, however, believe that historic theologies, including Christian, if they are speaking about the ultimate power and orderer of life in the world, must be open to revision and correction in the face of alternative views—views from other historic religions and the secular functional equivalents to theology.

In the realm of the moral, the theological sectarianism is particularly pernicious, as I have suggested above. Faithful witness to Jesus is not a sufficient theological and moral basis for addressing the moral and social problems of the twentieth century. The theologian addressing many issues—nuclear, social justice, ecology, and so forth—must do so as an outcome of a theology that develops God's relations to all aspects of life in the world, and develops those relations in terms which are not exclusively Christian in a sectarian form. Jesus is not God.

5.
CONCLUSION

What Lindbeck describes as a hope to me is a perilous fate, namely, that Christianity will find greater authenticity by becoming more sectarian. I have called sectarianism a temptation in theology, the Church and morality. It is a very seductive tempter. It can provide various forms of security. If being purely descriptive and historical in theology makes it scientific, then one has the security of being a scientist. If religion is passionate subjectivity and not related to anything objective such as the reality of a sovereign Deity, then whatever induces and nourishes those passions is free from critical scrutiny by other perspectives on life. If it is meaningful, one does not worry about whether it is true. If Christianity is simply a cultural linguistic community one can govern one's subjectivity by its meanings, learn its language and how to use it, and have a strong sense of identity with the Christian tribe, distinguished from the other tribes around. One can have the same advantages that there are to being a German instead of a Frenchman, or vice versa.

It is a temptation because it legitimates a withdrawal of Christianity from its larger cultural environs at least to the extent that the truth or adequacy of

Christianity is not subjected to critical scrutiny by other disciplines, other forces in the culture. To use Douglas Ottati's term, the sectarian temptation preserves the historic integrity of Christianity. It may do that, however, at the cost of making Christianity *unintelligible* in a world in which fewer and fewer persons are formed to the "Christian language."[9] It is seductive because it can provide reasons for not engaging in the fray of intellectual life, not engaging in the ambiguities of political and moral life. One only bears *witness* to a historic tradition, and the mark of authenticity is that of fidelity to the tradition. It becomes even more seductive if one is persuaded as Lindbeck is, that "continuing dechristianization will make greater Christian authenticity communally possible." (This reminds me of some passages in Luther where the number and vehemence of his enemies is adduced as a justification for the rightness of his position.)

I can use Ottati's too simple distinction between integrity and intelligibility to bring this lecture to a conclusion. Sectarianism preserves the identity of Christianity but at great cost to its intelligibility and to its participation in universities, politics and cultural life.

Readers of my recent work, and certainly critics of it, know what hearers of this lecture know, namely, that I find succumbing to the sectarian temptation to be pernicious. But the alternative to it is not without its risks. That is, a risk to the particularistic historic identity of the Christian religious tradition and the community. I cannot undertake a defense now of those risks; I have done so in too many printed pages already. I can only be assertive, and not justificatory, here. It is God with whom humankind has to reckon; God who is the source of all life, whose powers have brought it into being, sustain it, bear down upon it, create conditions of possibility within it and will determine its ultimate destiny. Theology has to be open to all the sources that help us to construe God's relations to the world; ethics has to deal with the interdependence of *all* things in relation to God. This, for me, necessarily relativizes the significance of the Christian tradition, though it is the tradition in which our theologies develop. God is the God of Christians, but God is not a Christian God for Christians only.

I close this academic lecture with a biblical verse which to me, as it did to my teacher from the eighteenth century, Jonathan Edwards, sums up the subject matter of theology and the spirit in which it should be done: "To the King of all ages, immortal, invisible, the only God, be honor and glory for ever" (1 Tim. 1:17).

9. Douglas F. Ottati, *Meaning and Method in H. Richard Niebuhr's Theology* (Washington: University Press of America, 1982), especially pp. 171–98.

Chapter 12

Christian Ethics

[In addressing the topic "Christian Ethics," other essays have been written that] deal with the ethics of various Christian traditions; this one attends to the patterns of Christian ethical writing, their elements and their relations to each other.

Themes. Writings that are systematic have organizing themes (metaphors, analogies, symbols, principles) around which other theological and ethical ideas and concepts cohere. The themes may be theological or ethical, or combinations of the two. Some examples follow: (a) The theme that backs H. R. Niebuhr's "ethics of responsibility" is anthropological; persons are responders or answerers more than "makers" or "citizens." The theological theme of "God acting in events" to which persons respond coheres with this, as do such procedures as the interpretation of events. (b) *Agape* is the supreme moral principle of Christian ethics for Paul Ramsey. Its supremacy is backed by his interpretation of biblical theology. Since it is a rule term for him, and since he believes that biblical ethics are deontological, his practical procedures for making choices cohere with his view of *agape*. (c) Luther's theology distinguishes but does not separate the work of God as creator and as redeemer. His ethics of the civic use of the law and of an agent-oriented freedom and love cohere with these themes. They are related to each other; Christians act out of freedom and love in obedience to the law and in their offices in orders of creation. (d) Augustine interprets human action as motivated by desires and directed toward ends. His view of rightly or wrongly ordered persons and acts coheres with his theological principle that all things are to be ordered proportionately in relation to God, the supreme good.

Base points. Comprehensive Christian ethical writings have four distinguishable base points, or points of reference. They are coherent insofar as the base points are organized around themes, as stated above. The base points are: (1) theological interpretation in a restricted sense—that is, the understanding and interpretation of God, God's relations to the world and particularly to human beings, and God's purposes; (2) the interpretation of the meaning and significance of human experience and history, of events and circumstances in which human beings act, and of nature; (3) the interpretation of persons or communities as moral agents, and of their acts; and (4) the interpretation of how persons and communities ought to make moral choices and judge their actions, those of others, and the states of affairs in the world.

1. How the interpretation of God is developed is critical for ethics. Process theology has implications for ethics that differ from those based upon an eternal and immutable divine order. The use of personal or interpersonal concepts to understand God and God's relations to the world will yield different ethics than a view of God as impersonal being. Christological choices are critical. If Christ reveals God to be primarily a gracious God, and if interpersonal concepts are used to understand God's relations to persons, one has ethics like Karl Barth's. If Christ is the one in and through whom all things are created, there is a Christological foundation for ethics of natural law, as in the Roman Catholic tradition. If Christ is the one through whom the divinization of man takes place, as in Eastern Orthodox theology, the ethical implications are different in yet another way.

2. The concepts or symbols used to interpret experience and events are critical. If God is acting for the liberation of human life, experience and events have a different religious and ethical significance than in an interpretation based upon an immutable moral order of creation. If events are interpreted on the basis of the great power of evil in the world, they have a different significance than in an interpretation that views the power of good to be more in control. Christological choices affect how experience and events are interpreted. If Christ is a new "seed" implanted in history that is "organically" spreading through life (e.g., Schleiermacher), events will have a different significance than in a view that sees the crucifixion as the primary way to understand them (e.g., H. R. Niebuhr on war). Judgments about eschatology affect the interpretation of events. If the coming of the kingdom of God is almost totally, or totally, a future event, eschatology will function differently in Christian ethics than in a view that sees the kingdom as the fulfillment of a historical end. If it is interpreted as a social ideal (e.g., Rauschenbusch) certain goals can be inferred from it to direct action; from other perspectives it stands basically as a critical principle relativizing and judging all human ends.

3. The interpretation of persons and their acts has ramifications for ethics. If human actions are strongly conditioned, or determined, by desires (e.g., Augus-

tine and Jonathan Edwards), Christian ethics takes a different shape from views that accent more strongly the freedom of the will. The decision that theologians make on various grounds about a theory of human action qualifies decisively the ethics they develop. Christological judgments are important here as well. If human beings are basically sinners, though justified by the work of Christ, persons and actions will be interpreted differently than in a view that stresses the present efficacy of redemption and sanctification.

4. Both the procedures and the content of the prescriptive or normative ethics in Christian writings require specific development. How they are developed depends on different sorts of choices that a theologian makes. One choice is of the fundamental shape of ethics; theologians back their choices in different ways. Paul Ramsey, for example, argues that Christian ethics is deontic because biblical ethics is. For others (e.g., Paul Lehmann), biblical theology supports a view of acting in events in ways consonant with God's humanizing purposes. For both theological and philosophical reasons other writers develop Christian ethics in a teleological manner. Interpretations of Christ make a difference. If Christ reveals the norm or ideal of true humanity, his life and teachings become morally normative and the procedures of moral life are discipleship or imitation and the application of his teaching to current actions. If his significance is primarily related to the redemption of persons, the norm is more that of dispositions from which moral actions flow; one gets a more "agent-oriented" ethics.

If the writings are both comprehensive and coherent, the four base points will be integrally related to one another.

Sources. Comprehensive Christian ethical writings use four distinguishable sources: (1) the Bible and the Christian tradition, (2) philosophical principles and methods, (3) science and other sources of knowledge about the world, and (4) human experience broadly conceived. Writers make judgments about these sources and about the weight or authority each has. Four kinds of judgments are made, namely, about which sources are relevant and why; which sources are decisive when they conflict, and why; what specific content is to be used from these sources and what is to be ignored or rejected, and why; and how this content is to be interpreted and why it is to be so interpreted.

1. All four kinds of judgments are made in the use of biblical materials and sources from the Christian tradition. Even if, as some argue, Christian ethics begins with biblical exegesis, choices are made about what biblical themes and passages are central. A basic choice is whether the biblical material will be used primarily for theological purposes that ground or back the development of ethics, or whether the moral teachings of the Bible will be treated as a revealed source of ethics. For example, the ethics of liberal Protestantism tended to use the New Testament, and particularly the Gospels, as a "revealed" source of moral ideals, ends, examples, and teachings. With the turn toward "biblical theology," ethics were grounded in various theological themes from the Bible, such as God acting in history, human beings as sinners, or the kingdom of God as breaking into history. Different theological themes from the Bible ground different emphases in

ethics. How the moral teachings in the Bible are related to the biblical theologies varies—e.g., for Barth they are instruction and give direction; for others they are ideals, principles, or rules.

Discernible differences can be found in writings from various Christian traditions; great theologians or historical movements establish patterns that persist. Examples: the use of natural law in the Roman Catholic tradition; the distinction between law and gospel and between the heavenly and earthly realms in the Lutheran tradition; the emphasis on following Christ as he is portrayed in the Gospels and on rigorous obedience to his teachings in the Radical Reformation tradition; the marked mystical aspects of ethics in the Eastern Orthodox tradition. Received traditions undergo development and change; an example is the rethinking of natural law in contemporary Roman Catholic theology in the light of more historical consciousness and stress on the "personal" character of human life.

2. Judgments are made about philosophical principles and methods. Writers sometimes explicitly adapt patterns from philosophy (e.g., Platonism, Aristotelianism, Kantianism, existentialism) because they believe they are consonant with a theology, or they use them to explicate the ethical implications of a theology, or they determine on philosophical grounds what the science of ethics is to which theology must be related. Sometimes the judgments about philosophy are implicit, sometimes they are defended on theological or other grounds.

Persistent themes in Christian ethics are developed differently, depending on philosophical choices made by the author. For example, love functions differently in Christian ethical writings that are deontic in mode from those that are primarily agent-oriented; in the former it is basically a principle or rule term, and in the latter it indicates a disposition of persons. Appeals to the Bible are not decisive in this matter; there is no philosophical theory of ethics in the Bible, and terms like love are used to refer to different aspects of moral life.

3. Applications of Christian ethics, no matter what choices are made on any of the previous items, use sources of information and insight about the sphere of activity that is attended to. Differences occur in part as a result of the different data that are used, even about the same general area of interest. For example, to understand persons as agents some writers turn to particular psychologists, others to particular philosophers. The choice of data requires defense on the basis of its adequacy. Concepts used to interpret information also vary; for example, Christians influenced by Marxist interpretations understand the relations between ethics and economics differently from those who judge modified free-market interpretations to be more accurate.

4. Broader understandings of human experience in general affect how Christian ethics are developed. Insight is drawn not only from academic disciplines, but also from literature and art, and from the residues of moral experience embedded in custom and habit. The choices affect some basic postures toward the world. For example, the weight of a writer's judgment on a continuum from determinism to radical freedom may be affected not only by philosophical and

scientific scholarship but also by the author's own experiences or by reflections gained from observations about historical events, etc.

All four types of judgments mentioned above are made about all four sources of Christian ethical writings.

Whether and how ethical writings are Christian depends upon the significance that Christ or Christology has for them. Christological judgments are critical to how ethical writings are Christian. Writers who view the Gospel narratives and teachings exclusively as a source for a sublime moral code, or for an ideal moral and social life, think in terms of the application of the teachings or realization of the ideal. For them, the significance of Christ is restricted to morality. For others, Christ is the revelation of the nature of God and God's relation to the world; for example, in Christ God is known as a gracious God who is "for man." Sometimes the focus is on the redeeming work of Christ; this calls attention to the efficacy of that work for the qualities of life of persons. Further judgments about the doctrine of sanctification will affect the interpretation of the Christian moral life. If the significance of Christ's work is forensic, the freedom of the Christian is stressed; if it is also efficacious in the reordering of motives and desires, claims are made for moral progress in Christian life.

Combinations and qualifications of these tendencies occur in various writings. The view of Christ as teacher and example might be backed, not by the judgment that is strictly moral, but by the idea that the form of God's revelation (i.e., in and through Christ) provides the pattern of life appropriate to those who believe in Christ and receive his benefits. Or, if the principal significance is what is revealed about God's goodness, the life and teachings can be signs or indicators of the kinds of deeds that those who respond to God's goodness ought to be doing. In the New Testament there are grounds for various foci of Christological development, and thus for different explications of what and how ethics can be Christian.

Chapter 13

Roman Catholic
and Protestant Interaction
in Ethics: An Interpretation

The aim of this article outreaches the present competence of its author. To peer retrospectively over 50, or better, 75 years of the relations between Roman Catholic and Protestant ethics suggests large research projects: a thorough study of the interpretations of Roman Catholic ethics by Protestant theologians, of Protestant ethics by Roman Catholic theologians, and of literature on ethics and moral theology from each tradition to analyze the use of sources from the other. Seventy-five (at least) years would be preferable to 50, for one should examine the books being read in theological schools in 1940, many of which came from the preceding decades. To describe the state of the exchanges, if there were any, in 1940 would only set the stage for an intensive examination of the literature in many Western languages in the last 50 years, and especially since Vatican II.

Were the treatments from each tradition stereotypical and very general until, let us say, 1960? Did writers from each tradition refer primarily to founding fathers or great synthesizers in each from ages past, or is there evidence that they examined contemporary writings? Were certain issues, theological and ethical, in focus? What reasons determined these foci? If one assumes a considerable development over the past three or four decades, whose writings from each tradition seemed to gain attention? What reasons seem to determine intensification of interaction? On what "levels of discourse" does the developing interaction occur? The moral level of judgments about war, abortion, economic issues, etc.? The level of philosophical justifications for the moral judgments? The level of theological backings for positions taken? If interaction was sustained by an incoming tide of ecumenism, has that tide ebbed? Are there practical moral questions regnant in current discussions about which one cannot divide opinion as characteristically Catholic or Protestant? If so, or not so, why? E.g., pacifism and just war? Are there theological issues which are accented in current discussions on which the house is not divided by traditional party lines? E.g., that of the particularity or distinctiveness of Christian moral outlooks and behavior in contrast to ethics as autonomous and Christianity as new interiority or as exhortative?

A further set of concerns evades competence for exhaustive interpretation. It pertains to background conditions shared by both traditions not only in Western culture and societies but also in Third World nations. For example, there are strong similarities in theologies and ethics of liberation written by Roman Catholic and Protestant theologians. To what extent is this due to shared social conditions? To shared intellectual input from theological, philosophical, economic, and sociological writers? Are larger social forces such as secularization in Western societies being responded to by both traditions—in similar or different ways? If Roman Catholic moral theology and ethics no longer shares the degree of consensus it had in 1940, i.e., if there is a "pluralism" in the Catholic Church, is this due to responses to different background conditions, to different movements in the literary and social world? Or would a more strictly academic, i.e., philosophical and theological, account be most adequate, if not sufficient? (In my judgment, most of the discussions of the social bases for theological and ethical preferences are exceedingly vague. Without any success I have over and over recommended Robert K. Merton's "Paradigm for the Sociology of Knowledge" in an effort to refine these analyses. See his *Social Theory and Social Structure* [Glencoe, Ill.: Free Press, 1949] 221–22.)

This introduction, with its caveats, resembles the opening section of many essays by Karl Rahner! Its justification is simply that it is "spading and digging" to locate what I am able to do in a more comprehensive context. If there are monographs that do what I propose is necessary for a competent treatment, unfortunately I do not know them.

PROFILE OF PROTESTANT DISCUSSION
BEFORE VATICAN II

If "Koch-Preuss" was used in seminaries in 1940, Roman Catholic clergy, and presumably the faithful they cared for, were taught that the division between Catholic and Protestant ethics was deep and broad. In less than four pages the assertions—and that is all they are—mark clear differences. I quote from only the first paragraph.

Catholic Moral Theology is based on the dogmatic teaching of the one true Church. Protestant ethics rests on arbitrary assumptions. . . . Catholics acknowledge an infallible authority in questions of both dogma and morals, whereas Protestants possess no objective rule for either, but are buffeted to and fro by winds of subjectivism and error.[1]

John Gallagher of the department of theology at Loyola University in Chicago in his forthcoming book demonstrates clearly that the "manualist tradition" is not as uniform as superficial impressions suggest, but my limited investigation indicates that Protestantism was either characterized in the mode of the quotation or blithely ignored. Whether Protestant views of Catholic moral theology were any subtler or more sophisticated than Koch-Preuss on Protestantism is a matter I shall attend to with admittedly selective evidences. The publication dates do not all fit precisely the prenativity of *Theological Studies,* but all precede Vatican II.

For the reader with only modest knowledge of Protestant and Roman Catholic theology, there are no big surprises forthcoming from this investigation. Most of the attention is on the theological level, i.e., on doctrinal questions that have been controverted since the Reformation. This level is intricately intertwined with the philosophical level; charges of distortions of theology and ethics because of the influence of Aristotelian, and to some extent Stoic, philosophy create both theological issues such as the relations between God and creation, and ethical issues such as the foundations of morality and the understanding of human persons. There are some, but remarkably few, discussions of differences on particular moral questions. All this reflects a conventional Protestant theological agenda, and also how ethics, in the context of Protestant theology, was more integrated into systematic theology than was the case in the Roman Catholic tradition with its sharper distinction between the areas of theological research and writing.

The relation of moral philosophy to moral theology or theological ethics is the fulcrum on which swing both the relatively extended discussions published by Karl Barth. His polemic is, however, directed more toward "neo-Protestantism" than toward Roman Catholicism. Indeed, on this point he wrote: "And if we were compelled to choose between the Neo-Protestant and the Roman Catholic solutions, in this as in so many other questions we should have no option but to prefer the latter."[2] At an earlier time he described Roman Catholic moral theology as a "bold union of Aristotle and Augustine," and after a very nonjudgmental summary of what he perceived to be the major features of this synthesis he lines out the issues: "Between the Roman Catholic view and our own stands a difference in the concept of God, of man, of the sin of man, and grace which comes to him."[3] While there is formal agreement on the definition of relations between

1. Antony Koch (adapted and edited by Arthur Preuss), *A Handbook of Moral Theology,* 5 vols. (St. Louis: Herder, 1918) 1:7. Chapter 3 is titled "The Differences between Catholic Moral Theology and Protestant Ethics."

2. Barth, *Church Dogmatics* II/2 (Edinburgh: T. and T. Clark, 1957), p. 529.

3. Barth, *Ethics,* ed. Dietrich Braun (New York: Seabury, 1981), p. 30. These lectures were delivered in 1928, but published in German only in 1973 and 1978.

moral philosophy and moral theology, the "intention and character" of the definition is materially very different.

Underlying the issues is "the fundamental Roman Catholic conception of the harmony, rooted in the concept of being, between nature and supernature, nature and grace, reason and revelation, man and God."[4] The order of being is the common presupposition in both philosophy and theology; metaphysics is "a basic discipline superior to both philosophy and theology." Barth's queries are epistemological, but freighted with theological and ethical implications. "Where and how," he asks, "is God knowable and given to us in his being and not in and as his act?"[5] In Catholic moral theology God seems to be grasped as an entity that humans can master, and such an entity does not deserve to be called God. It is impermissible, for Barth, to construct the order of obligation on the order of being, for then human beings have derived the obligation; it is grounded in human activity and not in the command of God. "Does not its command have to be one and the same as the divine act of commanding; indeed as the divine commanding itself?"[6]

The ethics of the divine commands of a gracious God that Barth developed so fully is, of course, backed not simply by his rejection of the analogy of being, but also by his view of revelation, his Christology, and other matters. It is clear that other Protestants shared some of Barth's criticisms of Catholic moral theology but came to positions different from his in their own ethical writings. I believe, however, that Barth's statement about a Roman Catholic conception of harmony could be said to underlie many of the Protestant charges. While other writers are not as vehement as Barth in his charge of human usurpation of divine prerogatives in moral theology,[7] the worry about absolutizing the relative based on natural law is quite pervasive.

Emil Brunner is particularly interesting on this point, since his systematic ethics combines a view of divine commands with a structure of orders of creation. If sin has corrupted all spheres of life—which he believes Thomas Aquinas and the Fathers hold at least about the economic order—then one must be wary of identifying any given historical order with the divine order. He charges that "modern Catholics" ignore this point. "Their idea of 'the Law of Nature' is so fully adapted to the actual state of things—think for instance of their doctrine of

4. Ibid.

5. Ibid., p. 31.

6. Ibid. Cf. Barth, *Church Dogmatics* II/2, p. 530 on the theme of harmony, and pp. 532–33 on the issue of human derivation of obligations. On the latter: "From the very outset man is assured of a right of consultation and control in God's command. Whatever else it may be and mean for him, it can never become for him a command that affects him personally and binds him unconditionally." What is common between the 1928 lectures and *Church Dogmatics* II/2 is the priority of divine act over being, and thus the language of divine commands. The latter discussion bears more marks of Barth's developed Christocentric theology; in Jesus Christ a divinely imperative obligation is part of the "divine act of the world's reconciliation with God as the act of His pure goodness" (p. 532).

7. See, e.g., Barth's discussion of casuistry as a procedure in *Church Dogmatics* III/4 (Edinburgh: T. and T. Clark, 1961), pp. 6–19, and the application of his criticism throughout his discussion of issues of taking human life (pp. 397–407).

private property—that the contradiction either disappears entirely, or is concealed by the formula: 'out of consideration for special circumstances.'"[8]

Reinhold Niebuhr makes a similar charge, though in one of his discussions his research led him to a qualification often cited in recent Catholic moral theology. In the first volume of *The Nature and Destiny of Man* he wrote: "The social ethics of Thomas Aquinas embody the peculiarities and contingent factors of a feudal-agrarian economy into a system of fixed socio-ethical principles."[9] In *Faith and History* he wrote: "It is certainly dangerous to fill the 'natural law' with too many specific injunctions and prohibitions." In his footnote to this passage he aptly notes "that Thomas Aquinas had less specific content in his natural law than is found in modern Catholic theory," and cites the oft-quoted passage from *Summa theologiae* 1–2, q. 94, a. 4, pertaining to defects as one descends from the common principle to the particular circumstances.[10] But Catholics are not the only ones who falsely absolutize the relative: "both Catholic and Protestant social theory tended to make the right of property much too absolute."[11]

Obviously backing the criticisms of absolutizing the relative are not only metaphysical and epistemological matters, but also a traditional Protestant view of sin, followed by correlative interpretations of grace. The discussion is, again, primarily on the theological level but has implications for ethics. For Barth the first consideration is, of course, grace, and sin is the second. For him human fellowship with God can be understood only as grace, which "rules out any attempt to snatch God's being beyond his act. . . . We could no longer understand grace as grace . . . if grace really shared its power with a capacity of our own nature and reason, if an ascent of man to God were really possible, and an order of obligation could exist, on the basis of a direct relation of man to God which grasps the divine being and thus bypasses grace."[12] The accuracy of this blunt insinuation directed to Catholic moral theology, of course, can be disputed, but the force of Barth's alternative frames a radically different view of ethics. His correlative view of sin is a traditional Protestant one. Sin must be viewed "much more sharply" than Roman Catholic doctrine views it. He rejects "any fitness of man for cooperation with God."[13] Thus justification and sanctification are the work of God alone and not of God and human beings together.

There is an air of Protestant conventionality about the discussions of sin and its outcome for ethics. The Lutheran Werner Elert, for example, summarizes

8. Emil Brunner, *The Divine Imperative* (Philadelphia: Westminster, 1947), p. 661 (endnote 8 to p. 399).

9. Reinhold Niebuhr, *The Nature and Destiny of Man*, 2 vols. (New York: Scribner's, 1945), 1:281.

10. Reinhold Niebuhr, *Faith and History* (New York: Scribner's, 1949), p. 182.

11. Ibid., p. 191.

12. Barth, *Ethics*, p. 31. Cf. *Church Dogmatics* II/2, 509–732, *Church Dogmatics* III/4, pp. 324–470, and *The Christian Life, Church Dogmatics* IV/4 (Lecture Fragments) (Grand Rapids: Eerdmans, 1981) for the implications of this for both ethical theory and "special ethics."

13. Barth, *Ethics*, p. 32. The discussions of sin in *Church Dogmatics* are, I believe, fundamentally consistent with this earlier discussion, but also set in different context because of the elaboration of the significance of a gracious God for moral life.

Catholicism in a way one could cite from many other sources: "In the final analysis, guilt consists only in the fact that man, who in things natural has remained essentially unharmed, suffers from one deficiency."[14] Reinhold Niebuhr states that the "official Catholic doctrine of original sin" does not differ greatly from Pelagianism. By its distinction between *pura naturalia,* the essential nature of humans, and a *donum superadditum* it incorporates the biblical idea of the Fall without dealing with the corruption of the essential nature of the human.[15] Various writers are more or less nuanced in their interpretations of sin in Roman Catholicism, and various citations from Aquinas are used to support their views. But the inference for ethics is generally the same: the Catholic doctrine of sin leaves too much confidence in human beings to know and do the right and the good.

Citation from St. Thomas is always interesting to observe. I found no Protestants who are worried about excessive claims of human capacity citing the following passage: "Yet because human nature is not altogether corrupted by sin, namely, so as to be shorn of every good of nature, even in the state of corrupted nature it can, by virtue of its natural endowments, perform some particular good, *such as building dwellings, plant vineyards, and the like;* yet it cannot do all the good natural to it, so as to fall short in nothing."[16] And all Protestant scholars surely knew that Luther, Calvin, Melanchthon, and others conceded that human capacities were present in a sufficient way to function in the civil use of the law. One can wonder to what extent the matter in hand has been, at least for some authors, a theological and religious one, i.e., a defense of salvation by grace alone so that no moral effectiveness could count toward the restoration of human relations to God. Or, whether the concern was more ethical in character, i.e., overweening confidence in human judgments about moral matters. The term "legalism" appears with frequency in some of the literature, and it seems to bear on both of these concerns. "Merit" is often the focus of attention.

Protestant theologians did not, on the whole, interpret Catholic moral theology as radically Pelagian, though certainly some popular Protestant interpretations did. Helmut Thielicke, e.g., writes "that Thomism does not present the doctrine of justification in such crude and deistic fashion that Christ is, as it were, only the initiator of justification, and that then, having started the movement, he withdraws . . . and leaves everything to the human action. . . ."[17] Thomism, he says very fairly, regards all merits attained by human beings as merits only through grace. Anders Nygren, whose *Agape and Eros* influenced many Protestant authors, wrote: "Mediaeval theology is a theology of merit. But this does not mean that it is not at the same time a theology of grace."[18] What Catholicism does

14. Werner Elert, *The Christian Ethics* (Philadelphia: Muhlenberg, 1957), p. 149.

15. Niebuhr, *The Nature and Destiny of Man,* 1:247–48.

16. Thomas Aquinas, *Summa theologiae,* 1–2, q. 109, a. 2. I do not find this cited in Roman Catholic authors either. Italics are mine.

17. Helmut Thielicke, *Theological Ethics,* 2 vols. (Philadelphia: Fortress, 1966), 1:74. The German edition of which the American is an abridgment was published in 1958.

18. Anders Nygren, *Agape and Eros* (London: S.P.C.K., 1953), p. 621.

is regard merit and grace as one, while from the Evangelical view they exclude each other.

One might think that the controversy over grace and merit would be of little interest to ethicians; the issue is primarily about how one is saved. But such thought would be a gross error, and ethical issues are joined between the traditions on this point. In the background is also the doctrine of habits and virtues that gives content to the view of the human in the Catholic tradition. Barth makes the charge with characteristic bluntness. The ethics of Aquinas as found in both parts of the second part of the *Summa* "has its basis in Aristotle and its crown and true scope in the religious life in the narrowest sense of the term, namely, the life of the clergyman and the monk."[19] One finds in Protestant literature charges of tendencies toward moral perfectionism, of a two-storeyed ethics, that result from traditional Catholic moral anthropology and cooperating grace. Reinhold Niebuhr's summary judgment, based on Thomas' *Treatise on Grace,* question 109, is not untypical. "The issue at stake here is whether man's historical existence is such that he can ever, by any discipline of reason or by any merit of grace, confront a divine judgment upon his life with an easy conscience. If he can it means that it is possible for a will centered in an individual ego to be brought into essential conformity with the will and power that governs all things. On this question the Catholic answer is a consistently affirmative one." Niebuhr cites from Thomas the necessity of continued divine help, but also the view that in the "redeemed state" human beings can be kept from mortal sin, "which is grounded in reason." "According to this formulation the conformity of the human to the divine will is well nigh absolute, and the only sin which remains is occasioned by vagrant impulses below the level of the will." In a kind of dialectical fashion, however, Niebuhr acknowledges the qualifications of this tendency in Thomas by quoting him: "Because man's will is not wholly subject to God it follows that there must be many disorders in the acts of reason."[20]

I have reviewed selectively and in a too perfunctory manner various Protestant attestations to Barth's series of charges quoted above: the differences are in "the concept of God, of man, of the sin of man, and the grace that comes to him." Important sources have not been cited, e.g., H. Richard Niebuhr's chapter on "Christ above Culture," Paul Lehmann's discussion of "the synthetic thrust" and his chapter "A Critique of Moral Theology," and some non-English works that I have reviewed.[21] It is important, while indicating similarities in these Protestant interpretations of Catholic ethics, not to oversimplify or overgeneralize them.

19. Barth, *Ethics,* p. 6.
20. Niebuhr, *The Nature and Destiny of Man,* 2:141. Niebuhr sees the worst tendencies finally affecting the Roman Catholic doctrine of the Church. "All Catholic errors in overestimating the sinlessness of the redeemed reach their culmination, or at least their most vivid and striking expression, in the doctrine of the church" (ibid., p. 144).
21. H. Richard Niebuhr, *Christ and Culture* (New York: Harper, 1951), pp. 116–48; Paul Lehmann, *Ethics in a Christian Context* (New York: Harper and Row, 1963), pp. 256–59, 287–325.

By far the majority of the Protestant interpretations use classical Catholic sources; the exceptions to this are interesting and important. Barth makes references to Mausbach; Brunner has a more interesting analysis of a difference between Aristotelian and Augustinian Thomists, and uses Cathrein, *Moralphilosophie,* 1924, as his source for the former and Mausbach, *Katholische Moraltheologie,* 1927, for the latter.[22] Lehmann's chapter on moral theology is a brief Protestant version of tendencies that were developing just before Vatican II; he uses Henry Davis, S.J., *Moral and Pastoral Theology,* as his example of the "manualist" tradition, and begins to trace the critique of such works from within Catholicism by discussing Gilleman's *The Primacy of Charity in Moral Theology,* Bernard Häring's *The Law of Christ,* and Dietrich von Hildebrand's *Christian Ethics.* (Space does not permit a comparison between Lehmann and the important discussion in Ford and Kelly of critical trends within moral theology.[23])

I stated above that there would be no surprises in this profile to a reasonably knowledgeable Catholic or Protestant reader. Indeed, something like Barth's agenda of issues frames three studies of Catholic and Protestant ethics that emerged in the 1960s, two by Roman Catholics and one by a Protestant, all Europeans.[24]

PERSISTENCE OF THE AGENDA

Franz Böckle, the Bonn Roman Catholic moral theologian, and Roger Mehl, the Strasbourg Reformed theologian, both produced comparative books based on

22. Brunner, *The Divine Imperative,* pp. 95–99. An interesting interpretive prerogative taken by Brunner is worth quoting. He quotes Mausbach: "Speaking from the Christian point of view, the inner surrender of the will to the Moral Law and to Good, the reverent love to God on the part of the creature, a love which is eager to serve, is essentially, and under all circumstances morally good, the opposite is morally bad." Brunner adds: "What the author really wishes to say is this: that everything is only good in virtue of this love, and that without this love it is not good. But this he dare not say."

23. See John C. Ford, S.J., and Gerald Kelly, S.J., *Contemporary Moral Theology,* 2 vols. (Westminster, Md.: Newman, 1958), 1:42–140.

24. In the Anglican moral theology tradition as well as in social ethics there has been historically much greater affinity with the Roman Catholic tradition than is the case with Continental Protestantism and its American heirs. From Richard Hooker forward, some notion of natural law gets approval, though its relations to gospel, to piety, etc., take different forms in different authors. In the period under consideration here, the work of Kenneth Kirk is notable: see, e.g., his *Conscience and Its Problems: An Introduction to Casuistry,* new ed. (London: Longmans, Green, 1936). Kirk differentiates his positions from Roman Catholic ones on some theoretical as well as some practical matters, e.g., birth control, but evidently in a continuing conversation with them. In social ethics the "Christendom Group," which was very active and identifiable until the late 1940s, had the idea of a natural order at the basis of its proposals for social reform. See, e.g., Maurice B. Reckitt, ed., *Prospects for Christendom: Essays in Catholic Social Reconstruction* (London: Faber and Faber, 1945), and V. A. Demant, *Theology of Society* (London: Faber and Faber, 1947). Archbishop William Temple's very influential book *Christianity and Social Order* (New York: Penguin, 1942) has a brief discussion of natural law in which he writes: "It is wholesome to go back to this conception of Natural Law because it holds together two aspects of truth which it is not easy to hold in combination—the ideal and the practical" (p. 60). All of these materials show, also, distinctively Protestant elements. None of them is very technical in a scholarly sense; they were written for quite practical ends. A breadth and depth of learning lies behind them, but what I have delineated as the conventional Protestant agenda is not a prominent feature.

lectures which focus on controverted issues. The agenda shared between them is significantly larger than the differences. Böckle's three chapter titles express it well: "Law and Gospel," "Precept and Order of Nature," and "Sinners and Sin." The structure of each chapter is basically the same: a summary of "the Protestant" view and the Catholic response. Böckle attends both to classic Protestant sources and to contemporary European authors. I cite only enough to illustrate, but not substantiate, my contention that a standard agenda of controverted issues provides the frame for analysis. In Böckle's chapter on "Law and Gospel" he summarizes "The Concern of the Reformers" in three propositions: "The Gospel as the message of redemption by Christ destroys every form of human self-justification"; "The Gospel does not take away the will of God, but directly preaches of its fulfillment through Christ and our sharing in it"; and "Insofar as the Gospel does lay down demands, these do not mean demands for action that we must accomplish as leading to our salvation; but rather the Gospel demands are a counsel pointing out things we may venture to achieve as a fruit of our salvation."[25] In his statements of a Catholic alternative he consciously bypasses three centuries of Roman Catholic textbooks because they are "over-freighted" with canon law, and their "narrowness and overemphasis" on law was partially anti-Protestant. His Catholic rebuttal relies largely on Augustine, Aquinas, and the Council of Trent. The discussion has moved far from the simplicity and dogmatism of the chapter on Protestant ethics in Koch-Preuss!

Mehl's book stems from Warfield Lectures delivered at Princeton Theological Seminary in 1968. Again a sketch has to suffice. The first lecture lines out the historical contentions about how ethics is situated in the theologies of Luther, Calvin, and "traditional" Catholicism. In his second chapter on "The Persistent Divergences" three of his four sections support my contention: "Nature and Supernature: The Anthropological Problem"; "The Problem of Natural Law and of Natural Morality"; and "Soul and Body; Virtue and Perfection: The Sexual Life." The fourth, in retrospect, might well reflect a special interest of the decade in which the lectures were delivered: "The Meaning of Secularization." Mehl in his final chapter notes two areas of convergence: the effects on ethics of biblical renewal, and new concerns in social ethics. The studies of biblical ethics by Rudolf Schnackenburg and Ceslaus Spicq, which impressed many of us Protestants, are his principal sources for the former, and the encyclicals of John XXIII and Paul VI for the latter.[26]

Josef Fuchs, S.J., in his *Natural Law: A Theological Investigation,* does not give as sharp and comprehensive attention to debates between Protestant and Catholic views of ethics, but it would be difficult to read his work without inferring that he seeks to justify natural law in the light of the criticisms of major Protestant theologians of this century: Barth, Brunner, Niels Søe, Thielicke, Schlink, Ernst Wolf, Reinhold Niebuhr, and others. One strand of the argument,

---

25. Franz Böckle, *Law and Conscience* (New York: Sheed and Ward, 1966), pp. 29, 30–31, 32.
26. Mehl, *Catholic Ethics and Protestant Ethics* (Philadelphia: Westminster, 1970).

in my judgment, is to establish biblical and theological grounds for natural law which temper many conventional Protestant criticisms. Like the works of Böckle and Mehl, the major topics can well fit Barth's list of issues; the argument, however, is more systematic and developed than theirs.[27]

The discourse in these studies is basically on the theological level, and how theological judgments affect justifications of ethical principles, moral values, and the nature of human action. All three authors turn to classic sources in both traditions to formulate the issues, and all three take into account significant writers in theological ethics among their contemporaries. There is ample evidence that Protestants are also concerned about particular moral teachings of Catholics during the period represented by these authors, e.g., Paul Ramsey's work on just war, discussions of birth control, etc. A hypothesis I hazard, however, is that one finds an increasing tendency in the literature by both Protestant ethicians and Roman Catholic moral theologians to leave these critical theological matters in the background. There are exceptions, such as Bernard Häring's major writings, *The Law of Christ* and *Free and Faithful*, essays by Charles Curran, and others. A perusal of decades of "Notes on Moral Theology" in this journal, however, backs my hypothesis on the Catholic side.

Quite different from these three books is one that was especially important at the time of its publication, namely Edward Duff, S.J., *The Social Thought of the World Council of Churches*. Duff's book provides the best available survey of its topic through the early 1950s. His principal heuristic device utilizes J. H. Oldham's well-known distinction between the "ethic of inspiration" and an "ethic of ends." The former is aptly characterized by Duff: it "insists that the fundamental and characteristic Christian moral attitude is not obedience to fixed norms or to a moral code but a living response to a living person, a fellowship with God who is sovereignly free and whose Will is sought for a present personal decision." This was a commonly held biblical-theological view among Protestants. The latter, in his words, "is based on an idea of the proper ordering of society and its parts whose overall purposes and particular functions are discoverable by a rational examination of their nature and operations," a more Catholic position. He demonstrates how a tension between these two types of ethics was present in the development of the World Council's "social philosophy,"[28] and notes how it issues in incoherence in social ethics. The purpose of the study, clearly, is not to examine various works by theologians; it is a thorough and judiciously fair assessment of somewhat unscholarly material. Not only its content but also the quite irenic spirit in which it is written marked a milestone in the conversation between the two traditions. The book aids the reader to see how matters discussed on the theological level make differences on the level not only of ethical theory but also of moral evaluations and prescriptions for society.

---

27. Josef Fuchs, S.J., *Natural Law: A Theological Investigation* (New York: Sheed and Ward, 1965).
28. Edward Duff, S.J., *The Social Thought of the World Council of Churches* (New York: Association, 1956), p. 94.

VATICAN II AND ECUMENISM

The literature becomes much more complex during and following the Second Vatican Council. There were stirrings for change in Catholic moral theology prior to that time which opened discussions within that tradition during and after the Council. Catholicism confronted "situation ethics" at least a decade before Joseph Fletcher's book by that title appeared. Ford and Kelly noted that "A feeling of uneasiness about moral theology has been in the air for some years. It is a feeling which cannot be brushed aside as mere murmuring by malcontents."[29] They provide a good list of the concerns: charity, the heart of the Christian life, does not vivify moral doctrine and teaching; the practice of virtue is passed over quickly because of the preoccupation with distinction of sins; scriptural and patristic sources are neglected; moral theology has been divorced from dogmatic theology; social obligations are not emphasized and an individualism reigns; the view of the human has not taken into account modern psychologies; the use of language about universal abstracts repels the modern mind; and the person of Christ has dropped from sight in the preoccupation with casuistry, legalism, and sinful deviation. A brief summary of the writings of important critics is followed by summaries of new approaches. (Bernard Häring's *Das Gesetz Christi,* which had already gone through four or five editions when Ford and Kelly published their book, is not mentioned. My impression is that of all the "new approaches," Häring's had the widest impact among priests and religious, at least, for well over a decade.) Ford's and Kelly's own reflections on the new approaches, while critical, are quite sympathetic. One does not find in their book any of the kind of vituperative dogmatism in favor of the old ways to which John Courtney Murray was exposed, and which one finds in the more recent events surrounding Charles E. Curran.[30] With reference to the traditional agenda of controversy, however, Ford and Kelly provide a practical, and not theological, defense of the past. "Just as one cannot incorporate the whole science of ascetics into the moral course, much less can one incorporate the dogma. . . . In teaching theology one must necessarily partition it."[31]

During the 1960s and 1970s occurrences other than publications affected the range and quality of Catholic and Protestant ethical interaction in North America, at least. In the areas of social action members of both communities participated together often, perhaps, finding greater affinity with each other than with many members of their own communions; one thinks of the peace and civil-rights movements. Catholic moral theologians began to participate in the American Society for Christian Ethics, and Protestant scholars read papers at the Catholic Theological Society of America. Roman Catholic students—priests,

29. Ford and Kelly, *Contemporary Moral Theology,* 1:42.

30. On Murray's case see Donald E. Pelotte, *John Courtney Murray: Theologian in Conflict* (New York: Paulist, 1976), pp. 27–73; on Curran's case see Charles E. Curran, *Faithful Dissent* (Kansas City, Mo.: Sheed and Ward, 1986).

31. Ford and Kelly, *Contemporary Moral Theology,* 1:100.

religious, and lay—were enrolled in graduate programs in universities that historically were Protestant; my impression is that fewer Protestant students received degrees from doctoral programs in moral theology in Catholic institutions. Dissertations often required research in materials from both traditions.[32] Syllabi for courses at college, seminary, and doctoral levels became more inclusive. Important faculties added members from each other's tradition. Books by both Protestant and Roman Catholic authors began to reflect the broadening and deepening of knowledge, and informally as well as formally new clusters of conversation partners developed. An unsuccessful series, Studies in Christian Ethics, published four volumes under the general editorship of Richard A. McCormick, S.J., Paul Ramsey, and myself; evidence of mutually knowledgeable writings appeared in more effective forms. Issues in social ethics such as war and peace, the economy, ecology, and oppressed groups such as women and ethnic minorities, as well as issues of medical research and practice and sexuality, drew attention like magnets from authors in both traditions; on many of them the division of opinion was no longer between Catholic and Protestant.

In *Protestant and Roman Catholic Ethics: Prospects for Rapprochement* I interpreted trends that were present in both traditions as moving toward at least common concerns if not common grounds. Put in a cursory manner, while Roman Catholics were moving from rigid and closed ways of thinking toward more flexibility, some Protestants were moving from the view Oldham and Duff characterize as "ethics of inspiration" to an appreciation for casuistry. These tendencies on the level of practical moral reasoning were supported by shifts in philosophical and theological thinking.[33] I noted in the Preface that by the time of the publication of that book the "flush of ecumenical enthusiasm" was gone. This was not a matter of regret, since finding a least common denominator between traditions is not desirable. The task, I wrote, "is to formulate the important questions and find the most adequate and coherent answers."[34]

The interpretive thematic structure of my *Protestant and Roman Catholic Ethics* cannot bear the weight of the proliferation of writings in ethics and moral theology in both traditions since its publication. Developments are too diverse, and there are strong defenses of more extreme positions than was the case in the materials I used. (Most of the developments have been chronicled in articles since Vatican II and in books that summarized recent discussion.[35]) In the remainder

---

32. I could cite many by both Protestants and Catholics. One that launched an important scholarly career was Lisa Sowle Cahill, "Euthanasia: A Catholic and a Protestant Perspective" (Ph.D. diss., Univ. of Chicago, 1976).

33. James M. Gustafson, *Protestant and Roman Catholic Ethics* (Chicago: Univ. of Chicago, 1978). The book is based largely on lectures delivered in January 1973.

34. Ibid., p. viii.

35. The flow of essays by Charles Curran through the years provides a very fine account of discussions. While the essays focus on Roman Catholic moral theology, they show a serious consideration of Protestant writings as a source for targeting issues in Catholicism and for Curran's constructive proposals. For examples only, see "Catholic Moral Theology Today," in Curran, *New Perspectives in Moral Theology* (Notre Dame: Fides, 1974), pp. 1–46; "The Stance of Moral Theology," ibid., pp. 47–86;

of this article I shall make insufficiently substantiated observations and interpretations that generally back this view.

First, there is no longer much interest in developing ecumenical consensus, per se, between Protestant and Roman Catholic ethics. As I noted above, from one perspective this is commendable; at its best, writers in both traditions are dealing with methodological, social, and moral issues regnant in our time which are shared by both communities. Evidence for this includes publications on ethical methods, including casuistry; on whether ethics is autonomous or necessarily confessional; on the use of biblical materials in ethics; and on matters of war and peace, the economy, liberation from various forms of oppression, and quite specific medical choices and general medical policies. For example, little is written by Roman Catholics on war and medical matters that does not take into account the prolific writings of the late Paul Ramsey, and little is written by Protestants that does not interact with the writings of Richard McCormick, Bryan Hehir, Charles Curran, and many others. Indeed, the generations of authors who did their graduate studies beginning in the 1960s find it natural to take account of publications from both traditions—sometimes in a polemical way and sometimes in an irenic way. Ecumenism generally has lost much of the vitality it had 20 years ago, but it is worth noting that on doctrinal matters efforts continue to overcome historic differences, e.g., on justification and sanctification, the sacraments, and biblical authority in theology. My impression is that no similarly concerted effort occurs on moral matters, on social-ethical issues, on matters of ethical method, and on theological aspects of ethics. Why this is the case I cannot fully explain.[36]

A partial explanation may be that within Roman Catholicism controversies have occurred which leave little time and effort for more ecumenical interests. To be sure, some Protestants have entered into these controversies as well. I have in mind not only divisions among Catholics on practical moral and social questions, but also on some quite recondite matters of method which are seen to warrant practical judgments, e.g., the principle of double effect, proportionalism, and

---

"Dialogue with Scriptures," in *Catholic Moral Theology in Dialogue* (Notre Dame: Fides, 1972), pp. 24–64; "Social Ethics and Method in Moral Theology," ibid., pp. 225–39; "The Relevance of the Gospel Ethic," in *Themes in Fundamental Moral Theology* (Notre Dame: Univ. of Notre Dame, 1977), pp. 5–26; "A Methodological Overview of Fundamental Moral Theology," in *Moral Theology: A Continuing Journey* (Notre Dame: Univ. of Notre Dame, 1982), pp. 35–61; "Three Methodological Issues in Moral Theology," ibid., pp. 62–89; and his book-length dialogue with Paul Ramsey, *Politics, Medicine, and Christian Ethics* (Philadelphia: Fortress, 1973). Two remarkably clear and informative brief summaries of issues are Richard M. Gula, S.S., *What Are They Saying about Moral Norms?* (New York: Paulist, 1982), and William C. Spohn, S.J., *What Are They Saying about Scripture and Ethics?* (New York: Paulist, 1984). See also "Notes on Moral Theology" through the years in this journal, and the useful series Readings in Moral Theology edited by Charles E. Curran and Richard A. McCormick (New York: Paulist, 1979).

36. In November 1987, Loyola University of Chicago sponsored a series of papers and a one-day symposium on Joseph Cardinal Bernardin's "consistent ethic of life." One paper was written by a Protestant, but it was noteworthy that in the discussion no interest was shown in ecumenical consensus. The concentration of discussion was on matters quite internal to Roman Catholic moral theology.

"consequentialism." (The latter seems to be a venial, if not mortal, intellectual sin.) I believe one could fruitfully interpret these internal Catholic debates on the continuum known from the history of moral theology: from laxism through probabilism and its qualifications to rigorism. I also believe that underlying various positions taken are not only intellectual issues but pastoral concerns: for some persons a fear of opening the gates of a dam so that prevailing undesirable currents of modern culture are not contained, for others a concern for the turmoils of conscience and suffering that rigorism can create.

Another partial explanation is that Roman Catholic moral theologians necessarily have to deal with the controverted issue of magisterial authority. To establish a magisterium of moral theologians with relative independence from the official magisterium takes great effort and concentration of attention. Some moral theologians who, under other conditions, might have interests in ecumenism have been put on the intellectual and institutional defensive.[37] Ecclesiological issues, and not only issues of ecclesiastical authority, have to be faced, e.g., that of who among the People of God are to participate in the formation of official moral teachings. Whose experiences ought to be taken into account? Perhaps Protestants have been reluctant to publish a great deal on these matters for fear of making life more difficult for their Catholic friends.[38]

There is no significant evidence that Protestant writers in ethics are any more interested in focusing attention on ecumenical consensus, per se, than are Roman Catholics. Where one finds a confluence of thinking, it is directed more by practical matters than by matters philosophical and theological. Evidence for this can be adduced from literature on liberation theology and ethics, feminist theology and ethics, and matters of human sexuality. Perhaps informal clusters of unity on such items have developed, and ecumenism among the participants is a by-product. My impression, however, is that at least some important intellectual issues, both theological and philosophical, are bypassed.[39]

---

37. See Charles E. Curran and Richard A. McCormick, S.J., eds., *Readings in Moral Theology No. 3: The Magisterium and Morality* (New York: Paulist, 1982).

38. Noteworthy for its direct and critical analysis of the Roman Catholic position (as well as others) on the abortion issue is Beverly Wildung Harrison, *Our Right to Choose: Toward a New Ethic of Abortion* (Boston: Beacon, 1983).

39. There is a wing of conservative Protestantism from which are coming works that are not in any sense anti-Catholic but are grounded in Protestant traditions of biblical theology as the basis for ethics. See, e.g., Donald G. Bloesch, *Freedom for Obedience: Evangelical Ethics in Contemporary Times* (San Francisco: Harper and Row, 1987). Bloesch states that his principal mentors in ethics are Karl Barth, Jacques Ellul, Reinhold Niebuhr, and Dietrich Bonhoeffer. The pattern of the book is more a description of an evangelical position contrasted with other positions (with expositions of a wide variety of materials) than it is a strongly developed apology for the evangelical position. For example, one finds summary statements such as the following: "Whereas philosophical ethics seeks to understand the good in the light of a general metaphysic or world view, theological ethics appeals to a definitive revelation of God in the sacred history mirrored in the Bible" (p. 19). Ethics in general refers to the meaning of the good: "Christian ethics . . . means the attempt to live the Christian life, a life reflecting the passion and victory of Jesus Christ" (p. 21). A "revealed reality, the living Word of God, . . . shapes moral decisions and guides moral reflection" (ibid.). There are brief discussions of some Roman Catholic writers in his section on contemporary ethical alternatives, but no ecumenical interest, per se, can be found.

Second, an issue that has always been present between Protestant ethics built on the principle of Scripture alone and the Roman Catholic tradition continues to be debated with great vigor. In Barth's terms it is the relation of Christian theological ethics to moral philosophy. There are various layers to the general issue. One is how the specifically Christian aspects of morality and theology are related to more general ethical themes. Indeed, within that layer one finds different answers to the question about what is specifically Christian. This opens another layer, which I shall look at separately: how the biblical material is to be used in moral theology and Christian ethics. It is important to note that there are differences of opinion in that layer between Roman Catholics as well as between them and some Protestants. For example, the use of biblical theologies as one basis for political and social ethics is present in a great deal of Catholic liberation theology. Social ethics developed from that base take quite a different form, and sometimes content as well, from social ethics based on natural law.[40] Other layers can be suggested by questions. What is the norm for the lives of individual Christians and for the Christian community? Is it conformity to Christ as revealed in the Gospels, a fidelity to him which is often also the way of the cross? Or is it a kind of deputyship of Christians in the world and its institutions seeking to bring events into accord with moral principles derived from nature, from creation? Ecclesiological questions come up. Is the Christian community to be a prophetic minority engaged in critical responses—responses based on its fidelity to Christ —to both general ethical theories and events in society? Or is it to be a community that is "worldly" not in a pejorative sense but in the sense of participating in policy formation and events in such a way that "compromise" of Gospel "ideals" and norms is required? Theological issues, in a very focused sense, are involved. Is the divine intention known in and through the divine ordering of creation? Or is it known almost exclusively through the historic revelation in Christ? How an individual theologian or a tradition interprets the relations between creation and redemption, how this relation is understood, in effect, in the Godhead has very important implications for ethics.[41]

Oliver O'Donovan, the Regius Professor of Moral Theology at Oxford, subtitled his book *Resurrection and Moral Order* as follows: *An Outline for Evangelical Ethics* (Grand Rapids: Eerdmans, 1986). While it is Christocentric like Bloesch's book, its argument is very different and much more complex. A major difference is O'Donovan's emphasis on the "created order," which is renewed in the resurrection of Christ and can be known through the Holy Spirit, which gives human beings access to it. Affinities with classic Catholicism, including patristic materials, are apparent; indeed, the argument builds upon some of them but in an "evangelical" way. For a more extended response to this book, see my review in *Journal of Religion* 68 (1988): 131–32.

40. For an interesting comparative analysis of this point, see David A. Krueger, "The Economic Ethics of John A. Ryan and Gustavo Gutiérrez" (Ph.D. diss., Univ. of Chicago, 1988).

41. Douglas J. Schuurman, in "Creation, Eschaton and Ethics" (Ph.D. diss., Univ. of Chicago, 1988), demonstrates this by examining two Protestant theologians, Emil Brunner and Jürgen Moltmann. The systematic question is how eschatologies affect ethics, with particular focus on whether the eschaton is interpreted as a restoration and fulfilment of all of creation or primarily of history. Comparable studies comparing Roman Catholic theologians with some Protestants would be instructive.

How ought Christian ethics to be related to philosophical ethics? This theme was introduced in my survey of pre–Vatican II Protestant theologians, and the discussion continues. Current discussion is, however, less on the theological and more on the methodological level. Indeed, my impression is that it has become a debate and is more intense now than it has been in the recent past. On the whole, Roman Catholic moral theologians have avoided defending intensely confessional positions—those which emphasize the distinctiveness and particularity in Christian ethics relative to moral philosophy. This, as all readers of this journal know, is in keeping with the mainstream of Catholic tradition, and with the mainline of the Reformation tradition. On the latter, one could cite Luther on the civic use of the law, Calvin on the natural law, and Melanchthon's ethical writings, as well as others.

Examples of recent Catholic publications can be drawn from both sides of the Atlantic. A very useful analysis of the issue was given by Charles Curran in which he both surveys the literature and argues his own position. His personal conclusion is that there is a Christian ethic insofar as Christians "reflect on action in the light of their explicitly Christian understanding of moral data, but Christians and non-Christians can and do share the same general goals and intentions, attitudes and dispositions, as well as norms and concrete actions." There is a Catholic ethic insofar as "Catholics act and Catholic theology reflects on action in the light of Catholic self-understanding, but this results in no different moral data although more importance might be given to certain aspects such as the ecclesial element."[42] After a mildly critical response, Richard McCormick concludes that "being a Christian means: (1) being human—in continuity with the human but in a context and atmosphere where grasp of the human may be intensified by Christian intentionalities; (2) being social—essentially a member of an *ecclesia* whose knowledge is shared knowledge; and (3) being individual——with existential calls and obligations not shared by others."[43]

Quite similar positions are expounded and defended from across the Atlantic. McCormick echoes quite accurately notes coming from his German Jesuit colleagues. Josef Fuchs concludes that "the newness that Christ brings is not really a new (material) morality, but a new creature of grace and of the Kingdom of God, a man of divinely self-giving love." The Christian realities do not bring a *basis* for morality different from truly human morality; "the meaning of the *Christianum* for our concrete living is to be found in its motivating power." There is a distinctive intentionality in the Christian life but not a different morality.[44] Bruno Schüller distinguishes, among other things, between exhortation and normative ethics; biblical ethics are exhortative, and normative ethics are to be tested

---

42. Charles E. Curran, "Is There a Catholic and/or Christian Ethic?" *Proceedings of the Twenty-Ninth Annual Convention of the CTSA* (1974): 153–54.

43. Richard A. McCormick, S.J., "Response to Professor Curran—II," ibid., p. 164.

44. Josef Fuchs, S.J., "Is There a Distinctively Christian Morality," in *Personal Responsibility and Christian Morality* (Washington, D.C.: Georgetown Univ., 1983), pp. 54–68; quotations are from pp. 61 and 63.

by universal criteria of truth.[45] Gerard J. Hughes summarizes his approach as follows: "In the end, my argument turns on the contention that belief in revelation is irrational unless that revelation somehow fits in with our antecedent convictions, and, in particular, with our antecedent moral convictions."[46]

The general tendency of this traditional Roman Catholic position is under criticism in vigorous ways at the present time, though not all Protestants are in agreement in the debate. Robin Lovin's study, e.g., of the social ethics of Barth, Brunner, and Bonhoeffer is grounded in a systematic question put to *sola scriptura* theologians. If Protestant ethics persists in rejecting natural law, or views that are in some way functionally equivalent to it, how can it contribute to public choices in a significant way?[47] The issue expressed in such a question has several dimensions. In my judgment, two of the currently most influential Protestant ethicians represent radical challenges to the traditional Catholic position and to Protestants such as Lovin: Stanley Hauerwas and John Howard Yoder.

The opening sentence of Hauerwas' *A Community of Character* articulates a motif that is central to his perspective: "Though this book touches on many issues it is dominated by one concern: to reassert the social significance of the church as a distinct society with an integrity peculiar to itself."[48] Yoder argues for radical reformation, not on the basis of historical precedents from the 16th century but on the basis of the truth of the biblical theology which he expounds and defends. As with Hauerwas, no short quotations grasp the full argument, but the following are representative. "The church precedes the world epistemologically. We know more fully from Jesus Christ and in the context of the confessed faith than we know in other ways. . . . The church precedes the world as well axiologically, in that the lordship of Christ is the center which must guide critical value choices, so that we may be called to subordinate or even to reject those values

45. Bruno Schüller, S.J., "The Debate on the Specific Character of a Christian Ethics: Some Remarks," in *Wholly Human* (Washington, D.C.: Georgetown Univ., 1986), pp. 15–42.

46. Gerard J. Hughes, S.J., *Authority in Morals: An Essay in Christian Ethics* (London: Heythrop Monographs, 1978), p. 10. The essays by Curran, Fuchs, and Schüller that I have cited are among those included in the useful anthology *Readings in Moral Theology No. 2: The Distinctiveness of Christian Ethics*, eds. Charles E. Curran and Richard A. McCormick, S.J. (New York: Paulist, 1980). Space does not permit me to interpret the differences between these authors or to develop their arguments for the conclusions I have noted. For other essays see ibid.

47. Robin W. Lovin, *Christian Faith and Public Choices* (Philadelphia: Fortress, 1984). Lovin's general concern is shared by many other Protestants. I addressed the issues in several dimensions in an uncharacteristically polemical lecture prepared for the 1985 convention of the Catholic Theological Society of America, "The Sectarian Temptation: Reflections on Theology, the Church, and the University." See Proceedings of the Fortieth Annual Convention (1985), 83–94. [Editors' note: This essay has been reprinted in the present volume and may be found on pp. 142–54.]

48. Stanley Hauerwas, *A Community of Character* (Notre Dame: Univ. of Notre Dame, 1981), p. 1. Similar statements can be found in many of his essays on social and theological ethics. E.g., ". . . [T]heology cannot begin a consideration of ethics with claims about creation and redemption, but must begin with God's choice of Israel and the life of Jesus. . . . [T]he first social task of the church is to be the church, which entails being a community capable of being a critic to every human pretension" (*The Peaceable Kingdom: A Primer in Christian Ethics* [Notre Dame: Univ. of Notre Dame, 1983] p. viii.)

which contradict Jesus."[49] An effect of such views is an aggressive prophetic ethics from an accepted "minority position" based on fidelity to the authors' interpretation of New Testament faith and ethics.

I noted that there are several dimensions to radical Protestant discussions of the issue under consideration. Morally, there is the dimension of what appears to be compromise of Christian morality in efforts to be relevant, or in Lovin's terms to be a full participant in public choices. Theologically, there is a dimension of confidence in the biblical revelation and its universal truth claims, and in which interpretation of it is correct. Philosophically, these authors find support in the writings of critics of "foundationalisms" in epistemology, of "rationalism" in ethical theory, and similar movements. They find support for their theological method in George Lindbeck's *The Nature of Doctrine*.[50] They are historicists in the senses that history rather than nature is the ground of their theology and ethics and that all truth claims are relative to the historic communities from which they come. Ecclesiologically, as Yoder argues, the believers' church represented by the disciplined congregationalism in some of Protestant history is normative.

Space does not permit further elaboration of current Protestant challenges to the traditional Catholic interpretation of the relation of Christian ethics to philosophical ethics. I am surprised, however, that there is so little Catholic criticism of these Protestant trends, and that fundamental theological matters receive so little attention. And there is evidence of considerable influence of these Protestant trends in some Catholic quarters, as well as Protestant quarters that have traditionally had more affinity with Catholicism on this issue. My perception of this aspect of recent discussions is one reason that the interpretive framework of my *Protestant and Roman Catholic Ethics* is no longer as useful as it was.

Third, as I noted, embedded in the issue of the relation of the particularly Christian to general ethics and moral philosophy is the authority and use of Scripture in Christian ethics and in Christian moral life. The literature on this topic by both Catholics and Protestants has increased significantly in the past 20 years. The topic can be divided by the following questions. (1) What interpretation of the ethics in the Bible is correct? (2) How are theological themes in the Bible related to its moral teachings? (3) Ought Christian ethics to be "biblical ethics," i.e., ought they to conform to the theology and the morality of the Bible? (4) If not, how ought the biblical themes be related to ethics? At the theological level? At the moral level?

49. John Howard Yoder, *The Priestly Kingdom: Social Ethics as Gospel* (Notre Dame: Univ. of Notre Dame, 1984), p. 11. Yoder's earlier book *The Politics of Jesus* (Grand Rapids: Eerdmans, 1972) contains a section entitled "Mainstream Ethics: Jesus Is Not the Norm" (pp. 15–19).

50. George A. Lindbeck, *The Nature of Doctrine* (Philadelphia: Westminster, 1984). Lindbeck's preference for a cultural linguistic view of the doctrinal task shares the "antifoundationalism" of the ethicians and in its penultimate sentence commends those "younger" theologians who are renewing "the ancient practice of absorbing the universe into the biblical world." (There are interesting affinities between Lindbeck's book and similar work by others and my *Treasure in Earthen Vessels: The Church as a Human Community* [New York: Harper, 1961]. What I called a kind of sociology of religion has now become theology, or at least a theological method.)

A cursory summary of "classic" Catholicism will have to suffice as a base line for my discussion. Clearly, the Bible functioned theologically in the determination of the ultimate basis of ethics; sacred doctrine comes only from revelation. The natural law participates in the mind of God, a gracious Creator, and God's end for the creation is only known through the revelation in Christ. Grace is available through Christ and through faith and the sacraments, and is efficacious in orienting and correcting Christians in their moral lives as they move toward their supernatural end. Biblical morality is, except in a few extreme instances, the same as morality derived from the moral order of the creation. The "hard sayings" of Jesus are not obligatory norms for all Christians; some have a special vocation to fulfil them.

There is no unanimity among significant Catholic moral and political theologians on the authority and role of Scripture in ethics. Bernard Häring's work, which in both of his extended systematic treatments is centered in biblical theology in a way that is distinctive, represents one point on a continuum. Various liberation theologies with their grounding in biblical theological themes, e.g., Exodus and the kingdom of God, like Häring's, are quite different from Bruno Schüller's relegating biblical ethics to exhortation.[51] The use of biblical themes as heuristic principles for understanding events in history and politics has no real analogues among moral theologians; none, to my knowledge, attempts to interpret the circumstances of individual moral choices in the light of what God is seeking to do in those events.[52]

Toward another extreme in the continuum are writings by Schüller, Fuchs, Hughes, and others for whom ethics in its material content is defensible without recourse to biblical revelation, or for whom biblical morality can be justified on

51. See Bernard Häring, *The Law of Christ*, 3 vols. (Westminster, Md.: Newman, 1963), 1:vii–xii and 35–53, for one example of his Christocentric biblical theology as a basis for ethics. See also Häring, *Free and Faithful in Christ*, 3 vols. (New York: Seabury, 1978), 1:7–25, for a more recent discussion of the authority of the Bible. After a brief interpretation of biblical themes relevant to ethics, he has a significant section "The Bible and Normative Ethics," in which he says: "Those authors who minimize or exclude a specifically Christian content of normative moral theology come from that tradition of manuals which presented a rather static code morality or an ethics of principles and norms which could be well controlled." He cites Franz Böckle, *Fundamental Moral Theology* (New York: Pueblo, 1980), which I could well have included in my discussion of Curran, McCormick, Fuchs, Schüller, and Hughes. "A moral theology of creative liberty and fidelity finds its distinctively Christian quality in the light of the dynamic dimensions and perspectives which we find in the Bible" (Häring, *Free and Faithful*, 1:23). I do not understand the reasons for what seems to be a studied ignoring of Häring by name and citation in major recent authors I have cited in this article, with the major exception of Curran, and a minor exception of periodic reference in McCormick's "Notes on Moral Theology" through the years. E.g., Fuchs's essay "The Law of Christ" makes no mention of Häring; see Josef Fuchs, *Human Values and Christian Morality* (Dublin: Gill and Macmillan, 1970), pp. 76–91.

52. Liberation theologians' use of biblical theology is exemplified in what has become the classic text, as well as in other books by other authors. See Gustavo Gutiérrez, *A Theology of Liberation* (Maryknoll, N.Y.: Orbis, 1973). My impression is that Roman Catholic discussions of political and social ethics can be distinguished into two strands theologically (and not merely by social theories and philosophical leanings): those grounded in biblical theologies and those grounded in more traditional natural law. The American Catholic bishops' letter on war and peace has both strands, quite unknitted to each other in my judgment. See *The Challenge of Peace: God's Promise and Our Response* (found in several editions and printings).

independent ethical grounds—even cases which have been exceptions in older traditions. This is not to say that for these authors biblical revelation has no theological and religious significance and moral effects, but clearly the function is very different from what one finds in Häring or in liberation theologians.

The role of the Bible in Christian ethics has been more consciously addressed by Protestants in the last decades, though the kind of concern expressed in Robin Lovin's study was present in the J. H. Oldham and John Bennett tradition of middle axioms, in the writings of Boston University ethicians such as Walter Mueldler, and other places. Some of the work attempts to relate both biblical theology and biblical ethics to more systematic ethical positions. For example, after the publication of a very useful survey article, "The Use of Scripture in Ethics," Allen Verhey wrote *The Great Reversal*, which is a study of New Testament ethics and a "modest proposal" for using them.[53] Verhey's work is a rare combination of competence in biblical scholarship and moral philosophy. Thomas Ogletree's contribution is systematically oriented from a phenomenological hermeneutic, and is a more comprehensive and systematic account, materially as well as methodologically, than Verhey's work.[54]

Two recent books by Catholic authors demonstrate ways in which the Bible has a different sort of usage in Christian ethics from those positions criticized implicitly (at least) by Fuchs, Schüller, et al. The subtitle of Lisa Sowle Cahill's *Between the Sexes: Foundations for a Christian Ethics of Sexuality* points to a contribution more significant than does the title. She carefully goes through the hermeneutical dilemmas in the use of the Bible and courageously makes informed judgments which are innovative; these lead her onward through her chapters on Genesis and the New Testament.[55] Her work, I think, is a model of ecumenically informed scholarship. More ambitious, but also more scattered because of multiple authorship and the book's organization, is *Christian Biblical Ethics* by Robert J. Daly, S.J., et al. The subtitle indicates their intention to take quite a different path than that suggested by Schüller et al.: *From Biblical Revelation to Contemporary Christian Praxis: Method and Content.*[56] Both of these efforts bridge gaps between what have been characteristically Protestant and Catholic approaches to the issues.

While extreme positions on the use of the Bible in ethics and moral theology— a *sola scriptura* approach on the one hand and the "autonomy of ethics" on the other—represent more traditional divisions between Protestants and Catholics,

---

53. Allen Verhey, "The Use of Scripture in Ethics," *Religious Studies Review* 4 (1978): 28–38, and *The Great Reversal: Ethics and the New Testament* (Grand Rapids: Eerdmans, 1984).

54. Thomas W. Ogletree, *The Use of the Bible in Christian Ethics* (Philadelphia: Fortress, 1983). Space does not permit more extended discussions of recent works by other Protestants. See the bibliographies in Verhey's *RSR* article (which includes Jewish materials) and in Ogletree. See also Charles E. Curran and Richard A. McCormick, S.J., eds., *Readings in Moral Theology No. 4: The Use of Scripture in Moral Theology* (New York: Paulist, 1984), for selected essays on the topic. For an analysis of alternatives, see Spohn, *What Are They Saying about Scripture and Ethics?* (n. 35 above).

55. Lisa Sowle Cahill, *Between the Sexes* (Philadelphia: Fortress, 1985).

56. Robert J. Daly, S.J., et al., *Christian Biblical Ethics* (New York: Paulist, 1984).

there is evidence of important efforts that cannot be stereotyped. This, I believe, is being done not for the sake of ecumenical consensus but out of efforts to find new resolutions to an age-old issue: the authority of the Bible for theology as well as for ethics.

From among other matters worthy of observation that would require emendation of my framework in *Protestant and Roman Catholic Ethics,* my fourth and final one is a growing interest in a cluster of items: the role of affectivity, the "heart," imagination, vision, virtues, etc., in ethical theory and in moral life. This interest stems from various sources: the importance of more complete human experience for ethics, not limited to cognition and logic; the limitations perceived in rationalistic moral philosophy and theology; the influence of certain theories of human perception; the recovery of the narrative character of religion; a new look at and emphasis on ethics of virtue; work done on the use of metaphors and symbols, and others. Critics of this interest worry about subjective and irrational tendencies that might be unleashed. For example, a statement by the Protestant Paul Lehmann, amply polemicized against by Paul Ramsey, indicated what critics worry about: "The theonomous conscience is the conscience immediately sensitive to the freedom of God to do in the always changing human situation what his humanizing aims and purposes require."[57]

Persons who address this interest have significant differences which cannot be developed in this article; what I want to note is that the interest is present and growing among both Roman Catholics and Protestants. Among Catholic authors three can be noted. Daniel C. Maguire developed a comprehensive interpretation of moral choices which draws on many sources and addresses many issues; imagination is only one of the vectors in his diagram. The accent on its role, however, in a larger scheme is distinctive. He discusses five aspects which can only be listed here: excitement, quiet, work, malleability, and a sense of the *kairos.* His contribution to the discussions of affectivity is also significant; he begins it with "All moral experience is grounded in affectivity, in the fundamental experience of personal value," and quotes Teilhard de Chardin, "Great truths are felt before they are expressed."[58]

Philip S. Keane indicates that a number of moralists now join in a criticism of excessive reliance on "discursive reason" in ethics and wants it understood that a focus on imagination does not mean that such an emphasis is wrong in moral theology; his purpose is not to attack moral principles but "to get at the 'more' . . . which imagination can help offer us."[59] The book draws from a number of

57. Paul Lehmann, *Ethics in a Christian Context* (New York: Harper and Row, 1963), p. 358. Ramsey calls Lehmann's position "act-agapism" or "act-koinonia" ethics: Paul Ramsey, "The Contextualism of Paul Lehmann," in *Deeds and Rules in Christian Ethics* (New York: Scribner's, 1967), pp. 49–103.

58. Daniel C. Maguire, *The Moral Choice* (Garden City, N.Y.: Doubleday, 1978); on "Ethics and Creativity," pp. 198–217; on affectivity, his chapter "The Feel of Truth," pp. 281–305; quotations are from p. 281.

59. Philip S. Keane, S.S., *Christian Ethics and Imagination* (New York: Paulist, 1984), p. 14.

sources to shape a brief account of the role of imagination in moral choices and illustrates it by addressing a number of current issues. For example, in the area of economic life he distinguishes three aspects of the role of imagination: it helps "to form a true and vital vision of the moral nature of economic problems"; it helps to overcome parochialism that stems from immersion in our own culture and economic system; and it helps to develop more flexible attitudes toward persons living in other systems.[60] Note the nub of the claims in this example, not untypical of claims made by others: a different vision, a freedom from the bondage of parochialism, and flexibility in attitude.

William C. Spohn's interest in affectivity particularly has led him to work within the context of a classic Jesuit project: the process of discernment. The resources on which he draws are both European and American, and both Catholic and Protestant. Discernment, he writes, "is precisely the reasoning of the heart." "It makes *judgments of affectivity* which are based on the central convictions of a person's character."[61] His proposal is developed carefully and he summarizes his conclusion as follows:

> Christian discernment brings to light rich elements in moral decision-making. Judgments of affectivity legitimately ground some moral decisions through the discriminating functions of memory and imagination. These judgments are evaluated not by formal logic but by aesthetic criteria: by the sense of self, the evaluation of events through biblical symbols, and the correlation of certain ways of acting and the configuration of Christian affections. Because these criteria are normative within the public tradition of the Christian community, discernment is not finally accountable only to itself.[62]

Ignatius Loyola and Jonathan Edwards, Karl Rahner and H. Richard Niebuhr—such are sources from which Spohn draws.

Space does not permit development of literature by Protestants which addresses and develops similar themes as those the Catholics are proposing. To readers of Christian ethics, affinities with the work of Stanley Hauerwas, with some aspects of my own work, and with that of others will be apparent. This represents a focus on a set of realities which are perceived to be present in moral experience, and both Protestants and Catholics seek the effective concepts to describe, analyze, and recommend consideration of them for normative ethics.[63]

60. Ibid., pp. 137–41; quotation is from p. 138.

61. William C. Spohn, "The Reasoning Heart: An American Approach to Discernment," in Frank M. Oppenheim, S.J., ed., *The Reasoning Heart* (Washington, D.C.: Georgetown Univ., 1986), pp. 51–73; quotations are from p. 52.

62. Ibid., p. 73.

63. Nontheological authors are within speaking distance of some of these trends in moral theology, e.g., Carol Gilligan, *In a Different Voice* (Cambridge, Mass.: Harvard Univ., 1982), and other feminist authors; with more philosophical rigor, Sabina Lovibond, *Realism and Imagination in Ethics* (Oxford: Basil Blackwell, 1983); and with magnificent erudition as well as philosophical acumen, Martha C. Nussbaum, *The Fragility of Goodness* (Cambridge: Cambridge Univ., 1986). Other citations could be added.

This account of interaction between Roman Catholic and Protestant ethics has not done justice to a great deal of literature. Important Catholic authors have been totally neglected: Germain Grisez, John Finnis, William E. May, Margaret Farley, John Boyle, David Hollenbach, many liberation theologians, and more. An equivalent number of important Protestant authors have been ignored or underutilized: Trutz Rendtorff, Paul Ramsey, John Bennett, Gene Outka, James Childress, Jürgen Moltmann, Robert McAfee Brown, and more. Important journal literature which reflects the work of lesser-known authors has not been mined. For this reason and others no theses are conclusively proved. A few plausible generalizations have been put forward: prior to Vatican II the interaction was distant and largely set by the traditional controverted issues between Protestant and Catholic theology; in the period I attended to in my *Protestant and Roman Catholic Ethics* convergences could be demonstrated in practical reasoning, philosophical backing, and theological reconsideration; more recently the theological issues have been subordinated to some degree to methodological issues, and on some of these the interaction is quite unselfconscious. One firm conviction comes forth: interest in ecumenism per se, i.e., in finding grounds for overcoming disagreements for the sake of greater unity of Christian moral witness, is dormant if not dead. Maybe it was never alive![64]

---

64. Only after submission of this article did I have access to John Mahoney, *The Making of Moral Theology: A Study of the Roman Catholic Tradition* (New York: Oxford/Clarendon, 1987). While interaction with Protestant theology and ethics is not given attention, the comprehensiveness and integration of its agenda—historical, ecclesiological, methodological, theological, and ethical—would modify some generalizations made in this article about current Roman Catholic literature and provide a framework for a fine comparative study of the traditions. See the review by James R. Pollock in *TS* 49 (1988): 762–63.

Chapter 14

Moral Discourse about Medicine: A Variety of Forms

I. INTRODUCTION

What are the boundaries of medical ethics? Who decides them? Is there a clear focus that identifies the presentations in the media, the articles in journals, and the scores of books as medical ethics? What do health professionals conceive the focus of medical ethics to be: clinical choices, research issues, health care distribution policies? Perhaps the more interesting question is, What is medical ethics *not*? Can sharp boundaries be defined between medical ethics and medical economics or sociology? Should cultural criticism of the role of biomedical research and medical care in our society be considered medical ethics? Is the decision process in the United States Congress and the National Institutes of Health that determines which diseases receive priority in biomedical research funding medical ethics, or is it medical politics? Are comparative studies of the justice of health care delivery systems between the United Kingdom, Sweden, and the United States studies in medical ethics, or studies in medical economics and politics?

Who has the authority to define the technical parameters and perimeters of medical ethics? Is it the various participants in medical practice and policy formation, or is it philosophers and theologians with their admirable penchant for conceptual clarity and precise distinctions? Does a sense that something is wrong with the distribution of biomedical research funding, the accessibility of health care, of the "medicalization" of society count as a moral concern? Or is such an uneasiness so inchoate or so conceptually muddled, that it can be ignored by scholars in medical ethics? Do inchoate promptings of moral uneasiness unduly extend the range of subjects to be taken into account in medical ethics? Or do the concepts and procedures of moral philosophy or moral theology define the ethical?

If the focus of medical ethics is clinical and research moral quandaries, can they be adequately grasped, understood, and explained without accounting for the sociology of research, of health care delivery systems, and of hierarchies of prestige and power in hospitals? Can they be understood and explained without taking into account medical economics and medical politics, or without taking into account changing cultural and personal values, individual aspirations and goals, and other elements of contemporary ethos? Are these relevant to moral judgments?

What happens to the scope of "medical ethics" when the high drama of extreme cases becomes the focus of attention? When court cases become prominent if not dominant data in ethics courses and articles? When moral philosophers and theologians, like so many psychiatrists, can be lined up to offer testimony for both the prosecution and the defense?

These questions come from the digging and spading, the ruminations, of one who has never been at the center of the field of medical ethics, but has been in and out of it since about 1961, before medical ethics became a growth industry. This article is not based upon comprehensive study of the large body of medical ethical literature, but upon broad though selective reading. Its title uses the term "moral discourse" precisely to espouse inclusion of a variety of literature. "Morally relevant discourse" might be even more appropriate, and certainly would be to any who desire to keep strict and technical limits to the language of ethics, to its concepts and procedures of argumentation. It does not take on the old problem of sharply distinguishing between the moral, the non-moral, and the pre-moral, but it appeals to a generosity on the part of readers to tolerate some ambiguity for the sake of clarity on a different level.

In literature about medicine, as well as literature about economics, politics, and other activities, it is possible to distinguish between four types of moral discourse. I shall call these ethical, prophetic, narrative, and policy discourse. The argument of the article is that if too exclusive attention is given to any one of the types, significant issues of concern to morally sensitive persons and communities are left unattended. My suggestion is that none of the types is sufficient in itself. The contributions of each type to the other and to a larger framework of medical moral literature are not fully developed here. What is common to the four types is a concern for various human values; each is prompted, in my judgment, by an uneasiness, a sense that something is awry. And each sees a different location for what is perceived to be inadequate if not wrong, and thus uses language or forms of discourse appropriate to that location. Each uses the data, information, sources of insight and concepts that are judged to be appropriate to the location or arena in which some wrong is intuited or perceived.

II. ETHICAL DISCOURSE

The center of ethical discourse, as I use the term, is the use of concepts, distinctions, and modes of discourse formulated over centuries in the disciplines of moral philosophy and moral theology. In contemporary medical literature all readers are familiar with the framing of problems and solutions by a relatively small set of concepts: rights, duties, obligations, competence, and justice. Also familiar are various allegedly helpful distinctions: between competent and non-competent patients, between active and passive euthanasia, between reversible and irreversible medical conditions, between various probabilities of effective outcomes of interventions, and the like. The modes of argumentation are often known by the typological and occasionally useful distinctions of moral philosophers, such as deontological and utilitarian. The quandaries that provoke reflection are typically those of conflicts of rights and duties, of degrees of acceptable risk, of allocation of scarce medical resources, of the moral status of patients— whether they have the capacities that mark them as persons, and the like. The procedure is often the classic one of casuistry, the application of principles to cases. Cases are developed by professional medical persons using information derived from clinical tests and from the experience of clinicians; comparison to other cases is often used to sharpen the similarities and dissimilarities between cases. The prognoses of various courses of action are considered. These prognoses are based upon medical science and clinical experience. Features are highlighted as salient which locate not only the medical but also the moral issue.

A procedure such as abortion can be addressed as a moral problem; within such a class of cases particular circumstances require a different degree of refinement of ethical analysis and choice. For example, the abortion issue is addressed as a very large class, and arguments for or against its moral licitness address all possible occasions for the intervention. If, however, the procedure is not ruled out as immoral, more refined ethical analysis is required to judge the moral propriety of a specific abortion in relation to specific fetal conditions or conditions of the mother.

Similar concepts and procedures are used in other critical choices that currently occupy physicians, ethicists, lawyers, and the public, for example, the appropriateness of using artificial procedures of nutrition in non-cognitive patients and, more controversially, of removing them once they have begun. The literature is replete with case studies; they are endlessly fascinating for many persons, because most focus on choices about death and thus have a sense of high drama.

Arguments about classes of cases or about particular cases often reflect preferences for different theories of morality, whether the debaters are conscious or not of them. For example, arguments appealing to rights have a different focus from arguments appealing to probable outcomes and qualities of life.

My favorite illustration of the above paragraph comes from discussions of proposed legislation, but the arguments reflected commitments to opposing views of the moral obligations of the medical professions. The legislation was the Uniform Anatomical Gifts Act; the discussants were colleagues in renal therapy. The surgeon at that time objected to the restrictions the Act placed on access to organs that could be used to save lives of other patients. The internist argued vehemently in favor of the Act, since it preserved the rights of the deceased and next of kin to determine the disposition of the corpse. The surgeon implicitly believed that the ethically sanctioned calling of the profession was to save the greatest number of lives possible, and thus the means to fulfill this vocation ought not be unduly restricted on moral and legal grounds. Clearly, the internist was defending a moral tradition which primarily honored the rights of individuals, even though choices made might deprive other persons of potential benefits. Different preferences for different ethical theories (or probably, in this case, preferences that were not for theories but for beliefs about morality) selected different aspects of the class of cases as the morally salient ones. In effect, the same information in each case received different degrees of moral valence as a result of different theories of morality.

Ethical discourse, as I use the term here, has as its purpose to decide how one ought to act in particular circumstances. The concern typically is to find moral justification for a particular intervention or for non-intervention. This is the great and important contribution of ethical discourse. A circumscription around salient features is usually rather clearly drawn. The principal agent is clear: the responsible physician. The circumstances deemed to be morally relevant are limited, though arguments occur over these limits. The primary object of the action is unambiguous; it is the patient. The alternative means of action are stipulated by the medical profession; the intention is certainly always to seek the best interests of the patient. Probable outcomes can be judged on the basis of similar cases. And if there is no clear and fully logical reason for one choice or the other, at least certain options are closed out. The prudential judgment takes place within limits, and the act or the inaction is done with relative certitude of its moral licitness. The risk of engaging in an unethical act is, if not eliminated, at least limited.[1]

Moral discourse, in this restricted sense of medical ethics, is obviously necessary, and its merits hardly need enumeration. The focus on particular acts and on a limited number of agents, however, requires assumptions that can be questioned from some other perspectives—perspectives that find other forms of moral discourse appropriate. There is not enough questioning of the propriety of high medical technology per se that is often the necessary condition for the existence of the

---

1. For an interesting, informative account of casuistry, its history and its current importance, see Albert R. Jonsen and Stephen Toulmin, *The Abuse of Casuistry: A History of Moral Reasoning* (Berkeley: University of California Press, 1988).

quandaries that have to be resolved. The technology which is interposed between the patient and a "natural" time to die, for example, is not brought under critical judgment. Certain personal and cultural values are assumed, e.g., that the preservation of physical life under conditions of unusual adversity and limitation is an individual and social good. The aspects of the patient's life story, his or her personal narrative, that are taken into account are limited; the relevant past tends to be brief. For example, a young physician was puzzled by an eighty-four year old patient's refusal of certain clinical tests. An older physician of Scandinavian origin asked a few questions and determined that the patient was an aged Scandinavian immigrant, and quietly said, "It is quite typical of a person his age from that culture to take a stoical attitude toward death." Also, the proper attitude of ethical discourse brackets emotions, affective responses, and physician's perceptions that cannot be reduced to data and concepts appropriate to ethical discourse. The ethical, in the eyes of some, becomes its own technical fix, eliminating the importance of compassion and other moral sentiments. The social and economic structure of health care in the society is often assumed as a given, even if it is deemed less than what is desirable. For all these and other limitations of ethical discourse, however, it is necessary, but if moral discourse is excessively limited to it, medical morality becomes myopic. (Later in this article an ethical approach to a policy issue is discussed).

III. PROPHETIC DISCOURSE

One can say that prophetic discourse tends to be "macro" in comparison with ethical discourse, which tends to be "micro." Prophetic discourse is usually more general than ethical discourse, and sometimes uses narratives to make prophetic points. It takes two distinguishable forms. One is indictment. Readers of the Bible know this from the writings of Hosea, Amos, and Jeremiah. The indictments are radical, i.e., they are not occupied with surface issues but expose the roots of what is perceived to be fundamentally and systematically wrong. Prophets are seldom interested in specific acts except insofar as they signify a larger and deeper evil or danger. The discourse usually is passionate and uses metaphors and analogies which stir the hearers' emotions. Often it is apocalyptic. Evidences are marshalled to sustain the indictment, and while some prophetic voices take counter-evidences into account and develop arguments, many do not. To the gloomy prophet much ethical discourse is simply re-arranging the deck chairs on the Titanic when it is already sinking. Or he construes developments to be on a course that is likely to lead to disaster if it is not halted. To the moral philosopher or theologian, the prophet's concerns often seem to be "global," her arguments poorly made, and her language too emotive.

The second form is utopian. The utopian prophet describes an alluring future in which ailments and maladies of persons and societies will be relieved and a healthier and happier condition realized. Utopian language, like the language of indictment, is often symbolic and metaphorical; it is visionary; it arouses human hopes; it raises human aspirations. To the policy maker the utopian prophet appears to be unrealistic; he seems unwilling to face the limits of the present time and does not have the patience to organize resources for the modest increments of improvement that can actually occur.

Ivan Illich's *Medical Nemesis* is announced by a paperback publisher in prophetic terms: "The most explosive, uncompromising . . . attack on the gravest health hazard we face today: our medical system" (Illich, 1977). Like many prophetic books it sharply divided the house between those who found it deceptive in its use of evidence, unnuanced in its arguments, and fear-mongering in its language, on the one hand, and those who were readily persuaded by its apocalyptic tone, on the other. Illich does not take up the kinds of clinical decisions that much of the literature of medical ethics addresses; he perceives underlying these and other problems a deeper evil, the system of modern medicine. Prophets frequently find a demonic or satanic reality that pervasively corrupts institutions and practices; Illich has his clearly in mind. And, like Hosea and Amos and Cicero of old, Illich has a way with words, using similes, metaphors, analogies, and literary references which are charged with passion and create affective as much as (or more than) critical intellective responses. A few quotations from his chapter "The Medicalization of Life" suffice to illustrate this.

He opens a subsection of this chapter "Political Transmission of Iatrogenic Disease" with a litany of events to show that medicine is now less concerned to enhance what occurs in nature and more concerned to "engineer the dreams of reason." The paragraph ends as follows.

> But any charge against medicine for the clinical damage it causes constitutes only the first step in the indictment of pathogenic medicine. The trail beaten in the harvest is only a reminder of the greater damage done by the baron to the village his hunt overruns (Illich, 1977, pp. 32–33).

One of the citations supporting the first of the quoted sentences is from a sociological article whose theme is that medicine is becoming a major institution of social control, either displacing or incorporating traditional institutions of religion and law, a place in which absolute judgments are being made by supposedly morally neutral and objective experts in the name of health. But note also the second quoted sentence, from which one infers that Illich's choice of language is meant to enhance a vision of innocent and powerless patients who are not fully aware of the greater damage being done by a powerful medical system of medical barons.

In a further section, "Terminal Ceremonies," Illich begins his discussion in this way:

> Therapy reaches its apogee in the death-dance around the terminal patient. At a cost of between $500 and $2,000 per day, celebrants in white and blue envelop what remains of a patient in antiseptic smells. The more exotic the incense and the pyre, the more death mocks the priest. The religious use of medical technique has come to prevail over its technical purpose, and the

line separating the physician from the mortician has been blurred (Illich, 1977, pp. 91–92).

Other authors who are concerned about terminal procedures, their costs, and their effects upon patients and others, describe the same set of conditions in less dramatic and affective language. Illich intends to affect the reader: procedures are death dances; physicians are priests in liturgical vestments; the scene is more exotic than a corpse on a pyre of sandalwood at the burning ghat in Benares; the role of the healer and burier can no longer be differentiated. The reader is presented with a redescription of events and conditions which allude to meanings of religious significance; an indictment of medicine is thereby implied if not explicit. It is not unlike the prophet Hosea's use of harlotry as a metaphor for religious negligence and disobedience among the people of Israel. Factual matters become charged with moral indignation through the similes and metaphors used.

Nor is it unlike a political speech by Cicero and countless politicians since his time. For example, in Cicero's speech against Lucius Sergius Cataline, he spoke in these terms:

> For imagine every type of criminality and wickedness you can think of: he has been behind them all . . . Whenever all through these years there has been a murder, the murderer has been he. Not one single act of filthy lechery has been committed without him being its guiding spirit (Grant, 1969, p. 97).

No medical ethical casuist uses this kind of language. But perhaps ethical discourse cannot readily indicate the systemic problems that Illich perceives, and it hardly arouses moral passions. Indeed, it deliberately seeks to bracket passions in favor of rationality.

Illich's is prophetic discourse in two important respects. He sees modern medicine to be at least as dangerous as it is beneficial, and goes beneath the symptoms presented to isolate the major source of many ailments, namely the social system of modern medicine. The dominant evil, the devil, is named. Also he uses the rhetoric of advocacy, and the language used is justified by its intended effect upon the reader. An indictment that might have been made in dry statistics and clearly developed linear argument is more forcefully made. One "feels" Illich's indignation, and he desires to arouse the reader's own.

There is value in Illich's prophetic address that ethical discourse does not achieve. Of course, the locations of the quandary are different. By locating problems systematically and socially, Illich at least calls attention to aspects of contemporary medicine that evoke uneasiness, and while his language is inflated from some perspectives, one is cognizant of aspects of modern medicine that might have escaped the attention of a morally conscientious clinician and a wider public. But Illich is hardly sufficient; his book does not aid the clinician in making a morally sound medical judgment, nor does it aid the policy maker in taking steps to improve medical research and care—steps that take one from where they are today to where they can and ought to be in a year's time.

Leon Kass would, no doubt, be appalled to see his work within the same class as Illich's. His prose is, except for an occasional flourish, undramatic; he is seldom given to hyperbole. His citations are less to current literature than to great classics of Western culture, and when a recent event is discussed it is used to point beneath itself to a deeper matter. He feels no need to bolster his articles with scores of citations to lend them authority as Illich does. He shows modesty about even his most dramatic forecasts, and is careful to modify any indictments with assurances that he appreciates the benefits of modern medicine and praises its accomplishments. Yet the reader senses a profound moral passion, a deep concern for the effects of medical experimentation and high technological care on humane values that Kass obviously holds very dear. He is prophetic. He exposes apparent assumptions that seem not to be radically challenged by scientists and clinicians; he peers into the future to question potential outcomes of courses of events if the present routes continue. And he has a vision of what constitutes the good human life; though it is not argued for, it is averred. This vision is a kind of normative backdrop against which problematic aspects of modern science and medicine are exposed by his descriptions and analyses. His call is to a heightened consciousness so that the humanness that is to be valued is not eroded by incremental developments oblivious to their wider and deeper consequences.

What I mean by prophetic discourse can be illustrated from a number of Kass's essays. Medical ethics literature is replete with articles about *in vitro* fertilization, as is the legal literature. Kass approaches it differently. He writes, "The first task, it seems to me, is not to ask 'moral or immoral?' or 'right or wrong?' but to try to understand fully the meaning and significance of the proposed actions" (Kass, 1985, p. 101). For Kass "meaning and significance" refers to a much larger cultural and human context than does the ethicist's conventional question: "Is the procedure immoral?" or "Can it be ethically justified?" Meaning and significance for whom and for what? In Kass's analysis it is for all humanity. The foreseeable consequences and predictable extension of developing life in the laboratory touch "even our common acceptance of our own humanity." "At stake is the *idea* of the *humanness* of our human life and the meaning of our embodiment, our sexual being, and our relation to ancestors and descendants." In thinking about immediate decisions, the kinds of decisions ethical discourse deals with, Kass warns that "we must be mindful of the larger picture and must avoid the great danger of trivializing the matter for the sake of rendering it manageable" (Kass, 1985, pp. 101–102).

The larger picture is further developed in a paragraph that provides the backdrop against which his moral concerns about particular practices become highlighted.

> Our society is dangerously close to losing its grip on the meaning of some fundamental aspects of human existence. In reviewing the problem of the disrespect shown to embryonic and fetal life in our efforts to master them we noted a tendency . . . to reduce certain aspects of human being to mere body, a tendency opposed most decisively in the nearly universal prohibition of cannibalism (Kass, 1985, p. 113).

The use of cannibalism to make a point about what underlies, in his eyes, *in vitro* fertilization is a powerful prophetic insight; it is jarring. Kass goes on to discuss prohibitions against incest and adultery, which "defend the integrity of marriage, kinship, and especially the lines of origin and descent." "Clarity about your origins is crucial for self-identity, itself important for self-respect." "It would be," he writes, "deplorable public policy to erode further such fundamental beliefs, values, institutions, and practices."[2]

In this discussion and in others, I maintain, Kass uses prophetic discourse. He peers through the immediate and confined things that ethical discourse focuses on to describe a more profound malady, one that is a threat to the whole of humanity. The things he values are stated; they are not argued for. And with a moral passion all the more eloquent because of its linguistic restraint he can evoke a vision of a pending crisis.

My impression is that utopian prophetic discourse in medicine is rarer than it was some years ago. Utopian outlooks may lie behind some of the inflated language that has been used to engage public support for certain research, e.g., announcing a "crusade" against cancer. Crusades have come to designate total war against an evil so great that any means of obliteration of the enemy is morally justifiable. A crusade provides support for more extreme measures than even a just war. Or we are titillated by the possibility of elimination of some death-dealing diseases, and evidences of radical containment, if not eradication, of small-pox and polio lend credence to other possibilities. Sub-titles of books intimate utopian possibilities, for example. Joseph Fletcher, *The Ethics of Genetic Control: Ending Reproductive Roulette*, or José M. R. Delgado, *Physical Control of the Mind: Toward a Psychocivilized Society*. Perhaps without a utopian vision some investigators and social planners would lose incentive to work and alter social arrangements.

Delgado is not an unmitigated utopian; he is cognizant of pending moral and social problems from increased use of physical control of brain activity. But, to this reader, he cannot restrain some unguarded dreams.

> We are now on the verge of a process of mental liberation and self-domination which is a continuation of our evolution. Its experimental approach is based on the investigation of the depth of the brain in behaving subjects. Its practical applications do not rely on direct cerebral manipulations but on the integration of neuropsychological and psychological principles leading to a more intelligent education, starting from the moment of birth and continuing throughout life, with the preconceived plan of escaping from the blind focus of chance and of influencing cerebral mechanisms and mental structure in order to create a future man with greater personal freedom and originality, a member of a psycho-civilized society, happier, less destructive, and better balanced than present man (Delgado, 1969, p. 223).

2. On pp. 310–311, Kass describes other features and potentialities that he values, e.g., "Through moral courage, endurance, greatness of soul, generosity, devotion to justice—in acts great and small—we rise above our mere creatureliness, for the sake of the noble and the good."

A reader's response to such a statement in part depends on his or her own moral sensibilities and aspirations for the human future. One can infer an intention on the part of the author, however; he desires to move us by an alluring future of greater personal freedom and originality, of a happier, less destructive society. Readers might have a response that is the reverse of the intended; his is another vision which could justify research and application that could destroy social fabrics and human values as it is pursued.[3]

Alluring visions of a better medical and social future are clearly ambiguous, but it is not necessary that their pursuit leads to blind neglect and destruction of existing values. Utopian prophets evoke hopes, and hope is a profound motivation for reducing the pain and suffering in the world.

Ethical discourse, because of the normal sharpness of its focus, does not stir the imagination to engage in larger medical pursuits; its normal language does not induce dreams. The issue is, of course, not only what evokes hope but what is the proper object of hope. My quotation from Delgado creates deep anxieties to persons who hold many values dear; it is also the case that a vision, perhaps judged to be utopian at one point in history, of a world without small-pox and polio, or of an agriculture that can provide nutrients sufficient for all humankind, has issued in benefits.

IV. NARRATIVE DISCOURSE

"Narrative ethics" is currently discussed and recommended by significant authors in religious ethical traditions, particularly Christianity. Oversimply, the principal line of argument is that we are members of moral communities, and the outlooks, values and visions of these communities are shaped by their stories. As we participate in a community and its formative narratives our own moral outlooks and values are shaped by its narrative. As such, this line of argument is descriptive, and its defense relies upon historical, sociological and social-psychological evidences. The critical issue, from a moral point of view, is what narratives ought to shape moral ethos and character. On certain theological grounds, it is argued that the Christian story ought to shape the Christian community and characters of Christian people, and even that the morality of Christians ought to be tested by its faithfulness to its own story.[4]

This larger thesis of narrative ethics is not the point of introducing it in this article, though one book I will cite provides a good example of medical education

---

3. For two forceful arguments against prophetic utopians, see Melvin J. Lasky, *Utopia and Revolution* (Chicago: University of Chicago Press, 1976), and Hans Jonas, *The Imperative of Responsibility* (Chicago: University of Chicago Press, 1984).

4. The most prominent proponent of this view in Protestantism is Stanley Hauerwas; his most systematic book to date is *The Peaceable Kingdom: A Primer in Christian Ethics*. His many essays on issues of medical care reflect this perspective.

as a process of internalization (and some resistance to it) that takes place as students are shaped by the "narrative," broadly conceived, of the medical profession.

Narratives are not arguments in the sense that ethical discourse provides arguments, though one must note the extent to which story telling (using various cases and experiences) occurs when clinical moral choices are discussed. At such a juncture the story functions similarly to parables in biblical and rabbinic literature; one asks a question of a wise person and hears a story which does not really prescribe precise conduct but illumines one's choice. The moral philosopher or theologian is often frustrated by the use of narrative; its logic is not that of moral arguments as normally conceived. The philosopher may abstract from the narrative an implied argument which might or might not be persuasive on her grounds. But the teller of the story would believe that important affective and descriptive overtones are thus dissolved by the abstraction.

Narratives can provide a more extended context within which the circumstances of a particular clinical choice are understood or in which a medical policy is proposed. Whether and how that larger understanding should be taken into account in a particular choice is a matter of dispute. A chapter by Renee Fox and Judith Swazey provides an example worthy of reflection, "The Case of the Artificial Heart." It is from one perspective a study in medical sociology, medical history, or even medical politics, but not in medical ethics. The central narrative follows the case of Mr. Haskell Karp, who received the first implanted mechanical heart (Fox et al. 1978, pp. 135–179). Around it is an interpretive report of an unfolding sequence of events which gives details about the competition between Drs. DeBakey and Cooley, along with other relevant aspects. Research has been done in primary documents, interviews conducted, etc. The chapter is not ethical discourse; it does not provide the kinds of arguments that scores of other articles on artificial hearts have done. At the end of a fascinating and informative account the authors close with a modest conclusion.

> In our view, this case and its outcome show that the medical and law professions, and the larger society to which they belong, have not satisfactorily dealt with the social, moral and legal issues involved in therapeutic innovation with human subjects (Fox et al., 1978, p. 197).

The technical medical "ethicist" could agree with that, and might press the authors for specific formulations of rules or guidelines to govern future events. But that would be to miss the point. Because of historical, sociological, economic, and other aspects of their account, the authors force the reflective reader into a much larger context of discussion that Fox has called in another place "medical morality" rather than medical ethics. Structures of institutions, sources of funding, competitiveness among investigators, motivations of desperate patients and their families, technological developments—these and other features frame specific moral medical choices. To separate the precise clinical choice from the more extensive factors leads to only partial understanding, if not gross misunderstanding, of the problem to be addressed. The authors' account points to many junctures in which critical choices are made, and the adequate moral response requires attention to the proper ends and means for each of them. Whether this wider context would make a difference in the clinical choice itself is not as clear.

Melvin Konner's narrative interpretation of his experience as a medical student after a decade of teaching and publication in anthropology is also morally significant. It is the story of becoming socialized into a profession by participating in its "narrative," and of Konner's resisting aspects of the resulting formation of professional character (Konner, 1987).

It not only portrays what happened to Konner but also records his apt perceptions of institutional arrangements, characteristics of various physicians and their conduct, the effects of strenuous pressures on young doctors, and many other things. It also describes the response of a mature and deeply humane student confronting the impersonal and objectified circumstances of a modern teaching hospital, and the effects of these circumstances on some patients.

Konner's is not a diatribe against the dehumanization of modern medical care in such institutions; he does nor argue from a theory of justice to portray injustices in health care; it is not a theory-laden book, not even theory from Konner's own discipline of anthropology. Its impact on the reader is all the greater because of that. The narrative portrays an ethos, a pervasive climate in large urban teaching hospitals; it has a prophetic impact. There is no theory about how the ethos is internalized in the becoming physician, though an anthropologist certainly would have one. There is no theory of "ethos" itself. But the reader feels the impact of the ethos on the development of the professional character of physicians. And Konner has his heroes, such as Dr. Ringler, who sustain outlooks, concerns, and relations that are commendable. But Konner does not explain how such persons have come to have and sustain commendable qualities against some odds. One gets a sense that by showing good qualities one knows them; there is no argument about why they are good.

Narratives like this stay close to experience; this is precisely their great merit. "Ethics" tends to abstract from experience; this is its merit. But both are important forms of moral discourse. The author of a narrative, in ways comparable to prophetic authors, can ask of the moral philosopher: What is the context in which choices are made? What are underlying social practices and assumptions, the accepted conditions, the institutional arrangements and the human emotions involved? Do they have to be addressed morally as much as the clinical case has to be? But none of the forms of discourse I have isolated is self-sufficient; they often overlap and supplement each other.

V. POLICY DISCOURSE

Literature on various aspects of medical policy is profuse. Some of it is descriptive, such as studies of the politics of biomedical research funding. Some of it is multidisciplinary, such as the reports of Presidential Commissions on various aspects of research and care. Some of it is ethical, such as distributive justice concepts framing alternative possibilities for health care distribution.

In this article I can only suggest a comparison between the approach to policy from a very disciplined use of ethical discourse and a hypothetical approach from the standpoint of persons who have institutional roles which require them to formulate policy within the limitations and possibilities of resources accessible to them. Gene Outka's oft reprinted article on equal access to health care serves as my example of a rigorous approach. It assumes a societal goal of assurance of adequate health care to all persons in the nation. In the development of his argument to justify the goal, Outka delineates the classic and standard concepts of distributive justice; similar cases should be treated similarly, but what constitutes relevant similarity? Need? Ability to pay? Social merit? He assesses the relevance of each of these conceptions and suggests institutional implications of his own conclusion (Outka, 1974). The great merit of this article is precisely that ethical discourse is dominant; it frames the analysis and proceeds with rigor and precision to disclose implications of various views of justice.

The contrast I wish to suggest is with an approach to the same subject in which the language and information of economics, politics, sociology and medicine would be dominant. Outka's article represents, properly, the standpoint of the ethical observer, an outsider to the institutions and roles through which choices have outcomes. His primary question is: What ought to be the case? Contrariwise, from the standpoint of various engaged agents (who are more likely to use the language of economics, politics, sociology and medical technology) the first question is usually: What is possible?[5] What resources are available or can be accumulated? What proper interests compete for these resources? What personnel and institutional arrangements are necessary? If it is not the prior question, the question of the possible is asked at least in tandem with questions more distinctively ethical. Information, relevant concepts, interpersonal sensitivities, relations to other institutions, etc., all have to be on the table for analysis. The ought questions are answered within possibilities and limitations of what is—the resources that exist or can be accumulated and organized.

Policy discourse, from the perspective of agents responsible for resource allocations, cannot be "purely" ethical. Enabling and limiting conditions ground possible courses of action. As theologians are wont to say, the good is sought under the conditions of finitude. Actually policy is seldom, if ever, determined by the conclusion of a formal ethical argument. But this does not eliminate the importance of the ethical analysis and argument; such argument articulates ends, refines the criteria for the moral choices embedded in the empirical, and facilitates moral self-evaluation. Policy discourse without ethical discourse easily degenerates into

5. In part these reflections stem from social roles I have had as a sometime member of the Advisory Committee to the Director of the NIH, and of the Board of a major not-for-profit health system in the Chicago area.

satisfaction with the merely possible, with assumed values and procedures, with the domination of the economic or institutional considerations. If ethical discourse can become encapsuled in its own concepts and modes of argumentation, so also can policy discourse unless it is subjected to the ethical discourse.

Prophetic discourse, such as Illich's, often looks global and unrealistic to the policy maker, but its perspective can function to jar institutions from blind acceptance of the status quo. Narrative can inform the policy maker of the larger and more inclusive "story" of which they are developing a sub-plot, but it is not decisive in determining what ought to be done. For example, board members and administrators of health systems would do well to read Paul Starr's historical and sociological account of American medicine to grasp what has brought them to their present circumstances (Starr, 1982).

VI. CONCLUSION

To focus moral discourse about medicine too exclusively on what I have described as ethical tends to lose sight of realms of choice and activity that are of great importance. Ethical discourse is not sufficient. But neither is prophetic, or narrative, or policy discourse. The location of choices, of the perceived moral uneasiness or possibilities, licenses each of the forms of discourse described. Perhaps, though it is not argued here, the location of the uneasiness should determine the concepts, approaches, language, and information that are appropriate, rather than a form of discourse determining what is and is not taken into account as morally relevant. At least there are different "moments" in medical morality when different forms are more appropriate. The contributions of each to the others in moral reflection about medicine is a topic for further investigation.

REFERENCES

Delgado, José. 1969. *Physical Control of the Mind: Toward a Psychocivilized Society.* New York: Harper and Row.
Fletcher, Joseph. 1974. *The Ethics of Genetic Control: Ending Reproductive Roulette.* Garden City, N.Y.: Doubleday Anchor.
Fox, Renee C., and Judith P. Swazey. 1978. *The Courage to Fail: A Social View of Organ Transplants and Dialysis.* 2d ed. Chicago: University of Chicago Press.
Grant, Michael, trans. and ed. 1969. *Selected Political Speeches of Cicero.* New York: Penguin Books.
Hauerwas, Stanley. 1983. *The Peaceable Kingdom: A Primer in Christian Ethics.* Notre Dame, In.: University of Notre Dame Press.
Illich, Ivan. 1977. *Medical Nemesis: The Expropriation of Health.* New York: Bantam Books.
Jonsen, Albert R., and Stephen Toulmin. 1988. *The Abuse of Casuistry: A History of Moral Reasoning.* Berkeley, Calif.: University of California Press.
Kass, Leon. 1985. *Toward a More Natural Science: Biology and Human Affairs.* New York: The Free Press.

Konner, Melvin. 1987. *Becoming a Doctor: A Journey of Initiation in Medical School.* New York: Penguin Books.

Outka, Gene. 1974. "Social Justice and Equal Access to Health Care." *Journal of Religious Ethics.* 2:11–32.

Starr, Paul.1982. *The Social Transformation of American Medicine.* New York: Basic Books.

Chapter 15

The Use of Scripture
in Christian Ethics

To embark on a paper dealing with a topic that has centuries of history, and volumes of explicit discussion, particularly in the recent decades, is to invite criticisms of partiality, of incompleteness, of ignorance of significant literature, and of failure to decisively settle complex issues debated from various interests and perspectives. In my case it is also to return to a matter on which I have written over several decades, beginning with an effort to summarize the judgements of my doctor father, H. Richard Niebuhr, on the subject in my "Introduction" to his posthumously published *The Responsible Self*. Off and on for many years I conducted seminars in which we examined both ethics in the Bible and the uses of the Bible in Christian ethics. One author who participated in one such seminar, William C. Spohn, has now published a revised edition of *What Are They Saying about Scripture and Ethics?* in which discussion is brought up to date and in which one chapter from the first volume, "Response to Revelation," is removed.[1]

In this paper I attempt to take a somewhat different approach to the use of Scripture in Christian ethics than I, and I think other authors, have done, though

---

1. William C. Spohn, *What Are They Saying about Scripture and Ethics?* (New York: Paulist Press, 1995).

it overlaps with the work of many others. Rather than begin with biblical themes and materials and "apply" them to ethics, I begin with questions of ethics and inquire how biblical materials might answer them. It is an elaboration of distinctions made previously between the moral and theological uses of the Bible. The moral has tended to focus on the ethical teachings and examples in the Bible to answer the question "What ought we to do?" The theological has been in focus on how the knowledge of God and God's purposes given in the Bible provide symbols and frameworks of meaning which assist in determining both the interpretation of circumstances and the ends towards which humans ought to be oriented. Its question, as asked by two Americans, H. R. Niebuhr and Paul Lehmann, is "What is God Doing?" In this paper, I attempt to state an agenda of the questions that Christian ethics, or more generally ethics, asks when it seeks to be comprehensive and systematic. On the basis of this agenda, I will argue that the Bible has different kinds of significance depending upon which item of the agenda of ethics is attended to, and that there are significant differences in how the Bible is used by authors on each agenda item. In the conclusion, I will make the case that the Bible has different contributions to different aspects of Christian ethics, and that, to take recourse to words used by H. Richard Niebuhr in his unpublished lectures, its authority is educative and corroborative, and not hierarchical as the ultimate justification of ethics.

Many persons, including me, have schematized the dimensions of ethics, or the questions that are asked when we engage in critical inquiry about the characteristics and aspects of moral experience. Here I adapt from William Schweiker's *Responsibility and Christian Ethics*.[2] Any such device is heuristic in purpose; thus no effort is made to defend this agenda as the only inclusive one. Schweiker writes that there are five basic questions: "what is going on? what is the norm for how to live? what are we to be and to do? what does it mean to be an agent? and how do we justify moral claims?" In a schematization, he calls these the interpretive, practical, meta-ethical, fundamental, and normative dimensions, respectively. I will use the questions, rather than the schematized appellations to organize the contents of this paper. My basic contention, to state it again, is that the use of Scripture will be different for each of these dimensions, and the kind of authority that it has for each will be different, particularly if we would enlarge this paper to an analysis of a wide range of Christian ethical literature.

THE INTERPRETATION OF EVENTS

What is going on? How this question is answered provides the depiction or construal of the events or circumstances in which action is taken, a *Gestalt* of that to which one is responding morally and in which one will exercise some powers

---

2. William Schweiker, *Responsibility and Christian Ethics* (Cambridge: Cambridge University Press, 1995), pp. 34–40, 230–231 (n. 4).

to affect or restrain a course of events or a pattern of relationships. Our principal question here is whether and how the Bible informs the answer to this question.

First, it is important to recognize that the interpretation of events and circumstances varies with the object of attention, and with the available and relevant information about it. The information and its interpretation vary according to whether the event or circumstances are primarily, for example, medical or military, ecological or political, interpersonal or institutional, or in some cases, combinations of these. Interpretation will also vary according to the perspectives of the analyst and potential actor, to the interests persons or institutions have, to the concepts and modes of explanation that are adopted from various academic disciplines that are used, and to the valorizations of different features being more or less causally determinative of the event. For example, an economist's interpretation of the same information that an anthropologist uses when studying the potlatch ceremony of the Pacific northwest Indians in the United States and Canada will lead to a different answer to the question, what is going on? This one example should suffice; various illustrations could be given *ad infinitum*, of the variations rooted in different problematic moral situations and in different interests and disciplines.

Our question is whether and how the Bible is used, can be used, or ought to be used to answer the question. That it is and can be used with different degrees of authority assumed by the hermeneutical practitioner is clear from a variety of evidence. In the United States, at least, I can see a television "prophet" interpret virtually any current critical event internationally or nationally from the perspective of the book of Revelation. The meaning and significance of what can also be interpreted politically and militarily are given by a framework of interpretation and orientation drawn from a biblical book.

Paul Lehmann, in his *Ethics in a Christian Context* as well as in *The Politics of Transfiguration*, uses both quite general theological principles, and some quite specific ones, to answer the question.[3] His well-known statement that God is acting to make and keep life human is quite general, though its application is illustrated; some specific applications follow with reference to liberation movements and even violent revolutions in the latter named book. Certainly, like the Protestant Lehmann, much of Roman Catholic liberation theology and ethics is biblically authorized by the theme of God's redemptive work in history taking place in all points where there is liberation from various forms of oppression. The authorization of this hermeneutical theme is exegetical, and whether the exegesis is well-defended, whether it is more a rationalization in theological terms for a deep and proper moral indignation, and whether it entails in its economic and political dimensions the kind of social analysis that is used are all matters of judgement and discussion.

The use of the Bible to interpret what is going on functions analogically, and the propriety of particular analogues is a matter of discussion. The television

---

3. Paul Lehmann, *Ethics in a Christian Context* (New York: Harper and Row, 1963); Paul Lehmann, *The Politics of Transfiguration* (New York: Harper and Row, 1975).

prophet virtually identifies nations and events with the state of the churches or the beasts in the Apocalypse; since such crude analogies have been used for so long for so many different events without the predicted outcomes one might think the effort would decline.

The more congenial analogical patterns are more or less complicated by the use of different foci on the content or purpose of what is deemed to be the biblically revealed divine presence or activity in natural and historical events. One can contrast Lehmann's humanization with Gustaf Wingren's interpretation of Law as God's ordering activity; with H. R. Niebuhr's conflation of creative, sustaining and redeeming dimensions of God's action in the same historical events; with Barth's assurance that God's commands and actions in the world will never deviate from the significance of God's revelation in Christ, or with Moltmann's eschatological focus. The use of the Bible interpretively depends, then, upon the biblical themes or symbols that are selected to provide a somewhat coherent account of what is going on. And the choice of symbols makes a difference not only to how what is going on is to be understood, but also with reference to the kinds of activity that should follow. Reinhold Niebuhr's "Christian realism," with the recovery of sin as a symbol for interpreting the roots of what can also be interpreted in economic and political terms, reasonably led to ethics of the resistance to evil; comparatively if weight is given to the presence of redeeming renewing work of God in all things made new, one might have a moral outlook of actualization of what are apparently beneficial potentials.

To conclude this section briefly, one can defend the view that the use of Scripture to answer the question, what is going on? will depend on (1) what authority is conceded to Scripture as a source of revelation of what God's activity or presence means, and (2) what themes from Scripture are used (and presumably defended) as the symbols for interpretation which provide the coherence of any outlook. Every Christian ethics that uses biblical material in this way also uses other sources of information, or concepts for understanding, and principles of explanation. The only exception to this would be some ethician who claimed such divine authorization as to eliminate all attention to "secondary causes," if he or she deemed God to be the primary and immediate cause, and sole source of the meaning of events. Thus, I argue, that any theological interpretation of what is going on that uses biblical materials necessarily has to find some corroboration or coherence with other interpretations of the same events based on other principles and valorized by other perspectives.

As a matter of empirical observation, I have the impression that most writers of Christian ethics, like most Christians, are not given to the use of biblical sources of answering this question as their first ones. Our first approach to answering, what is going on? is not, what is God doing. In modern culture psychological, sociological, economic, biological, and a myriad of other languages and sources of information dominate. Perhaps what is most often done is to reinterpret what has already been interpreted with another layer of meaning drawn from another source, the Bible. This will not adequately answer the question, what ought we to do, though it may set parameters and ends within and toward which that question is answered.

THE NORM FOR HOW WE LIVE

What is the norm for how to live? The answer to this question invites, on the face of it, more direct and specific moral uses of the Bible. First of all, the Bible has scores of norms, given some authority, about how we ought to live. That the Christian tradition has selected from those many norms or rules is clear. The cultic norms have been abrogated by Christian theology, while the moral norms of the Decalogue have continued to have authority. Compare the Christian abrogation of the cultic norms with the orthodox Jewish practices which claim that the aim of life is holiness, and that the dietary and many other norms eliminated by Christians are ways to holiness. And Christians who hold the Decalogue to authorize norms by which to live, have not followed the casuistic procedures for their application and development found in, for example, the Covenant Code in Exodus. Thus, just as selection from biblical sources is involved in the choice of metaphors, principles or events which provide a way of interpreting what is going on, so also selection is involved in biblical norms, and one distinction traditionally made is between the authority of moral norms from cultic norms. Here there is evidence that some relatively independent criterion of what constitutes the moral in distinction from the cultic has been invoked; thus the authority invoked is not only biblical, but mixed. Or it may be intra-biblical: one portion of the Bible supersedes another in authority.

Another sort of norm that is drawn from the Bible is that of persons, or one can say in the language of Karl Jaspers and others, paradigmatic persons. Saints and heroes, lives whose traits of character and actions are emblematic of what moral persons faithful to God or to Christ ought to be, function as biblical norms. Certainly the long history of an ethics of imitation of Christ, or of *Nachfolge Christi*, is present in the tradition and in some present forms of theology and Christian communal life. The narratives of the gospels as well as the recollections invoked in other New Testament literature are rich, alluring and also diverse. Is the normative form of how Christians are to live to be found in the narratives of the crucifixion, the cleansing of the temple, the healing of the sick and the blind, etc.? Similarly, if one finds the use of figures from the Jewish Scriptures as norms, which persons are chosen and which are rejected? The tradition has found ways to include among the saints Abraham, Moses, David, and others; one would be, I think, hard-pressed to make the narratives of David normative for how we ought to live without a considerable amount of moral editing.

It has been argued, quite persuasively, that the imitation of God as God is known through records of deeds and dispositions (loving, compassionate, etc.) is normative for Jewish and for Christian ethics. Certainly, as we have seen, one way to use the Bible in the interpretation of circumstances is to select passages which describe divine actions in events; in effect from the description, e.g., liberation, follows the norm, i.e., we ought to be doing the kinds of things God is now doing, or is believed to have done under analogous circumstances. As tedious as it may seem, the factor of selectivity has to be recalled again at this point. The narratives of the conquest of Canaan after the liberation from Egypt are plausibly accounts of Yahweh's activity; yet apart from their use to justify the Boers taking of Bantu lands and to some extent the immigrants to North America taking the lands of the native residents, they have not been invoked very often. An independent theological or moral judgement appears to have been made to judge certain of Yahweh's actions to be normative, and others not normative, or perhaps even nefarious and immoral.

The teachings of Jesus for many Christians, perhaps more lay persons than theologians, are assumed to be the norm by which Christians are to live. Certainly they are norms against which behavior has been measured to convict people of their hypocrisy and their inadequacy, driving them to despair and to a terrified conscience if they are scrupulously conscientious. But as everyone reading this paper knows, persons who focus on Matthew 5 and those who focus on Luke 6 readily foster two different, and perhaps incompatible, interpretations of the moral implications if not obligations that follow from Jesus' sayings. Without further analysis that would make my inferences from this more defensible, it is clear that the preference for Luke 6 over Matthew 5 is not based upon different assessments of the authority of Scripture, or upon the greater theological revelational authority of Luke's account from Matthew's account, but upon a moral preference that is related to particular contexts of Christian life and its circumstances.

Perhaps the feature of Christian ethics that is cited most often as its distinctive note is the centrality or primacy of love. The fact that love, *hesed*, is an abiding theme in Jewish Scripture is recognized, but it seems for various exegetical and other reasons to take on unique importance in Christian ethics. The New Testament is the source of ample evidence of its importance in Jesus' teachings, of his life being acts of love, of his life and death being revelations of God's love. Particularly I John 4 is a combination of theological and moral connections between God as love, the particularities of the Christian story, and the conduct expected of the Christian community. Indeed, the literature has come to view *agape* as a distinctively Christian term for love, and has interpreted its meaning in various ways. Is it always self-sacrificial and self-denying, or is it mutuality and self- and community-affirming? Does it direct our natural desire, *eros*, or does it run counter to nature in the name of an independently authorized norm? Is it a rule term, or a motive term? Is it a general principle which has to be applied in ways to, e.g., issues of justice? Or is it a power that informs intuitions about what is the neighbor's need? I need not rehearse any more questions that are answered in the ethical literature on love.

One needs, sometimes, to be reminded of a statement of H. Richard Niebuhr, "Though God is love, love is not god for [Jesus]."[4] A claim for the centrality of

4. H. Richard Niebuhr, *Christ and Culture* (New York: Harper, 1951), p. 17.

love for Christian ethics on the basis of biblical authority does not necessarily entail exclusivity—that all things have to, by one procedure or another, be normed by *agape*. This effort to norm all actions by *agape* issues in various application procedures, e.g., its "principalization" as in Paul Ramsey's efforts to apply it to cases rationally so that any moral ambiguity is overcome, or the love-justice dialectic of Reinhold Niebuhr in which the application is in morally ambiguous situations and one is always in a state of remorse if not guilt.

If the answer to the question, what is the norm for how we live, is "the Bible," the previous sketchy analysis has shown that selection must be made from the many different norms for action found in the Scriptures. The deference to the Bible as a source of moral norms varies with different accounts of its authority as revelation, and the authority granted to parts of it relative to other parts. The argument, made by some, that the Bible contains a divinely revealed morality, a set of norms or a norm which persons are obligated to adhere to, is countered by other arguments.

One is a Kantian style argument, e.g., in recent decades by Alan Donagan, *The Theory of Morality*, in which the author seeks to show that what he deems to be the major moral teachings of the Jewish and Christian traditions can be defended without recourse to biblical authority or to theological justifications.[5]

Another counter argument is made by Roman Catholic moral theologians who argue that for norms to be ethical, they must be universal and "natural"; they are, in Josef Fuchs's words, the *humanum* shared by all human beings; the *christianum* refers to the interiority of motivation that is the effect of the gospel and grace. Or, related, is Bruno Schüller's argument that the biblical morality might be the genetic source for moral norms, but their justification has to be universal and rational.

Another response to the issue of authority of biblical norms is to argue that they are obligatory for Christians, who have a distinctive way of life (though not an exclusive one) as a result of Christ's work in and for their sakes as persons and community. This claim, which is historic, has current justifications on various post-modern type convictions; morals are culture and community bound or related; to be Christian is to live out the particular ethos and norms that define the Christian community.

In summary, how any Christian community or how individuals use the Bible in their answer to the question, what is the norm for how we live, will depend upon various other judgements of quite different sorts. To say that the Bible provides the norm or norms for how we live simply begs scores of questions that must be asked with more precision than the sketch I have provided.[6] Whether biblical norms for conduct will in all occasions of action supersede other action

---

5. Alan Donagan, *The Theory of Morality* (Chicago: University of Chicago Press, 1977).

6. I have analyzed various answers to the question of whether there is a distinctive Christian morality, in "The Idea of Christian Ethics," in Peter Byrne and Leslie Houlden, eds., *Companion Encyclopedia of Theology* (London: Routledge, 1995), pp. 693–700.

guides which have some justification but do not cohere with the biblical ones, is generally, I believe, not the case. Thus, one can plausibly make a case for the notion of corroborative use and authority of biblical norms in relation to other norms. But whether this is satisfactory, and even what corroboration requires, will vary according to the religious and theological contexts in which persons are living and working.

HOW TO MAKE MORAL CHOICES

Schweiker's third question, what are we to be and to do? I interpret here to have particular relevance to how we become persons of certain characteristics and how we should make choices in quite particular circumstances. To some extent the "what are we to do?" has been noted in the discussion of Schweiker's second question. Here of course, our interest is in how the Bible is used, can be used, or persons claim it ought to be used to answer these questions.

First, I attend to Schweiker's question, "what are we to be?" The broadest context for discussion of answers would require delineation of various ideals of good character, of virtues, that have been developed not only in Western culture and thought, but also Asian cultures. And in Western, one would need to distinguish between Jewish, Christian, Islamic and various philosophical accounts. What Christians are to be requires comparison with other answers to indicate any distinctiveness, to show complementarity, or to demonstrate uniqueness. A question parallel to one asked above occurs here as well: ought Christians to be, morally, different from morally conscientious non-Christians? Or are virtues simply one, and the paths to their development different? These matters of wider comparative context are stated here only as reminders of what a more extensive discussion would require.

There certainly are traditions in which both what Christians are to be, and how they become what they are to be, are apparent. In Eastern Orthodoxy *theosis* is the central theological ethical connection; by participation in the mysteries a process of the divinization of persons, communities and finally the cosmos is occurring. "God became human that humans can be made like God," is one expression of this. Christians are to become God-like, certainly not in all the traditional features of the Deity (omnipotence, for example) but in those features which are both portrayed in Jesus Christ and his work. Christians are agents of renewal, redemption, restoration in a broken world. These terms require specification both of the how and where they are applicable and of the more particular traits they suggest, e.g., compassion, mercy, justice.

In various theological and ecclesial proposals, what Christians are to be suggests that the Spirit works through the processes that go on in the historic Christian community, not only through its sacramental life stressed in the Orthodox tradition, but in what is describable in quite naturalistic terms. Certainly in the nineteenth century Schleiermacher provided an interpretation of how the God-consciousness of individuals was shaped by their participation in Christ's own God-consciousness through the life and activities of the church. In one sense, what Christians are to be as persons and communities are loci of God-consciousness, and this state of being is then expressed in their moral activities in the world.

In our time, James B. Nelson used concepts from social psychology to interpret how the Christian can take on certain characteristics through participation in the life of the church.[7] The occupation with the role of narrative as giving shape to community, and through community to the shape of the character of Christians, as one sees it in some of Stanley Hauerwas's writings is another account of how Christians are to become distinctive as a people and as individuals. The process is not only described; it becomes one that is normed; Christians ought to be formed by the narratives and ought to be faithful to the narratives that inform them. This leads to distinctive, but not exclusive, virtues and characters.

The major theological issue that is answered somehow by asking how the Bible informs what we are to be is whether that ideal, that end, is unique, distinctive, or is the same as any other normative view of what persons ought to be, but arrived at through a particular tradition and set of practices. Thus, the use of the Bible to answer this question differs in different traditions and among different authors.

The second part of Schweiker's third question, "what are we to do?" requires different considerations. How that question has been answered and ought to be answered has a long history in moral philosophy as well as in Jewish and Christian ethics, and clearly there are differences of judgements. The purpose of bringing the question up here is to ask whether, or how, the Bible helps *to decide* what we are to do. To some extent, I have answered part of that under the matter of norms. Here, I want to ask whether or how the Bible addresses the *procedural question* of making choices and determining actions. Certainly, there is no *theory*, per se, in the Bible of how Christians are to make their moral choices.

I have already noted the importance of casuistry in the Covenant Code in Exodus; one can cite it in the Holiness Code in Leviticus and in other parts of the Jewish Scriptures. There is no part of the New Testament that develops applications of norms or rules and laws in such a systematic way as do those sections of the Jewish Scriptures. Surely, for some Protestants the use of such procedures leads to legalism with the double fault of usurping the divine prerogative in determining by human reason what ought to be done, and of tempting to works righteousness as a basis for salvation. But, it must be recalled, that casuistry thrived in the Catholic tradition, flourished in the Lutheran and Reformed traditions for a period of history, has been kept alive in the Anglican tradition into our own time, and recently been adopted by a variety of Protestants who found their received tradition to be intellectually sloppy in comparison with many moral philosophers and Roman Catholic theologians.

Biblical casuistry, as casuistry, as a process, is not significantly different in form and procedures from Cicero's casuistry, or from various ways in which civil law

7. James B. Nelson, *Moral Nexus* (Philadelphia: Westminster, 1971), passim.

applies either precedents or statutes to particular sets of circumstances. To be sure, Karl Barth and others have encouraged a "practical casuistry" which provides direction rather than closure, but this is in order to honor the freedom of God and not usurp God's prerogative to be the final determiner of what we ought to do. What can distinguish Christian use of casuistry is the content of the norms, rules, or principles that are applied. A recent example of this was Paul Ramsey's "in-principalization" of *agape* in such a way that *agape* via application of justice could justify war but not justify harm for noncombatants, etc.

I have, in previous publications, noted I Corinthians 7, and 10 and 11, as places in which the Apostle Paul seems to indicate that Christians, who have new freedom in Christ, are to take into account different points in determining how that freedom is to be used. One can see there an earlier example of what Barth called "points to be considered" in the course of listening for the Divine Command.

One can also find biblical passages which could be used to support a kind of moral intuitionism, not in the sense of justification of self-evidence of universal principles or values, but in the sense of perceiving what is the right action or the good end through the renewing and regenerative power of the Spirit. Certainly in later versions of Christian ethics, there are examples of how love knows what to do; Luther's tract on *The Freedom of the Christian* is a case in point.

Finally, the procedural answer is given in the use of parables, simply what the rabbis were masters of. Ask a moral question and the answer is a story. But the story is not a decision; it affects one's imagination, enlarges one's perspective, expands the considerations, and maybe even shocks the reader without telling her or him precisely what to do. In this respect parables function in the determination of what we ought to do in ways similar to the examples given in Cicero, or the effects of classic Greek dramas, or dramas and novels of later ages.

In summary, if one asks whether and how the Bible informs the procedures for answering the question, what are we to do, the answer is that it can, and does, with different examples. But, it is clear that there is no special authority to the Bible for determining how Christians ought to proceed to make moral decisions, unless there is a theology of some form of illumination which grants epistemological privilege to Christians in making moral choices.

INTERPRETATION OF MORAL AGENCY

What does it mean to be an agent? Schweiker's fourth question has been addressed partially in my answer to his third question. What is probed in this question is a philosophical, religious, psychological and ethical question debated since the first dispute between freedom and accountability on the one hand, and forms of determinism and excusability on the other. How one answers the question also depends on what use one makes of the verb, "means." Our question is whether the Bible provides answer to this question. Is there one biblical account of agency? Or are there different descriptions of human persons, their actions, the causes and meanings of their actions in various parts of the Bible? That there are different "theories" of agency coming from different philosophic, religious, and scientific viewpoints does not make an answer to this question easy. My conviction is that any interpretation of human agency in our time must take account of evidences offered by various studies of the human, from genetics to biopsychology, from anthropology to primatology, as well as from moral philosophy and theology.

It is safe, I believe, to assert that the Bible does not provide in any place what in contemporary terms could be called a "theory" of agency, or of moral agency. One does not have, as one does with, e.g., Alan Gewirth's *Reason and Morality*, a defended description and interpretation of the human as voluntary and purposive, which provides the grounding for his theory of ethics.[8] Nor does one have accounts of the biological grounding, if not determination, of moral desires, ends, and actions that various persons are publishing as a result of animal behavior and other studies. Just as the Bible describes certain virtues, or gifts of the Spirit, without a theory of virtue, so the Bible assumes moral accountability for both actions of persons and of communities without a systematic theory. Persons and communities, in the Bible, are accountable for their actions, and are punished and rewarded as a consequence of them. But, I, at least, cannot recall any discussion of the graded application of the role of desires in relation to the role of intentionality and will either to suppress desire or to provide direction to it.

One can infer, however, from a variety of biblical materials, that to be a human person, or a human community, means that one is responsible to other persons, the community, and ultimately to God for one's actions, and that there are laws and rules, ends and traits of character that function as norms by which actions are judged. There are ideals and ends, and paradigmatic persons which lure people and communities toward certain values. And there are very descriptive accounts of the forms of behavior for which persons are accountable that are punished by Yahweh, or which deter one's acceptability in the Christian community. In re: the former, the historical books of Jewish Scriptures are replete with actions by, e.g., David and members of his family and entourage that are morally despicable. In re: the latter, Paul's discussions with the Christians in Corinth depict the lines that ought not to be crossed in Christians faithfully acting out their freedom in Christ.

Perhaps most distinctively biblical about an answer to Schweiker's fourth question is the interpretation of humans as fallen and thus corrupt to degrees which vary according to exegesis of text, and also as graced or renewed, again with varying accounts of the behavioral or moral efficacy of grace or the power of the Spirit.

One can make the case that there is a distinctive answer to the question of agency in the biblical account of the fall of the human. To be an agent in the light of biblical accounts is to be disobedient to the commands of God, to be a mem-

8. Alan Gewirth, *Reason and Morality* (Chicago: University of Chicago Press, 1978).

ber of a "stiff-necked" people whose actions have to be deterred and directed by threats of divine punishment or promises of divine rewards, to be the "harlots" (Hosea) who know what God requires but be lured by false gods and false forms of life, to be stained so deeply that it took the death of Jesus on the cross to make humans right with God and enable them to a new life, etc. One need not rehearse the theological tradition with its continuing and varied accounts of the cause of sin, the nature of sin, and the effect of sin. One might, then, answer the question in this way: The Bible interprets the meaning of agency to be in a condition of bondage or sin which (to varying degrees depending on theological views) corrupts human action and causes moral wrongs against others as well as against the Deity. There is a condition of sin which, in various accounts, issues in sinful actions; sin has both a theological and a moral referent.

To make this claim, however, is not to claim that it is only from the Bible that one finds accounts of human corruption. Nor can one claim that the effects of human corruption that various biblical materials describe are different from effects of other accounts which interpreted human moral evil.

Now, to the claims for the efficacy of grace or renewal as a result of God's steadfast love in Jewish Scriptures, and the result of Christ's person and work in the New Testament. One might say that the Bible calls upon individuals and collectivities to acknowledge their waywardness and sin, and to repent. To repent genuinely is to be forgiven, and to be provided a newness, a capacity to turn from old ways to new ways, and even to receive the power of grace of the Spirit which transforms human agency. Again, the claims made for the moral efficacy of grace and the Spirit vary in different theologians, often depending upon which biblical accounts or passages they focus on. Are the behavioral claims to be interpreted, e.g., in Romans 7, as continuation of not doing the good one wills to do? Or are other Pauline and other claims for a radical newness of life which issues in the fruits of the Spirit to be stressed? Whatever the details of development, one can answer this fourth question by interpreting human agency as, at least for those who are *de facto* Christians (recalling Barth's distinction between *de jure* and *de facto*), graced by the goodness of God in such a way that actions are directed toward and by the Divine will or ends. And for some theologians, the universal claim is correct; to be an agent is to be graced by God so that one can know and do the good either by the continuing image of God in humans by creation, or by the universal effects of God's grace offered and given to all, even those who do not recognize it.

One other turn on the question, only mentioned heretofore, needs recall, namely that agency is not only individual, but collective. Institutions are agents, in that their exercise of powers is directed by ends and has consequences for others in various events. Certainly in the 20th century, both with Reinhold Niebuhr's interpretation of the aggrandized power of institutions to create havoc on human well-being and the liberation theologians' notions of "sinful social structures," the notion of the fall, or the fault, is used to interpret political, international, economic and other events involving groups and institutions.

Whether the symbols of sin and grace provide epistemological privilege, so that in the light of the Bible some things about human agents and events are known differently, more accurately, or more truly by those who orient themselves from the Bible, is an empirical question. In the United States, one is reminded of Reinhold Niebuhr's claim that revelation informs our understanding of experiences and events and in turn is confirmed by them. This claim was not endorsed by political intellectuals who called themselves "atheists for Niebuhr" but who were persuaded by the accounts of Niebuhr's Christian realism on other grounds.

JUSTIFICATION OF MORAL CLAIMS

How do we justify moral claims? Schweiker's fifth question opens the door to comparative analysis of different justifications of moral claims at various levels of specificity. One might include in the answers to this question the reasons for being moral at all. If one does this, various secular and religious responses can be listed: the reason for being moral is that morality serves individual and personal utility; it accords with human reason; it accords with human nature or nature writ large; it expresses the image of God in each human person; it is a response of gratitude and obligation for all the good that God has given to humans in creation and in redemption.

Or, one might construe the question to refer to the justification of particular moral rules, moral ends, or moral outcomes. Again, the breadth of comparative references can be great. One has utilitarian and deontic justification for moral rules; one also has justifications grounded in historic "revelations" in the Jewish and Christian Bible and in the Koran and other sources; one has justifications for rules, ends and consequences drawn from interpretations of the nature of humans individually, in interrelationships with each other and the social and natural orders.

Our more particular restatement of the question follows those of the previous questions. Does the Bible give justifications for moral claims? If it does, what are they? And, in what ways are they unique or distinctive? That the Bible does give justifications for moral claims is evident. Within the biblical materials, and carried on to our own time, is the claim that God commands certain moral obligations or certain human values and consequences of actions. The authorization is ultimately divine command, or divine revelation. What is revealed might be particular moral rules or ends, as in the second table of the Decalogue, or as in the words of the prophets. Or what is revealed is that God does command, and that one is to hear God's command as one is addressed through and by particular occasions of human moral choice.

Over and over in the history of Western morality persons have asked the "Euthyphro question" in one form or another. Is a moral claim justified because God commands it? Or does God command a moral claim because it is right, or good? Citations of alternate interpretations in the history of Christian ethics need not be rehearsed to establish the issue pertinent to this paper. Christians have chosen to justify moral claims independent of a theological authorization, or at least a theological authorization that is found in a particular historic text. Previously I have referred to both Josef Fuchs and Bruno Schüller as contemporary examples; one can add to that the names of Gerard Hughes, Charles Curran, and many others. For others the rightness of a moral claim must be backed by biblical texts, though as previously noted, the selection of texts is common practice.

Whether Christians *should* justify moral claims by the use of Scriptures depends upon, as seen in other parts of this paper, other theological choices that they have made. One claim might well be that the particularity of Christian belief, faith and community requires that authorization or justification of its moral claims be found in the Bible. They do not require that the morality claimed is unique in its substance, though there might be distinctive claims made upon Christians, e.g., love of enemies, a life of self-sacrifice or self denial. One thinks of Calvin (*Institutes*, Bk 3:7) who argues that the sum of the Christian life is the denial of ourselves, and of many other writings before and after the sixteenth century in which this is affirmed as the distinctive theme.

In sum, one can respond to the fifth question in this way: Christians can and do justify moral claims at various levels of specification on the basis of biblical authority. The authority might be a more literalistic reading of the Scriptures, or it might be a more general revelational authorization. Whether Christians ought to justify moral claims by using the Bible continues to be a matter of debate among moral theologians. This debate is not only reason vs. revelation; it is also a debate about Christology, interpretation of texts such as the Genesis source of humans being made in the image and likeness of God, about whether the Christian community is to be restrictive in its demarcations relative to other communities and thus pursue morality justified by distinctive biblical themes, and other matters.

CONCLUSION

If one does not first ask, what is the authority of the Bible for Christian ethics, but rather first asks what are the questions that ethics answers, and how does, can, and ought the Bible be used to answer them, a different approach to the discussion is established. I hope that the brief illustrations of various ways of addressing the authority of the Bible from the ethical questions has shown the variety and complexity of answers that do exist in history and in contemporary discussions.

To develop a systematic response to each of these from my own perspective would require at least the length of the present paper, and an elaboration of the theological grounding from which the response is made. I only suggest that the terms "corroborative" and "educative" authority would be appropriate, not only for my work, but probably for that of others who draw upon or are identified with different theological positions.

The reversal of the direction usually taken in discussions regarding the use of Scripture in ethics, i.e., by asking first of all questions of ethics and then how the Bible is used to answer them, is, at least, to its author, an energizing new way of looking at an age-old question. It complexifies the general problem by specifying various dimensions of it, and might have the effect of provoking more precision in the literature. At least this is the author's aspiration.

Chapter 16

A Retrospective Interpretation of American Religious Ethics, 1948–1998

In the 1960s, The Ford Humanities Project, under the direction of the Council of the Humanities at Princeton University, published a series of books assessing the status of various humanistic fields. The difficulties the sponsors of the project had in determining both how religion should be treated and what should be included are discussed briefly in the foreword to the second of the two volumes in the series that were devoted to religious studies (Ramsey 1965, vii–viii). This second volume was to review the state of scholarship in religion; Clyde Holbrook's book, *Religion: A Humanistic Field,* an earlier publication in the series, had provided "a full and wise discussion" of the question of whether the study of religion required creedal commitments and therefore would be incompatible with "free scholarly inquiry."

The Ramsey-edited book mirrors the pattern of the dominant Christian Protestant theological curriculum of the midcentury, and thus the dominant pattern of the teaching of religion in liberal arts colleges. The titles of the articles are "The History of Religions," "Old Testament Studies" (authored by Harry Orlinsky, the only Jewish scholar represented), "The Study of Early Christianity," "The History of Christianity," "Theology," "Christian Ethics," and "Philosophy of Religion." The publication of the volume had been held up because of the failure of the assigned author of the ethics article to submit a manuscript; I was given three months to provide one. The question immediately arose as to whether the article should be called "Religious Ethics." The same question was raised when the Department of Religious Studies was formed at Yale during the same period. My answer in both instances was that the term "Christian Ethics" reflected what had been done and what was being done, and when changes had occurred in materials studied and taught, in faculty trained and hired, the more inclusive term would be honest and should be used. I could safely write, "A totally ignored area is that of comparative religious ethics" (1965, 345). After a brief development of that sentence, I closed the paragraph, "Perhaps the comparative sociologists of religion, building from Max Weber's studies of the religion, ethics, and cultures of Judaism, Protestantism, Chinese and Indian religions will provide the literature that is needed" (1965, 345). In addition to comparative religious ethics, I looked briefly at the relations of Christian ethical publications to biblical, historical, and philosophical studies. I, and perhaps no other single person, could not now produce a survey article of the field of religious ethics comparable with what was possible in 1964. The academic study of religious ethics, like the fields of professional ethics, has become a rapid-growth intellectual industry in the past three decades.

In *Human Understanding,* a rich and multidimensional study of how academic fields and disciplines develop, Stephen Toulmin distinguishes between two "styles" of historical approaches to any science, the "internalist" that concentrates on the changing content and methods of a discipline or field, and the "externalist" that focuses on the relations of the discipline to its broader intellectual and social contexts (1972, 300). In every field there are intersections between the content and methods on the one hand and the broader intellectual and social contexts on the other. The state of our field as I surveyed it more than thirty years ago is a case in point.

"Internally," such diversity as existed had to be uncovered by looking at where ethics was studied under the aegis of various religious traditions—Protestant, Roman Catholic, and Jewish. The content was largely textual and dominantly theological or traditional; the methods varied according to the historic or currently dominant procedures in each tradition. Certainly the purpose of both research and teaching was more normative than descriptive or analytical. In Protestantism, the Social Gospel tradition continued, albeit in altered ways: authors were concerned to recommend policies on debated public issues. The most used textbooks of Roman Catholic moral theology had largely similar structures and not a great deal of diversity in outcomes. Ethics was studied and taught to help shape the moral lives of students, whether clergy or lay, and to affect the activities of religious institutions and persons as they participated in political and moral issues in the culture. Even the comparative analyses were largely in the service of systematic or normative interests, that is, to show one way to be preferable to alternatives.

"Externally," the seminaries were the dominant location of research and writing: At midcentury, what was to become the American Academy of Religion was the National Association of Biblical Instructors, and what was to become the Society of Christian Ethics was a group of us who met with a small subvention from the Hazen Foundation (usually gathering in the Auburn Room of Union Theological Seminary in New York) until Das Kelly Barnett conceived of a professional society.

The events that were to change the context drastically within a decade were only beginning: rapid development of religious studies, changes in theological interests (only some of which sustained themselves—for example, liberation theology and ethics), the Second Vatican Council, attention to the current British-American moral philosophy, feminism, the civil rights and antiwar movements, holocaust studies, and so forth. Activism largely replaced scholarly interests in many seminaries and churches. (Having been asked to spend an evening and morning with the staff of my denomination's social action agency, precisely to inform them of current movements in philosophical and theological ethics, I was told by one staff member that I was wasting their time—which led to my catching the 10 P.M. train back to New Haven.) Some colleagues—for example, John C. Bennett, Walter Muelder, and Roger Shinn—continued their great service to the churches and ecumenical movement while also contributing to the field; others turned their work almost exclusively toward more academically centered scholarship.

What we need is an account, carefully argued and developed in persuasive detail, of the intersections of these internal and external factors in the development of the field of religious ethics since my chapter on "Christian Ethics" was published in *Religion,* but this defies my competence—at least within the limits of the present context. My recent internal analysis of "The Idea of Christian Ethics," with an outline of continuing controverted issues, is found in the *Companion Encyclopedia of Theology,* but to keep within space limits, I have offered there no significant "externalist" foci. Limits of space also force choices for this article. An intellectual historian, rather than an ethicist, should write the dense narrative and critical interpretation showing (as Toulmin indicates) how conceptual change occurs and why, whether changes are more like evolution than revolution, how professional institutionalization and other political factors enter into the formulation of questions that are central, and how different scholars and authors have different audiences in view. Vignettes of particular periods, like 1948 to 1954, when I was a graduate student, and 1963 to 1967, when many interests changed, could be drawn with some thematic hypotheses about the relative importance of the internal and external factors at these points in time. At the other extreme from a careful historical study would be high-level generalizations about the relative weight that various internal and external factors have in directing the work in a field of scholarship that is not a discipline. In either case, to focus on intersections of the internal and external factors in a satisfactory way would require choices about just what (for example, change in content and method) was affected by which external factors and how. Cultural studies scholars, like the sociologists of knowledge who preceded them, are better at drawing background conditions, which plausibly have some effect on the intellectual or cultural product, than they are at explaining precisely what is determined by what in either direction across the intersection. An analysis of religious ethics would be no different.

With candid acknowledgment, then, of the limits of this undertaking, I will hazard some thematic interpretations of how "Christian ethics," as understood at midcentury and through the time of my survey published in 1965, became "religious ethics," as that is represented in the span of issues of the *Journal of Religious Ethics* [JRE]. Neither time nor space permits the scores of qualifications that each theme requires, and there is inevitable reflection of my own participation through fifty years. These themes could be tested by detailed comprehensive research, or they can function as heuristic devices that shed some light on very complex developments. Stated as trends, the themes are (1) from Christian ethics to religious ethics, (2) from normative ethics to descriptive, comparative, and analytical ethics, (3) from philosophical assumptions to critical philosophical consciousness, and (4) from the Social Gospel's agenda for social ethics to more and different practical moral and social issues. These thematic trends are not sufficient to interpret all the literary and curricular developments that have taken place, nor is it possible to provide more than illustrative observations to support them. To simplify my task, I will attend to changes in content and methods (internal factors) and attempt to show what changes occurred, why they occurred, and what differences they have made.

1. FROM CHRISTIAN ETHICS TO RELIGIOUS ETHICS

My observations about changes in the content of materials studied, taught, researched, and published precede my observations of changes in method. The enlargement of content of materials has taken place in two distinct ways: the addition of attention to the ethics of non-Christian religious traditions, and an expansion of "religion" from historic traditions to include a more generic reference to the religious or the transcendent dimensions of reality. Both of these expansions occurred as a result of several external factors. One was the fact that the study of religious ethics broke out more and more from its traditional social location in institutions for the training of clergy in the historic traditions and in departments of Bible and religion in Protestant church-related colleges and departments of theology in Roman Catholic ones. Other factors were the secularization of the religious commitments of many scholars and teachers; a flourishing ecumenism that extended from intra-Christian interests to intertradition foci; the increasing acceptance of the study of religion in public, and highly secularized, colleges and universities; and the involvement of ethicists from various historic traditions in public or semipublic discussions of practical moral and social issues.

For Protestants, the most obvious extension was into Roman Catholic moral theology, already reflected in my article in *Religion.* For many Protestant students of Christian ethics, knowledge of Roman Catholic material had been, if it existed at all, limited to some general knowledge of Thomas Aquinas and some acquaintance with the papal social encyclical tradition. Knowledge of Eastern Orthodox ethics was less; Nicolas Berdyaev, hardly a representative of the central themes of Orthodox ethics, was probably the only author from that background who was taught. With Pope John XXIII came a new openness on the Catholic side that was reflected in publications by Catholics such as Josef Fuchs, Bernard Häring, Charles Curran, Richard McCormick, and others. In addition to moral theologians, the systematic theologies of Karl Rahner, Bernard Lonergan, Marie Dominique Chenu, Henri de Lubac, and others had profound implications for Christian ethics, as did the biblical studies of Rudolf Schnackenburg and others. Nondenominational doctoral programs (actually deeply Protestant) attracted clerical, lay, and religious Roman Catholics; Catholic scholars began to attend the Society of Christian Ethics meetings; and papers by Catholic writers were read and discussed in various ecumenical and secular professional societies and informal groups.

As important as the expansion of materials studied was the change in student bodies, especially at the doctoral level. It is clear that far more Roman Catholic students enrolled in formerly Protestant-dominated programs than vice versa, but in many programs very different discussions of ethics took place, background familiarities differed, and mutual learning increased both inside and outside seminar rooms. This led to dissertation research and various publications that included both Protestant and Roman Catholic materials at various levels of the subject matter—for example, work on Rahner's theology in relation to ethics, comparative studies of Catholic and Protestant arguments about medical issues, the incorporation of materials from one tradition into constructive proposals that were dominated by the other, and so forth. The contributions of younger scholars to each other across former barriers have not only profoundly affected the movement from Protestant to broader Christian ethics, but have also inspired attention to other traditions as well—at least for purposes of classroom instruction, if not of research and writing.

Retrospectively, the absence of instruction in Jewish law and ethics outside Jewish educational institutions seems astounding. Certainly exchanges between Jewish and Christian theologians who published ethical writings occurred, for example, across Broadway in New York, but the Christian preference was for Martin Buber and Abraham Joshua Heschel rather than the rabbis who sustained and developed the legal casuistical tradition. Courses in Jewish ethics, some with dimensions of Christian comparison, began to be taught as departments of religious studies employed Jewish scholars and as larger numbers of Jewish students enrolled in historically Christian colleges. In spite of most scholars' limited knowledge of Hebrew, there has been marked growth in the number of anthologies, symposia, and discussion of topical moral issues (for example, birth control and other medical matters) by Jewish scholars. The erudition required to master the Jewish legal and ethical traditions is not readily achieved by non-Jewish scholars, and this has deterred growth in comparative work. No survey of religious ethics now, however, could ignore the available publications by scholars from each of the Jewish "denominations." Nevertheless, instruction in Jewish law and ethics continues to be unduly neglected in the training of scholars in religious ethics.

Expansion from Christian ethics to Islamic, Hindu, Buddhist, and Confucian ethics has developed noticeably, as shown by articles in the JRE. While, for example, the Laws of Manu or the Sharia were known superficially from courses in comparative religion, scholars of Christian ethics did not pay much attention to them, or to the religious traditions in which they function. Certainly some of this reticence was due to proper prudence and humility. Those who attempted to master enough Jewish ethics, not to mention the ethics of other traditions, to teach responsibly then faced daunting linguistic, historical, and cultural requirements to do justice to the texts and moral practices of these other religious traditions. Fortunately, specialists in these religions began to attend to their laws and ethics more specifically, and colleagues in ethics gained sufficient competence to describe and analyze texts and practices.

As their interests broadened to include other religious traditions, persons trained in Christian ethics moved with care into the more difficult venture of comparative religious ethics. The work of Sumner Twiss and David Little achieved this through the development of a philosophical framework, while James Smurl emphasized more the experiential and cultural contexts, and Robin Lovin and Frank Reynolds proceeded on the conference and symposium model, using particular beliefs and outlooks (for example, cosmogony) as a common basis on which to compare beliefs and ethics or morality. Comparative religious ethics currently faces the same plurality of ways of conceiving the area of comparative religion (or history of religions) that religious studies as a whole confronts, including the concern about imposing Western perspectives on non-Western cultures. Yet the development of religious studies as a field necessarily carries with it increased interest in and scholarly study of non-Western religious ethics and comparative analysis.

How Christian ethics expanded to religious ethics depended in part on operative definitions of "religion." Where religious studies turned from historically identifiable religious traditions and their ethics to functional interpretations of religion in which "the religious" or "the transcendent" was understood to be a dimension of any way of life, or of any comprehensive view that provided perspectives on the world, there was a different expansion of religious ethics. The functional interpretation (or if not the functional, some other generically philosophical account of "religion") took hold: Teachers of religious ethics developed courses in death and dying, aging, war, medical ethics, and sexuality as part of their portfolio of religious ethics. On this model, knowledge about, or references to, historic religious traditions was not a necessary part of the field. The "taint" of denominational adjectives—Protestant, Jewish, or Catholic—could be avoided while the moral passion or fervor of a committed reformer was presumably legitimated. Thus, the field, in the name of a generic description of religion, could become very normative indeed in communicating morally preferred policies or personal choices. This tendency, insofar as it developed, ran counter to the dominating scholarly tendency.

As I have indicated, the shift from theological and normative methods of Christian ethics to descriptive, analytical, and comparative methods took place during a shift in social location from institutions transmitting and developing particular forms of ethics in normative ways to religious studies in the context of the arts and sciences. A kind of emancipation went on to settle the doubts of secular scholars about whether religion could be studied in a value-free scholarly way, without creedal or religious commitments. If this shift comes under the mantra of "the Enlightenment project," it is now under critical scrutiny during the postmodernist era we are passing through. Thus, we turn to the second theme.

2. FROM NORMATIVE ETHICS TO DESCRIPTIVE, COMPARATIVE, AND ANALYTICAL ETHICS

The field continues to produce scholarly works as well as pedagogical activities that are normative, while also assuming the critical posture. It is not only books that seek to improve on a modern classic, for example, H. Richard Niebuhr's *Christ and Culture,* that demonstrate the continuation of the normative ethics of a particular religious tradition. Even the JRE itself, which was founded in part to foster new methods and approaches, contains critical and constructive articles designed to justify alternative normative positions or to demonstrate the flaws in such proposals from alternative normative perspectives. (In section 3, I will develop one aspect of the different configuration of the analytical and the normative, namely the use of different moral philosophies.)

Although many colleagues would not use the term "free scholarly inquiry" to describe their activities in this postmodern period, a major motive for the shift in religious ethics was to demonstrate that texts and moral practices could be studied without creedal or personal religious commitments. Several factors played into this shift. One was the acceptance on philosophical, anthropological, historical, or other bases of moral relativism. For some, moral relativism meant that no significant moral evaluations could be placed on the ethics of any religious tradition. For others, the position was less radical. It simply meant that one could understand and interpret moral teachings and ethical theories only in relation to the historical, cultural, and religious contexts in which they developed; relativism meant interpreting ethics in relation to particular contexts. Thus, studies of the Christian ethics of war took account of how the tradition of justifiable wars and their justifiable conduct developed in relation to the religious ideas of the time, the political, military, and other historic circumstances in which the church found itself, the alternative accounts of what Christian fidelity meant, and so forth. As John Noonan cogently argued, the teaching of the church on contraception, usury, and other practical matters changed over time in relation to changing contexts of ideas and of relevant information and social circumstances. Some historical studies were conducted in the service of larger moral interests, that is, to relativize the absolutes shaped in particular historical conditions and thus make possible revisions in current teaching or practice. Other studies were conducted out of intellectual curiosity—perhaps to interpret how moral teachings were affected not only by traditional ideas or by biblical and historical authority, but also by political, economic, and social conditions. An ethical text or moral practice can be understood more adequately if the context of its development and use are understood.

Another probable factor was the enrollment in religious ethics courses of students from different religious backgrounds or from secularized families. Religious studies, under the suspicion and scrutiny of skeptical colleagues, were careful to avoid the appearance of evangelizing. To demonstrate that religious ethics could be taught and researched in a descriptive and analytical way, just as moral philosophy could, was important for political purposes. The justification and defense of, for example, Christian ethics as better than other ethics would appear unscholarly, though the justification and defense of utilitarianism or Immanuel Kant in some moral philosophy courses would not.

It ought not to be forgotten, however, just how much new intellectual vitality and enthusiasm could come from expanding the range of materials to be studied and taught in ethics. (For example, although I never achieved competence to teach Jewish law and ethics alone, the zest that exploratory efforts evoked led, among other things, to my requesting permission in 1970 to review David M. Feldman's *Birth Control in Jewish Law* in *The Christian Century,* in an effort to get other Christians interested in the area.) The sheer joy of employing patterns of analysis that were developed in an area of one's established competence to materials from another area has been, I believe, significant for many teachers and scholars. Capacities to empathize as much as possible with religious ethical materials from different traditions have been cultivated by many colleagues.

Much of the material published in the JRE from its inception has represented this movement from the normative to the descriptive, comparative, and analytic approaches to religious ethics. Pluralism and diversity have been accepted in the materials studied; in the perspectives brought to bear on traditional materials, such as feminist or African American theological perspectives; in juxtaposing other types of study with ethical studies, for example, the literary critical and cultural anthropological approaches; and in the interactive relations with philosophy, sociology, and other areas that traditionally related to religious ethics. Thus, in addition to the multiplication of materials from Christian to other traditions, there has been an expansion of acceptable approaches to the field, foci of attention for research, and the methods and procedures used. Religious ethics is a field, then, that employs not only normative agendas, but also a variety of descriptive, interpretive, and analytical agendas. Just as social ethics has always been whatever someone calling herself a social ethics scholar does, so religious ethics has become whatever someone calling himself a scholar in that field does. The range stretches from authoritative interpretations of normative religious ethical traditions such as Eastern Orthodox Christianity or Judaism, to innovative normative reinterpretations of traditions, to various religiously and morally disinterested forms of inquiry which use different methods and procedures, for example, philosophical, empirical, or psychological.

3. FROM PHILOSOPHICAL ASSUMPTIONS TO CRITICAL PHILOSOPHICAL CONSCIOUSNESS

Absent carefully nuanced development and many qualifications, my argument concerning this theme may be even less sustainable than my arguments concerning the previous two. Some centers of scholarship have always been very conscious of the philosophical structures of their Christian ethics. Perhaps most obvious was the Boston University School of Theology, where the philosophical personalism of Borden Parker Bowne was explicitly adhered to by persons publishing in Christian ethics. Just as religious ethics currently develops in relation to *au courant* moral and political philosophy, so in midcentury various philosophical theories of value framed some of the Christian ethical writing. Changes in preference occur, as one can see in reading the work of Ramsey from *Basic Christian Ethics,* in which idealism was his partner, to later work in which John Rawls functioned in a somewhat similar way. George Thomas's *Christian Ethics and Moral Philosophy* was the only major publication in the middle decades of this century to focus on the topic of its title. There were philosophical theologies that only later added the implications for ethics to their explorations of the doctrine of God. Process theology, for example, produced almost no ethical work during the time it dominated theological studies at the University of Chicago. Graduate students in major doctoral programs were expected to know classics of Western moral philosophy and at least snippets from modern works. *Readings in Ethics,* edited by Gordon Clark and T. V. Smith, was the preferred anthology for graduate students' preparation for doctoral examinations in several programs known to me, just as later anthologies functioned for subsequent student generations. The title of this third section, then, is a slight exaggeration; what it indicates is a discernable shift to more explicit engagement with current trends in moral philosophy.

External factors that may have functioned to raise the level of philosophical self-consciousness were: better philosophical training for some graduate students; frustration with what Ramsey once called the "wastelands of relativism"; a growing awareness of the procedures of practical casuistry, which, with its distinctions and rules of application, characterized Roman Catholic moral theology; high motivation to show to non-religious scholars (although probably not many cared) that religious ethics could be philosophically rigorous; and increasing penetration of issues in medical and other arenas by religious ethicists as they began to meet growing interest in the same topics by moral philosophers.

The philosophical contexts about which sophistication developed were several. The current literature in Anglo-American moral philosophy was the major focus for many authors and teachers, but existentialism and German phenomenology informed the work of others. Degrees of competence in moral philosophies differed. Retrospectively, one can guess that many persons did not get beyond William Frankena's textbook, *Ethics*, with its version of a taxonomy of ethical theories. (Also, Frankena was the only philosopher publishing in that period who seemed interested in including Christian ethics in his publications, thus contributing such barbarous neologisms as "act-agapism" and "rule-agapism.") Indeed, in some writings in Christian ethics, ideal types were reified, and consistency within the framework of a chosen type of theory was made the measure of the quality of the work.

To a considerable extent, the study of moral philosophers did add to the rigor of religious ethical writing; this was beneficial both in fostering academic self-confidence, if not respect from other scholars, and in strengthening the field intellectually. In some instances, the work of one or another moral philosopher, or a version of moral philosophy, became a justification for a normative position, the standard for evaluation of the quality of religious ethics, or the internal structure of systematic proposals. More often, interests in moral philosophy induced critiques of constructive and systematic proposals, thus reinforcing the attitude of critical disinterested scholarship.

Indeed, in Christian ethical writing one can observe a kind of borrowed authority—borrowed from different moral philosophies and invoked to shape and justify constructive positions. A scan of bibliographies and footnotes over the decades creates the impression of efforts to keep religious ethics current with the changing fashions of moral philosophy. For example, at a meeting of the British counterpart of the Society of Christian Ethics in 1984, the moral philosophical background was still the more or less analytical tradition of Oxford and Cambridge; at a meeting in 1996, Charles Taylor, Alasdair MacIntyre, and the theologians influenced by them provided the frame of reference. The constructive ethics of persons like William Schweiker, working out of the hermeneutical tradition, is different from the work of Gene Outka. In religious social ethics, John Rawls has been the dominant external voice, as he has been in other movements. Current writing still differentiates itself from Rawls or supports him not by theological arguments, but by adopting the philosophical critiques of a Rawlsian perspective or undertaking to answer them. The interesting question is whether religious ethicists have to argue for a moral philosophical position on its own grounds before forming and justifying their religious ethical positions.

The growth in philosophical sophistication and self-criticism poses the question of what method and what content should determine the material and the procedures of research, writing, and teaching in religious ethics. In Jewish law and ethics, persons trained in moral philosophy and in religious ethics, as well as in Halakhah, approach traditional materials with a different agenda than traditional rabbinic scholars do. This both gives new insight into the material and makes it more accessible to a wider group of scholars in religious ethics. However, in Jewish law and ethics, as well as in Christian or other traditional approaches, this does not necessarily alter radically the internal, normative developments of the field, which have a constituency of committed religious adherents. When a religious ethicist writes from a normative position, whether conserving creedal and theological standards or revising them, is it legitimate for the theological or religious interest and ideas to determine the philosophical patterns? Or do the philosophical bases of critiques determine the worthiness of, for example, Stanley Harakas's publications on Eastern Christian ethics?

Just as the shift from normative to descriptive, comparative, and analytical ethics reflects the external factor of a shift in the desired readership and in the constituency of students, so also does the intensification of philosophical self-consciousness. Religious ethics was in the same trajectory as the rest of religious studies: For many, the aim for evaluation of publication and teaching was no longer to affect the moral communities of various traditions or ecumenical agencies. Rather, the developing academic-guild consciousness (which went well beyond religious studies) set the standards for self-evaluations and for external review. Writing ethics to be published in various religiously sponsored journals of opinion, if it occurred at all, came to be considered a para-academic vocation, not deserving of the plaudits of those who were attuned to the *au courant* philosophical issues in ethics. One outcome of this was a greater distance between the ways that Protestant and some Catholic constituencies of moral activists, on the one hand, and academic-guild religious ethicists, on the other, wrote about ethics. (I recall vividly when a new dean of Yale Divinity School responded immediately to a philosophically rigorous paper by David Little, "That's not ethics. Ethics has to do with prophecy. I learned that from Rabbi Heschel.") Writers like Ramsey, who sought to address both the academic and religious constituencies, were often dismissed by the latter. (See Ramsey 1967 for a passionate critique of both the methodology and the uncritical substantive biases of one of the major ecumenical ventures of the 1960s.)

Religious ethicists who continue to produce constructive works relate to philosophical works in different ways. Some, I believe, for reasons of philosophical persuasion, adopt a general or quite specific approach to shape their positions, for example, a hermeneutical theory or approach or a process philosophical approach. There is an integrated congeniality between the philosophy and the theological ethics. Others, such as those who adhere to a conviction that Christian ethics should be based on biblical exegesis, are less concerned with what philosophical suppositions are imbedded in their work. For example, traditional rabbis writing responsa are not concerned to engage contemporary philosophy. Still others might be convinced that the defense of a theology is the first order of business and that the theologian has to become her own philosopher, but with requisite critical self-consciousness. Indeed, normative religious-ethical publications are increasingly qualified by the general intellectual movement (for example, feminism) that shapes the philosophic and religious materials that are used.

Since midcentury, normative ethics has been characterized by increasing philosophical self-consciousness; they have also adhered to different philosophies. Gibson Winter's and Howard Harrod's use of phenomenology creates quite a different religious ethics from Outka's use of analytical materials. Engaging and finding

support from MacIntyre or Taylor is radically different from the shaping of a religious ethics that accords with the philosophical theology of Schubert Ogden, as
the work of Franklin Gamwell does. One has the impression that the authority of
philosophical ethics for both the critique and the development of religious ethics
is not settled after decades of more self-consciousness of the issues. Perhaps it ought
not be settled at the most abstract level, but discussed in relation to particular
aspects of religious ethics, for example, their moral anthropologies, their decision
procedures, their visions of the good, or their intended audiences and usages.

4. FROM THE SOCIAL GOSPEL'S TRADITIONAL AGENDA TO MORE AND DIFFERENT PRACTICAL ISSUES

Just as Roman Catholics brought traditional neo-Thomist manuals of moral theology into the period under discussion, Protestants brought the outlook and the
agendas of social ethics. Outlines of a number of textbooks were very similar: a section on biblical ethics stressing the idea of love, some brief forays into a few historic
figures, and then chapters on politics, economics, international relations, maybe
family, and maybe race. The historical background of this was the Protestant Social
Gospel movement, which had developed in the Progressive Era in response to undesirable social conditions in a period of rapid social change in America: industrial-
ization, urbanization, and immigration. Some of the classics of that era continue
to be reprinted, for example, Walter Rauschenbusch's *A Theology for the Social
Gospel* and at least selections from his great Roman Catholic counterpart, John A.
Ryan. Both of these authors not only attended to a religious and theological background but also addressed particular problems of economic justice.

Surely the motivation for teaching and writing in the first half of the twentieth century was to impel social reform and give some direction to it. It was, in
the best sense, a practical literature, and the classroom teaching was to train religious leaders with the aspiration that they would, in various ways, affect events
in society. This motivation and intention certainly has continued throughout the
period under consideration in this article. Several developments can be noted,
one of which was a somewhat higher degree of specialized competence in
the social and policy sciences. This can be seen, for example, in the Christian
Ethics and Economic Life Series, which began in 1949 and was sponsored by
the Department of the Church and Economic Life of the Federal Council of
Churches and its successor, the National Council of Churches. Ethicists were also
involved in specialized policy issues in international affairs through ecclesial and
para-ecclesial organizations. The renewed interest in the just war tradition led to
study of international politics, nuclear weapons, and guerrilla warfare as time
progressed.

Advocacy ethics in the Social Gospel period and through the century has been
written not only in policy modes but also in more prophetic modes, that is, by

using religious frameworks of interpretation to point out many instances of injustice and oppression in ways meant to stir the easy consciences of many religious people. The ethics of liberation theology has been more an indictment of injustice and evocation of indignation than an engagement in the detailed evaluations of the moral dimensions of particular economic and political policies. Religious narratives and symbolism are powerfully used to describe circumstances and events in their immoral and inhuman dimensions, and to critique social and economic policy proposals that are more technically informed by various policy sciences. Systemic evils, structured in social customs and institutions, that have justified oppression of various groups have become the focus of advocacy for radical social change.

New and different circumstances and issues have come to the fore. The previous paucity of literature on medical research and clinical practice by Protestant writers, compared with the current surfeit, offers a dramatic contrast. Joseph Fletcher's *Morals and Medicine* was virtually the only Protestant publication. For historical reasons, the Roman Catholic tradition had for decades produced writings on this subject that were both greater in number and more precise in their analyses and recommendations than anything Protestants had produced. Rabbinic decisors, in their responsa to inquiries about what practices were licit under Jewish law, were more similar to Catholic moral theologians than to Protestant ethicists. The interest in the ethics of medical research, care, and social policies now elicits detailed attention from writers in all the religious traditions. The series on religious traditions and health published by the Park Ridge Center is only one manifestation of this.

Just as external events and circumstances provoked the interests of the Social Gospel movement, so also the flood of developments in medical ethics was a response to rapid changes in medical technologies, medical research, and policies of health care delivery. Religious ethicists were initially more dominant in the discussion than moral philosophers. Perhaps this was due to the preoccupation of moral philosophers with general ethical theories, as well as the more practical orientation out of which religious ethicists came.

Medicine was the first growth area of applied ethics. Moral philosophers as well as moral theologians and other religious scholars became "ethicists," a new term and a new profession, as concern for the moral became widespread across selected areas of public life. Concerns about moral issues in economic life became focused on ethics and business, and religious scholars contributed to the discussion of applicable principles and procedures, of the characters of the agents, and of the transplantation of the issues of ethical theory (religious and otherwise) into this realm of practice. Programs in ethics and the professions, if not developed under the auspices of religious ethics, engaged increasing numbers of its scholars in their programs.

The rapid development of environmental ethics is the most noteworthy recent addition. In this sphere, as elsewhere, the impetus was external: growing consciousness of threats to the necessary conditions for biological diversity; pollution of air, water, and earth; the limits of natural resources in relation to rapid population growth. Secular voices, for example, Rachel Carson, raised the alarm, and the history of nineteenth-century American naturalists was retrieved and interpreted. Aldo Leopold provided a widely read and provocative depiction of a land ethic. Religious writers such as John Cobb, Paul Santmire, Rosemary Radford Ruether, Sallie McFague, Gibson Winter, Jay McDaniel, and, most recently and comprehensively, Larry L. Rasmussen brought various theological and religious perspectives from the Christian tradition to bear on both the interpretation of the issues and various levels of the prescription for remedying the deterioration. Comparable work has been done from other historic traditions as well. Environmental ethics was added to the standard litany of topics about which religious communities the world over are concerned.

Just as Social Gospel writers had to interpret in nonmoral and nontheological terms the circumstances to which they were responding, such as conditions in slums, so the religious ethicists who have engaged new areas of practical concern rely upon sources of information, theories of events, and multidisciplinary analysis of very complex aspects of nature, of social and economic and political life, of international relations, and so forth. How these necessary sources are evaluated, how choices are made among alternative interpretations, and how they are used for moral argument are important matters of discussion. As with moral philosophy, so also in these expanded areas of religious ethical writing, one question is whether the ethicist first determines which account of the circumstances or events is more reliable on "scientific" grounds, or first develops a theological or ethical perspective that is more determinative of her analysis and prescriptions. A further question is whether the nonreligious sources require revisions of the religious ethical prospective itself.

5. PLUS ÇA CHANGE . . .

While the change in substance and methods has been quite dramatic since the midcentury and since my survey published 1965, and while the events and circumstances that provide context for work academically, intellectually, religiously, socially, and scientifically have changed significantly, it is important to note the continuities.

Religious ethics has never replaced Christian ethics. Perhaps the most influential writers in the field are those who are expounding the particularity of Christian ethics, and a morality of conformity to and interpretation of the meaning of Jesus Christ, such as Stanley Hauerwas and the late John Howard Yoder. At least, with reference to the Protestant religious communities, the distinctiveness of moral witness that is adumbrated, its religious and theological authorization, and its rhetoric effectiveness are clear. This more confessional view is not disengaged from other scholarship in religious ethics. It is philosophically backed in its critique of the efforts of other Christian writers who develop bases for a universal morality, as well as in its constructive development of themes of narrative, community, tradition, and virtue. Indeed, the philosophical backing for the current argument to distinctiveness is probably more sophisticated than the assumptions that supported distinctively Christian ethics generations ago.

The same philosophical backing supports a similar interest on the particularity of the religious ethical outlooks, as well as the distinctiveness of patterns of activity in other traditions. To some extent, the growth of publication in Jewish ethics, and the applications of it and Jewish law to medicine and other areas, serves as an index of the limitations of "religious ethics" as a self-sufficient academic enterprise. Jewish scholars work, as they have for centuries, within the authorized tradition, using traditional rabbinic methods and texts. Current moral counsel or legal judgment follows and serves the Jewish community.

Thus, orientation by and toward a professional guild of "disinterested" scholars of religious ethics has never replaced orientation by and toward traditional religious communities. In some respects, the greatest advance in the period in question has been the explicit differentiation and development of cohesive independent expositions of "ethics" within the various particular traditions. In recent decades, for example, we have seen the first publications in English that develop and expound the ethics of Eastern Orthodox Christianity, in the works of Stanley Harakas and Vigen Guroian. Their publications, while set in a context that makes them accessible to others, are strongly addressed to the current generation of American adherents to their churches. In various areas of "applied ethics," there is a resurgence of emphasis on showing the members of Jewish, Roman Catholic, and other religious communities what their faith and loyalty imply for their moral lives and personal and professional choices. This material does provide data for comparative religious ethics and other approaches that one finds in the professional guild of religious studies scholars, but it continues the earlier interest of "Christian ethics" to inform religious leaders and parishioners of the bearing of their faith on individual and collective choices. There is probably a gap, however, between academic writers who are oriented toward religious communities and writers whose rhetorical skills and powers more effectively engage the "lay" mind and life. To be sure, there are scholars who play several roles, writing for different audiences through different channels, speaking to different groups in different sorts of discourse. But the interest in advocacy of religious and moral outlooks toward clergy and laity continues to be very much a part of the field of religious ethics.

Likewise, the focus on philosophical issues has never replaced biblical and theological concerns. Indeed, in the past decades, the body of literature on the use of the Bible in Christian ethics has grown significantly. Contributions have come from biblical scholars such as Victor Paul Furnish and Richard Hays, from scholars who combine biblical and ethical training such as Allen Verhey, and from ethical scholars such as Larry Rasmussen and Thomas Ogletree. To some extent, this development reflects the critical self-consciousness of the move toward "religious ethics"; what had been assumed about the use of the Bible now has to be examined and justified.

Perhaps theological concerns *per se* have received less attention from ethical writers than in previous generations. For example, both Reinhold and H. Richard Niebuhr were considered to be theologians in their time, though both are still studied for their contributions to ethics. The differentiation between theology and moral theology that some recent Roman Catholics have sought to mitigate by making ethics more theological is quite different from Protestant tendencies in which "ethicists" are more differentiated from theologians. One evidence of this is the recent symposium, *Christian Ethics: Problems and Prospects,* edited by Lisa Sowle Cahill and James F. Childress. It contains no articles on ethics and Christology, sin and redemption, eschatology, or other theological themes that formerly were part of American Christian ethics and that continue to be considered integral to Christian ethics in other parts of the world. At the same time, theologians such as McFague, Ruether, Edward Farley, Phillip Hefner, and Ted Peters are making significant contributions to ethics. (A currently significant theologian and former colleague told me that he had not read my work and explained that "if it had had systematic theology in the title," he might have looked at it. Such is the power of naming among specialists, even within theological communities—not to mention religious studies.) Among ethical writers who represent something of the older cohesion between ethics and theology are Gregory Jones and Gilbert Meilaender. Theologically substantive concerns have never fully atrophied in the face of methodological and other philosophical preoccupations.

Participation in the ethical dimensions of various professions and social interest groups has never replaced a concern to be clear about the Christian (with its variations), Jewish, Muslim, or other particular traditional approaches to topical moral issues. When representatives of these traditions participate in institutions such as the Hastings Center, the practical and theoretical questions about what is Catholic or Protestant or Jewish about medical ethics continue to be discussed. It is plausible to argue that for both intellectual and religious communal reasons, such joint participation has intensified the concerns about distinctiveness and particularity. Thus, we have books on Jewish medical ethics and papers contrasting the Lutheran to the Calvinistic approach to the same field. There are probably fewer publications now that make the case for "the transcendent" as a nonhistorical basis for "religious ethical" approaches to practical issues than there were twenty-five years ago.

Thus, overall, it is clear that the academic concern to create a field of religious ethics that is basically descriptive, comparative, or analytical has never replaced normative religious ethics; indeed, it may unintentionally have contributed to a resurgence of work that develops the particularly normative dimensions of various traditions.

This has been, then, an effort to sketch, in a highly generalized way, the intersections of internal and external factors as these intersections have functioned to govern the development of the field of religious ethics. Exactly how the internal changes are related to external changes needs, of course, further exploration. External aspects of the four developments I have traced surely include: the resurgence of emphasis on pluralism and particularism in modern societies; their revival in academic cultures through various postmodern and other critiques of "objectivity," "essentialism," and so forth; the sense that religious communities need a distinguishable place on which to stand to justify their participation in public life (consider the various programs, some handsomely funded, on religion and public life); and more general cultural drifts away from "liberalism" to more "conservative" values.

This essay, a pretentious overview of changes through fifty years from at least 35,000 feet, no doubt reflects the biases of its author, states much that is too obvious to have been written while saying too little about the qualifiers of each of its themes, is too skimpy in its citations and documentation, and fails to show precisely what external factors decisively altered what internal factors, and vice versa. Perhaps it carries too much the odor of an intellectual memoir by a participant observer without the discipline of that method of research. Yet whatever its limitations, it will have achieved a modest aspiration if it stimulates alternative accounts and more detailed study of our field by others interested in how an academic enterprise changes over decades of time.

REFERENCES

Cahill, Lisa Sowle, and James F. Childress, eds. 1996. *Christian Ethics: Problems and Prospects.* Cleveland, Ohio: Pilgrim Press.

Clark, Gordon H., and T. V. Smith. 1935. *Readings in Ethics.* 2d ed. New York: Appleton-Century-Crofts.

Feldman, David M. 1968. *Birth Control in Jewish Law: Marital Relations, Contraception, and Abortion as Set Forth in the Classic Texts of Jewish Law.* New York: New York University Press.

Fletcher, Joseph. 1979. *Morals and Medicine.* Princeton, N.J.: Princeton University Press.

Frankena, William. 1973. *Ethics.* 2d ed. Englewood Cliffs, N.J.: Prentice-Hall.

Gustafson, James M. 1965. "Christian Ethics." See Ramsey (ed.) 1965, 285–354.

———. 1970. Review of *Birth Control in Jewish Law: Marital Relations, Contraception, and Abortion as Set Forth in the Classic Texts of Jewish Law,* by David M. Feldman. *The Christian Century* 87.20:632–33.

———. 1995. "The Idea of Christian Ethics." In *Companion Encyclopedia of Theology,* edited by Peter Byrne and Leslie Houlden, 691–715. London and New York: Routledge.

Holbrook, Clyde A. 1963. *Religion: A Humanistic Field.* Englewood Cliffs, N.J.: Prentice-Hall.

Noonan, John. 1965. *Contraception: A History of Its Treatment by the Catholic Theologians and Canonists.* Cambridge, Mass.: Harvard University Press.

Park Ridge Center. 1984–95. Health/Medicine and the Faith Traditions Series. 13 vols. Edited by Martin E. Marty and Kenneth L. Vaux. New York: Crossroads; Valley Forge, Pa.: Trinity Press International.

Ramsey, Paul. 1950. *Basic Christian Ethics.* New York: Scribner.

———. 1967. *Who Speaks for the Church?* Nashville, Tenn.: Abingdon Press.
Ramsey, Paul, ed. 1965. *Religion.* Englewood Cliffs, N.J.: Prentice-Hall.
Rauschenbusch, Walter. 1917. *A Theology for the Social Gospel.* New York: Macmillan.
Thomas, George. 1955. *Christian Ethics and Moral Philosophy.* New York: Scribner.
Toulmin, Stephen. 1972. *Human Understanding.* Princeton, N.J.: Princeton University Press.

Bibliography of
James M. Gustafson

The following is a revision of a bibliography of Gustafson's works compiled by Chris Scharen in 1997.

I. BOOKS

1957

Coauthored with H. Richard Niebuhr and Daniel Day Williams. *The Advancement of Theological Education.* New York: Harper and Brothers. JMG is author of chaps. 7 and 8 and the appendix.

1961

Treasure in Earthen Vessels: The Church as a Human Community. New York: Harper and Brothers. Reprint, Chicago: University of Chicago Press, Midway Reprint, 1976.

1968

Christ and the Moral Life. New York: Harper and Row. Reprint, Chicago: University of Chicago Press, Midway Reprint, 1976.
· Coedited with James T. Laney. *On Being Responsible: Issues in Personal Ethics.* New York: Harper and Row, Harper Forum Books. JMG authored 3–18, 111–19, and 175–83. English edition, London: SCM Press, 1969.

1970

The Church as Moral Decision-Maker (collected essays). Philadelphia: United Church Press, A Pilgrim Press Book. (Referred to below as *CMDM.*)

1971

Christian Ethics and the Community (collected essays). Philadelphia: United Church Press, A Pilgrim Press Book. Paper edition with preface by JMG, 1979. (Referred to below as *CEC.*)

1974

Theology and Christian Ethics (collected essays). Philadelphia: United Church Press, A Pilgrim Press Book. (Referred to below as *TCE.*)

1975

Can Ethics Be Christian? Chicago: University of Chicago Press. Japanese translation, Tokyo: The Jordan Press, 1987. Excerpted in *Introduction to Christian Ethics: A Reader,* edited by Ronald P. Hamel and Kenneth R. Himes, OFM, 133–39. New York: Paulist Press, 1989.

The Contributions of Theology to Medical Ethics (Pere Marquette Lecture). Milwaukee: Marquette University Press. Excerpted in *Perspectives in Biology and Medicine* 19 (Winter 1976): 247–70.

1978

Protestant and Roman Catholic Ethics: Prospects for Rapprochement. Chicago: University of Chicago Press. Korean translation by Hee-Sub Kim. Seoul: The Christian Literature Society, 1984.

1981

Ethics from a Theocentric Perspective. Vol. 1, *Theology and Ethics.* Chicago: University of Chicago Press. Pages 287–93 reprinted in *On Moral Medicine: Theological Perspectives in Medical Ethics,* edited by Stephen E. Lammers and Allen Verhey, 293–95. Grand Rapids: Wm. B. Eerdmans Publishing, 1987.

"Say Something Theological!" (1981 Nora and Edward Ryerson Lecture at University of Chicago, April 25). Chicago: The University of Chicago Public Information Office. Excerpted as "Theology and Piety" in *Word and World* 3 (Spring 1983): 114–16.

1984

Ethics from a Theocentric Perspective. Vol. 2, *Ethics and Theology.* Chicago: University of Chicago Press.

1988

Coedited with John R. Meyer and coauthor of articles. *The U.S. Business Corporation: An Institution in Transition.* Cambridge, MA: Ballinger Press.

Varieties of Moral Discourse: Prophetic, Narrative, Ethical, and Policy (Henry Stob Lectures). Grand Rapids: Calvin College. Reprinted in *Seeking Understanding: The Stob Lectures 1986–1998,* 43–76. Grand Rapids: Wm. B. Eerdmans, 2001.

1994

A Sense of the Divine: The Natural Environment from a Theocentric Perspective. Cleveland: The Pilgrim Press.

1996

Intersections: Science, Theology, and Ethics (collected essays). Cleveland: The Pilgrim Press. (Referred to below as *ISTE.*)

2004

An Examined Faith: The Grace of Self-Doubt. Minneapolis: Fortress Press. This book contains a revised version of the Benjamin Warfield Lectures delivered at Princeton

Theological Seminary, March 2002, "Theology and Ethics, and Other Disciplines," and a revised version of the Uppsala lecture, "'The Almighty Has His Own Purposes': From Politics To Theology," listed below (2002).

II. ARTICLES (INCLUDES FOREWORDS, RESPONSES TO ARTICLES, INTERVIEWS, PARTICIPATION IN DISCUSSIONS, AND PUBLISHED SERMONS)

1951

"Our Covenant." *Chicago Theological Seminary Register* 41 (November): 8–10.

1954

"An Analysis of the Problem of the Role of the Minister." *Journal of Religion* 34 (July): 187–91.

1955

Coauthored with H. Richard Niebuhr and Daniel Day Williams. "Main Issues in Theological Education." *Theology Today* 11 (January): 512–27.

1956

"What Our Seminaries Are and Ought to Be Doing." *Advance* 148 (January 25): 16–17, 27.

1957

"Christian Ethics and Social Policy." In *Faith and Ethics: The Theology of H. Richard Niebuhr*, edited by Paul Ramsey, 119–39. New York: Harper and Brothers.
"When Is Self-Indulgence a Virtue." *Advance* 149 (February 27): 13–14, 28.
"Protestant Sociology of the Family." *Religious Education* 52 (March–April): 89–93.
"Decision-Making." *YWCA Magazine* (April): 15, 30–31.
"This New Word—'Automation.'" *Crossroads* 7 (July): 12–14.
"The Church and Business Culture." *Christianity and Crisis* 17 (December 23): 171–74.

1958

"Justice" and "Society." In *Handbook of Christian Theology: Definition Essays on Concepts and Movements of Thought in Contemporary Protestantism,* edited by Martin Halverson and Arthur A. Cohen, 191–93 and 351–54. New York: Living Age Books, Meridian Books. "Justice" reprinted, *Chaplain* 15: 43–45.
"Facing Our Fear of Social Change." *Crossroads* 8 (April): 9–11.
"Report of Workshop on 'Student Self-Images.'" *Bulletin of the American Association of Theological Schools* 23 (June): 221–22.
"Religion and Prosperity." *Challenge* (Institute of Economic Affairs, New York University) 6 (August–September): 35–39. Excerpted as "Does the Prosperous American Need God?" *Decatur Sunday Herald and Review,* November 16, 45, and "Do Prosperous Americans Need God?" *Trade Union Courier,* November 21, M-1 and M-2.

1959

"Conformity to What?" *United Church Herald* 2 (January 29): 12–13, 32.
"Education after Sputnik." *Crossroads* 9 (April): 8–11.

"Christian Attitudes toward a Technological Society." *Theology Today* 16 (July): 173–87. Reprinted, *CMDM,* 17–32; also in *Modern American Protestant Thought: 1900–1970,* edited by William R. Miller, 414–30. American Heritage Series. New York: Bobbs-Merrill, 1973.

1960

"Of Yale and the Church." *Signs and Times* (Student Publication of the Yale Divinity School) 1 (September 16): 1, 3–6.
"Sociology of Religion in Sweden." *Review of Religious Research* 1 (Winter): 101–9.

1961

"Bigger Churches, but Only If Better Churches." *United Church Herald* 4 (February 23): 8–9, 33–34.
"Christian Ethics." *Yale Divinity News* 58 (May). Three-paragraph brochure statement.
"Patterns of Christian Social Action." *Theology Today* 18 (July): 159–71. Reprinted, *CMDM,* 33–46; also in *Moral Issues and Christian Response,* edited by Paul T. Jersild and Dale A. Johnson, 13–21. New York: Rinehart and Winston, 1971.
"Religiosity: An Irritating Necessity." *Christianity and Crisis* 21 (July 10): 123–27.

1962

"The Living Past." In *Proceeding of the Ninth International Congregational Council,* 33–42. London: Independent Press. Also see "Ett levande förflutet." *Tro och Liv,* November 1963, 7–17.
"Bases of Church Unions Noted from Congregational Christian History." *Midstream* (Council on Christian Unity, Indianapolis) 2 (September): 18–32.
"Types of Moral Life: An Essay in Slight Exaggeration." *Religious Education* 57 (November–December): 403–10.

1963

"Introduction." In *The Responsible Self: An Essay in Christian Moral Philosophy,* by H. Richard Niebuhr, 6–41. New York: Harper and Row. Japanese edition with a brief foreword by JMG. Translated by Shin Chara. Tokyo: Shinky Shuppanso Publishing, 1967.
"The United Church of Christ in America: Actualizing a Church Union." In *Institutionalism and Church Unity,* edited by Nils Ehrenstrom and Walter G. Muelder, 325–51. New York: Association Press.
"Authority in Pluralistic Society." *Lutheran World* (Lutheran World Federation) 10 (January): 24–33. Also see "Autorität in einer pluralistischen Gesellschaft." *Lutherische Rundschau* 13: 35–49. Reprinted, *CMDM,* 47–61.
"Chief Justice Warren and His Startling Proposal." *United Church Herald* 6 (February 7): 12–14, 23.
"Teologi, Samfund och Samhälle i USA." *Vår Lösen* 54 (June): 253–59.
"The Clergy in the United States." *Daedalus* (American Academy of Arts and Sciences) 92 (Fall): 724–44. Reprinted in *The Professions in America,* edited by Kenneth Lynn, 70–90. Boston: Beacon Press, 1963, 1965. Also in *Social Compass* (International Review of Socio-Religious Studies) 12 (1965): 35–52.

1964

"The Church: A Community of Moral Discourse." *Crane Review* 7 (Winter): 75–85. Reprinted, *CMDM,* 83–95.
"Goldwater: Yes or No." *Christian Century* 81 (July 8): 879.

"Comments." Response to Thomas F. O'Dea, "Sociology and the Study of Religion." A Report on an Invitational Conference on the Study of Religion in the State University, *The Society for Religion in Higher Education*, October 23–25, 15–20.

1965

"Christian Ethics." In *Religion,* edited by Paul Ramsey, 285–384. Englewood Cliffs, NJ: Prentice-Hall. Reprinted, *CEC,* 23–82.

"The Ethics of Promotion." In *Stewardship in Contemporary Life,* edited by T. K. Thompson, 145–73. New York: Association Press.

"Theology and Ethics." In *The Scope of Theology,* edited by Daniel T. Jenkins, 111–32. Cleveland: World Publishing. Reprinted, *CEC,* 85–100.

"Christian Conviction and Christian Action." *Presbyterian Action* 15 (January and February): 14–15, 31; and 10–11, 30. Reprinted, *CMDM,* 97–108. Excerpted as "Churchmen as God's Deputies," *Presbyterian Outlook* 146 (September 14, 1964): 5–6.

"The Eclipse of Sin." *Motive* 25 (March): 4, 6–8.

"Context versus Principles: A Misplaced Debate in Christian Ethics." *Harvard Theological Review* 58 (April): 171–202. Reprinted in *New Theology Today No. 3,* edited by Martin E. Marty and Dean Peerman, 69–102. New York: Macmillan, 1966. See also "Situation Contra Prinzipien: Eine irreführende Debatte in christlicher Ethik." *Zeitschrift für evangelische Ethik* 13 (January 1969): 14–40; *CEC,* 101–26; excerpted in *Theology Digest* 14 (Autumn 1966): 188–94.

"Wondering about Death." *Yale Divinity News* 52 (May): 10–12. Sermon.

"Dialogue on the Moral Life." *Ecumenist* 3 (July–August): 75–78. Reprinted in *Catholic Mind* 63 (November): 37–41; in *Ecumenical Digest* 1 (April 1966): 14–19; and in *Readings in Biblical Morality,* edited by C. Luke Salm, 142–48. Englewood Cliffs, NJ: Prentice-Hall, 1966.

"Leaky Litany." *United Church Herald* 8 (September 1): 4–5. Editorial correspondence.

Coauthored with Robert C. Johnson. "The Study of Religion at Yale," *Reflection* 63 (November): 1–3.

"Christian Faith and Moral Action." *Christian Century* ("How I Am Making Up My Mind" Series) 82 (November 3): 1345–47. Reprinted in *Frontline Theology,* edited by Dean Peerman, 134–40. Richmond: John Knox Press, 1967. Also as "Christlicher Glaube und moralisches Handeln." In *Theologie im Umbruch* (Munich: Chr. Kaiser Verlag, 1968): 138–44.

1966

"Man—In Light of Social Science and Christian Faith." In *Conflicting Images of Man,* edited by William Nicholls, 51–70. New York: Seabury Press. Reprinted, *TCE,* 199–213. Excerpted in *Contemporary Religion and Social Responsibility,* edited by Norbert Brockman and Nicholas Piediscalzi, 153–63. New York: Alba House, 1973.

"A Theology of Christian Community?" In *Man in Community: Christian Concern for the Human in Changing Society,* edited by Egbert de Vries, 175–93. New York: Association Press. "Eine Theologie der Christlichen Gemeinschaft?" In *Die Kirche als Faktor einer kommenden Weltgemeinschaft,* 118–32. Berlin: Kreuz Verlag. In *New Testament Themes for Contemporary Man,* edited by Rosalie M. Ryan, 77–93. Englewood Cliffs, NJ: Prentice-Hall, 1969. In *CMDM,* 63–80. Excerpted in *Contemporary Religion and Social Responsibility,* edited by Norbert Brockman and Nicholas Piediscalzi, 53–64. New York: Alba House, 1973.

"A Look at the Secular City." In *The Secular City Debate,* edited by Daniel Callahan, 12–16. New York: Macmillan.

"The Voluntary Church: A Moral Appraisal." In *Voluntary Associations: A Study of Groups in Free Societies, Essays in Honor of James Luther Adams,* edited by D. B. Robertson, 299–322. Richmond: John Knox Press. Reprinted, *CMDM,* 109–37.

"Foundations of Ministry." In *The Church and Its Manpower Management,* edited by Ross P. Scherer and Theodore O. Wedel, 21–28. A Report of the First National Consultation on Church Personnel Policies and Practices. New York: Department of Publication Services, National Council of the Churches of Christ in the U.S.A. Reprinted, *Minister's Quarterly* 22 (Spring): 3–9; and in *CMDM,* 139–50.

"The Shouting of Slogans." *Commonweal* 83 (February 18): 582–83. Editorial correspondence.

1967

"Christian Style of Life: Problematics of a Good Idea." *Una Sancta* 24 (Resurrection): 6–14. Reprinted, *CEC,* 177–85.

"Love Monism." In *Storm over Ethics,* edited by John C. Bennett et al., 26–37. Philadelphia: United Church Press, The Bethany Press. Excerpted in *The Situation Ethics Debate,* edited by Harvey Cox, 79–82. Philadelphia: Westminster Press, 1968.

"Christian Humanism and the Human Mind." In *The Human Mind,* edited by J. Rolansky, 85–109. Amsterdam: North Holland Publishing. Excerpted, *Reflection* 65 (January 1968): 1–5. Reprinted, *CEC,* 187–204.

"A Community of Reflection." *Focus: A Theological Journal* 4 (Summer): 7–15.

"A Christian Approach to the Ethics of Abortion." *Dublin Review* 241 (Winter 1967–1968): 346–64. Reprint with slight changes, "A Protestant Ethical Approach." In *The Morality of Abortion: Legal and Historical Perspectives,* edited by John T. Noonan Jr., 101–22. Cambridge, MA: Harvard University Press, 1970. Also in *Abortion: The Moral Issues,* edited by Edward Batchelor Jr., 191–209. New York: Pilgrim Press, 1982. Also in *On Moral Medicine: Theological Perspectives in Medical Ethics,* edited by Stephen E. Lammers and Allen Verhey, 403–12. Grand Rapids: Wm. B. Eerdmans Publishing, 1987.

1968

Foreword. In *Responsibility in Modern Religious Ethics,* by Albert R. Jonsen, v–x. Washington, DC: Corpus Books.

"Moral Discernment in the Christian Life." In *Norm and Context in Christian Ethics,* edited by Gene H. Outka and Paul Ramsey, 17–36. New York: Charles Scribner's Sons. Reprinted, *TCE,* 99–119.

"Two Foci of Moral Development." In *The Acquisition and Development of Values: Perspectives on Research,* 24–25. Report of a conference. Bethesda, MD: National Institute of Child Health and Human Development.

"Two Requisites for the American Church: Moral Discourse and Institutional Power." In *The Future of the American Church,* edited by Phillip J. Hefner, 30–45. Philadelphia: Fortress Press. Reprinted, *CMDM,* 151–63.

"What Is the Contemporary Problematic of Ethics in Christianity?" *Central Conference of American Rabbis Journal* 15 (January): 14–26. Reprinted in *Judaism and Ethics,* edited by Daniel Jeremy Silver, 51–67. New York: KTAV Publishing House, 1970.

"New Directions in Moral Theology." *Commonweal* 87 (February 23): 617–23. Correction of printing error, 87 (March 15): 727.

"Two Approaches to Theological Ethics." *Union Seminary Quarterly Review* 22 (Summer): 337–48. Reprinted, *TCE,* 127–38.

"Toward Maturity in Decision-Making." *Christian Century* ("This Babel and Beyond" Series) 85 (July 10): 894–98.

"Kenneth W. Underwood, 1918–1968." *Journal for the Scientific Study of Religion* 7 (Fall): 286.

1969

"Faith, Unbelief, and Moral Life." In *The Presence and Absence of God,* edited by Christopher F. Mooney, 19–30. New York: Fordham University Press. Reprinted, *TCE,* 47–57.

"Political Images of the Ministry." In *The Church, The University, and Social Policy: The Danforth Study of Campus Ministries,* edited by Kenneth Underwood, 2:247–62. Middletown, CT: Wesleyan University Press.

"The Transcendence of God and the Value of Human Life." In *Proceedings of the Twenty-Third Annual Convention,* The Catholic Theological Society of America, 23:96–108. Yonkers, NY: St. Joseph's Seminary. Reprinted as "God's Transcendence and the Value of Human Life," *CEC,* 139–49; and in *On Moral Medicine: Theological Perspectives in Medical Ethics,* edited by Stephen E. Lammers and Allen Verhey, 121–26. Grand Rapids: Wm. B. Eerdmans Publishing, 1987.

"What Ought I to Do?" In *Truth and the Historicity of Man: Proceedings of the American Catholic Philosophical Association,* Vol. 43, edited by George F. McLean, 56–70. Washington, DC: The Catholic University of America, Office of the National Secretary of the Association.

"Why Read Barth's Ethics." In *Karl Barth and the Future of Theology,* edited by David L. Dickerman, 15–20. New Haven, CT: Yale Divinity School Association. Reprinted without footnotes, *Reflection* 66 (May): 10–12.

"Commentary." A response to Daniel Callahan, "The Sanctity of Life." In *The Religious Situation,* edited by Donald R. Cutler, 346–52. Boston: Beacon Press. Reprinted in *Updating Life and Death,* edited by Donald R. Cutler, 230–36. Boston: Beacon Press, 1968, 1969.

"From Scripture to Social Policy and Social Action." *Andover Newton Quarterly,* n.s., 9 (January): 160–69.

"The Relevance Gap." *Catholic High School Quarterly* 26 (January): 20–25.

"Bibliographical Notes on Medical Ethics." *Reflection* 66 (March): 6.

"Law and Morality." *This Is TCU* 11 (Spring): 6–7, 10–15.

"Theological Education as Professional Education." *Theological Education* 5 (Spring): 243–61. Reprinted in *Theological Education as Professional Education: The Report of a Convocation Sponsored by the Episcopal Theological School during Its Centennial Year Observance,* edited by Olga Craven, Alden L. Todd, and Jesse H. Ziegler, 105–23. Dayton, OH: The American Association of Theological Schools.

"A Protestant Response." A response to David Darst and Joseph Forgue, "Sexuality on the Island Earth." In *Ecumenist* 7 (September–October): 87–89. Reprinted as "All Relative Things Are Not Equally Relative." In *Sexuality on the Island Earth,* 28–35. New York: Paulist Press, 1970.

"'Responsibility' and Utilitarianism." A response to John Giles Milhaven, "Exit for Ethicists." *Commonweal* 91 (October 31): 140–41.

"Ethical Theory and Moral Practice." *Christian Century* 86 (December 17): 1613–17.

1970

Foreword. In *The Theology of H. Richard Niebuhr,* by Libertus A. Hoedemaker, vii–xi. Philadelphia: United Church Press, Pilgrim Press.

"Education for Moral Responsibility." In *Moral Education: Five Lectures,* 10–27. Cambridge, MA: Harvard University Press. Reprinted, *TCE,* 59–72.

"On the Threshold of a New Age." In *The Continuing Quest: Opportunities, Resources, and Programs in Post-Seminary Education,* edited by James B. Hofrenning, 13–22. Minneapolis: Augsburg Publishing House.

"The Study of Religion in Colleges and Universities: A Practical Commentary." In *The Study of Religion in Colleges and Universities,* edited by Paul Ramsey and John F. Wilson, 330–46. Princeton, NJ: Princeton University Press.

"The Theologian as Prophet, Preserver, or Participant." In *Christian Action and Openness to the World*, vols. 2–3, edited by Joseph Papin, 97–117. Villanova, PA: Villanova University Press. Reprinted, *TCE*, 33–46.

"The Burden of the Ethical: Reflections on Disinterestedness and Involvement." *Foundation* 66 (Winter): 8–15. Presidential Address, American Society of Christian Ethics. Reprinted, *TCE*, 33–46.

"Fragen zur Ethik der Revolution." *Lutherische Monatshefte* 9 (May): 237–41. Reprinted as "Ethik der Revolution." In *Zur Ethik der Revolution*, coauthored with Johan Marie de Jong and Richard Shaull, 9–24. Stuttgart: Kreuz-Verlag.

"Basic Ethical Issues in the Bio-Medical Fields." *Soundings* 53 (Summer): 151–89. Reprinted in *TCE*, 245–71, and in *Contemporary Issues in Bio-ethics*, edited by Tom L. Beauchamp and LeRoy Walters, 73–83. Encino, CA: Dickenson Publishing, 1978.

"The Place of Scripture in Christian Ethics: A Methodological Study." *Interpretation* 24 (October): 430–55. Reprinted, *TCE*, 121–45.

"Spring, 1970, and Theological Education." *Reflection* 68 (November): 3–7.

"The Conditions for Hope: Reflections on Human Experience." *Continuum* 7 (Winter): 535–45. Reprinted, *CEC*, 205–16.

1971

Foreword. In *The Ethical Demand*, by Knud E. Løgstrup, ix–xi. Translated by Theodor I. Jensen. Philadelphia: Fortress Press.

"The Relationship of Empirical Science to Moral Thought." In *Proceedings of the Twenty-Sixth Annual Convention*, Catholic Theological Society of America, 122–37. Bronx, NY: Manhattan College. Reprinted in *TCE*, 215–28; and in *Introduction to Christian Ethics: A Reader*, edited by Ronald P. Hamel and Kenneth R. Himes, OFM, 428–38. New York: Paulist Press, 1989.

"The Relation of the Gospels to the Moral Life." In *Jesus and Man's Hope*, vol. 2, edited by Donald G. Miller and Dikran Y. Hadidian, 103–17. Pittsburgh: Pittsburgh Theological Seminary, A Perspective Book. Reprinted in *TCE*, 147–59; and in *Christian Ethics: An Introductory Reader*, edited by Hunter P. Mabry, 173–87. Sapore: Indian Theological Library, 1987.

"Moral Authority of the Church." *Chicago Theological Seminary Register* 61: 1–14.

"We Live by Faith." *Presbyterian Outlook* 153 (November 22): 1.

"What Is the Normatively Human?" *American Ecclesiastical Review* 165 (November): 192–207. Reprinted, *TCE*, 229–44.

"What Does It Mean to Be a Moral Person?" *Face to Face* 4 (November): 19–21. Interview.

"Spiritual Life and Moral Life." *Theology Today* 19 (Winter): 296–307. Reprinted in *TCE*, 161–76; and in *Introduction to Christian Ethics: A Reader*, edited by Ronald P. Hamel and Kenneth R. Himes, OFM, 163–74. New York: Paulist Press, 1989.

1972

"The Relevance of Historical Understanding." In *Toward a Discipline of Social Ethics: Essays in Honor of Walter George Muelder*, edited by Paul Deats, 49–70. Boston: Boston University Press. Reprinted, *TCE*, 177–95.

"Toward Ecumenical Christian Ethics: Some Brief Suggestions." In *Transcendence and Immanence: Festschrift in Honor of Joseph Papin*, 33–37. Saint Meinrad, IN: Abbey Press.

Coauthored with Marc Lappe and Richard Roblin. "Ethical and Social Issues in Screening for Genetic Disease." *New England Journal of Medicine* 286 (May 25): 1129–32. Reprinted in *Bioethics*, edited by Thomas A. Shannon, 95–121. New York: Paulist Press, 1976. Also in *Contemporary Issues in Bioethics*, edited by Tom

L. Beauchamp and LeRoy Walters, 588–92. Encino, CA: Dickenson Publishing, 1978.

"Ethics and Faith in the Life of the Church." *Perkins Journal* 26 (Fall): 6–13.

"Will God Dwell Indeed with Man on Earth?" *Iliff Review* 29 (Winter): 6–13. Sermon.

1973

"Genetic Counseling and the Uses of Genetic Knowledge—An Ethical Overview." In *Ethical Issues in Human Genetics: Genetic Counseling and the Use of Genetic Knowledge,* edited by Bruce Hilton et al., 101–13. New York: Plenum Press. Discussion following article includes comments by JMG.

"Genetic Engineering and the Normative View of the Human." In *Ethical Issues in Biology and Medicine: Proceedings of a Symposium on the Identity and Dignity of Man,* 125–54. Cambridge, MA: Schenkman Publishing. Discussion following article includes comments by JMG. Reprinted, *TCE,* 273–86.

"Religion and Morality from the Perspective of Theology." In *Religion and Morality: A Collection of Essays,* edited by Gene Outka and John P. Reeder Jr., 125–54. Garden City, NY: Anchor Books.

Appendix (a statement about genetic screening). In *Genetic Mechanisms of Development,* edited by Frank H. Ruddle, 366–69. New York: Academic Press.

"Mongolism, Parental Desires, and the Right to Life." *Perspectives in Biology and Medicine* 16 (Summer): 529–57. Excerpted as "Mongolism och rätten att leva." *Vår Lösen* 63 (1972): 247–59. Reprinted in *Bioethics,* edited by Thomas A. Shannon, 95–121. New York: Paulist Press, 1976. In *Bioethics.* Rev. ed. (1981). In *Death, Dying, and Euthanasia,* edited by Dennis J. Horan and David Mall, 250–78. Washington, DC: University Publications, University of America, 1977. In *On Moral Medicine,* editd by Stephen E. Lammers and Allen Verhey, 475–88. Grand Rapids: Wm. B. Eerdmans, 1987.

"On Seeing the Kingdom." *Criterion* 13 (Autumn): 7–9. Sermon.

"The University as a Community of Moral Discourse." *Journal of Religion* 54 (October): 397–409.

1974

"The Church in Dialogue with Non-Christians and Humanists." In *The Church and Human Society at the Threshold of the Third Millennium.* Vol. 6, edited by Joseph Papin, 159–75. Villanova, PA: Villanova University Press.

"Genetic Screening and Human Values: An Analysis." In *Ethical, Social, and Legal Dimensions of Screening for Human Genetic Disease,* edited by Daniel Bergsma with Marc Lappe, Richard O. Roblin, and JMG, 201–23. New York: Stratton Intercontinental Medical Book Corp.

"Response to Professor Curran—I." In *Proceedings of the Twenty-Ninth Annual Convention,* Catholic Theological Society of America, 29:155–60. Bronx, NY: Manhattan College.

1975

"Ain't Nobody Gonna Cut on My Head!" *Hastings Center Report,* Institute of Society, Ethics, and the Life Sciences 5 (February): 49–50. Reprinted in *Cases in Bioethics,* edited by Carol Levine and Robert M. Veatch, 37–38. Hastings-on-Hudson, NY: Hastings Center, 1982.

"Society's View." *Medicine on the Midway* 30 (Summer/Fall): 6–8.

Coauthored with Chase P. Kimball and Patti Tighe. "Teaching Medical Ethics." *Medicine on the Midway* 30 (Summer/Fall): 16–21.

"What Ought to Be the Issue for Religion in American Society in the 1980s?" *Chicago Theological Seminary Register* 65 (Fall): 1–6.

1976

"Creative Teaching—Studies in Religious Ethics: Taking Human Life." *Horizons* 3 (Spring): 65–74.

"Ethical Guidelines in Management and Decision-Making for Long Term Care Patients." *Bulletin of the American Protestant Hospital Associations* 49 (Spring): 20–23, 29.

"Obligations to Future Generations." *University of Chicago Record* 10 (May): 67–69.

"Capital Punishment: Some Remarks and Some Responses." *Reformed Journal* 26 (July–August): 18–19.

1977

"Interdependence, Finitude, and Sin: Reflections on Scarcity." *Journal of Religion* 57 (April): 156–68.

"Extension of the Active Life: Ethical Issues." In *Extending the Human Life Span: Social Policy and Social Ethics,* edited by Bernice L. Neugarten and Robert J. Havighurst, 27–32. Washington, DC: National Science Foundation. Reprinted in *Philosophical Foundations of Gerontology,* edited by Patrick L. McKee, 155–69. New York: Human Sciences Press, 1982.

"Gospel and Law: A Central Question in Theological Ethics." In *In Libertatum Vocati Esti Miscellanea Bernard Häring,* edited by H. Boelaars and R. Tremblay, 15:101–19. Studia Moralia. Rome: Academia Alfonsiana. Translated as "Vangelo e Legge: Un Problema Centrale Dell'Etica Teologica." *Chiamati alla Liberti Saggi di teologia morale en onore di Bernard Häring,* 105–28. Rome: Academia Alfonsiana, 1980.

"Denial of God as God." *Criterion* 16 (Autumn): 6–9. Sermon.

1978

"Theology Confronts Technology and the Life Sciences." *Commonweal* 105 (June 16): 386–92. Reprinted in *On Moral Medicine: Theological Perspectives in Medical Ethics,* edited by Stephen E. Lammers and Allen Verhey, 35–41. Grand Rapids: Wm. B. Eerdmans Publishing, 1987.

"Response to Farley." Article by Margaret A. Farley, "Fragments of an Ethic of Commitment in Thomas." *Journal of Religion* 58, Supplement—Celebrating the Medieval Heritage, 156–59.

"Contribution of the Two Niebuhrs in American History." In Japanese. *Doshisha American Studies* 15 (May 31): 1–7.

1980

"Response." To Eberhard Jüngel, "Zur Bedeutung Luthers für die gegenwärtige Theologie." In *Referate am fünften internationalen Kongress für Lutherforschung,* 80–86. Göttingen: Vandenhoeck und Ruprecht.

"Theology and Ethics: An Interpretation of the Agenda." With commentary by Hans Jonas (203–17) and rejoinder by JMG (218–24). In *Knowing and Valuing,* edited by Tristram Engelhardt and Daniel Callahan, 181–224. Hastings-on-Hudson, NY: Institute of Society, Ethics, and Life Sciences. Reprinted in *The Roots of Ethics,* edited by Daniel Callahan and H. Tristram Engelhardt, 175–219. New York: Plenum Press, 1981.

"Religion and Morality." *Indian Philosophical Quarterly,* n.s., 7 (January): 207–28.

"Leadership of the Church in Social Concern." *Chicago Theological Seminary Register* 70 (Spring): 30–41.

"A Theocentric Interpretation of Life." *Christian Century* ("How My Mind Has Changed" Series) 97 (July 30–August 6): 754–60.

1981

"Ethics of Mechanical Ventilation." In *Clinical Use of Mechanical Ventilation,* edited by Christen C. Rottenborg and Enrique Via-Reque, 340–46. Chicago: Year Book Medical Publishers.

"Nature, Sin, and Covenant: Three Bases for Sexual Ethics." *Perspectives in Biology and Medicine* 24 (Spring): 493–97.

1982

Coauthored with Elmer W. Johnson. "The Corporate Leader and the Ethical Resources of Religion: A Dialogue." In *The Judeo-Christian Vision and the Modern Corporation,* edited by Oliver F. Williams and John W. Houck, 306–29. Notre Dame, IN: University of Notre Dame Press.

"The Minister as Moral Counselor." In *Seminary and Congregation: Interrelating Learning, Ministry, and Mission; Report of the 17th Biennial Meeting of the Association of Professional Education for Ministry,* 31–41. Pittsburgh: Dusquesne University. Reprinted in *Journal of Psychology and Christianity* 3 (1984): 16–22.

"Teologisk etik och vetenskaplig forskning." *Vår Lösen* 73: 572–77.

"Professions as 'Callings.'" *Social Service Review* 56 (December): 501–15.

"Nature: Its Status in Theological Ethics." *Logos* (University of Santa Clara) 3: 5–23.

". . . in the Face of Christ." *College People* (December): 26–31; also in *Criterion* 21 (Winter): 16–18. Sermon.

1983

Coauthored with Elmer W. Johnson. "Resolving Income and Wealth Differences in a Market Economy: A Dialogue." In *Ethical Issues in Business: A Philosophical Approach,* edited by Thomas Donaldson and Patricia H. Werhane, 382–92. Englewood Cliffs, NJ: Prentice-Hall.

"Ethical Issues in the Human Future." In *How Humans Adapt: A Biocultural Odyssey,* edited by Donald J. Ortner, 491–516. Washington, DC: Smithsonian Press. Translated, "Mänsklighetens etiska framtidsfrågor." In *Religion och samhälle: Dokumentation 2000,* no. 8, 1–13. Stockholm: Religions-sociologiska Institutet, 1982.

"Theology and Piety." *Word and World* 3 (Spring): 114–16.

1984

"The Bishops' Pastoral Letter: A Theological Ethical Analysis." *Criterion* 23 (Spring): 5–10.

Coauthored with Richard L. Landau. "Death Is Not the Enemy." *Journal of the American Medical Association* 252 (November 2): 2458. Reprinted in *Perspectives in Biology and Medicine* 41 (Fall 1997): 150–51.

1985

"Response to Critics." *Journal of Religious Ethics* 13: 185–209. A response to five articles on JMG's work in *JRE* 13/1 (1985).

"The Sectarian Temptation: Reflections on Theology, the Church, and the University." *Catholic Theological Society of America Proceedings* 40: 83–94.

1986

"Theology in the Service of Ethics: An Interpretation of Reinhold Niebuhr's Theological Ethics." In *Reinhold Niebuhr and the Issues of Our Time,* edited by Richard Harris, 24–45. London and Oxford: Mowbray.

"Christian Ethics." in *The Westminster Dictionary of Christian Ethics,* edited by James F. Childress and John Macquarrie, 87–90. Philadelphia: Westminster Press.

"The Vocation of the Theological Educator." *Austin Presbyterian Seminary Bulletin* 101 (March): 13–26. Reprinted in *Theological Education* 23 (Supplement 1987): 53–68.

Foreword. In *Studying People: A Primer in the Ethics of Social Research,* by Robert Reece and Harvey Siegal, vii–viii. Macon, GA: Mercer University Press.

"Persons in Relations: A Critique of Some Medical Ethics." *Monitor* 5 (November): 6–7.

1987

"Priorities in Theological Education." *Theological Education* 23 (Supplement): 69–87.

"An Analysis of Church and Society Social Ethics Writings." In *Church and Society,* 170–83. Geneva: World Council of Churches. Reprinted in *Ecumenical Review* 40 (April 1988): 267–78.

1988

Participant in discussion, "Religion and Education." *Daedalus* 117 (Spring): 1–146.

Participant in discussion, "Nuclear Policy, Culture, and History." Edited by Milton B. Singer. Chicago: University of Chicago, Center for International Studies.

"Human Confidence and Rational Activity: The Dialectic of Faith and Reason in University Life." *Cresset* 51 (September): 5–10.

"Response," "Discussion," and afterword. In *James M. Gustafson's Theocentric Ethics: Interpretations and Assessments,* edited by Harlan R. Beckley and Charles M. Swezey, 203–24, 225–40, 241–54. Macon, GA: Mercer University Press.

"Reflection on the Literature on Theological Education, 1955–1985," and "Opportunities of a University Divinity School." *Theological Education* 24 (Supplement II): 9–73 and 74–81.

"Epilogue: For Whom Does the Corporation Toil?" *Bulletin of the American Academy of Arts and Sciences* 42 (October): 10–31. Reprinted from Gustafson and Meyer, *U.S. Business Corporation* (1988).

"The Consistent Ethic of Life: A Protestant Perspective." In *Consistent Ethic of Life,* edited by Joseph Cardinal Bernardin, 196–209. Kansas City, MO: Sheed and Ward. Response to JMG by Lisa Sowle Cahill, 210–18, and by Cardinal Bernardin, 249–50.

1989

"Roman Catholic and Protestant Interaction in Ethics: An Interpretation." *Theological Studies* 50: 44–69.

Coauthored with Elmer W. Johnson. "Efficiency, Morality, and Managerial Effectiveness." *Bulletin of the American Academy of Arts and Sciences* 42 (April): 9–28. Reprinted from Gustafson and Meyer, *U.S. Business Corporation* (1988).

1990

"James Luther Adams: Ethics and Ethos." *Christian Century* 197 (February 14): 124–25.

"Den farliga människocentreringen." *Vår Lösen* 81: 104–14.

"What Is Distributive Justice." *Horizons* (The Workman's Circle) 1 (Summer): 18–20.

"Public Choice and Professors of Ethics: Closing the Gap," 1–14. Atlanta: Georgia Humanities Council.

"Moral Discourse about Medicine: A Variety of Forms." *Journal of Medicine and Philosophy* 15: 125–42. Reprinted in *ISTE,* 35–56.

"The Focus and Its Limitations: Reflections on Catholic Moral Theology." In *Moral Theology: Challenges for the Future; Essays in Honor of R. A. McCormick, S.J.*, edited by Charles Curran, 179–90. New York: Paulist Press.

"Man måsta jämföra: Om växter, djur och Människan." *Vår Lösen* 81: 518–28.

"Response to Hartt." *Soundings* 73: 689–700. Hartt, "Concerning God and Man and His Well-Being: A Commentary Inspired by Spinoza," 667–87. Issue contains four articles on JMG's *Ethics from a Theocentric Perspective.*

1991

"All Things in Relation to God." *Second Opinion* 16: 80–107. Interview.

"August Seventh, 1945." *Agora: A Journal of Interdisciplinary Discourse* 3 (Spring): 81–86. Reprinted in *Christian Century* 112 (August 16–23, 1995): 779–81.

"Ethics: An American Growth Industry." *Key Reporter* 36 (Spring): 1–5. Excerpted as "Booming Business of Business Ethics." *Business and Society Review* 81 (Spring 1992): 84–86. Reprinted in *Perspectives in Biology and Medicine* 41 (Winter 1998): 191–99.

"Response to Francis S. Fiorenza." In *The Legacy of H. Richard Niebuhr*, 73–82. Minneapolis: Fortress Press. Fiorenza, "Theology as Responsible Valuation or Reflective Equilibrium: The Legacy of H. Richard Niebuhr," 33–71.

"Theological Anthropology and the Human Sciences." In *Theology at the End of Modernity*, edited by Sheila Greeve Davaney, 61–77. Festschrift for Gordon Kaufman. Philadelphia: Trinity Press International.

1992

"Christian Ethics," "Jesus of Nazareth," and "Situation Ethics." In *Encyclopedia of Ethics*, edited by Lawrence C. Becker, 151–57, 644–47, and 1152–53. New York: Garland Publishing.

"Reflection on the Life of Gösta Ahlstrom." *Criterion* 31 (Winter): 22–25. Reprinted in *University of Chicago Record* 27 (January 21, 1993): 5–6; and in *The Broken Pitcher: Memorial Essays for G. W. A.*, edited by Steven W. Holloway et al., 32–37. Sheffield: Sheffield Academic Press, 1995.

"Response to Van R. Potter, 'Getting to the Year 3000.'" *Perspectives in Biology and Medicine* 36 (Spring): 339–44.

"A Response to the Book of Job." In *The Voice from the Whirlwind*, edited by Lee G. Perdue and W. Clark Gilpin, 172–84, 251. Nashville: Abingdon.

"Att forklara och värdera: En dialog mellan teologi och empirisk vetenskap." In *Etik, Religion och Samhälle*, edited by C. H. Grenholm and G. Lantz, 69–82. Festskrift till Ragnar Holte. Nora, Sweden: Nya Doxa. Swedish version of 1990 Arizona State Lecture published by ASU in booklet form; also in *Zygon* 30 (1995) and in *ISTE*, 11–34.

"A Christian Perspective on Genetic Engineering." *Cathedral Papers 4*, 1–5. Washington, DC: Washington National Cathedral. Reprinted in *Journal of Contemporary Health Law and Policy* 8: 183–200; in *Human Gene Therapy* 5 (1994): 747–54; and in *ISTE*, 73–85.

1993

Foreword. In *Hope Is Where We Least Expect It*, by Daniel E. Lee, vii–viii. Lanham, MD: University Press of America.

"Interdependence and Responsibility." *Living Pulpit* 2: 44–45.

"God, Nature, and Human in the Western Religious Tradition." In *Man and Nature: A Cross-Cultural Perspective*, 13–32. Bangkok: Chulalongkorn University Printing House. Thai translation, Bangkok: OSIS, 1990.

Foreword. In *Radical Monotheism and Western Culture,* by H. Richard Niebuhr, 3–8. New ed. Louisville, KY: Westminster/John Knox Press.

"G. H. Mead and Martin Buber on the Interpersonal Self." In *The Perceived Self,* edited by Ulric Neiser, 280–89. Cambridge: Cambridge University Press.

"Where Theologians and Genetics Meet." *CTNS Bulletin* (The Center for Theology and the Natural Sciences) 13: 1–9. Reprinted as "Where Theologians and Geneticists Meet." *Dialog* 33 (1994): 7–16.

1994

"Remembering H. Richard Niebuhr." *Christian Century* 111 (October 5): 884–86.

"Alternative Conceptions of God." Response to William Alston, "Divine Action: Shadow or Substance." In *The God Who Acts,* edited by Thomas F. Tracy, 63–74. University Park: Pennsylvania State University Press.

"Niebuhr, H. Richard" and "Niebuhr, K. P. Reinhold." In *Theologische Realenzyklopädie,* Band 24, Lieferung 3/4: 468–70 and 470–73.

1995

"Tracing a Trajectory," "Explaining and Valuing," and "Response to Rottschaefer, Beckley, and Konner." *Zygon* 30: 159–75, 177–90, and 221–26.

"Tracing the Order of Nature: Niebuhr and the Secular Mind." In *Faithful Imagining: Essays in Honor of Richard R. Niebuhr,* edited by Sang Hyun Lee, Wayne Proudfoot, and Albert Blackwell, 61–78. Atlanta: Scholars Press.

"In the Intersections: Reflections on Being an Intellectual Traffic Cop." *Criterion* 14: 7–14.

"Making Theology Intelligible: An Interpretation of H. Richard Niebuhr." *Reflections* (Summer–Fall): 2–8.

"The Idea of Christian Ethics." *Companion Encyclopedia of Theology,* edited by Peter Byrne and Leslie Hoalden, 691–715. London and New York: Routledge.

1996

"Styles of Religious Reflection in Medical Ethics." In *Religion and Medical Ethics: Looking Back, Looking Forward,* edited by Allen Verhey, 81–94. Grand Rapids: Wm. B. Eerdmans. Reprinted from *ISTE,* 56–72.

"Styles of Religious Reflection in Medical Ethics, Further Discussion." In *Bioetikk og teologi, Rapport fra Nordisk teologisk nettverk for bioetikks workshop i Stockholm 27.-29. September 1996,* edited by Lars Østnor, 12–26. Oslo: Nordisk Teologisk Nettverk for bioetikk.

"Possibilities and Problems for the Study of Ethics in Religiously Pluralistic Societies." In *Culture, Religion, and Society: Essays in Honor of Richard W. Taylor,* edited by Saral K. Chatterji and Hunter P. Mabry, 240–59. ISPCK, Delhi: The Christian Institute for the Study of Religion and Society.

1997

"The Use of Scripture in Christian Ethics." *Studia Theologica* 51: 15–29.

"Christian Ethics and Community: Which Community?" *Studies in Christian Ethics* 10: 49–60.

"On Being Called." *Journal for Preachers* 20 (Easter): 50–54. Ordination Sermon.

"Don't Exaggerate!" *Christian Century* 114 (October 29): 964–65.

1998

"Cosmic Theocentrism: Remarks on Stanley Harrakas, *Toward Transfigured Life.*" *Annual of the Society of Christian Ethics* 18: 23–27.
"A Retrospective Interpretation of American Religious Ethics, 1948–1998." *Journal of Religious Ethics* 25, no. 3 (25th Anniversary Supplement): 3–22.

1999

"Niebuhr, H. Richard." In *American National Biography*, 16:416–19. Cary, NC: Oxford University Press.
"Just What Is 'Post-Liberal' Theology?" *Christian Century* 116, no. 10: 353–55. Response by William Placher, "Being Postliberal: A Response to James Gustafson," *Christian Century* 116, no. 11: 390–92.
"Liberal Questions: A Response to William Placher." *Christian Century* 116, no. 12: 422–25.
"Memories of a Friend." In *Reflections on Bonhoeffer: Essays in Honor of F. Burton Nelson*, edited by Geffrey B. Kelly and C. John Weborg, 3–6. Chicago: Covenant.
"Teologie och etik utmanad av kulturell kontext: Ett Troeltschian imperativ." In *Nya vägar i teologin: Festskrift till Anders Jeffner*, edited by Carl Reinhold Bråkenhielm et al., 207–14. Nora, Sweden: Nya Doxa.

2001

"Preface: An Appreciative Interpretation." In *Christ and Culture,* by H. Richard Niebuhr, Fiftieth Anniversary Edition, xxi–xxxv. San Francisco: Harper. Adapted from Inaugural Lecture of H. Richard Niebuhr Lecture Hall, Yale Divinity School, October 2, 2001.

2002

"Charles Curran: Ecumenical Moral Theologian Par Excellence." In *A Call to Fidelity: On the Moral Theology of Charles E. Curran*, edited by James J. Walter, Timothy E. O'Connell, and Thomas Shannon, 211–33. Washington, DC: Georgetown University Press.
"'The Almighty Has His Own Purposes': From Politics To Theology." In *The Relevance of Theology: Nathan Söderblom and the Development of an Academic Discipline*, edited by Carl Reinhold Bråkenhielm and Gunhild Wingvist Hollman, 101–12. Uppsala: Uppsala University, Acta Universitatis Upsaliensis. Proceedings from a conference held in Uppsala, April 14–16, 2002, in commemoration of the centennial for Söderblom's appointment to the Uppsala faculty.

2003

"Implications of Theocentric Ethics for Church and Ministry: Ministerial and Congregational Activity," "Implications of Theocentric Ethics for Church and Ministry: Ethics," and "The Significance of the Work of H. Richard Niebuhr for Church and Ministry Today." *Prism: A Theological Forum for the United Church of Christ* 18, no. 2 (Fall): 3–13, 15–26, 27–40. Responses by Rosetta Ross, 41–44, and Paul Capetz, 45–50.

2004

"Forum on *An Examined Faith:* Doubting Theology." *Christian Century* 121, no. 136 (June 29): 25–36. Articles: "Conversations That Count" by William C. Placher; "Wisdom—Divine and Human" by P. Travis Kroeker; "A Faith Worthy of Doubt" by S. Mark Heim; "James M. Gustafson Replies."

III. EDITOR OF JOURNALS

1970

"The Sixties: Radical Change in American Religion." Special issue, *Annals* (American Academy of Political and Social Sciences) 387 (January). Foreword by JMG, ix–x.

1977

"Consent and Responsibilities in Medicine." Special issue, *Journal of Medicine and Philosophy* 2 (December). Editorial by JMG, 305–6.

1979

Coedited with Stanley M. Hauerwas. "Theology and Medical Ethics." Special issue, *Journal of Medicine and Philosophy* 4 (December). Editorial by JMG and SMH, 345–46.

IV. BOOK REVIEWS

1953

Review of *Social Responsibilities of the Businessman,* by Howard R. Bowen. *Christianity and Society* 19 (Winter 1953–54): 21–23.

1955

Review of *Congregationalism: A Restatement,* by Daniel T. Jenkins. *Church History* 24 (March): 79–80.

1956

"New Insight for the Minister from Recent Sociological Studies." Review of *Protestant-Catholic-Jew,* by Will Herberg, and other works. *Yale Divinity News* 60 (January): 5–7.

Review of *Christian Ethics and Moral Philosophy,* by George F. Thomas. *Chaplain* 13 (April): 43–44.

Review of *Ethics,* by Dietrich Bonhoeffer. *Advance* 148 (April 4): 21.

Review of *Baleful Legacy,* by Marion J. Bradshaw. *Christian Century* 73 (May 2): 555–56.

Review of *Faith Active in Love,* by George W. Forell. *Journal of Religious Thought* 13 (Spring–Summer): 148–49.

Review of *Fads and Foibles in Modern Sociology and Related Sciences,* by Pitirim A. Sorokin. *Christian Century* 73 (October 31): 1264–65.

Review of *Christian Social Ethics,* by Albert T. Rasmussen. *Advance* 148 (November 2): 23–24.

1957

Review of *New Lives for Old,* by Margaret Mead. *Christian Century* 74 (January 16): 79–80.

Review of *The Social Sources of Denominationalism,* by H. Richard Niebuhr. *Meridian* 1 (Spring): 3.

Review of *Sweden: The Welfare State,* by Wilfrid Fleisher. *Christian Century* 74 (April 3): 426.

Review of *Democracy and Dictatorship*, by Zevedei Barbu. *Christian Century* 74 (April 17): 492.

Review of *Edward Bellamy: Selected Writings on Religion and Society*, edited by Joseph Schiffman. *Christian Century* 74 (April 24): 534.

Review of *What the Christian Hopes For in Society*, edited by Wayne Cowan. *Union Seminary Quarterly Review* 13 (November): 57–59.

1958

Review of *Christian Ethics*, by Georgia Harkness. *Advance* 150 (January 17): 23.

Review of *Ancestors and Immigrants*, by Barbara Miller Solomon. *Christian Century* 75 (January 22): 105.

Review of *Professors and Public Ethics*, by Wilson Smith. *Church History* 27 (March): 85–86.

Review of *Constraint and Variety in American Education*, by David Riesman. *Christian Century* 75 (April 23): 512–13.

Review of *The Two Cities*, by John A. Hutchinson. *Union Seminary Quarterly Review* 13 (May): 68–69.

Review of *Social and Cultural Dynamics*, by Pitirim A. Sorokin. *Christian Century* 75 (October 15): 1182.

Review of *Sociology of Religion*, by Joachin Wach. *Christian Century* 75 (November 5): 1275–76.

Review of *After Utopia: The Decline of Political Faith*, by Judith N. Shklar. *Christian Century* 75 (November 12): 1305–6.

Review of *Temporal and Eternal*, by Charles Peguy. *Westminster Bookman* 17 (December): 16–17.

1959

Review of *The Structure of Christian Ethics*, by Joseph Sittler. *The Chicago Theological Seminary Register* 49 (January): 10–11.

Review of *The Human Condition*, by Hannah Arendt. *Christian Century* 76 (April 1): 391.

Review of *Love and Justice* (edited by D. B. Robertson) and *Pious and Secular America*, by Reinhold Niebuhr. *Union Seminary Quarterly Review* 14 (May): 59–60.

Review of *Communism and the Theologians*, by Charles C. West. *Interpretation* 13 (July): 345–48.

Review of *The Comparative Study of Religion*, by Joachim Wach. *Religious Education* 54 (July–August): 394–95.

Review of *Religion and Culture*, edited by Walter Leibrecht. *Theology Today* 16 (October): 400–401.

1960

Review of *Kontakt med Kyrkan*, by K. M. Olsson. *Svensk Kyrkotidning* (Swedish Church Times) 56 (March 17): 167–69.

Review of *The Theology of Dietrich Bonhoeffer*, by John D. Godsey. *Westminster Bookman* 19 (June): 12–13.

1961

"Nutida amerikansk teologi." Review of *Theology of Culture*, by Paul Tillich; *Radical Monotheism and Western Culture*, by H. Richard Niebuhr; and *Relativism, Knowledge and Faith*, by Gordon D. Kaufman. *Tro och Liv* (Faith and Life) 2: 66–70.

Review of *The Birth of the Gods*, by Guy E. Swanson. *Review of Religious Research* 2 (Spring): 176–77.

Review of *Japanese Contributions to Christian Theology*, by Carl Michalson. *Faculty Forum* 17 (May): 3.

Review of *The Protestant Search for Political Realism, 1919–1941*, by Donald B. Meyer. *United Church Herald* 4 (September 21): 30.

Review of *War and Christian Conscience*, by Paul Ramsey. *Religion and Life* 31 (Winter 1961–62): 133–34.

1962

Review of *The Living and the Dead* and *The Family of God*, by W. Lloyd Warner. *Religious Education* 57 (March–April): 151–52.

Review of *The Churches and Rapid Social Change*, by Paul Abrecht, and *Man in Rapid Social Change*, by Egbert de Vries. *Theology Today* 19 (July): 302–4.

Review of *What Is the Nature of Man? Images of Man in Our American Culture*, by Kenneth Boulding et al. *United Church Herald* 5 (July 19): 27.

Review of *The Achieving Society*, by David C. McClelland. *Religious Education* 57 (November–December): 471.

Review of *The Church as a Social Institution*, by David O. Moberg. *Religious Education* 57 (November–December): 471.

1963

Review of *Religion in American Life*, vols. 1, 2, and 4, edited by James Ward Smith and A. Leland Jamison. *Virginia Quarterly Review* 39 (Autumn): 645–51.

1964

Review of *An Apologetical Narration*, edited by Robert S. Paul. *Bulletin of the Congregational Library* 15 (January): 5–6.

Review of *Ethics in a Christian Context*, by Paul Lehmann. *Union Seminary Quarterly Review* 19 (March): 261–65.

Review of *The Immobilized Christian: A Study of His Pre-Ethical Situation*, by John R. Fry. *United Church Herald* 7 (March 15): 32.

Review of *Visible Saints: The History of a Puritan Idea*, by Edmund S. Morgan. *Journal of Presbyterian History* 42 (September): 216–17.

1965

Review of *The Communion of Saints: A Dogmatic Inquiry into the Sociology of the Church*, by Dietrich Bonhoeffer. *Theology Today* 21 (January): 527–29.

Review of *Toward the Recovery of Unity: The Thought of F. D. Maurice*, edited by John F. Porter and William J. Wolf. *Religious Education* 60 (March–April): 158–59.

Review of *The Secular City*, by Harvey Cox. *Wind and Chaff* 3 (October): 3. Reprinted as "A Look at the Secular City." In *The Secular City Debate*, edited by Daniel Callahan, 12–16. New York: Macmillan.

Review of *Racism and the Christian Understanding of Man*, by George D. Kelsey. *Drew Gateway* 36 (Autumn–Winter 1965–1966): 50–52.

1966

"How Does Love Reign?" Review of *Situation Ethics*, by Joseph Fletcher, and *Deeds and Rules in Christian Ethics*, by Paul Ramsey. *Christian Century* 83 (May 18): 654–55. Adapted as "Love Monism." In *Storm over Ethics*, edited by John C. Bennett et al., 26–37. Philadelphia: United Church Press, The Bethany Press, 1967. Excerpted, *The Situation Ethics Debate*, edited by Harvey Cox, 79–82. Philadelphia: Westminster Press, 1968.

Reviews of *Religious Behavior,* by Oliver R. Whitley, and *The Sociology of Religion,* by Thomas F. O'Dea. *Religious Education* 61 (November–December): 466–68 and 468–70.

Review of *Law and Conscience,* by Franz Bockle. *Commonweal* 85 (December 16): 328–29.

Review of *Contraception,* by John T. Noonan Jr. *Una Sancta* 23 (Christmas): 111–12.

1967

Review of *Evil and the God of Love,* by John Hick. *Union Seminary Quarterly Review* 22 (January): 182–84.

Review of *Theological Ethics,* by James Sellers. *Religious Education* 62 (January–February): 77–78.

Review of *Elements for a Social Ethics,* by Gibson Winter. *Journal for the Scientific Study of Religion* 6 (Fall): 283–84.

Review of *Christian Ethics and Contemporary Philosophy,* edited by Ian T. Ramsey. *Journal of the American Academy of Religion* 35 (September): 285–89.

Review of *The Seminary: Protestant and Catholic,* by Walter D. Wagoner. *Religious Education* 62 (September–October): 460.

Review of *New Congregations: Security and Mission in Conflict,* by Donald L. Metz. *American Sociological Review* 32 (December): 1015–16.

1968

Review of *Who Speaks for the Church?* by Paul Ramsey. *Ecumenical Review* 20 (January): 98–100.

Review of *The Social Construction of Reality,* by Peter L. Berger and Thomas Luckmann, and *The Invisible Religion,* by Thomas Luckmann. *Journal for the Scientific Study of Religion* 7 (Spring): 122–25.

Review of *Religion and Public Education,* edited by Theodore R. Sizer. *Harvard Educational Review* 38 (Spring): 391–96.

Review of *Absolutes in Moral Theology?* edited by Charles E. Curran, and *New Look at Christian Morality,* by Charles E. Curran. *National Catholic Reporter* 4 (October 2): 13.

Review of *Life or Death: Ethics and Options,* edited by Daniel H. Labby. *Commonweal* 89 (October 4): 27–30.

1969

Review of *Building the Human,* by Robert O. Johann. *Thought* 44 (Summer): 309–12.

1970

Review of *Birth Control and Jewish Law,* by David M. Feldman. *Christian Century* 87 (May 20): 632–33.

Review of *Abortion: Law, Choice and Morality,* by Daniel Callahan. *National Catholic Reporter* 6 (August 7): 9–10.

Review of *A Rumor of Angels,* by Peter L. Berger. *Journal of the Scientific Study of Religion* 9 (Fall): 255–56.

1971

Review of *Black Self-Determinism: The Story of the Woodlawn Organization,* by Arthur M. Brazier. *Encounter* 32 (Spring): 181–82.

Review of *The Moral Rules,* by Bernard Gert. *Commonweal* 94 (August 20): 434–35.

Review of *Toward a New Catholic Morality,* by John Giles Milhaven. *Theological Studies* 32 (September): 523–25.

Review of *Fabricated Man: The Ethics of Genetic Control,* by Paul Ramsey. *Theological Studies* 32 (September): 521–23.

Review of *Cognitive Structures and Religious Research,* by W. Widick Schroeder. *Chicago Theological Seminary Register* 61 (September): 39–42.

Review of *The Ethics of Necropolis,* by Max L. Stackhouse. *Andover Newton Quarterly* 12 (November): 118–20.

Review of *Prudence Crandell,* by Edmund Fuller. *Review of Books and Religion* 1 (December 15): 5.

1972

Review of *The Power to Be Human,* by Charles C. West. *Theology Today* 28 (January): 504–6.

Review of *Catholic Ethics and Protestant Ethics,* by Roger Mehl. *Religious Education* 67 (March–April): 154–55.

Review of *Surviving the Future,* by Arnold Toynbee. *Worldview* 15 (April): 49–50.

Review of *Ethics in a Permissive Society,* by William Barclay. *National Catholic Reporter* 8 (April 28): 16.

1973

Review of *A Theory of Justice,* by John Rawls. *Theology Today* 30 (October): 306–12.

Review of *The Groundwork of Christian Ethics,* by N. H. G. Robinson. *Theological Studies* 34 (December): 745–47.

1974

Review of *Faith and Morality in the Secular Age,* by Bernard Häring. *Commonweal* 100 (April 12): 140–41.

Review of *Ambiguity of Moral Choice,* by Richard A. McCormick. *Religious Studies* 10 (June): 252–53.

Review of *Human Medicine,* by James B. Nelson. *Theological Markings* 4: 52–54.

Review of *Baker Dictionary of Christian Ethics,* edited by Carl F. H. Henry. *Calvin Theological Journal* 9 (November): 253–57.

1975

Review of *The Politics of Transformation,* by Paul Lehmann. *Theology Today* 32 (July): 197–98, 200, 202.

1976

Reviews of *The Ethics of Jonathan Edwards: Morality and Aesthetics,* by Clyde Holbrook, and *Jonathan Edwards: Theologian of the Heart,* by Harold P. Simonson. *Religious Studies Review* ("Notes on Recent Publications") 2 (January): 51.

Review of *Bibliography of Bioethics: Vol. 1,* edited by LeRoy Walters. *Review of Books and Religion* 5 (Mid-January): 1.

"The Editors' Bookshelf, Theological Ethics." Annotations of twelve books. *Journal of Religion* 56 (April): 214–16.

Review of *The Social Gospel in Canada,* edited by Richard Allen. *Religious Studies Review* ("Notes on Recent Publications") 2 (October): 58–59.

1977

"Bibliographical Resources for 'Bioethics.'" Annotations of four resources. *Religious Studies Review* ("Notes on Recent Publications") 3 (January): 63.

Review of *The Radical Imperative: From Theology to Social Ethics,* by John C. Bennett. *Journal of Religion* 57 (April): 192.

Reviews of *Christian Social Ethics in a Revolutionary Age,* by Carl-Henric Grenholm. *Journal of Religion* 57 (April): 190–91, and *Religious Studies Review* ("Notes on Recent Publications") 3 (April): 128.

Review of *Freedom and Morality,* edited by John Bricke. *Religious Studies Review* ("Notes on Recent Publications") 3 (July): 191.

Review of *War and Christian Ethics,* edited by Arthur F. Holmes. *Journal of Religion* 57 (October): 428–29.

"The Editors' Bookshelf." Annotations of sixteen books. *Journal of Religion* 57 (October): 437–39.

Review of *In Search of a Responsible World Society: The Social Teaching of the World Council of Churches,* by Paul Bock. *Chicago Theological Seminary Register* 67 (Winter): 54–55.

Review of *Abortion: The Development of the Roman Catholic Perspective,* by John Connery. *National Catholic Reporter* 13 (July 15): 13.

1978

Reviews of *Ethics in the New Testament,* by Jack T. Sanders, and *The Ethics of Freedom,* by Jacques Ellul. *Journal of Religion* 58 (January): 76–77, 77–78.

Review of *Christians and Marxists,* by José Miguez Bonino. *Journal of Religion* 58 (April): 220–21.

Review of *U.S. Foreign Policy and Christian Ethics,* by John C. Bennett and Harvey Seifert. *New Review of Books and Religion* 2 (April): 6.

1979

Review of *On Human Nature,* by E. O. Wilson. *Hastings Center Report* 9 (February): 44–45.

Review of *Sedgwick's Ethics and Victorian Moral Philosophy,* by J. B. Schneewind. *Journal of Religion* 59 (April): 250–51.

Review of *Authority in Morals: An Essay in Christian Ethics,* by Gerard J. Hughes. *Heythrop Journal* 20 (October): 421–23.

Review of *The Future of Voluntary Organizations: Report of the Wolfenden Committee. Social Service Review* 53 (December): 672–74.

1980

Review of *The Human Mystery,* by John Eccles. *Perspectives in Biology and Medicine* 23 (Summer): 660–62.

Review of *Jewish Bioethics,* edited by Fred Rosner and J. David Bleich. *Hastings Center Report* 10 (December): 42–43.

1981

Review of *Medicine and Religion: Strategies of Care,* edited by Donald W. Shriver. *Quarterly Review of Biology* 56: 513.

1982

Reviews of *Ethics,* by Karl Barth, and *The Sufficiency of Hope: The Conceptual Foundations of Religion,* by James L. Muyskens. *Ethics* 92 (April): 585–86 and 585.

Review of *Felix Adler and Ethical Culture: Memories and Studies,* by Horace L. Friess. *Ethics* 92 (July): 779.

Review of *Jonathan Edwards: Art and the Sense of the Heart,* by Terrence Erdt. *Journal of Religion* 62 (October): 433–34.

1983

Review of *Struggle and Fulfillment: The Inner Dynamics of Religion and Morality,* by Donald Evans. *Journal of Religion* 63 (July): 327–28.

Review of *Fundamental Moral Theology,* by Franz Bockle. *Encounter* 44 (Autumn): 405–6.

Review of *The Nuclear Delusion: Soviet-American Relations in the Atomic Age,* by George F. Kennan, and *Beyond the Cold War: A New Approach to the Arms Race and Nuclear Annihilation,* by E. P. Thompson. *Bulletin of the Atomic Scientists* 39 (October): 35–36.

1985

Review of *The Imperative of Responsibility: In Search of an Ethics for the Technological Age,* by Hans Jonas. *Bulletin of the Atomic Scientists* 41 (April): 58–59.

1986

Review of *Between the Sexes: Foundations for a Christian Ethics of Sexuality,* by Lisa Sowle Cahill. *America* 154 (January 25): 54–55.

1987

Review of *Voluntary Associations,* by James Luther Adams, edited by J. Ronald Engel. *CTS Register* 77 (Spring): 34–35.

1988

Reviews of *Resurrection and Moral Order: An Outline for Evangelical Ethics,* by Oliver O'Donovan; *Wholly Human,* by Bruno Schüller; and *Richard Niebuhr: A Lifetime of Reflections on the Church and the World,* by Jon H. Diefenthaler. *Journal of Religion* 68 (January): 131–33, 133–34, and 181–82.

Review of *The Prophethood of All Believers,* by James Luther Adams, edited by George K. Beach. *The Unitarian Universalist Christian* 43 (Spring): 52–54.

1989

Review of *Conscience and Casuistry in Early Middle Europe,* edited by Edmund Leites. *Journal of Religion* 69: 579–80.

1990

Review of *The Making of Moral Theology: A Study of the Roman Tradition,* by John Mahoney. *Ecumenical Review* 49: 74–76.

Review of *Ethical Writings,* by Jonathan Edwards, edited by Paul Ramsey, vol. 8 of *The Works of Jonathan Edwards. Journal of Religion* 70: 479–81.

1993

"Scientific Dreamers and Religious Speculation." Review of *Science as Salvation: A Modern Myth and Its Meaning,* by Mary Midgley. *Christian Century* 110 (March 10): 269–74.

1995

Review of *How We Die: Reflections on Life's Final Chapter,* by Sherwin B. Nuland. *Perspectives in Biology and Medicine* 39 (August): 139–41.

"Commandments for Staying Human." Review of *The Decalogue and a Human Future,* by Paul Lehmann. *Christian Century* 112: 1247–49.

1997

Review of *Being and Value: Toward a Constructive Postmodern Metaphysics,* by Frederick Ferré. *Common Knowledge* 6 (Spring): 145.

Review of *The Origins of Moral Theology in the United States,* by Charles E. Curran, and *Feminist Ethics and Catholic Moral Theology,* edited by Charles E. Curran, Margaret Farley, and Richard A. McCormick, SJ. *America* 177, no. 11: 24–26.

2003

Review of *All Things New: Reform of Church and Society in Schleiermacher's Christian Ethics,* by James M. Brandt. *Bulletin of the Institute for Reformed Theology* 3, no. 2 (Spring/Summer): 11.

Index of Names

Index of Subjects

abortion 6, 56–74, 103, 112, 117, 185
adequacy criterion. *See* sources, four
affections, 81–82, 88–89
agape. See love: as *agape*
agency, moral/ human, 88, 113, 132, 207–9
Aggiornamento. *See* Vatican II
American Academy of Religion, 214
Anabaptists, 142, 151, 158
Anglicanism. *See* Church of England
anthropocentrism, 76–78, 92–94, 118,
　　122–24
autonomy, moral, 61–63

base points, four, 16–23, 81, 156–57
Bible, 38, 147, 177–78, 198–212
biomedical ethics, 52–74, 76 111–25, 183–97
Buddhism, 150, 218

calling
　　God's, 7, 73–74
　　professional, 126–38, 181
casuistry, 16, 170, 172, 185–86, 206–7, 221
Catholic Theological Society of America, xx,
　　170
character, 14, 31–32, 40–52, 147, 192, 202–8
christology. *See* Jesus/Christ
church, 25–51, 142, 144, 148, 173–77
Church of England, 99, 106–7, 144, 167 n.24
coherence criterion. *See* base points, four
command, Divine, 6–8, 16–22, 37, 41, 163,
　　207, 210
common good, 117, 128–29, 132–33, 136–38
Confucian ethics, 218

conscience, 8–9, 19, 180
consequentialism, 114, 173
context, 1–24, 136–39, 193–94, 205, 218–21
contraception, 39, 104, 117, 241
covenant
　　between God and humans, 206
　　between humans. *See* marriage
creation, 35–36, 77, 82, 89–97, 110, 114–23,
　　148, 152, 154, 160, 174–78
cross, crucifixion, 13, 51, 156, 174, 202
culture, 79–84, 96, 123–25, 132, 142–59, 219

death, 7–8, 36, 67, 139–41, 150
deism, 165
divine command, ethics of, 6–9, 18, 21, 163,
　　210
dogmatics, relation ethics, 8, 10, 74, 170
Down syndrome, 52–74

Eastern Orthodoxy, 156, 158, 205, 217, 227
ecclesiology. *See* church
ecumenism, 161, 170–73, 180–82, 215–17,
　　223
empirical data. *See* sciences
end. *See telos*
eros. See love: as *eros*
eschatology, incl Kingdom of God, 90, 121,
　　123, 125, 156–57, 174 n.41, 175, 201
　　See also human life: future of
essentialism, 115–19
euthanasia, 65–67, 112, 185
evolution, 93, 119, 191
existentialism, 1 n.1, 10, 158, 221

259

right to life, 52–74

sanctification, 157, 159, 164, 172
sanctity of life, 67
sciences, 48 n.14, 60, 79, 85–97, 118–22, 140, 145–46, 152–53
Scripture. *See* Bible
sectarianism, 78, 142–54
senses, six, 88–89
sexuality, 29–30, 38, 96, 98–110, 121–22, 179
sin, 36, 98–110, 120–31, 184–88, 231–32
situational ethic. *See* context
Social Gospel, 12, 214, 224–26 (*cf* Rauschenbusch, Walter)
Society of Christian Ethics, 215, 217, 222
sources, four, 81, 157–59, 201

Stoicism, 162
suffer(ing), 32, 35–36, 55–57, 67, 73, 83–84, 88, 192

telos, 96, 112, 117, 121, 123
theology, 85–97
Trent, Council of, 168

utilitarianism, 114, 185, 210, 220
utopianism, 13, 135

Vatican II, 143
vocation. *See* calling

war, 13–14, 17–18, 78, 161, 169–71, 207, 219, 224